The Sacred Journey

Books by Robert B. Clarke

Published by Hampton Roads Publishing Company, Inc.:

The Four Gold Keys: Dreams, Transformation of the Soul, and the Western Mystery Tradition (2002)

An Order Outside Time: A Jungian View of the Higher Self from Egypt to Christ (2005)

Published by Hologram Books, LLC:

The Royal Line of Christ the Logos: A Jungian View of the Roots and Meaning of the Orthodox/Gnostic Christian Mystery (2010)

The Grail, the Stone, and the Mystics: A Jungian View of the Medieval Spiritual Mysteries (2010)

The Sacred Journey: Part One, Jung and His Discoveries; Part Two, Blavatsky, Nietzsche, Marian Visions, UFOS, and Aliens (2010)

The Sacred Journey

PART ONE

Jung and His Discoveries

PART TWO

Blavatsky, Nietzsche, Marian Visions, UFOS, and Aliens

Robert B. Clarke

Hologram Books
1270 Roberts Mountain Road
Faber, Virginia 22938

Photo of Carl Gustav Jung (LC-DIG-ppmsca-07205) from the
Library of Congress Prints and Photographs Division.
Cover images provided by istockphoto.com
Cover and text design by Jane Hagaman

For information visit:
www.hologrambooks.com
or write:

Hologram Books
1270 Roberts Mountain Road
Faber, Virginia 22938

ISBN 978-0-9842612-2-2
10 9 8 7 6 5 4 3 2 1
Printed on acid-free paper in the United States

Contents

Part One
Jung and His Discoveries

Part Two
Blavatsky, Nietzsche, Marian Visions, UFOS, and Aliens

Part One

Jung and His Discoveries

Chapter 1

First Steps on the Royal Road

Freud and the Denial of the Spirit

Sigmund Freud (1856–1939), considered by many to be the father of modern psychology, wrote: "The interpretation of dreams is the Via Regia [Royal Road] to the knowledge of the unconscious in mental life." But a Royal Road must surely lead to royalty ultimately. With Freud it leads to little more than a sewer, or, at best, to a dark, dismal cellar that is the repository for repressed wishes and shocking fantasies that consciousness cannot face, which then fester into obsessional neuroses.

The truth is, Freud took only the first step along the Royal Road, believing it to be not only the whole of the road, but also the whole of an extremely limited unconscious realm. It is like setting out along the road to Rome, but coming to the sewage works on the way, and taking it to be the whole of Rome. You may build your life's work on your assumption, as Freud did, and while you may be right to a degree in your assessment of the nature and function of the sewage works, you nevertheless completely miss Rome itself and its meaning. Furthermore, Rome is bound up with and expresses a version of eternal truth: If you take the sewage works to be the destination of the Royal Road, you miss even the real meaning of the sewage works, which can only be understood in the context of its association with Rome and its people. By itself the sewage works would be meaningless.

As I awoke one morning, in that brief instant between sleep and waking, a sentence flashed up from the unconscious that was not in any way the product of consciousness. It said, "Freud is the beginning of wisdom, but he is also the ending of wisdom." How very true this is, and how succinctly the unconscious put it. Freud begins on the Royal Road to wisdom, but then almost immediately stops, believing there is nothing more.

Because of this, wisdom then ends with Freud and his theories. Indeed, wisdom is lost.

It took the genius of Freud's early collaborator, Carl Jung (1875–1961), to discover that we must travel an exceedingly long journey beyond the sewage works to reach the true royalty, one that radiates with the brightest of all lights (though it also has its corresponding darkest of all darknesses). Freud warned Jung that they must be on guard against such dangerous superstitions as religion and the occult, but Jung eventually found he could not deny the real meaning of the archetypal/spiritual material that was coming to light, and this led eventually to the break with Freud. While Freud stopped at the sewage works, Jung went on to Rome.

I find it somewhat ironic that Freud referred to knowledge of the unconscious as the "Royal Road," for a royal road is a royal line, precisely what the unconscious referred to in one of my dreams. Jung was overhead, showing me a river of blue blood running from ancient Egypt to Christ. This was a line of divine incarnations from the realm of the spirit, whereas Freud's Royal Road is extremely limited, involving only personal psychology. In my dream the royal line, though involving the human psyche, develops into the structure of successive incarnations of what Eastern philosophy calls the Higher Self, the immortal figure to which we are all attached, different versions of which have appeared worldwide.

The psychology expounded by Freud limits everything to the personal psyche, and this in none too positive a light. Indeed, the conflict between Freud and Jung, two totally different views of reality, is Aristotle and Plato all over again, and perhaps even more so. Aristotle was ever the realist and materialist, whereas Plato's whole philosophy is based upon the reality of the spirit. This is what separated Freud and Jung.

Mankind generally came to think like Freud in the twentieth century, landing us in one unholy mess, severely limiting the evolution of the spirit that is meant to take place through matter, thereby obstructing the continuing purpose of evolutionary Creation. The total human psyche, so much more than a mere mind, is the means by which the spirit is able to experience matter directly. In extremely rare circumstances, God is able to use it to incarnate into the world. Jung realized this fully, and it forms the main message of his work, whereas for Freud spirit and soul and God Himself are delusions, and are even symptomatic of sickness of the mind. (Religion, including both orthodox and Gnostic streams, always taught that a human being consists of eternal spirit/soul possessing mind in worldly time and reality. Science in the twentieth century believed only in the mind.)

Psychology, the "science of the psyche" ("psyche" means "soul"), is a relatively modern phenomenon, and Jung himself states that had modern Man not lost belief in mythic/spiritual reality, psychology as a science would probably not have come about. It would have been unnecessary. According to Jung, it is only because modern Man became so mythically poverty stricken and starved of religious meaning and its living symbolism that he was forced to make his way, half blindly and half unconsciously, to the very roots of religious experience in the unconscious.

Nevertheless, we can say this was bound to happen, since Man cannot exist indefinitely suspended between simple, literal religious belief and dissociated atheism. Psychology only began as a science in the second half of the nineteenth century, when Man began to lose religious foundations and develop scientific ones. Sooner or later, real knowledge of spirit and soul as living realities accessed through the unconscious had to become known as facts experienced, bringing higher conscious awareness in its wake. With Jung that time had finally arrived.

Freudian reductionism had a tremendous influence upon the twentieth century, being one of the chief causes of the spiritual, social, and moral sickness of modern times. Before considering Jung, we must first look briefly at Freud, to properly value Jung's move to the archetypes of the spirit and to the deeper meaning of the human soul. This is not to say that Freud's contribution to human knowledge is therefore nonexistent or worthless. Jung himself called Freud a great man who helped open up the human psyche. Freud's true contribution is that he realized the overwhelming importance of dreams as messages from the hidden part of Man, but he largely misinterpreted their meaning, and denied the possibility of messages from beyond Man, which dreams sometimes are.

We must also remember there is a difference between psychology and psychiatry, the former being the study of the human mind in general, and the latter the treatment of mental disorders. Before personal psychology was brought into psychiatry, mental illness was considered to be due to physiological causes. Freud was one of the early figures to realize that the unconscious—which he termed the "subconscious"—plays a large and significant role in mental illness, and that it expresses itself in dreams, giving clues as to the real nature and cause of the illness. However, although he brought personal psychology into the picture, Freud's interpretations were extremely limited, considering what we now know concerning both personal and depth psychology.

Freud, who was Jewish, was born in 1856 in Moravia, which later became part of Czechoslovakia. At the age of four his parents took him to live in Vienna, where he was raised. However, Freud's early history does not concern us here, except to say that he became a fanatical atheist when quite young, and remained one for life.

Freud first studied physiology under the eminent Ernst Brucke, the most important teacher of his life, according to Freud himself. In 1885, he obtained a small grant to work with neurologist Jean-Martin Charcot, at the Salpetriere mental hospital in Paris. Charcot, who used hypnosis to treat his patients, was also much interested in hysteria, having discovered that it is due to certain obsessions taking possession of the mind (or the brain, as he would perhaps have seen it). Another of Charcot's pupils, Josef Breuer, found that certain pathogenic symptoms were due to the patient's earlier traumatic experiences. These influences formed the foundations of all Freud's later theories, although Freud does seem to have taken part in some of the important earlier work done at the Salpetriere.

In 1886, Freud set up his own private practice and commenced his research, eventually coming up with the sexual trauma theory of hysteria. He noticed that his neurotic patients had very vivid dreams, and that some of the contents corresponded to symptoms of their illnesses. Freud also realized that dreams often express what the conscious mind represses. Repression and dreams became the central part of Freud's work. This led to his book, *The Interpretation of Dreams* (1899), which Jung called "an epoch making work," adding that it was a masterful attempt to grapple with the mysteries of the unconscious on a sound scientific basis. Jung points out that whereas in ancient times dreams had been very highly valued, and were even believed to reveal the will of the gods, official science in the nineteenth century refused to take them at all seriously in any way. So Jung considered Freud's discovery of the meaning of dreams an important link with earlier times. Nevertheless, it is necessary to say again that Freud did not ascribe sufficient meaning to dreams, even misinterpreting many of the contents, thereby rendering them and the whole of the unconscious of much less value, failing to realize the true and full significance of what he had discovered, or rediscovered.

Jung once commented that the human psyche is not merely a hormone, but a whole world in itself, and that rationalistic thinking psychiatrists must come to realize they have other predecessors than the relatively recent ones such as Mesmer, Charcot, and Janet. The other predecessors to which Jung refers are the mythmakers, alchemists, Gnostics, and all of the initiates into the world's religious and esoteric Mysteries who have their foundations in processes of the unconscious; not least the

Hebrew prophets of the religion of Freud's forebears, which he had come to so vehemently reject. In fact, Jung states that the religions have always been the best and truest psychotherapeutic systems, but that modern psychology had completely failed to realize this. Consequently, psychiatrists needed to unlearn what they had learned and begin again, otherwise they would remain as neurotic as some of their patients

Jung said this in 1934, but unfortunately for the most part things today are as bad as ever they were. Jung was not listened to. Psychotherapists did not stop thinking neurotically. Even Freud's somewhat shallow interpretation of the unconscious is too deep for many modern doctors of the mind, who treat only consciousness. Psychology without the psyche, as Jung put it.

For Freud the unconscious was merely personal, soon coming to an end, tapering off from consciousness like a tail, whereas for Jung the reverse is true. It is consciousness that is the extension, while the unconscious spreads out not only to the collective levels, but seemingly to spiritual infinity and a "timeless" eternity. Jung came to realize that the personal unconscious is just a mere iota in the collective unconscious, which appears to have no limits, surrounding the world of consciousness and the universe of matter. The unconscious, Jung explained, is not just *below* consciousness, it is also above and around it. In *An Order Outside Time* I wrote the following to try to illustrate this:

> Imagine an iceberg floating on the sea, partly submerged in the water. That is like the human psyche, partly in the world of consciousness, and partly in the realm of the unconscious. If we take the tip of the iceberg above the sea to be personal consciousness, then everything above it, the dry land, the air, etc., would represent the reality of the world and impersonal, collective consciousness. The iceberg below the water level, however, which is much larger than what shows above it, would then equal the personal unconscious, which, like the iceberg, is much larger than the part of the psyche above, and which constitutes consciousness. But the submerged iceberg is in turn only an extremely small content in the great depths of the ocean, and in the same way the personal unconscious is merely a small drop in the waters of the collective unconscious. This might be better termed the "eternal unconscious," for it spreads out to an eternal reality of spirit and soul.

The personal psyche is part of the totality of the Self, though it is impossible to say how much of the full collective unconscious, or spirit/soul reality, it takes up. It reaches down into the soul depths that permeates all matter, but also up to the spirit heights, and is certainly immortal. There is a personal level of the Self, so that it functions like a guardian angel above us, but also a wider aspect, so that at lower level it is Son of the Earth Spirit/World Soul and divine Son of God at cosmic level. I call these Lower Self and Higher Self respectively. We find examples of the phenomenon in the world's myths and religions at various levels of development, particularly in the ancient world, seen with Horus, Tammuz, Adonis, Apollo, Dionysus, and so forth—and for Western culture with Christ. The Higher Self is a complexity of all opposites, and the unification of his parts in inner processes brings him forth through the collective unconscious as *an actual experience*. This was the great truth that Jung was fated to discover (or rather rediscover, for ancient Man had known it to high degree). Jung's work began with psychology, but became increasingly religious as he continued, activating and experiencing spirit/soul reality.

(As I wrote the above, the unconscious broke in with its contribution, the words "a chip off the old block" springing up into my consciousness. This says it perfectly; the human personality is a chip off the old block that is the Higher Self.)

One value of Freud, Jung pointed out, is that he demonstrated that we each have a dark, powerful, shadow side, and that we are capable of much filth and evil. We are not as good and superior as we think we are. Indeed, man may have too much darkness within his nature to survive in the long run. But Jung saw this is not the whole picture: By recognizing and accepting the truth about ourselves, we are able to fight to win redemption, both for ourselves and our world. Indeed, Jung added that had the inferior shadow side of Man been the largest and most important aspect, mankind would have long since perished.

Jung also said Freud always had the clinical picture of neurosis before his eyes, the very condition that makes people ill. Consequently, Freud judged life accordingly, always seeing the negative side of everything. Added to this was his rationalistic temperament, causing him to explain away deep and complex phenomena such as art and religion as due to repression of the sexual instinct, hatred of the father, and a childish need for the father. Freud was not really interested in philosophy in its original and true meaning, and he admitted to Jung that it had never occurred to him to read Nietzsche, the German philosopher whose views ran counter to Western Man's traditional way of thinking at that time.

Freud and Friedrich Nietzsche were more or less contemporaries. Freud, born 1856, was raised in Vienna. Nietzsche was born in Rocken,

Prussian Saxony, in 1844. Both were under the influence of the same Austro/Germanic culture of the time. Nietzsche caused something of a stir with his atheistic, anti-Christian notions, being fashionable among intellectuals, though neglected by the world at large. Some of Freud's friends and associates must have been reading him, even if they disagreed with his ideas. So it was much of a surprise to Jung when Freud admitted his lack of interest in Nietzsche.

However, it seems that Freud did read Nietzsche in his later years, of which Jung was apparently unaware. Freud comments that the philosopher's ideas agreed "in an astonishing way" with the findings of psychology—meaning Freud's atheistic/materialistic interpretations. Indeed, both *are* similar to a degree, though from the different angles of the sex and power instincts. Each was proclaiming "God is dead" in his own way. Nietzsche was actually, though largely unknowingly, undergoing the individuation process of the unconscious himself, the main product of which was *Thus Spoke Zarathustra.* Nietzsche's Superman—the Ubermensch, or Overman—whom his prophet Zarathustra heralds and proclaims, was not just an *idea,* but a developing psychic/spiritual reality within Nietzsche—the Higher Self of which he would have totally denied the possibility.

Nietzsche, coming from a long line of Lutheran pastors, had intended being one himself. He was intensely religious when very young. But Darwin's theory of evolution and "natural selection"—which was soon interpreted as "survival of the fittest"—together with other discoveries of science and the consequent rationalism, were to destroy all concepts of God and the spirit for him. Declaring, "God is dead. God remains dead. And we have killed him." Nietzsche developed his philosophy of "Will to Power" and the "Superman," from which the Nazis drew some of their "ideals." (However, Nietzsche was not anti-Jewish and people who met him were surprised to find him much more pleasant than his writings.)

As for Freud, it was Jung's opinion that he was a destroyer of the false, hypocritical, and sickly sentimental values of the Victorian age, and therefore a liberator breaking the chains that bind us to the past in negative ways. But he was not, Jung believed, a bringer of new ways and new truths. I believe that this is so from the wider view of history, but in the more limited sense, Freud did bring a new way. Along with others, Freud was part of that great tidal wave of nineteenth century materialism that was to deluge the twentieth century to devastating effect, altering the thinking of the whole of Western civilization to an extreme and negative degree. For while the nineteenth century had hung on to the remnants of medieval values in many ways—and not always to its detriment—there was nevertheless that great force of scientific-rationalism, based largely upon genuine scientific discoveries, that nothing could oppose and which was due to conquer Western culture—and eventually the whole of the world

With big business, political materialism, and shallow intellectualism as bedfellows, scientific-rationalism swept away the old religious order that had existed for many hundreds of years, which ironically had given birth (through learning) to the modern science that was to destroy it. Freud was a significant part of that new scientific force, and so floated in on the tide, so to speak. Although encountering much early opposition to his ideas, he could not help but win in the long run, as the whole tide was carrying him along, supporting him

The young Shelley had written a pamphlet while at Oxford University many decades before, called *The Necessity of Atheism* (for which he was expelled), which reveals the route that intellectual thought was taking. Many other thinkers—scholars, scientists, philosophers, etc. —were coming to similar conclusions, and when Darwin in the 1850s demonstrated that nature functions on a system of natural selection—survival of the fittest—the old beliefs and ideas of God and Creation were shaken to the foundations. If it was left to Nietzsche to finally declare his "God is dead" in resounding terms, Freud was only too happy to ram home the notion.

Freud came upon the scene just as scientific-rationalism, which had for some time been in the process of usurping the throne formerly occupied by God, was gaining momentum. While I am highly critical of Freud's narrow rationalism and reductionism, in his day the old guard rejected him for quite the opposite reasons—for coming up with the "mystical" promulgation there could be any real meaning to dreams and the "subconscious." Yet Freud was eventually to gain not only respectability but worldwide acclaim, while Jung, quite literally the hope of mankind (which the unconscious itself states) was largely isolated as an outsider during his lifetime.

Jung did not, by and large, fit the negative mood of the materialistic age, and was accused of being occultist, mystical, and unscientific. He was also too optimistic and enlightened, speaking of the soul and the spirit as realities that can actually be experienced through the unconscious. The Higher Self, of which Christ is still the main symbol for the West, was for Jung the true ruler of each human soul. He would quote Meister Eckhart (c. 1260–1328), who stated that God must be born into the soul of Man again and again, and this is as the Higher Self. (We today say Higher Self, after Jung and Madame Blavatsky, who took the term from Eastern religion, while the Gnostics called the figure the Anthropos, Monogenes, and the Logos or Word—these latter from the Greek Mysteries—but to mankind generally the figure has always been seen a god.)

Freud's Neurosis of Religion

As this book is concerned with the wider, religious aspects of the unconscious, and as Freud's views are so counter to Jung's (and to my own), Freud's central theories on the causes and treatment of mental disorders at the personal level do not concern us here. It is Freud's ideas on religion, and therefore on the nature of full reality itself and Man's place in it, that are of importance to us

It has been observed that Freud saw history as a war between science and religion, a war that science must at all costs win. Calling himself a "Godless Jew," Freud believed religion to be not merely an illusion, but far worse, a dangerous neurosis that had to be cured at all costs. Religion, he proclaimed, was due to the repression of the sexual instinct, though he also came up with various other causes, such as wish-fulfillment, hatred of the father, and (contradictory to this) the need for the father as in childhood. He stated that just as religion in the individual is tantamount to the formation of a neurosis, so religion in general is the universal obsessional neurosis of Mankind. He further insisted there are clear similarities between the rituals of religion and the ceremonials that neurotics display in their illnesses.

It obviously did not occur to Freud that people all over the world, in all ages, have taken part in religious rituals because of the satisfying feelings of wel-being, meaningfulness, and right order they give, as well as the numinous ones of holiness and sacredness. If, therefore, neurotics indulge in "ceremonials" that resemble religious rituals, perhaps it is an unconscious attempt to try to bring about similar health-giving effects. It is not that religious ritual can be reduced to neuroses, but that the neurotic person (or the neurosis itself) unconsciously attempts to bring about the order and health of the religion. In other words, religion is not the descent into chaotic neurosis; rather chaotic neurosis tries to achieve the higher state of wholeness felt with religion. The true holy man achieves a state of perfect peace, for he has brought all of the conflicting parts of matter and spirit together in a state of unified wholeness. (In old age, Jung was spiritually enlightened and attuned to holiness, while Freud was atheistic, pessimistic, neurotic, and bitter.)

As is well known, sufferers from mental disorders often become interested in religion. Again, Freud reduces this to an attempt by the weak and helpless sufferer to find some comfort and security. This may well be so, but behind it all is the fact that religion *offers* that help, because it is the system of healing and salvation for Mankind stretching back thousands of years to his most primitive beginnings. Religion, if genuinely felt, heals, because it is in harmony with processes of the collective unconscious, which aim at unification in the Higher Self. The human psyche is directly attached to the eternal realities of spirit and soul through the unconscious, and although the dark, negative side of the unconscious may rebel violently against the religious position at times, it is nevertheless accompanied by feelings of wondrous meaning. Atheism means division, the splitting away of ego-conscious from wider spirit reality, and this is one of the chief causes of neurosis. Splitting away from the spirit causes disturbance and pain, whereas the unification of these opposites brings at least some degree of harmony and peace.

Christ states he brings division, but this means the powerful and responsible state of higher conscious awareness that can choose to defeat its own selfish and evil impulses, rather than being their victim. With this power to discriminate and to choose his good over his own evil, Man gains enormously in moral strength and well-being. It is a huge leap forward in evolution.

The greatest fact of the human psyche is that it is connected to and is part of the Higher Self, which is nothing if not a *religious* phenomenon. This is exemplified by Jesus the man connected to the higher Christ, and in the Greek Mysteries, the mortal "eidolon" connected to the immortal "Daemon." To think or exist atheistically divides us from our true foundations in that higher immortal. It is as though a second split away from Time itself were to believe that the second is the only reality. I personally have experienced the phenomenon of the inner processes through the years, and an iota of experience is worth a wagonload of rationalistic hypothesizing.

Jung states that atheism causes a profound disturbance within the Self, as it involves the denial of the fundamental autonomy systems of the unconscious. Yet Freud claims religious beliefs to be the delusions and wish fulfillments of Mankind, and that we seek the protection of God the Father in the same way that the terrors of childhood cause us to seek the protection of the personal father.

In this, Freud is altering his opinion somewhat from his position above. Religion is now no longer due to obsessional neurosis, sexual repression, etc., but to the longing for an eternal Father to protect us, just as in childhood we need the personal father for this. If this were so, the need would be a natural one and there would be nothing delusional or neurotic about it, as the need and wish for something—whether in a state of helplessness or not—in no way implies that the thing needed and wished for does not exist. In fact, it is more than likely that it does. So while the need and wish for Him does not prove God, it certainly does not disprove Him, as Freud would have it

But again, Freud misses the point. Man has a developed mind that is able to see way beyond his immediate situation; to the past, to the future, and to ideas of infinity and eternity. With this highly evolved conscious awareness, Man does not merely search for meaning and answers to the riddle of the universe through idle curiosity, *he is meant specifically to do so*. That is what his developed consciousness is for. In fact, it is when Man does *not* search for meaning and for God (in some form) that he restricts himself to the level of the lower animals, and it is actually then that life becomes flat and meaningless, and neurosis, or worse, sets in with the dissociation. We are all agents of the Higher Self on Earth, and through us the Self is able to experience the world of matter. In exceptional cases the divine Self, the cosmic Logos, who is part of God, may descend to the human individual in the unconscious, amounting to God's incarnation. Ironically, this phenomenon was highly developed in Freud's Jewish forebears, specifically in the prophets, but he had completely dissociated himself mentally from this possibility

Elsewhere, Freud says that the "slaying of the father" is the real reason why Christ and all other youthful gods of mythology who die young must be sacrificed in atonement for the act. Yet does not the young, dying god simply mean the slaying of the Son, rather than of the Father? How can we with any seriousness interpret the sacrificial crucifixion of Christ as atonement for the mental slaying of the personal father, which is what Freud means? But Freud then goes on to say that the worship of Christ *is* the attainment of the death wish against the father, for a Son religion replaces a Father one, intimating a death wish against God the Father, and therefore really the personal father. Similarly, when Mithras slays the bull, he is slaying the personal father.

This is rationalistic misinterpretation gone mad. In the first place, Christ does not replace God, but is coexistent with him, and with the Holy Spirit they form the Holy Trinity, the Three-in-One Deity. So Father and Son are really One, the "One God with two faces," as the ancient Egyptians expressed it. Secondly, the slaying of the bull actually means the overcoming of the sexual impulse, and has nothing to do with the father. And what of the hero's slaying of the dragon, which is usually done *on behalf* of the High God, who is the Father? Even when Christ defeats Satan, *"that old serpent,"* in his temptation, it is in the interests of God the Father. Many religions, in fact, have glorified the divine Father/Son combination, and sometimes Father/Mother/Son.

Freud mentions Adonis being killed by a wild boar as an instance of the wrath of the Father, who takes animal form to wreak vengeance on the son. However, in mythology, boars and pigs are often great danger to the god-hero because they are symbols of the dark, instinctual side of the unconscious, or of the dark Self specifically. The dark god Set was associated with the pig in ancient Egypt, and as such he blinds his twin, Horus, in one eye. If an Egyptian happened to be touched by a pig he would immediately go and wash, or even jump into the river Nile, for the pig was an abomination—as also with Jews and Muslims

In my own individuation process, the sight of a pig—or even a rasher of bacon—was the cause of much worry because it is associated with the dark, instinctual powers of the unconscious. When Adonis is killed by a wild boar, it means he has failed in his heroic task, and the instinctual powers have defeated him. Mithras' slaying the bull means that he, on the other hand, defeats the rampant powers of sexuality that assail him, threatening to destroy his spirituality. This is symbolized sometimes as leaping over the bull, although then the defeat is not permanent, so that the bull will come to challenge again in the future. The Mesopotamian hero Gilgamesh has to defeat a menacing bull in his quest, sent by the scorned temptress goddess he has rejected.

Ironically, this defeat does involve personal sexuality here, one of the few times Freud does *not* ascribe a sexual basis. So the time when Freud could have brought in his sexual theory with much validity he fails to do so, interpreting the symbolism instead as a death wish against the father. Freud always reduces mythology and religion to personal psychology, to repression and neuroses, in effect lessening the wonder, the magic—and, it must be said, dark terrors of the spirit—to personal psychology, usually to sexuality, though he does not with Mithras and the bull when he should.

Freud says that there will be nothing left but despair for Mankind and civilization when the lofty hopes of religion are discovered to be mere illusions. He personally, however, is free from such bondage, and so too must we all become. (This was also part of Nietzsche's message.) But perhaps Freud's most telling statement of all is when he says that because religion is thought to be uplifting and beneficent, it must not at the same time be taken to be true. Such false beliefs taking the place of science, he continues, is an invasion that cannot be tolerated, that must be repulsed at all costs. Here we have it; science has now become God for Freud. How dare ideas of God and religion take the place of science almighty? All attacks on science on its throne must therefore be strenuously opposed. (See Freud's *The Future of an Illusion* 1928.)

As we can see, for Freud there is only material reality, with science the ruler of it, and all things must bow down to science. Yet as we know, science is only a method of measuring and assessing reality, it is not reality itself, not even the material side of reality. Science is only the grocery list, not the groceries themselves.

In rejecting the literal form of religious belief, Freud failed to search for its deeper meaning, and science has rushed in to usurp the authority once rightfully held by God. But if science replaces God for Freud, then sexuality replaces the Holy Spirit as the creative force of God. Freud became as possessed—even as inspired, in a sense—by lower sexuality as the saints were by the Holy Spirit.

Jung states that Freud reduced the numinous, archetypal, and therefore spiritual contents of the unconscious to human ones of the individual psyche. Discovering the ancient archetype of incest, he found something that could express the primordial and the collective, under the spell of which he then fell. Jung comments that Freud never asked himself why he was compelled to talk continually of sex and very little else. Jung realized Freud had simply substituted the lower dogma of sexuality for the higher one of religion, and was endeavoring with much effort to escape from the mystical side of his own nature, of which Jung had witnessed clear indications since their first meeting. Freud, like Nietzsche, possibly had a very religious soul, but like Nietzsche was dissociated from it. This caused the soul to rebel and affect both of them in negative ways.

Since time immemorial, religion in one form or another was always king and ruler, from the most primitive tribe to the highest culture. Freud saw this as sort of half intentional and half unintentional brainwashing, completely failing to realize there really *is* another reality of spirit and soul existing behind the physical universe that affects every person through the unconscious, for good or ill. This has a numinous, magical quality about it that Man often experiences in dreams, and sometimes evens in visions and trances. As Jung says, for too long modern Man dismissed dreams as chaotic nonsense until Freud found deeper meaning in them. But Freud saw only limited, negative meaning, though certain dreams fitted in with his own theories when the patient happened to be suffering from a certain type of disturbance. Overall, he was wrong as to the immense significance of the unconscious and the dreams it produces. In the final analysis we can say Freud was right in a small way but wrong in a big way.

He did help to open up the deeper layers of the human psyche, but he also helped to lure Mankind into a dangerous state of psychic/spiritual dissociation. He took the first step to wisdom and gnosis, but then immediately stopped, declaring the unconscious to be a tail that tapers off. In reality, consciousness is the tail to the collective unconscious, and matter to the eternity of spirit. Consciousness and matter taper off from spirit reality. Freud was to eventually attain almost unbelievable success, with world fame that ensures his immortality, yet in denying any deeper meaning to Man and ultimate reality, he missed the greatest treasure that can be known.

What is so mightily ironic is that these treasures are to be experienced through dream processes of the unconscious, the very domain that Freud was instrumental in discovering. He was sitting on the divine source itself, or the Royal Road to it, but all he could see was the personal cesspit, which does exist as part of the much greater whole. Jung pointed out that when Freud revealed all the filth of the human psyche, the Western world became fascinated and attracted to it, and the upshot was that an uglier face was put on the world. This is what happens when religion dies and reality is reduced to mere matter and morbid complexes of the ailing human psyche.

Despite Freud's negative reductionism and other limitations, Jung considered him a great man who rediscovered the value of dreams and who opened up the unconscious to Man's conscious experience. Nevertheless, Jung comments that nineteenth-century rationalism never let go of Freud, causing him to remain oblivious to the deeper archetypal contents. Jung concludes that such a materialistic attitude towards reality is completely out of step with the nature of the collective unconscious.

Freud was very neurotic, suffering fainting fits, and he constantly smoked cigars that eventually gave him cancer of the jaw and palate. Even then, after several operations, he still could not give up the cigars. Freud had been largely instrumental in opening up the unconscious, but he erected bulwarks against experience of the religious archetypes, the "black tide of occultism" as he called it. The splitting off from and denial of these contents, especially when activated, results in neurosis, and the more the contents tried to come through to Freud's consciousness, the higher he made the bulwarks. The same happened with St Paul: The more religious contents tried to break through from the unconscious, the more Paul set up barriers and persecuted the Christians. Finally, he was struck down when the archetypal Christ burst forth upon him on the road to Damascus. But Paul changed his conscious attitude and his values and, coming to accept the phenomenon that Christ represented, grew to be a greater personality, whereas Freud, refusing to open the gates, remained a neurotic smaller personality, unable to grow.

As said above, Freud probably possessed a deeply mystical soul, Jung observing certain religious symptoms break through in him on certain occasions. But Freud was divided against himself, setting up his scientific-sexual theory and damming up the archetypal contents that bring direct religious experience. Jung says his own patients started to heal when they began to experience the archetypal material from the collective levels of the unconscious, but some patients had no talent for assimilating them, and so remained ill.

Chapter 2

The Beginning of the Light

Jung and Freud inhabit different worlds, different universes, different realities. Freud's reality is totally limited to matter, so that even the mind, the psyche, ideas, philosophy, art, and so on, are at bottom merely products of matter and limited to it. In complete contrast, Jung's reality is open and unlimited. Spirit and soul are as real as matter, and although the way to these is through the collective unconscious, the true and full nature of the ultimate things so transcends mortals that they cannot be fully known. Yet we may experience the archetypal contents as symbolic images: They confront us through the unconscious in dreams, and the myths and religions of the world provide the evidence of these phenomena. Nevertheless, while Jung would admit, or even proclaim, that Freud's theories are valid to a degree (as part of a much-greater whole), Freud would not, and could not, return the compliment concerning Jung's discoveries.

As Freud bases everything on the sexual instinct, his direct opposite is actually Alfred Adler, for whom the power instinct is the primal force of life. Jung accepts both of these instincts as obviously tenable within their respective spheres, but realizes there are yet other instincts in Man, including that of religious meaning, and that all must be included in the totality of the whole psyche, the limits of which cannot be ultimately determined. Thus Jung transcends all of the lesser lights, who form their psychological theories around just one aspect of the totality. Jung, furthermore, is concerned not only, or even primarily, with the sick psyche, but also and mainly with the full, healthy psyche and its meaning in the eternal scheme of things. Consequently, from quite an early date he linked psychology up with religion. In fact, he could not help but do so, as he discovered that the farther into the unconscious we go, the more it functions in a mythological/religious way, on both the positive and negative sides.

This was an extremely important breakthrough, demonstrating in a scientific way that spirit and soul—and as Jung was to further discover, the Higher Self and God—are truths experienced through processes of the collective unconscious. No one had been able to prove the validity of these experiences on a scientific basis before, as studied processes of the human psyche attached to spirit reality. In so doing, Jung opened a new door, though really a very ancient door, the entrance to the cave of treasures insisted upon by the religious Mysteries. Yet though mystical in the light of its actual connection with spirit/soul reality, Jung's approach to the work was empirical and "scientific." He knew that he must keep on this track if his discoveries were to be taken seriously, let alone accepted. (By and large they were not, and are still not by psychology in general.) His findings were not based upon philosophical conjecture, but rather upon scientific investigation and experience, a point he often stressed. My own individuation process, as recorded in my first book, *The Four Gold Keys,* showed me that Jung's discoveries are *realities* that may be experienced.

Religious processes in the unconscious can be proven just as surely as neuroses can be, yet Jung was forced to declare that he had had his fill of isolation caused by the failure of others to comprehend what he had discovered. Jung was largely rejected because people could not understand him and the tremendous significance of his discoveries. Also, society was very much attracted to the filth dug up by Freud, and to his rationalism and negativism (which have a certain pseudo-intellectual attraction) and certainly also sexuality. A light such as Jung provided was not only misunderstood but largely unwanted in the overwhelmingly materialistic twentieth century. It was Freud who fitted the bill. However, things are perhaps opening up somewhat in the twenty-first century.

Jung was born in 1875, the son of a poor country pastor, and grew up mostly in the rural Klein-Hunigen, outside the Swiss city of Basle. A number of his uncles were also pastors, but he had no wish to follow in their footsteps. Jung's childhood companions were mostly rough country boys, which gave him a solid grounding in the soil that he never lost.

As a youth, Jung discovered he possessed what he called his No. 1 and No. 2 personalities, No. 1 being concerned with the world and his interest in science, while No. 2 was an ages-old man from the past. No. 1 regarded No. 2 as a realm of inner darkness, whereas Jung realized that although not clearly defined, in No. 2 "light reigned," as in a great royal palace. Jung had a dream at that time, where a mighty wind and a swirling fog invaded everywhere menacingly, and he had to cup a small light in his hands to protect it. Suddenly, a huge, dark figure loomed up behind Jung, and he knew that as the small light was his ego-consciousness, it must be protected from both the dark and light sides of the great forces of the unconscious no matter what. He also knew he must go forward into the world, to develop his No. 1 personality, though at the same time he was aware that he must never deny No. 2 and what it represented, which involved timeless reality.

This is the sort of thing that caused me personally to become mesmerized by Jung in the first place; he corresponded so closely to my own inner depths that they immediately recognized themselves in Jung and his work. I too have always vaguely felt the presence of a "wise old man" within my depths, who is "as old as the hills," and whom I now realize represents the timeless wisdom of the unconscious that Jung called "the personification of spirit." My first encounter with Jung brought a feeling that was magical, and though transference was involved, there was nevertheless much more to it. (Transference is a sort of projection unconsciously made from the patient onto the psychoanalyst, and also we could say from pupil to master, chela to guru.)

I remember that as a teenager I would doodle a head that had two profiles, each facing the opposite way. One was a young man, obviously identified with my conscious self, but the other was a white bearded old man, a philosopher or holy man. When I first saw Jung, on film, he may not have been literally white bearded, but he was certainly the personification of the "wise old man" figure I had always known within my depths.

When it came to the choice of career, the two personalities in Jung—we could say the world and the spirit—pulled opposite ways, though No. 1 eventually won the struggle and he decided to devote himself to scientific knowledge. He wanted most of all to become an archaeologist (my own wish when I was young), but as this was not possible for various reasons, including financial ones, Jung finally settled on becoming a doctor. No. 2 personality would rise up at times, and being ages-old, was in accord with the medieval world, personified for Jung by Faust. Consequently, Jung became captivated by the Middle Ages and Faust. He felt that Goethe had answered his own age with his great work, *Faust,* and so he looked on Goethe as a sort of godfather, the figure of authority over him. Actually, a rumor circulated for decades that an ancestor of Jung's had given birth to an illegitimate child by Goethe, which would have made the poet the great-grandfather of Jung. But although Freud referred to Goethe as "your ancestor" in correspondences with Jung, the latter discredited the idea in his later years. (The original Faust appeared in a medieval story, while Goethe wrote his version in the eighteenth and nineteenth centuries.)

Nevertheless, despite all of this, No. 1 personality still dominated, and Jung went to study medicine at the University of Basle in 1895.

Also at this early period, Jung began to study Nietzsche, and it seemed to him that his No. 2 personality corresponded to Nietzsche's *Thus Spoke Zarathustra* (1883) in the same way that it corresponded to Goethe's *Faust*. Both of these works are actually based upon processes of the unconscious, as both Zarathustra (more strictly the "Superman," the "Ubermensch") and Mephistopheles, the dark figure experienced by Faust, are examples of the Higher Self brought forth after long periods of inner development; only, they are negative instances. They are negative, Jung points out, due to the negative state of the collective German soul at those respective times, of which Goethe and Nietzsche are individual examples in personalized form. Both needed to have had certain negative values, or negative goals, for such figures as Mephistopheles and the Superman to have developed through the unconscious in the form they did.

Jung realized that *Zarathustra* was morbid and so feared that his No. 2 figure could also be morbid (in the medical sense). He also knew that Nietzsche had no chance of communicating his *Zarathustra* to others—Nietzsche did not even understand it himself—so Jung "slammed the door" on Nietzsche, deciding that the only way to get such phenomena across to people is by giving them evidence. Only with evidence can you demonstrate the truth of anything. (Even then, the evidence may not be understood and there may still be rejection, as Jung was to discover.)

At this early period, Jung saw Christ as the "mouthpiece of the Holy Ghost," and if the phenomenon could occur once in history, then it could occur at all times and in all places. He read books on spiritualism, and seven volumes of Swedenborg, among many other works, and though considering himself a Christian, it was in a much profounder sense than in the usual manner, so that nobody understood what he was talking about when he spoke of religion. As for science, he believed that it provides knowledge of sorts, but gives no insights of the deeper kind that ultimately matter more than cold material facts. Furthermore, he could see no reason why such things as ghosts and similar phenomena should not exist. These things were taken for granted in the rural area where he was raised, but here in the city where he now lived, he found people were dull, rationalistic, and limited in their thinking concerning such matters.

As regards his career, Jung knew he would have to specialize, and reading a book on psychiatry, his heart began to pound. He knew he had found the only possible way for him to go in life, though others doubted *his* sanity when he revealed the decision, for psychiatry was considered nonsense, and the mentally sick incurable. They were mostly to be isolated away like criminals or lepers, and anyone who willingly became involved in such work must be as unstable as some of the patients. Nevertheless, Jung was sure that it was the way for him, and, strangely, he could feel No. 1 and No. 2 become unified within himself. Finally, he obtained a post as assistant to psychiatrist Eugene Bleuler, at the Burgholzi Mental Hospital, Zurich, which he took in December 1900. He would remain there for nine years

The Key to the Cure

Psychiatry at that time was based largely upon physiological thinking, and only the conscious mind of the patient was assessed. The fuller psychology of the patient was not, by and large, taken into consideration. However, in that same year, 1900, Jung had already discovered Freud was doing just that, using dreams to investigate the personal unconscious of the mentally ill, and this became tremendously important to him in his own work. For his part, Jung realized that as each case is different, the treatment itself must be different; and with each individual, individual methods must be used to help them grow out of their illness naturally. Even today, this approach in psychiatry remains almost unique.

There is an example of Jung's approach right at the outset of his career. Jung tells of one of his first patients at the Burgholzi hospital, an old woman of seventy-five who had been there for most of her adult life. She was insane and had been bedridden for forty years, and when she ate, she let the food drop into her mouth from her fingers, like a child eating spaghetti. Even when not eating, she still made strange motions with her hands, which no one understood or cared about. No one on the staff now remembered her case history, or indeed, bothered to look into her illness in any way, but Jung was finally able to find the answer in some yellowed old records. These stated, among other things, that she had repeatedly made the motions of a cobbler drawing his threads through the boots he was working on.

The old woman died soon afterwards, and when her brother attended the funeral, Jung enquired of him what events had led to her insanity. The brother replied that she had been deeply in love with a cobbler who rejected her, and that this had affected her so much she had lost her mind. So Jung had the answer. All these years later she still did the cobbler motions to keep some sort of contact with the man she had loved, though sadly not to fulfillment.

Such stories are heart-rending, but this and many similar cases taught Jung that no matter how meaningless or crazy the antics of the insane seem to be, there is always a kind of reason behind them, if only it can be found. Jung's method, if he had a "method," was to get to know the patient's story, which alone would reveal what had so devastatingly shattered them and their lives. And he knew that the cure, if it came, must involve the full personality, the human drama set against the backdrop of the eternal drama, so to speak. But essential to all of Jung's psychological work was the finding of the key that would unlock the door to the personal mystery of the patient. From the beginning of the twentieth century Jung was treating patients therapeutically, reaching back into their history, which remained a somewhat unique approach for some time.

Jung's patients were to consist mostly of nonbelievers, those lost sheep who had lost their faith and their way, for their lives and reality itsel, had become limited to the level of the personal ego. This is the real reason why people become neurotic. They become stuck in their own limited selves. Jung saw that his task was to extend his patients' personalities to include deeper and wider truths. All the necessary material to accomplish this, and very much more, is provided by the unconscious itself, though not the personal unconscious chiefly, but the collective unconscious, from where the healing contents flow. Healing really begins when people start to experience the nonpersonal archetypes, which have always filled myths and religions with symbolic content. That is when the neurosis usually begins to disappear, though different patients may require varying periods of time for the cure to take full effect. Jung found that the unconscious produces the meaningful religious symbols that consciousness has lost, or lacks to a meaningful degree. Nevertheless, there were always patients who could not understand or come to accept these, and the neurosis would therefore remain to eat away at them. As Jung was to write, the psychic processes of the unconscious are Gnosis in high measure, upon which is based Christianity's symbolic message. Nothing invented by consciousness could even closely compare to the richness of these inner processes, found in myths everywhere (1953).

Jung knew this applied to all the religious systems, of course—that they are true systems of healing—but he also realized that any resistance by the unconscious of a patient must be taken very seriously. Not everyone will be able to "take" the unconscious and its processes, and a dangerous psychosis may well be lurking in wait, so that it would be imperative for it to remain buried and covered up. Mostly, however, his patients were able to find within themselves what they had lost in the Church, or in other forms of religion, although to varying individual degrees. The logical consequence of all this is that if enough people experience the psychic phenomenon and are brought together, because the experience is religious in its deepest and truest sense, it may form a new religion, or further develop an existing one. However, though the Jung Foundations and Institutes that were to form were a good beginning, these now seem to lack the fire and true understanding of Jung's own personality.

Some interest has recently developed concerning the Higher Self, where this is seen as a sort of guardian angel that may bring healing and comfort. This is correct because the Self does have this personal level that is close to the conscious personality, of which consciousness is part. But as Jung himself stressed, the full meaning of the Higher Self is in cosmic aspect, where at ultimate level it is the divine Son of God. The effect of such holiness should be to herd us back to religious worship, for only the numinosity of religious symbolism is able to express the intense sacredness involved. This seems to show that the true meaning of the Higher Self has not been appreciated or fully understood in the modern world. Incredibly enough, there has been a return to the traditional religious forms in large numbers in the United States, seeming to suggest that the archetypal forces are at work in the collective unconscious, trying to restore religious order. And indeed, that is what my dreams have been saying for a number of years. Nevertheless, the simplest form of the new upsurge, Fundamentalism, is *too* simple to have lasting effect. Far greater understanding is required. There is also the phenomenal success of *The Da Vinci Code,* due to the activated archetype in the collective unconscious. Only, because the true, spiritual meaning has not been understood, a lesser, mundane one has been unconsciously substituted and projected.

Jung himself was illuminated as though by the divine light of a Daemon, indeed, of a Savior, and thereby became a great light for modern Man to follow. This light, which glows in the dark depths of our being, of all Being, is the eternal light that is inextinguishable.

(As stated, ego-consciousness was called the eidolon in the Greek Mysteries, and the Higher Self, the Daemon.)

A Case of Dissociation

People often live their whole lives and never question the fundamental nature of the reality around them, of which they are part, nor even the society to which they belong. Some even exist contrary to their true natures, unaware that their true selves—and how and what they should be—may be different from what their present personalities have become. Jung relates the case of one particular patient at least three times in his works, and it is worth mentioning here because it illustrates perfectly this unknowingly being divided against ourselves. When a sufficient number of individuals are affected, the rot sets in for the whole culture.

This patient was a young Jewish woman, very beautiful and the daughter of a rich banker, but suffering from a deep neurosis. Jung found her highly intelligent, but nevertheless concluded that her intelligence was superficial. She had been educated in the modern, over-intellectualized manner, due mainly to her father, who had himself rejected the religious beliefs and traditions of his forebears. The daughter had had a long line of lovers in her young life, and indeed, another psychiatrist was now sending her on to Jung because he too was falling for her, placing both his marriage and his career in jeopardy.

After the first consultation, Jung found himself looking down on the girl, for he could not help considering her shallow and superficial. However, that night he had a dream in which he kneeled before her, which told him he had been mistaken and had seriously underestimated her.

So at the next consultation Jung probed deeper into her background, and it turned out her grandfather had been a zadig, a holy man of the Jewish faith who experienced visions, and further, came from a long line of similar holy men stretching back many generations. But the girl's father had turned his back on all of this, betraying both God and the faith, as Jung puts it, plus generations of his forebears. He had raised his daughter the same way, with the same shallow values, and giving her an education to match.

The trouble—and the cause of the young woman's deep neurosis—was that she possessed the soul of a saint and was meant for holiness. It was in her very blood; she was a true daughter of her forebears. But the way she had been brought up and was living cut her off from the deeper meaning of her soul, in total opposition to its real needs. Her true inner self had no outlet, no chance of expression. So a great chasm had opened up between consciousness and the unconscious, and this always means a neurosis; the wider the chasm, the deeper the neurosis. Jung says she thought she was in the middle of things, with her "modern" values and the way she lived, but she was really hopelessly lost. She had everything the modern world believes we need for happiness; beauty, wealth, high intelligence, and a more than abundant love life. Yet she was not happy, and indeed, was in danger of falling to pieces.

Jung was easily able to restore her to health, however. When he put her in contact with her own inner depths, where her true spiritual nature lay stifled and repressed, her neurosis automatically vanished. The split, the dissociation in her total being, was healed.

Not everyone possesses the soul of a saint, of course, as this young woman did, but we nevertheless do have souls, and as Tertullian (160–220 A.D.) points out, "The soul is naturally religious." The people of the ancient world knew that, as did all other peoples until our dissociated modern age. Even the West knew it—once

Jung's patient reminds us of another young Jewish woman of that time, and closely so in certain ways. This second figure, Edith Stein, was born in the 1890s in Breslau, which was then part of Germany. Edith was well educated and noted for her intellectual brilliance, though she was also considered kindly and warm-hearted. She was to write a number of noted works on philosophy, her stance at that time being staunchly atheistic.

Nevertheless, she eventually became a Catholic nun, having experienced a revelation in which she suddenly understood the immense significance of "Christ in the mystery of the Cross." She then chanced upon the autobiography of St. Teresa of Avila, which deeply affected her, and which she came to love dearly, so that when she became a nun she chose "Teresa" for her Baptismal name, becoming later Sister Teresa Benedicta. She was to become a very devout personality, but one with a humanity and simplicity that everyone who met her not only admired, but much loved. She appears to have been that rare combination of brilliant mind and truly humble soul, and looking at her photograph now, her face is lovely. Both the high intelligence and gentle, special quality of soul shine through.

Yet she was to die at the hands of the Nazis simply because she was Jewish. She had been sent to a convent in Echt, Holland, where her sister, who had also become a nun, joined her. Eventually, the two were arrested and sent "Eastwards," which to the Jews meant to Auschwitz, and there the sisters were gassed on August 9, 1942. (What is especially significant for me is that this was my own date of birth. Edith Stein—St. Teresa Benedicta—and her sister were being murdered as I was being born.)

Jung's young patient and Edith Stein were similar in that both were at first existing completely contrary to their true natures, for each had the soul of a saint but were living superficially and atheistically. (Both possessed Jewish "soul," of course.) Edith was beatified in 1987 and canonized in 1998. Unfortunately Jung does not tell us what eventually became of his young patient.

In another work *(The Grail, the Stone, and the Mystics)* we look at the visions of St. Teresa of Avila, which brought about the transformation in Edith, as these clearly contain symbolism of an individuation process, which makes the visions perfectly valid and tenable. An individuation process would almost certainly have been taking place in Edith unconsciously, and probably also in Jung's patient, for this may occur in suitable personalities no matter how estranged the ego may be from it in consciousness, and indeed, may become the imperative need.

I must leave off momentarily here to tell a dream I have had that is highly significant to this work.

> *There is a large, Old English sheepdog in a small room, about six feet away from where I am sitting. The dog then becomes a lion, complete with heavy mane, and picking up in its jaws this manuscript on which I am presently working, which is lying on a small table across the room, the lion brings it over to me, laying it on my lap. I am very concerned as to whether the lion, having its ferocious side, will attack me, but it actually sits quite close, smiling, though eager for me to press on with the work.*

The dream means that I have the full backing of the unconscious for the manuscript, and indeed, it is eager for me to press on with it. The lion is a well-known symbol in mythology and in alchemy, in the latter for Mercurius, who in turn symbolizes the collective unconscious in dual (indeed, many) aspects. That is why I wonder whether the lion is friendly or is going to attack me, for being dual in nature, the unconscious may be friendly and helpful, or conversely, very dangerous. The alchemists taught that the lion needed to have its paws cut off in the opus, which meant that the unconscious had to be rendered harmless and friendly in order for the work to continue. In the Bible, Samson and David both slay a lion at the beginning of their stories, really individuation processes, as does Herakles in the Greek myth, and Gawain in his quest for the Holy Grail, and all with the same meaning.

The lion is also a symbol of Christ, and Vishnu in India, as it was of Horus and Iu-em-hetep in Egypt. As Christ is the main symbol of the Higher Self for Western Man, so too were these figures for their respective cultures. Furthermore, the lion was a sheepdog at first in my dream, and a dog is also a symbol of the Self in first phase, on the male, spirit side. The dog-spirit has been known in mythology and folklore, and therefore in the unconscious processes, from most ancient times, the Egyptian gods Anubis and Apuat being examples. In fact, Horus, the Higher Self as divine Son, was said to be Anubis in one form. In central America the dog-headed god, Xolotl, accompanies Quetzalcoatl to the Underworld. My own dog played a significant role in my own individuation process as guide and companion.

A woman I know awakened to find a lion in bed with her, purring away. She had earlier experienced a bear. These are main symbols of forces through the unconscious and we find them several times in the Bible and throughout alchemy. Before slaying Goliath, David kills both a lion and a bear, actually to save a lamb from them, i.e., the divine child. Ezekiel sees a lion and a bear as part of his visions, as does Jeremiah.

The full backing of the collective unconscious for the work is very welcome, as it would be difficult for me to continue if the opposite were the case. All sorts of obstacles would be placed in my path; I would be drained of enthusiasm, concentration, and energy, and would be unable to carry on finally. However, as I say, the unconscious seems especially eager for this work to be done. (Since writing this I have dreamt of the lion sitting in front of me, facing outwards away from me, as though to guard and protect me.)

Chapter 3

Jung Discovers the Collective Unconscious

The Freud/Jung Association Begins

When Jung read Freud's *Interpretation of Dreams* in 1900, he was unable to understand most of it because he lacked any real experience of the subject. On re-reading it in 1903, however, he found that it fitted in with certain ideas of his own that had formed in the interim. He also read Josef Breuer and Pierre Janet and found much valuable material in their works. Yet Jung found he could not agree with Freud that the basis of every repression is sexual. He had seen many cases himself where the cause was not sexual, so even at the beginning of their association there were differences between the two doctors in their ideas. In fact, Jung himself reminisced at the age of eighty-six that although he had liked Freud very much at their first meeting, he could nevertheless see that in certain ways a wide gulf divided them.

Be that as it may, Jung took up the fight on Freud's behalf in the medical world, as the latter was not merely being rejected, but worse, ignored. Actually, Jung had first been tempted to publish his own findings without mentioning Freud, as though he were unaware of him and his work. But he knew this amounted to a lie, and in any case, his No. 2 personality interceded, refusing to let him do it. So he wrote a paper defending Freud, the upshot of which was that two eminent professors wrote to Jung, warning him that if he continued to defend Freud, his whole career would be at stake. Jung continued to do so, and after he published his own work, *The Psychology of Dementia Praecox* (schizophrenia), Freud invited him to Vienna for the first historic meeting in 1907.

As well as liking Freud, Jung was greatly impressed by him, though it was not easy to make him out, not easy to assess him. They talked for thirteen hours virtually nonstop, with Jung still having doubts about Freud's exclusive sexual theory. Indeed, Jung tried to raise objections to this on many occasions after this first meeting but Freud merely reminded him of his lack of experience; he would come to see things differently in the future. This was always to be a serious matter of contention between the two men, and even that was not really the main one of all, or was only a part of it. Time would show that not only the nature and meaning of the human psyche, but of the whole of reality itself was different for both men, and so the break was inevitable right from the beginning.

Jung realized this a few years later, when Freud asked him to promise not to abandon the sexual theory, but to make a dogma and a bulwark of it against the "black tide of occultism." Freud, having lost God, was substituting and deifying sexuality in His place. By "occultism" Freud meant everything that is not strictly material, rational and scientific, and it included religion preeminently and most definitely. Though not fully understanding what he was seeing, Jung had observed certain eruptions of a religious nature breaking out in Freud from the beginning, springing up from the unconscious, that he was repressing with the bulwark of his sexual theory.

As a matter of fact, the most powerful weapon the instinctual depths use against the religious impulse is sexuality—spiritual and sexual impulses are not merely opposites at the personal level of the unconscious, but also and more importantly at the collective level. Freud could never see this and would always strenuously deny that the collective unconscious exists. Jung speaks of the devastating conflict between love of God/spiritual meaning on the one side, and the desires of the flesh on the other. Jung later explained that for Freud, the lost God above now had to be sought below, and on the personal level, which meant that for him sexuality replaced God. For Freud, sexuality came to have the emotional numinosity of the lost God. Lower sexuality, which is felt as personal, of course, is in no way qualified or adequate to replace an eternal God. It caused a neurotic bitterness in Freud that Jung continually observed. Freud, whose role was to try and cure the sick, was himself suffering from neurosis, which had "the most troublesome symptoms," as Jung put it.

We must seriously ask if Freud with his materialistic/atheistic outlook merely confirmed the pessimistic fears of some of his patients that reality was without spiritual meaning, which condemned them to the same matter-only existence to which he himself was condemned, when their souls were crying out desperately for higher meaning. His treatment surely could not have helped Jung's patient, the Jewish girl who possessed the soul of a saint. Freud's insistence on sexual causes of neurosis would have been catastrophic for her, because sexuality was one of the forms of materialism she was drowning in. It was precisely the opposite remedy—religious meaning, which Freud totally denied—that was her cure. Jung always insisted that a change began to occur in his patients when they started to experience the religious archetypes from the nonpersonal levels of the unconscious. Freud believed that everyone is neurotic and merely accepted the situation, whereas Jung asked why the natural state of mankind had to be neurotic. Why should mankind not meant to be mentally healthy, as with the physical body? If we become neurotic, why is it not possible to cure that neurosis just as it is possible to cure physical illness?

Jung had come to understand the problem of the opposites of love and power, and he fully realized that just as Nietzsche had glorified power, Freud was now deifying sex. Thus Freud was prompted to try to extract the promise from Jung to defend the deified sexual position at all costs, a promise which Jung could not give. Freud was to demand this same promise from all those who wished to work with him in the years that followed, and almost all gave it. Freud had deified sexuality, as he had exalted science, believing that nothing must be allowed to knock these new gods off their thrones. By this time, Jung had begun to realize there are historical layers to the psyche.

Jung dreamed of two human skulls in a cave under the cellar of a house. He realized this was possibly giving him some answers to the many questions he had been asking concerning the lower strata of the human psyche. When he related the dream to Freud, however, the latter kept urging him to look for a secret, mostly unconscious death wish in it. So Jung, still feeling unable to challenge his mentor, stated that it perhaps meant a death wish towards his wife and sister-in-law, the first people that sprang to mind. Jung told Freud what he thought Freud wanted to hear, so that he would be satisfied with the answer. But Jung had realized the dream must refer to the successive layers of the human psyche, some obviously very deep and archaic.

Some writers have seen a "Freudian slip" in Jung's answer to Freud, which must reveal a death wish towards his wife. Others have suggested the reply was a "sideswipe" at Freud. One psychologist even claimed it to be a sort of therapeutic lying involving the solution to Jung's "split personality" —saying that by lying to Freud, and therefore hiding a secret, Jung thus healed the split within himself. (To be perfectly honest, I am still trying to figure out what on earth this psychologist could be talking about, though whatever it is, it is not the answer to Jung's answer to Freud. Jung had to suffer this sort of thing for most of his life. I personally have spent thirty years experiencing the depths of the unconscious and beyond, and it is my honest opinion that the people who know least about the human psyche, and indeed, the unconscious, are certain modern psychiatrists, so called doctors of the mind.)

A house, in dreams, represents the psyche, or fuller personality, of the individual, for just as we live in our house, so we inhabit our psyche. Skulls in a cave under the deepest layer of the house would therefore allude to something even older below or beyond the personal psyche, something collective and archaic. As for the cave in the dream, it is well known in mythology as the "Earth-womb," in which serpents, dragons, genies, and trolls reside, as well as being the entrance to the "hidden place" where is found the great treasure, sometimes a god. Mithras, for example, is born in a cave, as is Dionysus in the Orphic myths. So too is Christ in some Gnostic and apocryphal versions of his myth (*The Gospel of James* and *The History of Joseph the Carpenter,* etc.). Even in the traditional version, the original Aramaic word for "stable," *katalemna,* can also mean "cave." So we can see to what deeper meaning Jung's dream alluded, and he, with what must have been bated breath, obviously began to suspect as much himself.

The Breakthrough (The Door Opens)

We now come to those discoveries of Jung that are surely the most significant of the past few hundred years. The future of Western civilization literally depends upon them, and I am not overstating the case. My pronouncement is based solidly upon years of warnings (and much else) from the collective unconscious itself, experienced in my own dreams, that I have to take seriously. Jung's discoveries can lead us to a new and deeper understanding of religion, of our own Western spiritual heritage, and to new association with and further development of the spirit, ultimately meaning a new association, a covenant, with God. If we fail in this most important of tasks, Western civilization will collapse into chaos. That is what the unconscious itself states, though it also offers the opportunity for the necessary leap forward

For Jung, the dream of skulls in the cellar was the turning point, for it revived his old interest in archaeology and the ancient world. He began to read books on Babylonian myths and other material, including certain Gnostic works. It all had a peculiar effect on him. A work by the

German mythologist, Friedrich Creuzer, *The Symbolism and Mythology of Ancient Peoples,* had a particular relevance. Jung says reading it was like being in a madhouse and treating as patients all of the figures encountered in mythology. But then something clicked, and he suddenly saw the connection between the psychology to be observed in ancient mythology and that of primitive peoples; there were distinct similarities. He knew he had discovered something important.

Also at this time he looked at material published by an old "revered and fatherly" friend, Theodore Flournoy, which contained the schizophrenic fantasies of an American girl, a Miss Miller, which too were clearly mythological in nature. These consisted basically of three main fantasies; the first a poem she composed in three stanzas, "Glory to God"; the second a poem in ten verses called "The Moth and the Sun"; and the third a fantasy of an Aztec god she called Chiwantopel. Jung immediately recognized that although these fantasies appeared to be schizophrenic delusions, they consisted of material that forms the basis of many myths of the world. They were therefore not strictly "delusions," which would have no reality at all, but were archetypal and so actually did exist at another level of reality, as contents of the collective unconscious. The problem was, they were breaking through to Miss Miller's conscious mind almost uncontrollably, threatening to overwhelm it, as usually happens in cases of schizophrenia or psychosis. "The Moth and the Sun" obviously spelled great danger for the young woman, for we know what happens to a moth when uncontrollably drawn to a bright flame.

In these fantasies, Jung saw the mythological/psychological motif of the Sun-hero who descends into the depths of the feminine collective unconscious, the World Soul, on the "night-sea journey," in which the terrible dragon may be conquered and spiritual rebirth attained. In Miss Miller's fantasy however, Chiwantopel fails and an earthquake engulfs him. Consequently, Jung feared that catastrophe would befall Miss Miller herself, foretold by the moth and the flame and the fate of Chiwantopel.

We must remember that Jung was just beginning to understand these things and still had an immense amount to learn. The failure of the hero/Self in his quest, while meaning collapse of that particular individuation process, does not automatically mean the destruction of consciousness. Although the moth/flame motif warned that Miss Miller was in grave danger, it is yet possible to scrape through such a situation safely. This may have been the case with Miss Miller, and indeed, one report says that she later made a happy marriage. So the situation apparently did not end in tragedy, as Jung believed it would.

Whatever her outcome, Jung having studied the Gnostic, Egyptian, Babylonian, and other material from world mythology, and seeing similar material in the fantasies of Miss Miller and other patients, plus the motifs found in the psychology of primitives, suddenly realized they all had similar themes and certain related symbolism. Obviously, all those individuals in world cultures who had produced the myths could not have been mentally ill, and in fact myths are far too healthy and ultimately wise for that to be so. The similar material in the mentally sick patients, Jung concluded, had to be breaking through uncontrollably from another, nonpersonal level of the unconscious, the conscious minds of the patients being unable to assimilate the contents successfully. That alone could be the answer.

Jung worked on these elements for some time, and the end result was his book, *The Psychology of the Unconscious,* later retitled *Symbols of Transformation.* This is a great work—first published in three parts, between 1911 and 1913—for within its pages Jung explores the true nature of mythology and religion, great literary works, primitive cultures, and many other relevant items from the view of psychology and the collective unconscious. This was quite revolutionary for its time, and indeed, for the most part even now. Jung further realized in this work that libido is a primal force that is psychological, and even spiritual in a sense. It is not necessarily sexual, although it can be so channeled.

Jung had found the key to the great mystery of myth and religion, why Man has always felt compelled to record myths and enact rituals. Further pieces of the puzzle would take their own time to arrive; but it was all potentially there. Even at this early time Jung came to realize that the world's myths and religions—indeed, all its esoteric Mysteries—are based upon direct experiences of spirit and soul coming through from the collective unconscious to the personal unconscious.

Jung further demonstrates in the book that the conquest of the Great Mother depths is a necessity of personal development, certainly in the individuation process, and is only partly the task of winning freedom from the personal mother. Yet he eventually came to realize that the same symbolism would arise in a hero who had never known a personal mother (or even, we must add, if personal mothers did not exist at all). So the mother archetype has to be collective ultimately, being on a much larger scale than at the level of the merely personal mother. Archetypal motifs involving the hero are in this way nonpersonal and belong to the structure of fuller reality itself.

One well-known motif of the collective unconscious is the winged or feathered serpent, known to both the Americas and the East. I remember seeing writer Graham Hancock on television, stating there must have been a very ancient preexistent culture that gave all of these myths and motifs to the world. He mentioned both the serpent and the winged/feathered serpent specifically as prime examples of motifs found in myths universally. But the preexistent culture of which he spoke is actually the collective unconscious. Wings, and therefore birds, symbolize higher spirit, and the serpent the chthonic soul depths, so the winged serpent represents the unification of both. The symbol means the unification of the opposites in the Higher Self, which is why in Central America the Savior figure Quetzalcoatl was symbolically the Feathered Serpent (or Plumed Serpent).

As said, archetypal material may be experienced chaotically, and people may be overwhelmed, but the symbolic contents are also experienced during the hero's quest through the unconscious, Jung's individuation process. The difference is that the hero is able to assimilate the contents without being overwhelmed by them, and they do, in fact, expand his personality, while with the mentally ill person they may shatter an already weakened consciousness. The archetypes, then, constitute great danger, a devastating assault on ego-consciousness in its state of weakness, but the initiate who is able to rise above and contain the contents, grows in gnosis (knowledge) and personality. He may then wear the lion skin, like Herakles, the lion symbolizing the unconscious force he has defeated, or rather gained and unified with. The dangerous pouring through of unconscious contents was symbolized in my own dreams, at least in one way, by my being on an island with the sea waters rising up threateningly, so that I had to go up on higher land. But unless the patient's psychiatrist knows all of this, which in all probability he or she will not, it will be interpreted as the delusional hallucinations of a sick mind, even in a "hero," having no basis in reality whatsoever. Jung became a master of this inner knowledge and so could help his patients assimilate the archetypes, and therefore find healing and grow as personalities

It all started to come together for Jung with these realizations; he had *the* answer, *the* key, to the great mystery of the human psyche, to the real meaning of myths and religions, and to the deeper meaning of life itself. After all, while the discovery of the personal unconscious may be of major importance for mankind, the further discovery of another reality to be reached beyond that, entirely different in nature to the physical universe, is world-shaking in its implications. Yet Man in the past always knew of this other reality, whole cultures being constructed upon experience of the spirit/soul archetypes

Dreams Foretell the Break with Freud

Jung had dreams and certain experiences concerning Freud at this early time, 1911, which presaged the split between the two men. Jung's unconscious would have known he was outgrowing Freud, and the archetypal dreams themselves were strong omens. For his part, Freud had come to believe Jung had a death wish towards him, he being the "father" and Jung the "son," so to speak. Freud even fainted a couple of times because of this. The first occasion was when Jung began discussing recently discovered peat-bog corpses while they were having dinner together. As Jung chatted on about them, Freud became progressively agitated, eventually becoming so overwhelmed he fainted. Afterwards he told Jung that he, Jung, obviously had a death wish towards him, which amounted, in Freud's neurotic thinking, to the slaying of the father impulse. Jung was naturally somewhat amazed that Freud's death-wish fantasies could be so intense as to cause him to faint, though it is true Freud had fainted on a number of other occasions when his emotions became too overwhelming for him.

Freud's second faint concerning Jung was during a congress in Munich, when someone remarked that Akhenaten, the Egyptian Pharaoh, had destroyed his father's cartouches on the steles due to his negative attitude towards his father, and that his monotheistic religion was therefore due to a father complex. Jung was coming to realize that the secret to such figures as Akhenaten lay at a much deeper level than mere personal complexes, so he argued that Akhenaten had been a highly religious man and had held his father in honor (which is certainly the case). Furthermore, Jung went on, most other pharaohs chiseled out the names of their fathers, inserting their own simply because they were all incarnations of the same god. It was common practice, and, very significantly, rechiseling also happened in many cases where the previous pharaoh had not been the personal father. So with Akhenaten and the other examples of rechiseling, there are no grounds whatsoever for suspecting "father complex."

In any case, at this point Freud fainted off his chair, and so Jung picked him up and laid him across a sofa in the adjoining room. Jung states that as he did so, Freud in his weakness looked up at him as though he, Jung, were the father, and Freud the helpless son. As Jung points out,

Freud's fantasies of father murder were the basis of both fainting incidents, although Jung would also have unconsciously represented, potentially, the deeper powers of the unconscious that Freud was blocking out. Considering Freud's obsessive need to possess authority and to be right at all costs, especially over his sexual theory, and considering Jung's future great discoveries, which Freud would have sensed unconsciously, it is small wonder that Freud felt so deeply threatened by Jung, who was to prove a greater light.

We could say it is perhaps true, in a sense, that Jung did have a death wish—not against Freud's personal life, but against his authority. Jung himself says they were in their work like father and son, as well as like master and apprentice, but the point had been reached where the son had outgrown the father, and the apprentice was growing into a greater master than the present master was, or could ever be. In that sense, therefore, Jung had to be rid of Freud—I am speaking of the full situation itself and not of Jung's conscious thoughts—so that Jung could grow to his own true stature.

Jung had two particular dreams that highlighted the true situation, over which he was still somewhat confused and puzzled. The first dream concerned an old Austrian customs official who was peevish and vexed. It turned out at the end of the dream that the figure had really been a ghost from the past and Jung concluded that this represented Freud and his limited attitude. Jung's second dream was of a medieval knight in shining armor, over which hung a white tunic displaying a red cross. This, Jung realized, was a Grail Knight, concerned with the quest for the Holy Grail. There was a world of difference between the meanings of the two dreams, and Jung knew that Freud, the small, peevish, long-dead figure from the first dream, could never understand the breathtaking implications of the Grail Knight of the second, whose quest was essentially a holy one.

Jung had always loved the Arthurian/Grail legends, always sensing they contained a special, deeper meaning, and he was now feeling a desperate urge, a yearning, to find similar meaning that, as the dreams were demonstrating, lay way beyond Freud's understanding. Jung had long been forced to sacrifice his own ideas before Freud's authority to large degree, and had understood this was the price required by Freud for the collaboration. But this state of affairs could not last indefinitely, as the unconscious was now telling him.

The final break with Freud came when Jung stated in *Symbols of Transformation* that incest also has a wider, spiritual significance, and claimed that religious/mythological symbolism generally has origins in a wider, nonpersonal unconscious. He knew this might cost him his friendship with Freud, and it did, for Freud would tolerate no opposition to his own theories, no matter how genuinely those differing ideas were felt. Jung's wife, Emma, believed Freud, though disagreeing, would understand and be magnanimous, but Jung knew better, and when the book was published, the friendship was over. The book was generally declared to be nonsense in any case, and most of Jung's colleagues and friends in psychology deserted him.

So, strictly speaking, Jung did not break with Freud, it was Freud who would not tolerate Jung after he had openly declared disagreement with certain of Freud's theories. Of course, Freud must have felt relieved to be rid of the man who was upsetting him so much as to cause fainting incidents. But it is also true that the unconscious itself would have brought about the necessary break sooner or later, and indeed, deep down Jung must have known that the break would occur with the publication of his book. Freud, though doing important pioneer work, was less gifted and a lesser light than Jung, and the truths that Jung was to discover were incalculably greater than Freud's limited and ultimately negative view of the human psyche and of full reality. Plus, Freud had blocked off from his conscious mind all of the archetypal material that Jung now proclaimed in his book.

Nevertheless, at first Jung tried to offer Freud openings, making statements and concessions that could have smoothed the ground between them, and indeed, Freud seemed to respond. But it was merely a front; privately he was very angry and upset. The situation gradually worsened, becoming quite difficult and openly hostile between the two. Jung wrote a letter to Freud, stating that if he would persist in playing the role of the authoritarian father, or treating his pupils as patients and stressing all their faults, he would continue to produce either "slavish sons or impudent puppies" as followers. Furthermore, as Freud remained on top as father, "sitting pretty," Jung suggested that instead of attacking everyone else's failings he should take a good look at his own.

This letter to Freud has been called "amazing," "reacting with ferocity," "a massive over-reaction," and "behaving like a florid fool and the brutal fellow that he is." Personally, I think it rather mild considering all of the tension and hostility that had built up between the two men, which must have been ready to explode. They finally agreed to cease all further correspondence. In future years Jung did write to Freud a couple of times or so concerning medical matters, but Freud never replied.

It is true Jung was considered hot tempered at times by some who knew him, particularly in his earlier years, but this was only part of his basically honest and forthright nature. He told people not to take this surface attitude seriously, that deep down he held no animosity. And this must have been so, because to explore the depths of the collective unconscious with an unfriendly basic nature would have brought negative results. This did not occur—in fact, Jung experienced the most positive results possible, highly religious in nature. No one could have written books of such depth of understanding and of genuine humanity had he been the cruel and ferocious personality some have accused him of being.

It has been suggested that Jung was perhaps like the medieval mystic alchemist Paracelsus (whose forename was Bombastus, hence "bombast"), forthright and even explosive at times on the surface, but possessing a great and truly human heart underneath. Jung says himself that the bombast in Paracelsus was most probably caused by the powerful tension that contact with the collective unconscious brings, and he seems to have understood the same concerning himself. As a matter of fact, those who claim that Jung's manner was too rough at times are mostly those who were hostile to his theories, or who have not understood them. Others found him quite engaging, and still others mesmerizing and loveable. (I have been experiencing the same conflicting opposites of the collective unconscious myself for thirty years but have nevertheless remained the same shy, charming, affable, adorable soul I always was—at least, that's *my* opinion.)

Jung Undergoes the Individuation Process: Dreams and Visions Erupt

Isolated after the break with Freud, Jung felt disoriented and helpless in a world that was largely alien. Yet he felt that he was serving a higher will. He now had to fight on behalf of his own discoveries, and ironically, was to investigate the higher, deeper, and wider aspects of sexuality through the unconscious, particularly in alchemy, carrying on work begun in a sense by Freud. It may be that Freud could have done some of the later work himself, had not his reductive and materialistic prejudices made it impossible. Higher sexuality involves the Sacred Marriage between the eternal opposites of masculine spirit and feminine soul, the *Hieros Gamos*, upon which the greatest religious truths are based.

Jung was to spend the next fifty years investigating the deeper and wider reaches of the unconscious, which stretch out to goodness knows where—certainly, it is at least a parallel reality to the known material universe. As he did so, Jung correspondingly grew himself as a personality, becoming the "wise old man," seer, and prophet, and even, it seems at times, holy man. He grew into what he studied and experienced, so that he seems to be the personification of the collective unconscious itself. This is *mana*, of course. In his work and his discoveries, Jung was to run counter to the twentieth century and Western civilization, for while the latter moved ever further away from religion and plunged into scientific-materialism—and indeed, into materialism in all of its forms—Jung found himself heading the other way, back to the irrational, the mythological, the mystical, the religious; as realities discovered through the collective unconscious, though done by means of scientific investigation.

Always cautious in his writings, Jung wished to present his case as empirical evidence, for only evidence will convince modern Man. Even then it is a long shot when it involves the unconscious, unless people should happen to have direct experience of these things themselves, which few actually do. By far the most difficult thing for modern Man to accept, apparently, is that religion has its basis in fact, that it has always arisen through original experience, and therefore need not depend upon mere faith. It is irrational fact involving unconscious/spirit reality, but nevertheless fact.

At the end of 1912, Jung had a dream of a white bird, probably a dove, which changed into a little girl with golden hair, aged about eight, who spoke of a male dove and "the twelve dead." I have been visited by the same archetypal child myself several times over the years, and each time she had golden curls and was aged about eight, though I have also seen the corresponding boy child, actually more often. These are the male/female sides of the Self as they first appear in human form. One of the dreams of the girl with golden curls appears later in chapter 5, under the sub-heading The Star Above.

Jung could not help pondering just to what the twelve dead spoken of by the girl in his dream could allude, thinking of the twelve disciples, the zodiac, and so forth, but could find no satisfactory answer. He then had another dream, of rows of tombs that revealed mummified corpses on stone slabs. These included one from the nineteenth century, one from the eighteenth century, and then going back to finally a crusader knight from the twelfth century. The corpses each came alive and clasped their hands when Jung looked at them, though the crusader barely moved his finger, thereby showing it was only just stirring. Jung felt very disturbed by it all, though he suspected that it must have profound meaning. In fact, he felt so disoriented that he checked over all the details he could remember of his whole life, to try and find some item that could be responsible for his present state of disturbance, but nothing seemed to fit.

This deep uneasiness led him to build little houses and a castle out of stones, bottles, anything he could find, and he eventually found he was constructing a little town. He had done this as a boy and felt he was now making contact with his young life again, and greatly enjoyed doing it. Jung was beginning to construct himself into a more total personality, for as part of the individuation process our past, present, and even future must be made one. Furthermore, building houses and a town symbolizes construction of the Higher Self, as I know from my own processes. (A town I built in my processes was called "Robertsville" by the unconscious.)

One modern writer states that Jung's dream about the "twelve dead" and the crusaders reveals how he was trying to cope with the break with Freud, again displaying total lack of understanding. The dream has nothing to do with Freud. It shows that Jung was now touching upon lower, archetypal layers of the unconscious that descend and recede back into history, that still exist in that timeless other reality that Jung was stirring up. In a sense, it is waking the dead; that is, from the view of consciousness; from the view of the collective unconscious itself, the archetypal contents merely slumber until their possible awakening, or reawakening. Naturally, it was causing Jung to feel very disturbed, as waking the dead would do.

It really quite literally meant awakening the medieval past spiritually, in order to continue the royal line of spirit that runs through the Western collective unconscious. This began in ancient Egypt, running through the Hebrew prophets and up to Christ. The medieval mysteries of alchemy, the Holy Grail, and the visionary processes of the saints and mystics, had continued this line to a degree. Holy Ghost movements had sprung up all over Europe based upon the quaternity structure, the unification of the masculine Trinity with feminine World Soul as 3 + 1. But it had all eventually died in the ages of reason and materialism that had followed. At least, it had sunk back to the depths of the unconscious/spirit. It was now becoming Jung's task to bring the royal line to life again through depth psychology, which is why part of his work for many years was to study alchemy.

Some time after these dreams, in 1913, Jung's visionary and prophetic powers became fully activated, although at first he himself did not understand just what was happening. Travelling on a long train journey, he was suddenly overwhelmed by the vision of a flood covering all of Northern

Europe, though the Alps of Switzerland had grown higher to rise above the flood. Many thousands of drowned bodies were floating in the seas, which had turned blood red, and the debris of a civilization that had collapsed into chaos could be seen everywhere. The vision lasted for about an hour, then passed, but a couple of weeks later Jung saw the same vision again. He knew that whatever this alluded to was certain to occur He concluded it must allude to himself, that he was in danger of succumbing to a psychosis. (Had this been so, the Swiss Alps rising above the chaos would have meant that he, a Swiss himself, would eventually, as consciousness, surmount the chaos that surrounded him.)

Not long after this, Jung had a further dream, repeated three times, in which a whole land was covered with ice, killing off all the green vegetation. In the last of the dreams, the freeze descended from the cosmos, but unexpectedly Jung then saw a tree whose leaves turned to grapes, "full of healing juices." He plucked these and handed them around to the crowd that had now gathered there.

Soon afterwards the First World War broke out, and so Jung realized that his dreams and visions had alluded to that. He was to understand later that a flood is a very ancient symbol used by the collective unconscious to represent the overwhelming of a culture by negative forces from the collective depths, and the subsequent collapse of that culture into chaos. But Jung's disturbing experiences did not cease there, and he was continually bombarded with them, forcing him to conclude he was going insane, as others including Nietzsche have done under the great onslaught of archetypal material from the unconscious. Furthermore, although Jung as yet would not have realized it, certain alchemists, who experienced processes of the unconscious themselves in dreams, had also suffered a similar fate. One of them, Heinrich Khunrath, stated, "Not a few have perished in our work." Although the poisonous substances sometimes used in the opus, the work, fatally affected some alchemists, others were severely affected mentally by forces from the unknown depths, just as many shamans have been.

So Jung did Yoga exercises to try and keep the visions under control, yet he was careful not to stop them altogether (if, indeed, they could have been stopped), for he knew that to dissociate himself from them completely could cause a serious neurosis, as it had done with Freud. On the other hand, being overwhelmed by them would mean being shattered by a psychosis. He was also well aware that he could cause mass psychosis that could run riot in others; that he could be stirring up a psychic epidemic just as dangerous as a physical plague in medieval times.

Jung realized that at all costs he must learn to interpret his visions and their symbolic contents or they would overwhelm him. So he knew it was imperative to go down to meet the contents squarely. Nevertheless, he also knew there are occasions when contact with the unconscious must be strictly avoided, as in cases of latent psychosis, and Jung seriously wondered if this was not the present danger to himself. Whatever the case, he was aware something tremendous was happening now, and it was perhaps too late to get out of it. Besides, he needed to gain control over these invading powers not only for his own good, but for the sake of his patients, for how could he help them if he was unable to handle the material himself?

He then had two other experiences—this was at the end of 1913—the first of which occurred while sitting at his desk. All of a sudden, he found himself plummeting down to black depths below, to a cave where there was a dwarf and a red crystal. Then, lifting a stone to reveal another cave beneath, he saw the body of a blond youth, wounded in the head and floating by in the waters of a stream. A huge black scarab, a red Sun rising from the water, and a stone, from which spurted gallons of blood, followed the youth along the stream.

Some days later, Jung had a dream the essence of which was that, with a brown-skinned primitive as companion (or accomplice), he shot and killed the blond-haired Germanic hero, Siegfried. After this the rain came down in heavy torrents, and Jung felt full of remorse and guilt that he had killed something so "great and beautiful."

Jung knew the first vision referred to a solar myth involving a Sun-hero, and that both the scarab and the rising Sun alluded to rebirth. In ancient Egypt the scarab represented Khepru, God as the self-creating force (the scarab reproduces from out of itself), while the rising Sun symbolized God rising from the Underworld at every new dawn, although sometimes it was God as his Son, Horus. In fact, one form of God in Egypt was as the Red Sun, called the Red God. (Christ was also the rising Sun to the first Christians.) Beyond this Jung was mystified.

On waking from the Siegfried dream, Jung had the overwhelming feeling that he would be compelled to shoot himself unless he could interpret the meaning of the dream correctly. He never said why he would be forced to shoot himself, only that the shooting would definitely happen if he failed to fully understand. Thankfully, it suddenly dawned on him that the experiences, though having a personal aspect, were mostly of a collective nature, and that Siegfried represented the Germanic desire to dominate and "heroically" impose its will. Jung understood that he consciously shared this desire of the "ego's will," but now saw that it represented a view, a wish, that was neither desirable nor possible, either for himself or for Western Man generally. Siegfried, in short, was too primitive a form of hero. The dream was therefore stating that this inflated standpoint of consciousness had to die, symbolized as the killing of Siegfried, who was a too archaic type of god. Jung concluded there are higher things than heroic idealism and the will of the ego, and as the brown-skinned primitive companion represented his own dark shadow, there should now follow a better relationship with the unconscious. Rain, by the way, is a very good sign in dreams, meaning that things are now going well, or soon will be. Snow means the opposite, for while rain causes things to grow and blossom, snow can kill them off. Nothing grows well in snow.

Incidentally, the modern critic of Jung mentioned earlier sees both the dwarf in the cave in the first experience, and Siegfried in the dream that followed as representing Freud. The dwarf because Freud was only five-feet seven tall while Jung was six-feet one, and Siegfried because Jung killed him off, supposedly becoming full of guilt and remorse because of the split with Freud and the desire to polish *him* off. Again, this displays total lack of understanding of the archetypal nature of the unconscious and how it expresses itself. These critics find it impossible to see beyond Jung's personal psychology and supposed resentments and complexes. What is actually involved is another archetypal and apparently eternal reality of spirit and soul that Jung was experiencing. Jung was breaking into that other reality—*it* was breaking into *him*.

The early visions of Jung, along with his realization that mythology is the key to the collective unconscious—and vice versa, that the collective unconscious is the key to mythology—constitute the turning point, the beginning of something truly great. Jung's dream of the Egyptian scarab and the rising Sun pointed to spiritual rebirth, first of all in the personality of Jung. But as contents of the collective unconscious were involved, the rebirth was not limited to Jung, just as when Moses experienced God (and the Higher Self) it was not limited to Moses alone but concerned the whole of the Israelite people, and even the whole of mankind. Jungian psychology is not just a method of treatment for personal mental problems, it is a new way—and yet the age-old way—to God; and also, we must never forget, to the Devil. Jung connects us to the immortal side of our nature, for we are the mortal part of that immortal, the Self. In order for him to have established this truth, Jung had to pass through the highly dangerous, tortuous fires of the unconscious realm and not only survive, but flourish.

As must be clear, Freudian theories are totally inadequate to deal with the contents of such visions, and attempts to interpret them along those lines entirely miss the mark. Jung actually says Freud could not interpret archetypal "big dreams," and so would therefore retreat into his sexual dogma, the limits of his psychological horizon being much too low and narrow.

Chapter 4

The Four Gold Keys

Jung had another dream at this time in which he was in a sort of a crater on the Moon, or in "the land of the dead," where he saw a "wise old man" figure with a white beard, together with a beautiful young blind girl. These called themselves Elijah and Salome, and accompanying them was a large, black snake. Now, the "wise old man" and the girl often appear together in unconscious processes and they represent the opposites of spirit/meaning, and soul/life. Jung called the "wise old man" archetype "the personification of spirit," but was of the opinion that Salome was blind in his dream because, representing the anima, she could not see the meaning of things. These figures are found together when a certain psychic/spiritual stage has been reached, meaning a union of the opposite sides, partly at the collective level. The snake has a variety of interconnected meanings, and it is found frequently as the counterpart to the hero in myths. The snake may represent evil, but also wisdom, for as scripture says, "*Be ye therefore wise as serpents*" (Matt. 10:16). In ancient Egypt, the positive Uraeus serpent encircled Pharaoh's crown in protection, whereas the evil Apep serpent, representing chaos and destruction, had to be fought and defeated.

In later dreams, Jung experienced the figure of a winged old man who had developed out of the Elijah figure, whom Jung called Philemon. Philemon radiated an Egyptian/Hellenistic/Gnostic aura, and while his wings were those of a kingfisher, he also had the horns of a bull. He brought Jung a bunch of four keys, which is actually a highly significant event. As Jung says, psychologically this figure represents superior insight and knowledge, and indeed, is that "personification of spirit." We meet him in many myths, legends, and religious texts. One example is Jethro, who teaches Moses the religious Mysteries, and whose daughter, Zipporah, Moses marries. Jethro and Zipporah form the "wise old man" and girl archetype, and Potipherah and Asenath with Joseph in Egypt, and Lao Tse with the dancing girl in China, are other examples.

Many critics, including Freud, have accused Jung of imagining himself a prophet and redeemer, not realizing that it was mastery of the collective unconscious that made prophets and redeemers of Moses, Jesus, the Buddha, and all the rest. However, Jung always stressed that he was no more than a psychoanalyst doing his job, though we know he was much more.

Another archetype then began to appear to Jung at this early time, which seemed to come from out of the Earth. Jung called it Ka, after the Egyptian figure of the Earth that embodied Pharaoh's soul. This figure was connected with metals and announced to Jung that he was the one by whom the gods are buried in gold and gems. Jung was able to integrate all of the archetypal contents in the years that followed through his studies into alchemy, for alchemy teems with symbolism of the collective unconscious. When I first discovered Jung and began my individuation process, the archetypal "wise old man" figure in my dreams took Jung's form, and at times even seemed to be Jung himself (my anima figure, the female archetype, was a woman I called Julie). Just as Philemon brought the four keys to Jung, so I received four gold keys from Jung, who was in fact dying, at which I realized that I must continue the work begun by him.

Now what does this mean, to receive four keys from the "wise old man" spirit figure? Jung does not say. But the keys in my dream were on a gold key ring, and this gives us some answers. The four gold keys with the key ring constitute a mandala, as well as meaning the squaring of the circle, and if spread out to the cardinal points would form a variation of what is perhaps the main Gnostic symbol of wholeness, o and + combined as in the Celtic cross. The symbol is extremely ancient, and Jung says that it is probably the main symbol of the collective unconscious.

The very fact that Jung's Philemon seemed to be Egyptian/Hellenistic/Gnostic points to all of this. The Church did not continue and further develop the hidden mystery that is approached through the unconscious—was not aware of it, apparently—and alchemy was chiefly concerned with the lower spirit Mercurius and the Philosopher's Stone, though the alchemists were eventually forced to parallel these with Christ. Philosophical alchemy was not merely involved with archetypal processes, it was completely dependent upon them, though mostly projected into matter. The Church, on the other hand, projected the divine mystery outward—into the spiritual heavens (with some justification) though having come to Earth in an incarnation. It failed to realize that the mystery also lies within Man, through the human soul; indeed, *within* the Earth Spirit/World Soul. (Certain Church Fathers knew the real and deeper meaning of the Christ phenomenon, Origen, Clement of Alexandria, etc., but this appreciation was to gradually fade.) The Church, therefore, must now accept the unconscious depths (through which the spirit heights are reached) as part of its whole mystery, for they form the foundations out of which all genuine religions grow. It was Jung's fate to revive the royal line through the unconscious from ancient times and to continue it, or rather *to make the continuance possible.* I too became deeply involved with the work, as have others.

Salome, the girl/anima in Jung's dream is the part of the World Soul that splits off to become personalized in a human individual, and in all living creatures, and in fact, even in what we call dead matter, for all Creation is animated with soul, i.e., Life. In the first dream of my processes I was informed that even empty space is alive, and therefore contains soul, and the latest discoveries of science have indeed found that empty space is "something" and contains some kind of living force.

Jung says he eventually came to understand how a man's unconscious contains the archetypal feminine figure, the anima/soul, playing a relatively important role. The corresponding male figure in a woman's unconscious he termed the "animus," adding that while the anima tends to be represented by a single figure, the animus appears in several forms. However, in my own experience, the anima, like the animus, also appears in several and even many forms.

Jung adds that for many years he would turn to the anima when he felt emotional disturbance and ask her just what she was doing now, just what did she know? He would use her as intermediary and psychopomp (guide) to the collective archetypes, which is a main role, but the time came when he no longer needed to do this, as he eventually learned how to deal with the unconscious directly, without the help of the anima as intermediary. The anima is tricky and can lead a man into all sorts of false ideas and moody emotions, though she obviously has her very positive aspects, essential for life. As said, she can lead ego-consciousness down to the unconscious depths, as well as communicating unconscious contents to consciousness. But Jung eventually learned to deal with the archetypal contents directly, and as he says, it is then that the anima loses her fascination and numinosity for consciousness.

It is usual for the anima to be projected onto a real-life woman, and this happened in my own individuation process. There was a time when I would have literally died for this outer figure, when all of life seemed to depend completely upon her, but when I reached the higher levels of the processes, her fascination faded somewhat. I then found it amazing that my anima could ever have held such magic and power for me. But it is plain to see why a man can sometimes be led to ruination by such a real-life woman upon whom he has projected the anima, despite his efforts to break free. (The same holds true for a woman with the animus, of course.) Unfortunately, the anima is usually in a negative state until redeemed, and so it is a somewhat negative or even bad type of woman onto whom the projection is made. Yet she too may well be a special type who contains within her own nature the possibility of redemption. This is the basis of the Gnostic and Greek myths where Sophia or Mary Magdalene, "a sinner," are obvious examples. Mary also represents the collective soul, the dragon/prostitute found in mythology generally that may be transformed into the Goddess of Wisdom. This happens to Sophia in certain myths.

Here is the dream where I receive the four gold keys from Jung.

> *I am in a small, old castle where I nurse C. G. Jung, who is very old and ailing. Suddenly, a hazy vision appears before me, coming from out of another reality. I see four gold petals form, like a cross with arms of equal length. Jung, who is unable to see because his sight is fading badly, asks, "What do you see before you?" When I reply, "Four gold petals, forming a cross," he says, "That is it. It is done." (Or "It is finished.")*
>
> *I then help him up a flight of stairs, but at the top he dies, his blue eyes staring blankly. His body then falls over the rail, from the landing to the ground floor below, where it splatters. At first I am very concerned that his body will be something of a mess now at his funeral, but then I think, "What does it matter what his body looks like? His spirit is intact and is now floating upwards."*
>
> *I then realize I have received four gold keys on a gold key ring from Jung, and I say, or the dream causes me to say, "How strange that I am Jung's follower and successor, considering our very different lives and backgrounds."*

The small, old castle resembled Jung's medieval style house at Bollingen, which Jung had built as a 3 + 1 structure to represent the quaternity nature of the Higher Self. My vision of the four gold petals forming a flower/cross is reminiscent of the Golden Flower of Chinese Taoism and alchemy, one of the main Eastern symbols of the Higher Self. As Jung states, the inner immortal in Western man must be developed in a similar way to the Golden Flower, but as a Christ-form to fit both our Western traditions and the needs of the developing religious spirit in the West.

Since earliest times gold has symbolized the things most precious to Man, and in an earlier dream, Christ became a golden cloud that enveloped me. The meaning of four gold keys on the gold key ring is similar to the four gold petals forming a cross; the wholeness of the Self with his four emanations, his fourfold structure, which is also the squaring of the circle. As said above, the cross within the circle was perhaps the main symbol of the Gnostics, but it is actually much older and we find it in certain forms at the very beginnings of ancient Egypt and other early cultures. Matriarchal worship preceded the patriarchal in these cultures, and so the first form of the symbol in Egypt was the Great Mother of the Great Bear Circle over the Four Quarters of the Earth. Later, when Patriarchal, Heaven itself was a circle supported by the four pillars of Shu, or again over the four quarters of the Earth. Other versions are Ezekiel's chariot with four wheels, and wheels with four faces; the Buddha sitting on a circular podium with a pillar at each corner; and the Four Sons of Horus, called Quebhsennuf, Tuamutef, Hapi, and Amset, rising from the Waters on a lotus. The symbol is universal, and we will see various other examples later.

The gold keys have a specific meaning themselves: they unlock doors that lead through the unconscious to the eternal reality of spirit and soul, the reality of the Higher Self. I remember reading that in ancient Israel, a newly installed High Priest would receive four special keys from his predecessor as the authority of his office, and this would originally have derived from similar inner processes. As we know, St. Peter received the keys of the kingdom from Christ, which must be based on the same tradition. *"And I will give unto thee the keys of the kingdom of heaven"* (Matt. 16:19). Jung reports an alchemical text that states that the door to the greatest treasure is opened with four keys.

So Jung received the keys from his winged "wise old man" figure Philemon, "the personification of spirit," and then I received them in turn from Jung, who was a representation of spirit to me. Victorian mythologist Gerald Massey gives a piece of information that is very relevant here:

"In the coming forth to day from out the dark of death which is the resurrection in the *Ritual,* Atum-Iu, the closer and the opener of Amenta, carries in his hands the keys that close and open the Underworld. These are the Ankh key of life, and the Un-sceptre, with which Amenta is closed and opened. These are repeated in the Book of Revelation as the keys of death and hell" (Massey 1907). *Ritual* is Massey's shorthand for the Book of the Dead.

In other versions it is Shu who provides the keys to unlock the gates to the Underworld, the unconscious/spirit, the keys again being in the form of the Ankh cross (although Atum-Iu may refer to Shu, who was Son of Atum). This is actually the cross and circle combined, as are the keys on the ring that I receive from Jung. Amenta, the Egyptian Underworld, was the lower realm of the unconscious, and just as the Egyptians stated that it was necessary to descend to the depths of the Underworld to reach Heaven, so in the unconscious processes it is experience of the lower depths that brings forth the spirit heights. As Alan Alford says in *When the God's Came Down* (2000). the Underworld was like the letter J in that it was necessary to descend the lower curve in order to ascend the stem to the spirit heights.

Two types of keys are indicated in Massey's quote, but the meaning is the same as those Jung and I receive in our dreams, though the latter have associated meanings. Christ's words in Revelation (1:18) are, *"I have the keys of death and Hades,"* (which in Egypt would be Amenta, and in the modern world the collective unconscious). An old Jewish saying was ". . . the keys of four things are in the hands of God alone." This implies four keys and could refer to this very same process.

Jung recently visited me in a dream, wearing a tam (a round flat hat), which had the edges folded over on four sides to form a square, the squaring of the circle, just as the four keys on the key ring denotes. As he left, Jung said, "I'm off to see the Holy Ghost." Now, it is the function of the Holy Spirit to spiritualize mankind—I am speaking of the actual psychological process, not just a belief that this may occur as an outer event—and this is, in fact, what Jung does, or what the unconscious processes do. Jung connects us to the immortal aspects of our nature and thereby spiritualizes us (to varying degrees depending upon each individual). In this sense he is doing the work of the Holy Spirit. Jung in my dreams is "the personification of spirit," but sometimes I could swear that it is Jung himself; perhaps he has become blended with the Holy Spirit in higher reality.

In *Psychology and Religion: West and East* (1958), Jung states that for Christianity the Holy Spirit is the breath of God that brings healing. The Holy Spirit is the Third Person that binds together Father and Son, so that these three are nevertheless One. Because this force can descend into the human psyche, Man shares in the Holy Spirit with Father and Son.

This is the Paraclete that Christ said he was leaving for us, sometimes called the "Comforter." Jung says the Cosmic Man, the ultimate Higher Self, has been known for two thousand years, having merged with our concepts of God and Christ, and that the stigmata of the saints shows them to be carriers of the Christ or Anthropos image. These, he says, are symbolic examples of the Holy Spirit at work in Man.

As pointed out, in Egypt the god Shu provided the keys to the Underworld, and he was actually called "the breath of Ra." Shu was identified as part of God even more so than the divine Son Horus in a sense, in that he merges with Ra "as a flame of fire merges with the Sun" —he was also divine Son himself in earliest times. Shu was therefore in this aspect the Holy Spirit that brings the keys of the mysteries of the Underworld to the initiate.

The Christian Holy Spirit, called the "breath of God," seems to identify it with Shu as the same spirit force of God. And just as Shu provided the keys to Amenta, so it was the Holy Spirit that provided them for Jung in the form of Philemon, and for myself in the form of Jung.

Jung mentions the alchemist Michael Maier (sixteenth century), who says that God is the Sun, and as it turns, it spins gold, which falls to and affects the Earth. In this way, God is the gold that becomes gold within man. This is the same as God as the fire of the Holy Spirit, whom Jung says is sometimes represented as a winged old man, in alchemy Mercurius as the god of revelation. Together with the King and his Son, the three form the alchemical Trinity.

Considering what he says above, Jung must have known that it was the Holy Spirit that visited him, providing the keys that lead to the great mysteries of eternal spirit and soul, and ultimately to God. Jung was always very cautious about revealing his personal experiences, even in his autobiography, but he must have known the tremendous significance of it all. He must have known that the Holy Spirit had descended upon him. But as the world, and particularly his fellow psychologists, would not accept even the simpler things he had discovered concerning the psyche, they certainly would not have accepted the ludicrous claim that he was working under the direct supervision of the Holy Spirit. Yet such indeed appears to have been the case!

It became Jung's task to develop the Higher Self in Western Man on the lines laid down by our religious past, which as stated reaches back to ancient Egypt, source of the royal line or river of true blue blood. Receiving the four keys myself from Jung, I can only conclude that I am meant to continue with the great task, to whatever extent I am able. When I look back now, I fully realize that I too have been under the influence of a higher force. The divine child coming from across the waters (in a previous dream I had) is further proof that this is so, for it means the birth in time of the Self. Later dream visions reinforce this conclusion.

In the present dream, when I help Jung up the stairs, he is beginning his ascent to that higher reality. Then comes the parting, and when I speak of his spirit ascending, his material body goes in the other direction, to the ground below. His body splattering alludes to its decomposition, but as I say in the dream, what does that matter now? It is his surviving spirit that is important, that is now ascending to higher spirit reality, to merge, it seems, with the Holy Spirit. So the Jung in my dream appears to be Jung as himself, but as part of the Holy Spirit.

Active Imagination, Spirits, and Mandalas

One of Jung's methods of treatment was what he called "active imagination," a sort of meditation in which the patient—or anyone else who wishes to try it seriously—concentrates to let consciousness become largely oblivious to outer surroundings, thus allowing unconscious contents to rise up. This is what happened when Jung, sitting by his desk, let himself sink to the cave in the depths below, where he then experienced the corpse of the blond hero, Siegfried, and the black scarab.

Jung had a young pupil who tried active imagination. The young man found himself going through rooms deeper and deeper until he finally came to a central one where a young boy sat smearing himself with excrement. This frightened the pupil so much that he never tried active imagination again. Jung says the child smearing itself meant an unconscious psychosis, which at all cost must remain covered up. So it was wise to let active imagination alone in this case. Jung comments that the young man was the only one of his pupils ever to become a Nazi.

My Own Experience of Active Imagination

Early in my individuation process I tried active imagination once, achieving good results, but whenever I tried it again I found I was putting too much of conscious thoughts and wishes into it. So I went back to using dreams as my source of material from the unconscious, which I suspect that the unconscious preferred, as these are uninfluenced by the wishes of consciousness. However, my one sortie into active imagination produced some striking archetypal material.

I see a small, round pool of water, about three or four feet in diameter, and a black bird, perhaps a raven, is marching around it, strutting comically. Suddenly, a fish pops up out of the pool and covers the bird's beak with its mouth, and this warns the bird off. The fish then takes me down into the pool, where the water is clear at first, but as we go down deeper and deeper, things become darker, and we are apparently now in the deepest depths of the sea. In fact, we are actually going back through time, and finally we come to the creation of the world, where everything is volcanic in black and red, the black being cooled rock, and the red still fire and molten rock. I then see a dinosaur, probably the archetypal dragon, silhouetted in black as it stands on the black rock, with the glow of the red heat behind it.

We then go forward in time to the first civilizations of the Fertile Crescent in the Middle East, Mesopotamia, Egypt. Everything is bright daylight now, and I see people on the old roads, journeying to and from the ancient cities. Then again travelling through time, the fish and I are in the Europe of the Middle Ages, perhaps the Germany of about the twelfth or thirteenth century, and I see what resemble Teutonic Knights riding across the plain (these could be Knights Templars.) I then see God ride down from the skies, and as well as being bearded, he has Sunrays coming from out of his head; he is therefore the Sun-God. As he reaches the land, the Earth, he becomes his own divine Son, now beardless, and he rides across the plain to a cottage that is perhaps on the edge of a wood. Snow White of the fairy tale comes out of the cottage and into the garden, where she meets the Son of God. As they hold hands as sweethearts, I hear the old song "Ah, Sweet Mystery of Life (At Last I Found Thee)."

This is indeed the sweet mystery of life, of Creation; small wonder I could not get much out of active imagination after this; I was given the highest possible archetypal meaning on the very first attempt. The World Soul evolves to a high level and then the High God of spirit descends. Becoming his own Son, he unites with the pure soul of the Earth, the World Soul, personified as Snow White, in the *Hieros Gamos,* or Sacred Marriage. This is the goal seen in many myths and religious processes of the world; what greater meaning could there be?

As for the details of the inner vision, they are well-known symbols in themselves. The pool that becomes the sea refers to the collective unconscious—throughout mythology and the Bible the hero or prophet encounters a lake, pool, or well, sometimes with a woman (the anima) there; Isaac meets Rebekah, Jacob meets Rachel, and so on. The raven has negative connotations, being, amongst other things, associated with the Devil and the dark forces. In certain Mysteries, however, the raven is the first stage of the dark and dense material that must be transformed into the white dove, representing the highest stage. The raven's head was a main symbol of alchemy, the *caput corvi,* and it, or the raven itself, meant the Earth Spirit Mercurius in lowest and heaviest form. We also find the raven with the biblical Noah and Isaiah, and with the earlier Gilgamesh, again as dark counterpart to the white dove.

The fish is a main symbol of the Savior-Self, called the Dag in ancient Babylonia and by the Jews, and the Ichthys by the Greek world—the Savior from the depths of the unconscious. Christ the Ichthys is the most well-known fish of all, Eucharistically eaten. The first symbol of the ancient Christians was the fish. Often the Savior comes forth from the Mother-Fish, a form of the Great Mother in the waters, the great unconscious.

The Savior as fish reaches back to the first culture we know of, Sumeria, where Enki, later to become Ea and then Oannes in Babylonia, was "The Sublime Fish." In India, the first form of Vishnu was the Savior-Fish, the Matsya, while in ancient Egypt the divine Son, Horus, was "The Fish of the Inundation," and "The Fish in the Form of a Man." Even today, the Savior of the Dogon people of West Africa, Nommo, is a fish. So while the raven is a creature of dark heavy matter, even of the Devil, the fish is a symbol of the Savior—often the Great Mother as Mother-Fish gives birth to the Savior-Fish.

In my vision, the fish takes me through the depths of the sea, the collective unconscious, through time to the creation of the world, where I see the black dinosaur/dragon, the creative principle of the Deity manifested in its lowest, and therefore animal, form. Later, Man has evolved to the level of the first civilizations where there is the brightness of higher consciousness. Then it is later still, probably medieval Germany with the Teutonic Knights, or Templars, and this may be because, while all other countries are Motherlands, Germany is the Fatherland, and therefore alludes to the masculine principle; to God the Father here. And sure enough, the Sun-God, the High God of Spirit, comes riding down from the heavens, becoming his own divine Son as he reaches Earth, beardless now to distinguish the Son from the bearded Father. As for the Sunrays emanating from the head of God, the Hindu Brahma is said to have seven rays emanating from his head—in contradistinction to the seven-headed dragon of the instinctual depths.

The divine Son then unites with Snow White, the pure and virginal

World Soul; and she must be purified and virginal, otherwise God will not and cannot unify with her as his own good and perfect Son. All of this is a process that takes place through the collective unconscious, the "other reality" of spirit/soul existing behind the physical universe, although in the dream it takes place in the outer world.

The vision is the essence of the Christian myth, and we see it more plainly in the Gnostic versions where Christ unifies with Sophia, goddess of Wisdom, or with Sophia as daughter of the Great Mother, or even with the Virgin Mary or Mary Magdalene. Similarly, Horus marries his mother, Isis the Virgin, in one Egyptian myth. This is the end purpose of Creation, for the World Soul must unify with God—through God as the Son—just as in nature male must unite with female for totality and wholeness. The dragon and Snow White represent the opposite extremes of the same feminine spirit, and the former must transform into the latter. This is the relevance of the redemption of Mary Magdalene, first phase the harlot, second phase Mary the Virgin—the harlot redeemed becomes the Virgin (though again these may be separate and opposite aspects of the feminine spirit).

What more could I achieve with active imagination? The above tells us the whole purpose of Creation—and individuation.

Seven Sermons to the Dead

To return to Jung's experience, an incident occurred in 1916 that demonstrates the archetypal depths Jung had activated. His house suddenly became filled with spirits, and certain other connected supernatural events were witnessed not just by him but also by his family. These spirits were from the "land of the dead" as Jung puts it, that supernatural domain of which shamans speak. Just before this, Jung had experienced his soul flying away from him, which he recognized as a highly significant event, as it established a connection with the "land of the ancestors," giving the contents, the "dead," the opportunity to come forth to *this* reality.

Jung's eldest daughter saw a white specter, his next eldest daughter had the bedclothes snatched away twice in the night, and his young son experienced an alarming dream of a fisherman catching a fish, and then the appearance of the Devil. The boy insisted on brightly crayoning this down on paper the next morning, an occurrence that according to Jung was completely out of character; he had never done it before. Finally, the room they were all in became filled with spirits, perhaps heavily felt rather than seen, and as the atmosphere rose to fever pitch, the spirits suddenly cried out they had not discovered in Jerusalem what they had sought, and had therefore returned.

Jung literally there and then began to write his work, *Seven Sermons to the Dead,* which flowed out of him like "a rushing stream," and straightway the room cleared and the spirits were gone. He says himself that taken scientifically, all of this may seem incredible, but it had happened as he said and therefore should be accepted as one of those inexplicable, paranormal incidents that sometimes do occur.

(Personally, I have only had one definite experience of spirit during waking hours, but supernatural contents have certainly come through during the night, having risen from the deeper, collective unconscious. Several times over the years, my darkened bedroom became awhirl with eerie contents, not seen but deeply felt, the room being ready to burst with the uncanny atmosphere. A few seconds after I first awakened, it would all die down and become still, like a boiling kettle of water calming down when the heat is turned off. I had brought these seething spirits up from the depths and beyond, and they took a short time to sink down again. I have heard family members—and even my dog—disturbed in their sleep because they were being affected through the unconscious by the spirit. The next day, no one ever remembered—or at least, never mentioned—anything, and things went on as normal. But make no mistake, these things are *real* and do happen.)

It is always necessary to keep the two different worlds of the conscious and collective unconscious separate, so that while investigating the latter, we remain grounded in the former, even though our way of thinking, our whole attitude and values, must be altered. Jung says he had the realities of his work, his patients, and his family to keep him anchored in *this* reality firmly, and that is how it must be. Jung underwent the original spiritualizing processes of the unconscious, and knew that he must devote his life's work to them, to make them a reality that could then be scientifically studied and assessed.

In the next few months after the above experience, archetypal material flowed into and out of Jung, causing him to write it all down on 1,330 sheets of paper, This was done in the manner of the Gnostic texts, and the *Seven Sermons to the Dead* was attributed to Basilides, the great Alexandrian master of the second century A.D. (It was common practice to ascribe Gnostic works to past authorities; for instance, the *Gospel of Philip,* though a later work, was attributed to the disciple of Jesus.)

Jung also began to paint and study mandalas, the holy circles that express the full Higher Self, to which consciousness is attached and is a part. All of this activity, really adding up to Jung's individuation process, continued for some years, Jung gaining the wisdom of the unconscious through direct experience as time passed. Then in 1926, another piece of the jigsaw puzzle of what had become his great quest came to him, this too concerning mandala symbolism. Soon after he painted a mandala, a holy wheel that seemed somewhat Chinese in character, he received a manuscript from the Orientalist Richard Wilhelm. *The Secret of the Golden Flower* (1931) concerned a thousand-year-old Chinese Taoist/alchemical treatise, the contents of which confirmed Jung's own conclusions about how mandalas circulate around a center. This information supported his own work on how the conscious personality is connected to an inner center, and how this center, rather than consciousness, is the authority of the psyche. He then had a dream in which he found himself in a dimly lit city, and, coming to a square, saw an island in the middle on which there was a single, blossoming magnolia tree. This center was bathed in bright sunlight, and the tree itself was the source of the light. The city was Liverpool, the liver being "that which makes to live." So the whole scene expressed a mandala in which the island with the magnolia tree was the center that is the Self.

All of this meant something very important, but being untrodden territory, Jung still lacked sufficient understanding, and there was no one involved in similar work to whom he could turn for advice. He was compelled, therefore, to go on totally alone.

He had come to realize that myths are based upon collective processes of the unconscious/spirit; indeed, that the unconscious *is* a process itself, and that ego-consciousness may be transformed by association with it. Other parts of the jigsaw puzzle were also beginning to fit into place. True enough, the material coming to light could be found in the fantasies of the mentally insane. Yet that was not necessarily detrimental to the material itself. We could say that the realities of the outer world are also chaotic to the minds of the insane, but that does not mean the realities of the world in themselves are chaotic and have no order. As our minds absorb, integrate, and make sense of worldly contents, so they may do with contents from the otherworldly realm of the unconscious, as long as consciousness is sufficiently strong and wise to accomplish this. Mandalas, Jung realized, are highly symbolic expressions of a great mystery that lies through and beyond the human psyche, or soul. Now this very old Chinese alchemical work was substantiating some of Jung's own ideas and theories concerning these.

However, despite his newly gained insights and understanding, he still felt he remained largely in the dark.

On top of this, there is much danger and suffering in the work, much dread and fear, as ego-consciousness knows it is jumping into a different reality, one of a completely different nature to the outer world. As said earlier, it is a well-known fact that shamans, alchemists, etc., were sometimes seriously injured mentally in the processes, and so the dangers are obviously real. Yet at the same time there may be wonderful excitement as it is gradually realized that something very special and of the highest importance is taking place, something numinous and magical. Jung felt all this to his very depths, as I did myself as I journeyed through it myself, and as may everyone who travels the dark and dangerous unknown on the individuation process.

As symbolic material comes through from the unconscious of all descriptions—light and dark, good and evil, from the basely instinctual to the highly spiritual—consciousness is filled with wonder and awe, especially when it is checked with similar material in the myths, religions, and esoteric Mysteries of the world. This is it. It all fits. You have the key, the answer to the tremendous problem of the meaning of human existence, to all of the religious Mysteries that mankind has known, and you will never have to look elsewhere. They are all based upon the same archetypal material that is now coming through from the unconscious/spirit to your experience, material of things much greater than Man, so that it has to be assimilated in the correct way, with true humility and even worship. As Jung says, we must shrink to the size of a pea before such wonders.

Gradually, the personal inner self grows, undergoing a transformation of personality in the sense that it now thinks and functions in a religious/mythological way, the way in which Man used to think before the dissociated modern age, though now in an updated way and with real knowledge and understanding. Consciousness cannot help but think differently as it has been to the divine source and *experienced* it all, and has not only survived but thrived. Reality itself has changed and the personality with it, now having gnosis, and the Great Man, the Self, becomes known as a reality, even as Christ. This is not to say that consciousness is thereby free from its own foolishness at times, for we remain what we were and are, fallible and faulty human beings. Yet now spirit and soul are real, the Higher Self is real, God is real, and we are content to be the tiny iotas we truly are before such wonders. All of this comes in time. Jung, while progressing and growing, still had some way to go.

When Jung broke with Freud he plunged into the darkness, the vast unknown, full of dangers that would very possibly result in madness. Jung felt he was in complete isolation and had only his intelligence, instinct, and insight, plus a large portion of courage, to aid him, and so when visions symbolizing wholeness and a certain kind of holiness came to him, he could not help but feel them to be an act of grace. Even so, he did not as yet realize the full significance and implications of the collective unconscious, for although he knew that spirit reality does exist, other pieces of the jigsaw puzzle still needed to be fitted, and more had yet to be investigated.

Chapter 5

Further Archetypal Discoveries Unfold

Researches into Alchemy

During this period (1926) Jung had a number of strange dreams, two of them very crucial, he felt. In the first, there was an annex to his house, wherein he found a large library full of books, some of which were volumes containing curious illustrations and symbols he did not understand. In the second dream, Jung found himself near a sunlit Verona in wartime—this would have been the First World War. A peasant accompanied him as they crossed a bridge and entered the courtyard of a large manor house, where Jung suddenly realized they were somehow trapped in the seventeenth century and would remain so for some years. Yet Jung was certain in the dream that one day in the distant future he would escape out of that place and time. These dreams were nothing if not prophetic, for they presaged Jung's investigations into alchemy, which would actually last some years. However, I have delved deeply and long into the archetypal meaning of alchemy in another work, *The Grail, the Stone, and the Medieval Mystics,* so I will mention only certain relevant points about the subject here.

When Jung first looked at alchemy, he considered it largely nonsense, though at the same time something deep down inside of him seemed to argue that it was not. Reading Richard Wilhelm's, *Secret of the Golden Flower,* a work that searched deeply into Chinese alchemy, Jung was deeply impressed and it caused him to place an order with a bookseller for any books about alchemy that the bookseller might come across. Fairly soon, Jung was sent a collection of texts contained in the *Artis Auriferae Volumina Duo,* dated 1593, which he tells us are classics of alchemy, and which he intended to study if only to be able to dismiss the whole subject once and for all. Nevertheless, for a couple of years Jung could only look at the pictures, continuing to think of alchemy as mostly confused nonsense, though inexplicably at the same time increasingly finding the book hard to put down. Something drew him to it, and finally, unable to resist any longer, he submerged himself completely into deeper study of the contents.

Slowly but then more rapidly it came to dawn on Jung that everything in the texts was symbolic, and therefore contained real and deeper meaning, but in such strange a language that it all needed to be deciphered. Eventually he was to realize that the curious illustrations he had seen in the books in the library in the first of the dreams were alchemical symbolism, and that the dream of being trapped in the seventeenth-century manor house referred to his deep involvement with alchemy that was to continue over so long a period of time. In all, the task of deciphering the meaning of the texts, and of coming to a full understanding of alchemy itself, was to take him over ten years.

It gradually became clear that the processes of alchemy correspond to the deeper processes of the unconscious, but that the alchemists, who were undergoing the processes within their own depths had, partly unconsciously, projected it all into the outer processes of matter. Yet although most alchemists were unaware of the projection, certain others do seem to have realized it, and indeed, were forced to, coming to posit their Philosopher's Stone as a symbolic parallel to Christ, thus the "lapis-Christ parallel," (though it would perhaps be truer to say that the unconscious did so itself). As we now know, Christ and the Philosopher's Stone both symbolize the Higher Self, developed and brought forth in the psychic/spiritual processes, but at different, even opposite levels, the *filius microcosmi* countermatched by the *filius macrocosmi*. The *filius microcosmi* basically meant the divine Son, the Logos or Higher Self, produced out of the higher spirit or God, while the *filius macrocosmi* meant the Son, or Lower Self, produced from the lower Earth Spirit/World Soul.

After this, Jung felt that in the alchemists he possessed historical antecedents for his own discoveries in his psychological work, and that alchemy actually forms the link between Gnosticism, original orthodox Christianity, and modern depth psychology (I must add that medieval mysticism and the Holy Grail were perhaps even higher and better links in certain ways).

I remember that when I was just getting into the study of Jung's works—and of my own unconscious—I had a dream in which I came across a certain book in a public library. Even before I opened it, the book seemed to emanate a strange aura, sort of supernatural, and when

I did open it, I found it full of curious illustrations that I at first thought stylized. But that was not it, and though I persisted, I found it impossible to figure out just what the strange drawings and engravings really meant.

About two weeks later in real life, I visited a library in the city where I live (not the one in the dream), and there on a shelf I found Jung's book *Psychology and Alchemy* (1953), of the existence of which I had hitherto been unaware. Looking inside, I found it full of the strange illustrations as in the book in my dream, and I thought, "So *that* is the answer." This was precisely what I had seen in my dream, and the illustrations in the book were the symbolic ones of alchemy. I then began to have dreams containing alchemical motifs, though at the same time I was having ones with Christian and Gnostic themes. This is very similar to Jung's experiences, of course, all those years earlier, of which I was unaware at the time I had the above dreams.

In one dream containing alchemical symbolism, I sang four songs, about the Sun, the Moon, a wedding, and a river. I had this dream a few weeks before the one about the strange book. When I came to study Jung's book, I found one of the illustrations was of the unification, the marriage, of the Sun and Moon over a central river, which was actually what I sang about in my earlier dream. Here is the dream:

> *I am on a stage in a theater and I start to sing to the audience. I sing four songs, or maybe just a line from each, in the following order: "(The Bells are Ringing) For Me and My Gal," "Up a Lazy River," "Moonglow," and "Stardust."*

I did not know it at the time but the four songs represent the unification of the opposites in alchemy. The third and fourth songs, "Moonglow," and "Stardust," suggest Sol and Luna (Sun and Moon), two favorite symbols of the alchemists for the eternal opposites. The first song "For Me and My Gal," is about a marriage, of course, and "Up a Lazy River" denotes the eternal river, the way between the opposites that unifies them.

As said above, some time after this dream I acquired *Psychology and Alchemy*, in which I found an old alchemical engraving of the Sun and the Moon, and a river flowing between them. This is what the East means by Tao, the Way—that is, the way to unite what are separated. This is also the way that lies between them, as well as being the Way, the Path, to travel. Below the engraving in the same book Jung quotes an allegory of the psychic union of opposites from the *Rosarium Philosophorum* (1550).

"O Luna, folded by my embrace, / Be you as strong as I, as fair of face. / O Sol, brightest of all lights known to men. / And yet you need me, as the cock the hen."

The Sun has always symbolized masculine spirit and the Moon feminine soul, and since earliest times their unification has been the goal of the esoteric Mysteries, based upon unconscious processes, so that the alchemists were essentially carrying on those traditions, though not always realizing it.

Alchemical symbolism has become constellated in the Western collective unconscious, just as Christian symbolism has, the one being the underside that complements the other. My dream processes contain many examples of both.

This, to say the least, was a great coincidence, to find Jung's book after having the dream, if indeed, coincidence was involved. Considering Jung's similar experiences, I am forced to conclude the unconscious is sometimes aware in advance of things of which consciousness has as yet no inkling.

When the alchemists practiced their art, which, of course, involved investigations into matter through chemical processes, the nature of matter was unknown. So the unconscious found it an excellent means of symbolizing its own processes to the alchemist, who, being unaware of the existence of the unconscious, believed that the strange and numinous dreams and visions which began to break through were due to his work in the laboratory. (The alchemists relied very heavily on dreams.) Yet a few alchemists were wise enough to realize that if any transformations were taking place at all, they were not of base metals into gold, but rather of base material man into a spiritualized state. The alchemists were thus divided into two groups, those who sought the physical gold, and those who sought the spiritual gold. The latter group proclaimed, "Our gold is not the common gold."

There were thus the *philosophical* alchemists who sought the Philosopher's Stone, the "Stone of the Wise," "the stone that hath a spirit," which could bring riches and health, but even more so spiritual treasures. There were many other names for the desired "gold," or goal. As said, some even realized that the ultimate product meant a super-spiritual entity, a Redeemer, that paralleled Christ, hence again the "lapis-Christ parallel." Ironically, modern science and modern man generally, came to believe only in the reality of the physical alchemy that became chemistry. It even became possible to produce gold from other materials. Yet it had always been possible to produce the *spiritual* gold as a symbol of the Self, through inner processes of the unconscious as a psychic/spiritual phenomenon. And indeed, still is. Though it is possible to produce gold from other materials today, the process is apparently too costly to be economically viable. But how much more precious is the product that is "not the common gold," and that symbolizes the Self as a Redeemer, a Savior?

The alchemists said the spirit contained within the Philosopher's Stone—within the whole of matter—was Mercurius, who, like the Stone, was called "the thousand named." Because Mercurius represented all sides and possibilities of what we now call the collective unconscious, or at least its lower depths, he was said to be "good with the good and evil with the evil." So when evil, Mercurius opposed Christ as a type of Antichrist, but when good was a lower approximation to Christ, hence again the "lapis-Christ parallel." This is why Merlin the Magician as an expression of Mercurius is said to be both good and evil.

As a type of divine child, Mercurius was the *filius* or "son" (of various types and names), called "the age-old son of the Mother," although the Mother or World Soul was actually the feminine form or side of Mercurius. But essentially Mercurius was the spirit in matter that needed to be freed by the alchemical work. While sulphur was the "red" of alchemy and salt the "white" (thus male and female), they were actually two sides or aspects of Mercurius, who as "peacemaker" unified them in the alchemical marriage. As I have said elsewhere, Mercurius is really a later form of the Egyptian god Osiris, Lord of the Underworld (the unconscious/spirit). As Osiris countermatched God as Ra, so Mercurius was the lower correspondence to God (as to Christ) as the spirit in matter. Mercurius was even said to be a lower version of the Holy Trinity—he was both threefold and fourfold in different aspects. Not only good/evil and male/female, he was also solid/liquid and indeed, many twinned opposites, and so was symbolized as quicksilver. As masculine spirit he was "living fire" and as feminine spirit "divine water." A "bringer of light" to those with lofty motives, he came as a "diabolical seducer" to those whose motives were base. This is why Mercurius says, "I beget the light but darkness too is of my nature."

Mercurius was not the actual light, but the *bringer* or *herald* of the light, the light itself being Christ. This exemplifies how the Lower Self begins the inner processes while the Higher Self completes them, just as John the Baptist says he baptizes with water but one will come who will baptize with fire. (In Egypt the dog-god Anubis, connected with Osiris, carries a lamp to light the way for the coming of the divine Son Horus.) Mercurius comes as the *filius*, the Self as divine child, but he was also *all* of the many contents that make up the Self, and indeed, many others, called the *prima materia.*

One symbol of Mercurius was the snake—people today often dream of snakes—which had both positive and negative aspects, and in his threefold form he was three serpents, of which I personally have dreamt. Another form of Osiris, as guide through the unconscious, was the hare, and Mercurius too appears as guide in this form—again, this is the case in my own dream processes. Just as Osiris was "Lord of Green Vegetation," so Mercurius had the title *Spiritus Vegetativus,* "Spirit of Life and Growth." In another form Mercurius was the unicorn, which had to be tamed, but he was also the stag, with the unicorn then representing the higher spirit. This is why there is an alchemical engraving of a stag as soul coming face to face with a unicorn as spirit in the forest.

Another symbol of alchemy was the severed head, sometimes identified with the alchemical vessel as the *corpus rotundum,* in which all of the materials to be worked upon were assembled. The Golden Head of Osiris became all important in the earlier Greek alchemy, but in medieval alchemy it was "the black head" of Osiris, or "the black Osiris." This equalled the "raven's head," the *caput mortuum,* or *caput corvi,* which intimated the *nigredo,* the terrible "blackening." It really expressed a state of great depression and melancholia, the very dangerous time when strange dark contents flow up from the depths of the collective unconscious. Assailed, consciousness feels this as a tremendous onslaught, causing the alchemists to lament, "Not a few have perished in our work."

The period of the nigredo was said to last forty days, the same period of time for the sufferings of Jesus in the wilderness in his temptation, when he too is assailed by dark contents. We find the same sufferings with Osiris in the Underworld, with David in Psalms, in the writings of Nietzsche, and in the inner processes of many saints and mystics—certainly in my own—all representing the journey of consciousness through the dark depths of the collective unconscious. Just as these figures had to endure the darkness to reach the light, so the black raven in alchemy, sometimes a creature of the Devil, had to be transformed into the white dove through the work. (After the biblical Flood, Noah sends out three white doves and a black raven to see if the deluge is over, this being a quaternity structure of 3 + 1, with the black raven as the recalcitrant fourth.) These are just a few of the many hundreds of symbols that abound in alchemy, and as I pointed out above, I delve into this much more deeply and wider in the chapter, The Great Mystery of Alchemy, which appears in another of my works, *The Grail, the Stone, and the Mystics.*

Tails, Faust, and Mephistopheles: Heads, the Symbolic Christ

His studies into alchemy caused Jung to feel a close relationship to Goethe once again, who had been an alchemist immersed in dream processes over many decades—the alchemists tell us that dreams were the source of their symbolism. The product of this was Goethe's classic work, *Faust,* which he called his "main business," and in which the devilish figure Mephistopheles appears to Faust to tempt him with worldly rewards in return for his soul. Jung had long wondered what the "secret" of Goethe was. With his deep study of alchemy in terms of processes of the unconscious, he now knew. He also realized that the same processes have been the basis and inspiration of the world's myths, religions, and esoteric Mysteries. These had become activated—alive—again in Goethe and in Nietzsche, come to that. Both these were negative examples of the phenomenon. Jung says throughout his many writings that Mephistopheles was the real product of Goethe's work, and that Mephistopheles actually represents the dark shadow side of the unconscious content, the Self, though he hardly mentions the effect it all had on Goethe. In other words, Mephistopheles must have happened to Goethe himself; Goethe must have produced Mephistopheles as a negative form of the Self in his own alchemical/dream processes.

A figure such as Mephistopheles as a psychic companion would drive any normal person to insanity or suicide, so what actually happened with Goethe? Actually, it does not appear to have affected the poet unduly—as far as we know. But then Jung does mention somewhere, concerning Goethe and Mephistopheles that great poets are not normal personalities and can get away with what other people cannot. This in my opinion fails to answer the question. In the work, Faust finally manages to cheat the Devil to retrieve his soul, which Jung considered totally unconvincing, spoiling the otherwise complete validity of the work as a genuine individuation process of the unconscious. Yet still we must ask, did Mephistopheles happen to Goethe himself? Was he condemned to facing Mephistopheles for the rest of his life, at least in dreams?

Jung believed that besides the developing myth of Christ, the religious problems of the West are bound up with *Faust* and Mephistopheles, and indeed, with Nietzsche and Zarathustra. But Jung also felt that Faust and Mephistopheles corresponded to the No. 1 and No. 2 personalities within himself, which must have been exceedingly worrisome for him—as Faust says, "Two souls, alas, are housed within my breast." Faust, in his hubris, causes the death of two elderly people, Philemon and Baucis, who "give shelter to the gods," which then can only mean catastrophe for Faust. The unconscious/alchemical process can now only be of a lower negative type, the higher spirit side having been "killed off" as it were. So instead of developing a Savior in the processes, Faust brings forth Mephistopheles, the dark shadow that countermatches the Self as Savior. This surely must have happened to Goethe himself

Realizing that the same fate was possible for him—for anyone undergoing the inner processes—Jung consciously strove for all the things that Faust had discarded, including the positive values that a civilization needs to rise above the selfish, destructive levels. Though actually feeling the danger of this negative spirit within himself, Jung nevertheless knew that in a certain sense Faust with Mephistopheles has a certain value, in that it highlights the serious problem of the enormous shadow in modern Man. It is a dire warning of just what we are all capable of falling into. Jung says the hubris that was in *Faust* (therefore in Goethe), and in Nietzsche and Wagner possessed the unconscious of the whole German people in the first half of the twentieth century, leading ultimately to two horrendous World Wars.

For thirty years of my own individuation process I too had the "fear of Faust" within me, the fear that in the end I could have a Mephistopheles as the Devil on my shoulder. The alchemists were filled with the same fear, and so held up all the Christian virtues as their guide; Jung himself made sure he followed their example. Much later he wrote to a young clergyman that his thoughts were circling around God like the planets circle around the Sun, and with the same irresistible attraction. We should all—especially those who undergo the individuation process—hold up the Christian virtues as guides by which to live.

While Jung continued his long study into alchemy, he was at the same time still investigating the meaning of Christ as both a psychological and a mythological figure, reaching backwards to ancient roots, and forward to further development of Christianity itself. This would be a positive achievement in contrast to Mephistopheles, who was a negative one. Since Jung's day, however, sadly and dangerously, the term "Christian civilization" has become archaic and meaningless. Was it really only half a century or so ago that the term still had some validity and relevance? Nevertheless, it is very difficult to envisage what other symbolic form but Christ the cosmic Self, the Logos, as Son of God could take, or be, for the West.

Yet against all that could have logically been expected at one time, America suddenly seems to be becoming more spiritually alive; at least in certain ways, which is actually how the Holy Spirit works. When a culture starts to degenerate, becoming sunk in materiality, as America has certainly become (as has Europe, with the rest of the world hastily following suit), there may be what Jung calls the enantiodramia, the swing of the pendulum from one extreme to the other. In fact, this *has to* occur when a culture is sinking into a hylic state, otherwise it will finally collapse into chaos, as many myths around the world tell us has happened to certain cultures. In other words, the opportunity for respiritualization, and therefore for regeneration, is presented due to certain workings of the spirit through the unconscious. Whether this is solidly grasped or let pass is always uncertain. But the chance is there.

What may now occur in the Western soul is the reactivation of the Savior archetype in highest form, i.e., as the cosmic Logos, which would mean the further development of the spiritual royal line of Christ. (The New Age worship of Earth is totally inadequate to bring about the necessary respiritualization.) The cosmic archetype would then come through to certain people as direct inner experience. As Jung says, "The symbol of 'Christ' as 'Son of Man' is an analogous psychic experience of a higher spiritual being that is invisibly born in the individual. . . ." *Alch. Stud.* (1968). He mentions the Chinese Taoist/alchemical text, *The Golden Flower,* which states of the Higher Self, "Without beginning, without end, without past, without future." This reminds us very closely of what was said of Melchizedek, the mysterious priest-king and Messiah figure of Israel, of whom Christ was after the order of: *"Without father, without mother, without descent, having neither beginning of days, nor end of life, but made like unto the Son of God."* (Hebrews 7:3). Jung continues to say that nothing less than Christ's Second Coming can turn the destructive tide.

In the ancient world, the archetype of the Higher Self had already been constellated in the Gnostic image of the Anthropos in Jewish traditions, and prior to that in the Egyptian myth of Horus (and Iu-em-hetep, Khonsu etc.). But with Christ, the Logos archetype had become the psychic dominant all over the Roman Empire. Jesus the man, the Jewish prophet, was to represent that archetype with Christ, and fulfill the great religious need of the age.

This really meant, Jung says, the deified Augustus being opposed by Christ as Son of God, and that the Messiah problem—and answer—of the Jewish people was thus made universal. Just as the Roman world had become crushed by power worship (exemplified by the figure of Caesar) and the masses rendered soulless, so the same problem has arisen in the modern world, with the corresponding need and expectation for redemption. Jung believed that UFO phenomena are the result of this need, though seen in technological terms due to our scientific age. Certain of my own experiences seem to substantiate this view. Nevertheless, it is also true that Christ is still alive as the archetypal image for Western man in the unconscious, as I can well attest from my own processes. In fact, I know of several people who have experienced Christ directly in dreams, therefore the reactivated "Christ within."

Here is a dream to show how Christ may appear during the individuation process:

> *My father takes me to ancient Palestine where we wait by a roadside for a procession to come along that is being led by Christ. Crowds of people have gathered and are also waiting, but we manage to get a place at the front, where there are stone pillars so many feet apart along the road. As Christ comes into view, I wonder if he will notice me because of my sufferings, but when he reaches where I am standing, he becomes a golden cloud of light, which then comes and envelops me.*
>
> *I have to cover my eyes with my hands because the cloud is so bright and radiant, and an angelic choir sings from above. Then Christ, who has become human form again, holds my hand and takes me flying through the air to the town that is just to the south of where I live. Here, from above, we watch a Salvation Army procession as it marches through the streets, and Christ seems to be showing me that I must bring salvation to this place.*

The personal father in these processes represents the male line of spirit, whereas the personal mother represents the soul line of the feminine depths. This is why in older societies boys were taken from their mothers at puberty to be instructed in the spiritual mysteries, not being allowed to see their mothers, and sometimes any females, for the time of the initiation period. It is also why Jesus, as a boy of twelve, rejects his mother in the temple.

As with other dreams involving the Christ figure, I must ask if this is the original Christ, or the Holy Spirit taking his form, or the Self as a Christ parallel or equivalent. I can only say I am unsure. To the visionary saints and mystics the figure they saw was simply Christ and they were blissfully untroubled by the questions we must ask today. Yet in trying to ascertain the truth, perhaps we are in that sense lessening the mystery and its meaning. Perhaps I should just accept the figure as Christ and not spoil the impact with too many questions that are futile in any case.

The radiance of Christ in the dream is so brilliant with light that I have to cover my eyes, and this makes me wonder more seriously if it actually was the original Christ, who will have become an eternal form of the Son of God in spirit reality, of the Logos. Furthermore, he instructs me to bring salvation to the town a couple of miles south of where I live—where the woman who is my anima figure lives in real life—the soul depths not yet being part of the totality of the Self in my processes. The Self is a *complexio oppositorum,* a complexity of opposites *par excellence,* which (or who) has parts reaching down to the animal and insect levels as well as up to God Himself: he is literally part of God come forth, like a Son. Christ in my dream is apparently pure spirit, representing only that side of the Self, the higher spirit side, and yet complete in spirit reality. This is not the Lower Self, the Osiris of the lower unconscious (or the lower form of Horus); this is the higher, divine Son and part of God.

Jung says the divine figure experienced within the human soul is able to manifest and become amenable to understanding due to the presence of the psychic archetype. Thus the basic truth of Christianity, expressed partly in Church dogma, has its foundations in the unconscious, and is not something merely invented by conscious thought (1959b, 1963b).

As well as dealing for some time with the question and problems of the suffering Christ, who atones for the sins of the world, Jung was also concerned with the light and dark sides of God, though still partly in connection with the suffering Christ. When God incarnates as his own good Son (as the Self) he comes to share the fate of suffering humanity (this takes place through the unconscious as an actuality). But Jung saw Job in the Old Testament as a sort of prefiguration of Christ. The suffering Job believes that the light side of God will help him against the dark side of God, or at least, will comfort him in his sufferings. (There are other prefigurations in the Old Testament, most specifically King David, whose story involves an incarnation with crucifixion and much suffering. This is why Christ is "Son of David" in the Bible. Sonship is much more than a biological one. Joseph in Egypt is another example.)

Jung put all of the Job material, plus his personal ideas on the religious problems of mankind in the modern world, into his book *Answer to Job.* The work was largely pounded when published, particularly by the clergy, who obviously and not unexpectedly did not understand the contents and their significance. It is a personal view by Jung, but it also expresses the symbolical/mythological viewpoint from the unconscious itself as Jung understood it. Symbolic truths are more valid than rational truths in a sense, since they express the very essence of a thing and cover the full meaning of a situation, the rational *and* the irrational. The essence of at least part of the book is that, because Job, and therefore Man, suffered from God, then God as the incarnated Christ must suffer from Man. This happens, in Jung's view of the situation, as a process through the unconscious.

I could not say that I agree with this entirely, for Christ is of a royal line of divine incarnations that has several antecedents, and suffering is part of each incarnation. In mythology and the Pagan Mysteries alike we find the tortured, dying, and resurrecting god, Osiris, etc., but sometimes "hanged on a tree," like Christ; Odin, Dionysus in certain versions of his myth, and so on. Joseph in Genesis tells Pharaoh's baker, *"Yet within three days Pharaoh shall lift up thy head off thee, and shall hang thee on a tree; and the birds shall eat thy flesh off thee."* (Gen. 40:19). So the crucifixion of Christ is not specifically connected with Job, as Jung suggests, but is rather the age-old suffering of the death and resurrection processes. Jung actually knew this, so his theory concerning merely Job is a bit of a mystery, though the latter does fit the same archetype. However, many other issues are raised in the book and it is a work of some importance.

Studies concerning Christ as a symbol of the Self were put into Jung's book *Aion* (1959), in which he elucidates the psychic structure of Man as it first descends into the unconscious, and then inwardly expands outwardly to the Higher Self. Jung gives as an example of this as the "Moses *quaternio*," explaining how some of the principle figures in the story of Moses represent this psychic structure as it descends and ascends in the unconscious. He also examines the Christ and Antichrist dilemma, stating that Christ is still the hero of Western culture, the Lord of the Tetramorph, at the center of the mandala of the four symbols of the evangelists (three animal-headed and one man-headed), exemplifying the Higher Self.

Jung warns of the backlash of Antichrist due to the poor understanding of what Christ really means, which will result in Christ's subsequent loss. Jung quotes the scriptures, *"This is Antichrist, who denieth the father and the Son"* (John 2:22), and *"Every spirit that disolveth Jesus . . . is Antichrist . . . of whom you have heard that he cometh."* (John 4:3). The spotless Christ who is merely projected into the clouds, and who is consequently largely misunderstood, was bound to create the backlash sooner or later. This began at the time of the Renaissance and has gained momentum ever since. The French Revolution, the enthronement of "Reason," and the Enlightenment, were foretastes of the present age of disillusionment that is "anti-christian."

Our one real hope, Jung stresses, is a new understanding of what Christ means as a symbol of the cosmic Self. Antichrist is just as much a symbol of the Self as Christ, as they represent the two halves of the same archetype, the two sides of the same coin; but we must understand that they are *inner* realities. That is to say, although they are immortal phenomena in themselves, existing in eternity, they may be experienced through the unconscious under special circumstances. God is not only *real*, but is *dark* as well as *light*. It is equally possible for Man to feel God's angry fist as it is his benign hand. God's right hand is Christ, but His left hand is Antichrist, and both are realities.

God is a paradox, and if Man fails to accept His light side—while recognizing His dark side—he will experience that dark side. On top of this, Man is capable of an infinite amount of evil himself, usually projecting it onto others if he recognizes it at all. (There is a strong tendency in Man today to deny real evil, which means that it more easily runs unchecked.) The reality is that Man is burdened with both his own evil and the evil side of God, and his only real defense consists of his own good and the good side of God. *But he must be aware of all of this.*

Life, says Jung, is thus a great problem for Man in that he is burdened with the opposites—not only his own, but God's. Jung saw that Man has become increasingly unaware of this greatest of problems, rather than more aware of it, as should have been the case. So not only does Man refuse to accept the burden of the great religious problem, he is dangerously unaware that the problem exists. Perhaps Man has to sink even lower into the quagmire before he realizes he needs a line from above to pull him out. Perhaps Man needs to suffer utter despair to be forced to seek the true meaning of his life and of his soul. But in the meantime he is riding high on sensation and the things of the world, too high to realize there are deeper realms that are neglected and festering. This is mass-mindedness, dissociated from deeper and fuller archetypal/spirit reality. The unconscious Man must be added to the conscious man to make him whole, and that involves ultimately the religious and spiritual side of reality.

The Church itself, according to Jung, should be truly monotheistic and recognize that both the light and the dark, the so-called eternal opposites, are of God. The incarnation as seen by the Church is full of contradictions, but the symbol of wholeness, the cosmic Self, unites the opposites so that they can exist together in the meaningful whole without clashing, although Man must always make moral choices, of course. Jung points out that for Creation, the development of consciousness was an extremely important step—perhaps *the* most important step—and he saw Christianity as an essential higher development of this. His great fear was that modern Man may fail to understand his own great purpose, and fall to the dark shadow on the principle that dark follows light. In other words, we have had Christ, now it is Antichrist. One thing he was certain of is that there will be a great change in Western civilization, either a further development or collapse. The essential thing is for Man to realize that he is centerd in God, not in matter (or himself), and that meaning and healing come from things beyond himself and his own little conscious ego.

People now seem to be involving themselves in religion and spirituality in certain ways, especially in the United States, although this is partly unsatisfactory. But they are nevertheless thus taking on the great religious problem of modern life. Fundamentalists may seem ridiculous in their literal acceptance of biblical assertions, but we can understand their preferring to do this when the only other option they see is atheism, and therefore ultimately chaos. Personally I prefer some of the fundamentalists to some of the New Age followers, who have rejected the higher spirit and God, thereby sinking back into the Earth in regression. We must remember that it was always taught in the Mysteries that the Earth must be redeemed by the higher spirit of God, which requires first of all the acceptance of God.

The Fish Below

Jung's *Aion* is largely concerned with the symbol of the fish, for he recognized the immense significance of the fish in the myths and religions of the world as a main symbol of the Self as Savior. As a fish comes from the depths of the sea, so the Self emerges from the depths of the unconscious. However, the Self as Savior is twice born, coming as the divine child from the sea (the World Soul) but also from the heavens as Son of the Father, sometimes represented by a star. Jung understood that all of the myths of the fish, and certain religious rituals involving the fish, are based upon archetypal processes of the unconscious, and that we may find similar symbolism in our dreams today.

A young friend of mine, knowing nothing whatsoever about the fish symbol, dreamt of a fish that was somehow sevenfold. This matches Ea of Babylonia (originally Enki of Sumeria), "The Sevenfold Fish," "The Sublime Fish," and "The Fish with Seven Fins." Other forms of the archetype are Vishnu as the Matsya fish connected with the seven Rishis in India, and Christ on the shore of the Sea of Tiberias cooking fish for the seven fishermen disciples. St. Augustine said that Christ himself was the fish that was cooked.

Of Christ the fish, Jung says in *Aion* "The image of the fish came out of the depths of the unconscious as an equivalent of the historical Christ figure, and if Christ was invoked as the 'Ichthys,' this name referred to what had come up out of the depths. The fish symbol is thus the bridge between the historical Christ and the psychic nature of man, where the archetype of the Redeemer dwells. In this way Christ became an inner experience, the 'Christ within.'"

The fish gods generally are born from the Great Mother, who is in some way the sea, "the Waters" (the collective unconscious), and who is sometimes a fish herself, the Mother-Fish. This is seen with Artegartis, whose son was Ichthys, which means "fish." In fact, the first symbol of Christ was as the Ichthys, the Fish. There was also a Mother-Fish, Rema, whose son was the fish-god, Rum, or Rem. Christ the Ichthys, "drawn from the deep" according to St. Augustine, is therefore Son of the Mother in this aspect. The Assyrian/Babylonian Oannes, the Man-Fish (later form of Enki/Ea) is depicted coming from out the mouth of the Mother-Fish, as is Vishnu in India carrying the Word, and there are early depictions of Christ coming from out of the Fish.

The fish-mouth itself, placed in the heavens as the star Fomalhaut in the constellation of the Southern Fish, was sacred, and besides giving birth to the Savior-Fish was also the primordial door out of which the soul of life of the world poured forth as water, the life force of the unconscious. The fish-mouth was also the entrance to this Underworld. An early fish of Wisdom was female, called Nina, a goddess, after whom great Nineveh was named, but Ea, the Sublime Fish, who was god of Wisdom, is certainly older as the Sumerian Enki.

Neith was a type of the Mother-Fish in ancient Egypt. She had several forms but as the Mother-Fish gave birth to seven crocodile sons. Sebek as crocodile Savior was her main son in this form, though in another she was Mother to the great Horus. These sons were later merged as Horus-Sebek in certain cults. Horus was "The Fish Who Came with Water," "The Fish of the Inundation," and "The Fish in the Form of a Man." Actually, both Hathor and Isis bring forth the divine Son from the sea as a fish in certain myths, though Hathor also brings him forth in the heavens as the cosmic form of the Son. One form of the fish in Egypt was the An, while E. A. Wallis Budge informs us that the Oxyrhynchus fish was worshipped all over Egypt. When Osiris is murdered and dismembered by Set, it is this fish that swallows the phallus. Another form in Egypt was the Abtu fish, and this is possibly from the same root as the abode of Enki, Abzu, and of Ea, Absu; the An and Abtu fish were said to be on either side of the solar boat of the Sun God, Ra. All of these fish are connected with a Savior.

Centuries before Christ, the expected Messiah for the Jews was called the "Dag," meaning "fish," this probably from the Assyrian fish god Dagon—Dagon itself is possibly a merging of "Dag" and "On," the latter perhaps being connected to the An fish (and Oannes). Dagon later became a fertility god of the Philistines. There seems to be a common root for many of the very ancient gods of the Middle East, and Adonis, and Bacchus among others,were also symbolically the fish. Later we see a fish, fetched from out of the sea, on the Grail Table next to the Holy Grail. The Islamic Self figure, Khidr, the Verdant One, is also connected with a fish, as is the god Vatea of Polynesia, half man, half fish, and sevenfold as many of the fish gods are. Even Noah is connected. Noah is taken from Nu of early Egypt, who has seven companions with him in his boat, as does Noah. Nu is the personification of the primordial ocean, called the Nun, the symbol of which is the fish. (See *An Order Outside Time* for a full investigation of the archetypal fish symbol.)

In another work, *The Royal Line of Christ the Logos,* I mention the experiences of a woman I know who has experienced some very significant dreams, though she knows nothing of dream symbolism or mythology. An initial dream disturbed her by its strangeness and great power. In the dream it was night, and as Jane looked through her bedroom window, a brilliant Moon glowed over a pool that, though dark, receded into far greater depth and darkness (so it could have been the sea). In the water was an immense silver fish, a Mother-Fish, while smaller upright goldfish stood around the side, probably seven in a line. Then little crocodiles, shining luminous green, came out of the pool and ascended the stairs of Jane's house to her bedroom. I asked her if there were seven crocodiles, to which she answered "I would say there were." This Mother-Fish matches Neith with her seven crocodile sons, or the archetype that these represent, still as alive as ever after thousands of years, again demonstrating Jung to be correct on the continuing relevance of the fish symbol.

In a later dream, Jane saw a sort of large green sea-horse, and it is a fact that Sebek, crocodile Savior son of Neith was referred to as the "dragon-horse" at times in Egypt. Jane has also seen a polar bear in a dream and this too reflects an early form of Great Mother worship. The archetype, repressed with later masculine worship, particularly Judaism, Christianity, and Islam, is now resurging.

Later still Jane dreamt of a golden dog on a lovely sunny day, though there was also a lot of blood and corpses around. The golden dog is a symbol of the Self in highest possible form, as Savior, the golden dog being first form of the Self in processes of the unconscious. The blood means spirit, and corpses point to death and resurrection in the transformation processes. Neith was, as said, mother of the Golden Horus, so Jane's whole set of dream visions seem to be a modern repeat of Great Mother Neith, first in lower aspect as genetrix of seven crocodile sons, and later in higher form, mother of the Golden Horus, represented by the golden dog (of whom Christ is a later development). The latest dream symbolism Jane has experienced is the unification of red and white, the symbolism found not only throughout the Bible, but in ancient Egyptian texts and later with the Holy Grail, alchemy, the medieval mystics, and so forth. White is feminine, symbolizing matter/soul, red is masculine, meaning higher spirit. In the Mass the white bread is solid and the red wine liquid, again opposites to be unified.

Jane was raised a Catholic and eventually became a teacher in a Catholic school, and so the lower soul depths are responding with their own deeper symbolism, actually from ancient Egypt. Egyptian Mysteries, as we have seen, were the foundation of the great Mystery of Christ, so it is all on the same royal line of the spirit through the unconscious, the archetypes still alive today as ever.

The story of Jonah, who enters into the belly of a fish, and then exits again after three days (as does Herakles), is probably based on that of Oannes the Man-Fish, the later form of Ea. (The New Testament mentions a whale, but in the original Old Testament text, the Book of Jonah, only a fish is mentioned.) The name "Jonah" is almost certainly connected with "Oannes," as is the name and character of John the Baptist. The Greek for "John" is *Ioannes,* almost the same as Oannes. The early Christians were called Pisciculi, "little fishes," and the Pope's seal ring has (or anyway once had) the sign of the fish displayed on it, which has to represent Christ as the Ichthys. There is a depiction of an upright fish, i.e., Christ, at Kells in Ireland, with seven figures bowing before it. Jung tells us that the alchemists declared the fish must be edible, which means in a form that can be assimilated to consciousness, and to eat the Eucharist fish of the Church is to integrate Christ the Self into ourselves as an *inner* fact of the unconscious. So, all told, there is much evidence to substantiate Jung's discovery of the fish as symbol of the Higher Self in or through the unconscious, which was put so often into mythology and sacred texts.

There exists an illustration of Isis seated with the infant Horus on her lap, while resting on her head as her symbol (and perhaps also that of Horus) is a fish. Isis is thus a form of the Mother-Fish here. This is given in a book dated 1869, *Ancient Pagan and Modern Christian Symbolism.* The author, Thomas Inman, erroneously states that the fish is associated with Isis because of its sexual and fertility associations. He even takes seriously the opinions of a surgeon friend of his that in hot weather the private parts of the human anatomy take on a fish odor; in the East this would be accentuated. So this is why Isis and other goddesses are associated with the fish, or are mothers of the fish gods. In other words, they were thought to smell like fish. However, Inman says that Christian fish symbolism itself is not due to any such causes or interpretations. If Christ is the fish, he comments, it is because of Pagan contamination! It seems that a century-and-a-half ago, reductive rationalism was even then attempting to demolish the sacred meaning of myths and their symbolism.

The fish was well-known in alchemy and had to be salted to be made edible. Salt symbolized wisdom and so the fish content, to be in positive form, had to be salted in order to be integrated. The fish symbolized the *Filius Sapientiae,* the Son of Wisdom, Wisdom partly being represented by the Mother-Fish. She was thus *Sapientiae Dei,* the feminine side of Mercurius.

A modern example of the Savior-Fish in mythology is Nommo, seen with the Dogon people of Mali, West Africa. The myth says Nommo came down from the star Sirius (or Sirius B its companion star) in a boat with seven companions to teach the Dogon culture and spirituality. Nommo is depicted as a fish, and like Christ is crucified and resurrects. However, Nommo seems to be a mixture of Christ and the Egyptian god Num, the later form of Nu, who is actually the origin of Noah. The symbol of Nu was the fish, and a title of Nu as Num was "Master of the Waters," which just happens to be the title of Nommo.

Jung continued to be deeply occupied with the processes of alchemy in relation to unconscious/spirit, which was expressed in his complex work *Mysterium Coniunctionis.* He subsequently had a dream that had two important features. These were his father's fish laboratory, and a "reception room for spirits." The fish laboratory, Jung concluded, alluded to his own preoccupation with Christ the Ichthys, while the "reception room for spirits" indicated the alchemical spirit, which he was still investigating, actually activating the deeper layers of the unconscious in his search.

Jung's father, the pastor, had forced himself to accept Christ on faith, but had been heavily burdened with much doubt because of it, and so Jung reasoned this was why the fish laboratory belonged to his father in the dream. This "wound" of Jung senior had been passed on to Jung the son as a problem to solve, as both personal and collective tasks. The problems of one generation, if not resolved, are passed on to the next generation in some form or other, because ultimately mankind must answer those problems or fail to progress; at least in that particular way. This is how Jung saw these things

The Star Above

Quite often, the fish exemplifying the aspect of the god from the lower spirit, or soul depths, the Lower Self, is countermatched by a star expressing his cosmic aspect, the Higher Self. This is seen with Christ the Ichthys, who also has his Star of Bethlehem, the "Star in the East" symbol above. *"Where is he that is called King of the Jews? For we have seen his star in the east, and are come to worship him."* (Matt. 2:2). Oannes the Man-Fish, later Babylonian form of Ea, is sometimes depicted with the tail of a fish and then with a fish's mouth below and a star hanging above; fish and star are thus countermatching symbols.

Horus was "The Fish of the Inundation," while the star Sirius (as Sept) was "Herald of the Birth of Horus" and "Star of the Annunciation." Both Horus and Christ are the Morning Star. A star represented Pharaoh in his god aspect.

Jung tells us that a star was always connected with the birth of a Messiah, and Num. 24:17 says, *"There shall come forth a star out of David."* Christ says, *"I am the root and offspring of David, the bright and morning star."* And referring to the initiate into his Mystery, *"And I will give him the morning star."* (Rev. 2:28). Zarathustra, the Persian prophet, was born under a star that shone brightly for three days and nights, so brightly in fact that it frightened the villagers, who fled until the star finally faded. Assur of the Assyrians had an eight-rayed star as his symbol, as did Sydic of the Syrians. The Wichita Indian Savior of North America, the Flint Man, came as a star that fell to Earth. St. Nicholas von Flue (1417–1487) continually saw a star in visions, and he had even seen a bright and luminous star while in his mother's womb. The connection between the fish and the star is excellently expressed by the Dogon of Mali, just mentioned above, who say that when a star heralds the coming of Nommo, it will be "The Day of the Fish."

So the fish and the star symbolize lower and higher aspects of the Savior/Self, although the fish can alternatively be the Mother-Fish that gives birth to the Savior—or to seven crocodile sons. These symbols are still produced today by unconscious/spirit reality in its messages to us in dreams. The lower archetypal depths wish to see the light of consciousness, but the higher, infinitely brighter light of God must rule. Always the higher spirit must redeem the lower spirit of the Earth.

Here are a couple of dreams from my processes in which stars appeared:

> *I look up at the night sky and see a round, white star move slowly across the heavens from right to left. This seems to last for minutes. I realize that it is a very important and meaningful omen.*

The star is a well-known symbol the world over, going back to primitive times, for the birth of a god or special being, thus heralding his advent in worldly reality. Not only would early man witness a moving star in the outer heavens as a real event, he would also experience it as a content and omen in his dreams and visions, as in mine here.

The unconscious chooses signs and symbols that best fit the situation, and a moving star portending the arrival of a special being is most appropriate.

> *I am sitting on the front step of a cottage with a lovely little girl who has golden curls, and who laughs happily. The girl's mother then comes and puts a woollen, fishnet blanket around the child. This is on a sunny day, but somehow we see beyond the clouds to where the sky is dark, or perhaps it has become night. Suddenly, we see a shooting star travel across the heavens from right to left, but then I tell the girl to look to the left, where a second star moves across from left to right, though this second one is partly covered by a dark cloud and is somewhat hazy. The stars then meet in the center of the sky and merge, pulsating and flashing like a neon light.*

The lovely little girl with golden curls is the female side of the divine child. Jung saw this very same child at the beginning of his own processes just before the First World War. The child here is brought a woolen fishnet blanket, which alludes to the lamb and the fish, symbols of aspects of the Self as Savior, i.e., Christ., by her mother, who represents the feminine spirit, the World Soul. We could say that the Lamb represents the Son of the Father, and the Fish the Son of the Mother.

A star heralds the approach or coming forth of the Higher Self, but there are two stars in the present dream, coming from either side of the sky, meaning both light and dark aspects. The second star being partly obscured by the dark hazy cloud further indicates this, and the two stars merging and pulsating means their unification into wholeness, the two sides of the Self unified.

In *The Sirius Mystery* (1976) historian Robert Temple mentions a dark, hazy star in the ancient Egyptian texts and concludes that it alludes to the star Sirius, or to its satellite Sirius B, Sirius being "binary" or twofold, or even ternary, threefold. But as the above dream indicates, the myth is actually expressing symbolism of the collective unconscious, light and dark sides of the Self. The ancient Egyptians could not have known of Sirius B in any case, and as Robert Temple points out himself, (though not realizing the full significance of what he is saying) Set, the evil twin of Osiris/Horus, is said to be a dark and hazy moving star in the myth. Again, this means the dark aspect of the Self. The contents of my dream demonstrate excellently how the mythology of ancient Egypt was based upon processes of the unconscious, and this is actually true of myths worldwide.

Chapter 6

The Trinity and the Quaternity of Wholeness

"Being One I Became Three"

—Egyptian text (Budge 1904)

Three and Four in Unconscious Processes

As part of his studies into alchemy and the archetypal Christ, Jung was deeply occupied with the symbolic numbers three and four. The fourfold structure of the Self as the quaternity is one of Jung's major discoveries. The numbers three and four constantly reoccur in dreams and throughout mythology, religious doctrines, alchemy, ancient philosophy, the esoteric Mysteries, legends, and fairy tales. In fact, one of the main goals of these traditions, if not the *main* goal, is the unification of three and four, sometimes as seven but also expressed as 3 + 1, i.e., the quaternity. We can look at this and some mythic/religious examples in a little depth here, for not only does it form part of Jung's discoveries, it is the structure that connects Man with God and the World Soul, and therefore with eternity. It is important, furthermore, to remember that conscious Man does not invent archetypal symbolism; it is the unconscious/spirit itself that provides this in the first place, largely through dreams. As with the rest of this book, I add to Jung's examples some of my own findings.

As well as higher archetypal structures being based on three, four, 3 + 1, 3 + 4, and so on, we find that the fundamental nature of the human psyche consists of the same pattern. As early as 1921, Jung published *Psychological Types*, in which he states the human psyche has four functions; sensation, thinking, feeling, and intuition. Sensation tells us something is there, thinking tells us what it is, feeling gives the emotional tone and the value of it, and intuition is the "sixth sense" we may unconsciously employ concerning it. The four functions are best seen as the four cardinal points forming a cross.

The conscious primary function at north, whichever it is, will always have its direct opposite sunk in the unconscious at south as the opposing fourth—the "recalcitrant fourth," as Jung puts it—and this will always desire to go off wildly on its own. After all, it is always the opposite in nature to the primary function. Thinking, for instance, will be diametrically opposed in the unconscious by an undeveloped feeling. The fourth may also be contaminated with the repressed shadow, and so felt to be the very Devil himself. The other two functions at east and west are auxiliary ones, and during the individuation process these may be unified to consciousness with effort. But the fourth is always much more difficult to win over, having, as Jung says, the "all-or-nothing" nature of an instinct. The fourth may again appear as a woman in a man's dreams, and presumably as a man in a woman's, though this is a different aspect or set-up to the structure just given with the recalcitrant fourth. In both cases the structure forms a 3 + 1 quaternity.

But the matter does not stop there; in fact it really just begins. In dreams, three figures or structures often refer to spirit, although it depends upon the context and the situation. Obviously, if I am with two companions so that we make three, it does not refer to spirit, and so only in specific circumstances does it do so. (This example would probably refer to myself as primary function, with the two auxiliary functions represented by my two companions.) Three aliens appearing in a dream, however, (which I have seen) would by contrast mean spirit. In one dream I saw an alien with three eyes in a vertical line, which I knew signified spirit, while in another, a light with three arms, which held bulbs that suddenly lit up, became three strange men, again representing spirit.

Abraham's experience when he entertains three angels at Mamre probably has the same Trinitarian meaning.

"And the Lord appeared unto him in the plains of Mamre: and he sat in the tent door in the heat of the day; and he lifted up his eyes and looked, and, lo, three men stood by him: and when he saw them, he ran to meet them from the tent door, and bowed himself toward the ground." (Genesis 18:1–2).

This is almost certainly the meaning of the Magi, the *"wise men from the east"* bringing the three gifts of gold, frankincense, and myrrh to Christ at his symbolic birth, again referring to Trinitarian spirit. Man has always felt the need to arrange his higher gods in Trinities and triads, and these have usually been counterbalanced by lower trinities and quaternities, based, we can be sure, upon archetypal structures experienced through the unconscious, though some of these would perhaps have been seen as outer manifestations. The alchemists speak of a dark chthonic trinity, for example, and Mercurius, the spirit of the Earth/unconscious is in one form the three-headed serpent, or three snakes. The caduceus, the two snakes entwined around a rod, associated with Mercurius and Hermes, probably originates from this, for the head of the central rod may well have been a snake originally, making three snake heads, the chthonic trinity. We encounter the chthonic trinity in Dante's *Inferno,* and Cerberus, the three-headed dog that Herakles fetches up from the Underworld in the Greek myth, has the same meaning. As the Egyptians, Sumerians, and other cultures knew, both the soul depths and higher spirit, and, indeed, Heaven itself, were to be reached through the Underworld, i.e., the collective unconscious, and all of the countermatching symbolism expressing soul and spirit arose from there.

The Trinity as an archetype, in Jung's opinion, may not merely engender a possible spiritualization of the personality, but may actually *enforce* it. However, if the effects of the Trinity begin to affect the health of the individual, because it is too overwhelming and therefore dangerous to consciousness, the Trinity will recede and let the opposite, worldly, life dominate again. Georg Koepgen, who collaborated with Jung for a time, writes, "The Trinity is a revelation not only of God but at the same time of Man." (1939). Jung continues to say that religion touches the human soul to a large degree, though today history is the only one of the sciences (apart from depth psychology) to pay any attention to the Christian Trinity or to religion generally. Yet the Trinity is a phenomenon that may be experienced directly through the unconscious, and while history cannot validate the Trinity as reality, and does not particularly wish to do so, depth psychology does accomplish precisely this.

The original doctrine says the Father and Son sent the Holy Ghost, and the fact is, it does seem to proceed from both, in a sense. The Father is One, but then the Son manifests from the Father making Two, or the Other. The Third is then the force that unifies both, so Jung's reasoning goes. "Out of the Father comes the Son," completed by the Holy Spirit, all becoming the Holy Trinity. Yet experience seems to show that the Third may act independently, and Christ himself says that while Father and Son may forgive sins done against them, the Holy Spirit will not. The Trinity certainly appears in dreams, or the Trinitarian force of spirit, and may be opposed by the chthonic trinity or triad from below in response—or it may occur the opposite way. I had a dream in which I travelled to Australia where black three-legged creatures came up out of the ground. Then in the following dream, three-legged flying saucers, definitely connected with the Holy Trinity, appeared overhead in the skies, still in Australia. These dreams involved countermatching Trinitarian forces of spirit, from the lower Eart, and from the higher celestial realm. (The full dreams and interpretations are given in part 2 of this work.)

Now not only do threefold structures appear in our dreams but sometimes fourfold ones in some way, this also being the case in myths, religious texts, etc. There is always uncertainty between three and four in the Mysteries, and Jung points out this is why there were three and four colors in alchemy, three and four procedures, or sometimes 3 + 1 in some way. As Plato says at the beginning of the *Timaeus*, "Three are there, but where is the fourth?" Plato's whole philosophy was based upon Trinitarian thinking—experience really—while that of Pythagoras was largely quaternary, or fourfold. But let us look at how three becomes four at higher level.

When part of God breaks away and by means of the Holy Spirit comes through the collective unconscious to incarnate in a human individual, who is a material entity, of course, the divine Three—Father, Son, and Holy Spirit—become Four in a sense, for the human individual here represents the realm of matter. This is why the fourth is occasionally a man in mythic/religious structures, though sometimes this is said to be an angel. For example, Christ at the center of the four symbols of the Evangelists, which are lion, eagle, ox, and angel, a 3 + 1 structure called the Tetramorph. Christ is thus "Lord of the Tetramorph." This is similar to the prophet Ezekiel's quaternity vision involving three animals, lion, ox, eagle, and man, although Daniel has four animals, lion, bear, leopard, with the recalcitrant fourth a beast, said to be "dreadful and terrible." In ancient Egypt, the quaternity nature of Horus was expressed by his four sons, again represented as three animal-headed and one man-headed, the fourth actually being female originally.

In the same way, Christ's four brothers in the Gospels could refer to the same quaternity nature and may even be 3 + 1 in that the fourth is called Judas, i.e., recalcitrant as Judas Iscariot. "*Is not this the carpenter's son? Is not his mother called Mary? And his brethren, James, and Joses, and Simon? And Judas?*" (Matt. 13:55). In fact, the first three are mentioned here together, while Judas is separated. Elsewhere, in the Gospel of John, Judas Iscariot is referred to as "Simon's son," and so here is not the brother of Jesus, who is son of Joseph. Yet Judas could still be a recalcitrant fourth symbolically, because all four brothers may not be real life ones, though two, James and Joses, have to be. In Central America myths, the Savior figure, Quetzalcoatl, has four brothers or agents who rule over four regions, expressing his fourfold totality.

Come to think of it, in Egypt the four sons of Horus are originally his brothers. However, the fourth with Horus was a sister first of all, and as said previously, the fourth to the male Trinity is often female. This is because the initiate may in his processes bring the feminine World Soul to unify with the Trinity, or with threefold masculine spirit. The Higher Self, as Christ, is manifestor for God the Three-in-One Deity, become Four because he is now unified with the feminine element (Mary Magdalene or Sophia in the Gnostic texts).

Jung says that God, the Three-in-One Deity, is in other circumstances made into a quaternity by the Devil, the Devil being God's "recalcitrant fourth" here, the "Ape of God" that makes the Trinity into Four according to the Gnostics. So while God is at north, Christ and the Holy Spirit are at east and west, with the Devil at south. These can be moved around to different aspects of the phenomenon. For example, God is the Father, with Christ, the embodiment of love, at His right hand, and the Devil in his denial at His left. Then the Holy Spirit according to this would be the fourth below that makes up the quaternity. Jung quotes Koepgen, who writes, "The existence of Satan, however, can only be understood in relation to the Trinity." (1939). But the Devil and the feminine element are never, as far as I know, in the same quaternity schema, because although both exemplify the Earth and matter, it is in different aspects or ways.

Some critics assign Jung's positing of the Devil as God's recalcitrant fourth to his "hatred" of Freud, or even as bitter hostility towards God. But we must ask, did the Gnostics, the Egyptians, and all of the other mythmakers, prophets, and initiates into the sacred Mysteries of the world also have hatred for Freud and hostility towards God, seeing they came up with the same symbol? Though Jung's popularity has greatly increased with the years, so has the inanity of some of his critics. How they can make "animosity" or "hatred" of Freud, or "hostility towards God," out of the quaternity structure is simply beyond my comprehension.

In a number of medieval depictions there is a heavenly male Trinity with Mary completing the four of wholeness. At the Musee de Cluny in Paris, an enclosed figure of the Virgin Mary opens up to reveal Father, Son, and Holy Spirit. Thus Mary completes the Trinity as a quaternity. Jung mentions a Christian quaternity of Holy Ghost (dove) at north, Virgin Mary at south, Christ at east, and God at west. These can be moved about with just as much authenticity.

Jung says that the Church often makes the Devil, the recalcitrant fourth to the Trinity, into a mere shadow, but points out that evil is just as real as good, good and evil being the opposite poles of a moral judgment. If evil lacks substantiality, then so too must good. The alchemical Mercurius is threefold as the "three-headed serpent," but he is also *quadratus*, the fourfold Mercurius

Jung further remarks that it is certainly odd that the Church Fathers so violently attacked the divine principle of a quaternity, seeing that the central symbol of Christianity itself, the cross, is a definite quaternity. With Christ and his total affirmation and love, must also come Satan with his complete dissent and opposite of love, this meaning not only a further differentiation of Man, of his consciousness, but also of God. Jung concludes that the Devil must be added to the divine principle of the Trinity to make God in his wholeness a quaternity (in our thinking—but during the unconscious processes it is reality experienced), just as we must see the total human psyche as a quaternity if we wish to have a true concept of the wholeness of it.

Jung has also been accused of blatant contradiction in positing both the Devil and the feminine principle as the fourth of the quaternity, but this again displays complete lack of understanding of the archetypal position. As said, they are simply different aspects of the full situation, for while the Devil is "Prince of this world" and tempts Man with the worship of it, matter is at the same time largely feminine, Mother Earth, World Soul, and so on. Indeed, the words "mother" and "matter" are from the same root. In alchemy, Mercurius was the masculine Earth Spirit, while the World Soul, the *anima mundi*, was the feminine side. Or Mercurius was himself masculine/feminine. These are facts experienced through the collective unconscious itself, and are therefore expressions of it, not just the opinions of consciousness. No one invented or merely postulated them—not Jung, the alchemists, the Gnostics, or anyone else—they *experienced* them

Three as masculine spirit and four as feminine matter/soul need to be unified in the processes, but this is not to say that the feminine element cannot be threefold itself, as a lower trinity or triad in countermatch to the higher Trinity. I have seen three female figures from the lower depths in dreams many times as well as three male ones (sometimes hostile), therefore lower trinities or triads. And as said above, the chthonic trinity is sometimes three snakes or a three legged creature or three savage warriors or three witches, etc.

As to the number four itself, while it sometimes refers to matter/soul, as with the four quarters or directions of the World Soul, it also refers, as we have seen, to the quaternity of 3 + 1. Jung tells us that while the Son of Man and the quaternity are present in Daniel and Ezekiel, (as 3 + 1) they are more strongly stressed in the apocryphal *Book of Enoch,* where the prophet travels on visionary journeys. He encounters "the four hollow places" of the Underworld in which the spirits of the dead reside awaiting the day of Judgment, but afterwards sees "four faces of God." The "four faces" are archangels singing praises, with the fourth one separate, actually "fighting off the Satans," therefore making the structure 3 + 1. This angelic quaternity of Enoch's, consisting of Michael, Gabriel, Raphael, and Phanuel, comes forth with the Head of Days, and Jung says this means the four faces/angels represent a differentiation of God, his manifested structure, and that God wants to become Man here.

So Enoch journeys to the heavenly four quarters above, as well as to the Earth's center, these movements forming a mandala, the quartered circle. Enoch as ego-consciousness has become caught up in the divine drama, which may happen to anyone who goes to these extremes, who reaches these levels, with the inner processes. In Christian terms Jung calls it being crucified with Christ, adding that the priest dividing the fontal water into a cross, sprinkling it to the four directions in the *benedictio fontis,* may refer to a similar fourfold structure of the Higher Self. It is symbolism occurring as part of an individuation process that descends to the World Soul and up to the heavenly realm. Make no mistake, Enoch does literally experience these figures and structures as part of his processes. It is a fact that around the world from ancient times the Higher Self figure as Savior has been expressed by the number four, often as 3 + 1.

From the lower angle, Mary is the matrix or vessel from which the Savior is born, "the flower of the sea where Christ lies hidden," as she has been called. This is equalled by the *rotundum* in alchemy, which is quartered by the four cardinal points and from which the Philosopher's Stone is said to arise. In medieval mysticism the King of Glory reposes in the rose that is supported by the four evangelists, while it is well known that in the East, as well as in ancient Egypt, the gods are born from the fourfold lotus; also seen in alchemy. According to Pythagoras the soul is a square, and Jung says the quaternity comes forth out of the World Soul (this must be the lower quaternity).

To certain Gnostics, the Anthropos (Self) was a city with his four limbs as four gates. To other Gnostics, the Monogenes, a type of Anthropos, rested on a platform supported by four pillars. As well as four colors of alchemy that were of the Stone, there were also four stages (and three stages), the *nigredo, dealbatio, rubefactio,* and *citrinitas.* Paracelsus, the medieval alchemist, speaks of Archeus, the Great Man in alchemy, a type of Anthropos, composed of four parts and being "the great Cosmos." This sounds like the Logos, the Higher Self in cosmic form, who disperses parts of himself into all mortals.

The Mountain of the Adepts in alchemy was four-stepped but enclosed a seven-stepped Temple of the Wise, with a phoenix, which rises from its own ashes in renewal, on the apex. All was lit by the Sun and Moon, and at the four corners were depicted the four elements. Very similar to the phoenix was the Ortus of alchemist Michael Maier, which combined in itself four alchemical colors; black, white, red, and yellow. Like the phoenix, the Ortus consumed itself and then was born anew, thus symbolizing resurrection. (The phoenix was a symbol of Christ's resurrection.) The Ortus was said to reside in Africa, because the Dark Continent represented the "dark and hidden land," the collective unconscious. Relevant here is that Maier says the fourth was to be experienced through the "seven planetary spheres," intimating the Higher Self, who undergoes resurrection in his processes, and who is fourfold and sevenfold in varying aspects.

The Kabbalah has four Guardian Angels that guard the Four Corners of the Earth, which roughly correspond to the Four Maharajas of esoteric Eastern philosophy, the Four Holy Ones connected with Karma, Humanity, Cosmos, and Man. In Buddhism, there are the Four Truths and the Seven Ways, and also the Seven and Twelve Nidanas. The three of spirit and the four of matter/soul, when added together give seven, but the number of the supreme totality is twelve. None of this symbolism, confusing at times, is invented by consciousness, but is rather experienced through inner processes.

Let me add here that in dreams stretching over many years I have covered the world in all four directions, from the North Pole to the South Pole, from the Far East to the Americas, finding myself in many of the countries in between, but basically forming a cross. This symbolized covering the lower, soul side of the collective unconscious, the World Soul, which has a fourfold structure, such as Enoch's four hollow places of the Earth. I experienced many strange and dangerous things, but the experience of one content, or side, of the unconscious usually invokes the appearance of the opposite side, and so the bringing to light of the soul depths invokes contents from the higher realm of the spirit in response. Further, the unification of contents of the soul depths causes the World Soul to bring forth the Son of the lower depths, who copies and countermatches the divine Son of the Father above. This is why the Philosopher's Stone, symbol of the lower Son (the *filius*), was posited as directly countermatching Christ in the "lapis-Christ parallel."

Other Trinities/Quaternities

As mentioned above, the prophet Daniel has dream visions in which he sees four beasts rising up from the sea—lion, bear, leopard, and a fourth beast *"dreadful and terrible."* (Dan. 7:7). This is followed by the Son of Man coming with the clouds of Heaven, who then joins the Ancient of Days sitting on his throne. The sea symbolizes the World Soul, the collective unconscious, and the four beasts represent the quaternity of the Lower Self brought forth as the lower Son; i.e., the Son of Man here. *"I saw in the night visions and behold, one like the Son of man came with the clouds of heaven, and came to the Ancient of Days, and they brought him near before him."* (Dan. 7:13).

Thus Daniel's Son of Man quaternity is similar to those of Christ, Horus, and Ezekiel, the difference being that where the Fourth is a terrible beast with Daniel, it is human or an angel with the others. Quaternities often vary in this way, or countermatch each other. The Ancient of Days is said to be God, and the archetypal pattern of appearances of the divine Father together with the Son can be traced back through the Old Testament to the beginnings of Egypt. God in Egypt was fourfold in one aspect, but he also says, "Being One I became Three." Nevertheless, in other circumstances he was termed "The God with Two Faces," because here he contained Father and Son within his fullness. He was also called "The Aged One" in Egypt, matching the Ancient of Days with Daniel and Enoch.

Another three-becoming-four incident occurs in the Book of Daniel, in which three men, Shadrach, Meshach, and Abednego, are cast into the fiery furnace by Babylonian emperor Nebuchadnezzar's guards. But when Nebuchadnezzar takes a look to see if they are now ashes, he is astonished because the three figures, instead of being shriveled, have been joined by a fourth. This figure is actually called a "Son of God." *"He answered and said, Lo, I see four men loose, walking in the midst of the fire, and they have no hurt; and the form of the fourth is like the Son of God."* (Dan. 3: 25).

Though the three figures with the Son of God could be seen as a 3 + 1 quaternity there is yet a deeper meaning. The number three and fire both allude to the higher masculine spirit of God, while the number four and water refer to lower feminine spirit or soul, ultimately the Great Mother. Thus Son of God with fire and the number three (three figures) involves the Higher Self, and the Son of Man with water and the number four (four beasts) involves the Lower Self. This seems to represent a whole process, from above and below, *par excellence,* uniting the Son of the Father with Son of the Mother, and, of course, three with four into seven; i.e., the Seven Powers of the Self.

Scholars have not made much (if indeed, anything at all) of this reference to the Son of God here in Daniel, nor of Melchizedek, another biblical character who is a divine figure. Yet these, as Higher Self figures in highest aspect are indeed true Sons of God and prefigurations of Christ. Christ is even referred to in the scripture as being "*. . . after theorder of Melchizedek.*" (Heb. 7:17.)

The three, triad or Trinity, while in a sense being whole unto itself, is nevertheless not ultimately whole as a total reality—not even God, it would seem. Just as every man has a female in his unconscious, and every woman a male, so it seems that the feminine spirit is connected to God, and of course, God to the feminine spirit.

As said above and as Jung mentions, while Plato's philosophy rests on Trinitarian thinking, Greek thought as a whole was of quaternary nature, particularly the Pythagorean school, which based much on four. In fact, Jung has been accused of being a Pythagorean who deifies the number four. But it is not a matter of belief or postulation, rather of direct experience of these things—in other words, of gnosis.

We can see the quaternity archetype expressed around the world in myths, largely in animal forms. The four sons of Horus in Egypt were ape, dog, hawk, and man. I actually saw these in a dream vision, but the fourth, the man, changed into a woman, and as said, the fourth in the myths was originally female. Another quaternity of Egypt on the same model consisted of the gods Ra, Set, and Shu, with the goddess Tefnut as fourth—this was when Set was in positive form earlier; Horus later replaced him. These four were part of the fuller Seven Spirits. The monotheist Pharaoh Akhenaten reached a similar structure with Ra, Horus, and Shu contained in the Aten Sun-disc, thus forming the Holy Trinity, but then the goddess Tefnut connected with these; thus quaternities of 3 + 1. Of the seven gods in Japan called the Kami, a special four are three brothers with their sister Iznani. There are similarly a special four of the seven Nommo gods of the Dogon people of Mali, in West Africa. Prajapati, in India, makes himself fourfold and is then reborn in the seven Rishis. The same expression is seen when Rabbi Abba writes that while the Tetragrammaton (the name of God) is fourfold, it nevertheless has seven eyes.

We have seen that with Ezekiel, the four are lion, ox, eagle, and man, and with Daniel, lion, bear, leopard, and a beast "dreadful and terrible."

In India, they are cow, eagle, ape, and serpent. In China, stag, phoenix, tortoise, and dragon. In Assyria, the structure was reversed and three were man-headed and one animal-headed. With the Aztecs the four were house, flint arrowhead, cane, and rabbit; and in Persia the god Ahura Mazda shows Zarathustra four metals, gold, silver, steel, and iron, which will compose the mound of the one Solar God.

The Tat-Cross of Ptah in Egypt meant God in his four divine forms, while in the Mysteries, on the fourth night of the *Ritual* (in the Book of the Dead), the Four Pillars were said to be erected upon which the future kingdom of God the Father was to be founded. It was on these four pillars in Amenta, the Underworld, that the firmament rested, the "Heaven of the four quarters." So the foundations of Heaven were fourfold in the Underworld. In the inner processes the higher spiritual must always rest upon solid foundations below.

In a pyramid text of Pepi I, Fourth Dynasty, it states, "Homage to thee, O thou who hast four faces . . ." meaning God. Later, the Gnostic Valentinus derived the primordial four from the original "dual being," the Anthropos or Self, and as said above, for the Gnostics in general God was "Four," the fourth sometimes being the recalcitrant "Ape of God." (Valentinus had a dream in which a divine child appeared, saying, "I am the Logos." This was Christ the cosmic Self now born into the soul of Valentinus.)

These are just a few examples of how the fourfold structure or constituents of the god have been experienced and symbolized across the world. As can be seen, they are often of a 3 + 1 nature, though not always so, and are sometimes part of the full Seven Powers or Spirits. The four "angels" with Enoch are actually part of the seven archangels, of course.

Here is a dream that exemplifies the unification of the three and four in the Self at animal level:

> *I am taking my dog for a walk on his lead, though he is also my old she-cat. Both are now combined and unified into one creature. He is somewhat dirty because I have allowed him a lot of freedom of late, but then he had to be allowed some freedom. Still, I will have to bath him later. Then I see my dog's and cat's four sons, all pups, though one is different from the rest, and stands out as "Zephael, son of the Dark Angel," so the dream says.*

My masculine dog-spirit and feminine cat-soul have become unified, which means that the spirit and soul sides of the Higher Self are now unified at lower level. Throughout my individuation process it has been necessary to keep my dog tightly on his lead, which means that I protect the developing Self from the dirt, desires, and dangers of the world, though of late I seem to have been somewhat lax. Bathing means to wash off the dirt, and therefore the crass worldliness, and we find a comparison in alchemy with the alchemical bath, the *ablutio,* which produced the One white color that contained all other colors, sometimes called the "Peacock's Tail." This basically means the unification of all the opposites in the One, ultimately the Higher Self.

Though my fourth is "son of the Dark Angel," this may allude to man as representative of dark matter. However, the "Dark Angel" that is "prince of this world" is the very Devil himself, in which case the fourth certainly would be recalcitrant.

Jung says the 3 + 1 quaternity of Ezekiel is the symbol of the Higher Self, and that the quaternity that exemplifies Yahweh consists of three animal symbols and one human, the latter representing Satan as "godfather" to Man in spiritual aspect.

Many psychiatrists have been of the opinion that Ezekiel's visions were the products of a severely disturbed mind. The truth is, Ezekiel must have possessed a highly developed and extensively broadened consciousness, which enabled him to successfully assimilate such complex symbolic contents from the unconscious. He must have experienced the Higher Self as divine Son, and through him, God. But it is quite in keeping with the dissociated, over-rationalized thinking of modern psychiatry that a prophet of God and leader of his people should be so misunderstood as to be classified insane.

Some while ago I had a dream of a dog with a broken leg. A couple of days later I sent for a plumber and we somehow got to talking about dreams. He told me of one he had the previous night, where he was trying to push a small four-wheeled cart but was having trouble because one of the wheels was broken. Sitting in the cart was a dog. Obviously, the meanings of our respective dreams corresponded precisely and we had apparently both tuned in to the same archetypal situation. As said above, a dog is one of the main symbols of the Self in first form, called in the Mysteries a dog-spirit. In a sense, three is its number, as three is the number of masculine spirit, and so what is needed for wholeness in the dreams of the plumber and myself is the fourth, which is "broken." However, from another angle the Self is fourfold, Christ on the cross, etc., and the four legs of my dog, and the four wheels of the cart express this—Marduk in ancient Babylonia was accompanied by four dogs with the same meaning.

The Gnostics said that the "Christ within," the Anthropos, of each person is not different from others; all people share the same figure as it is collective. In other words, all souls are contained within the Logos. The plumber and I were experiencing the same Higher Self, symbolized by a dog, though the crippled fourth, while having the same meaning, was expressed differently. This is what Jung meant when he said dreams often show a three and four situation.

As to the archetype of the Self within Man, two thousand years ago certain Gnostics, and even some of the more orthodox Christians, realized that Christ was, or at least symbolized, the "Christ within." He therefore indicated or equaled the Anthropos figure, though this in no way contradicted the fact that Christ in ultimate form was the Son of God above. The Gnostics also realized that in a variety of forms the symbol of the Anthropos, the crossed or squared circle, springs up from within Man, denoting order and wholeness; that is, the unification of spirit and matter/soul. Nevertheless, when in Egypt the circle of Heaven was unified with the square of the Earth, the circle of Heaven was considered superior. Always we see this archetype, or archetypal situation, at work in Man, expressing things of far greater issue than mere Man himself. We can see from all of this that the archetype of a totality divided into four reaches far back into antiquity.

The lower spirit, or soul depths, produces a Son in the processes to countermatch the higher Son of God. This lower Son of the Mother is dual in nature and it is this Son who in negative aspect is a sort of Satan, Set in Egypt, Mephistopheles with Goethe, etc., and who becomes the recalcitrant "fourth" according to this schema; and there are other variations. As said above, Jung has been accused of being a Pythagorean who deifies the number four, but Pythagoras came across this great truth of the quaternity himself, actually contrasting with Plato whose thinking was and remained Trinitarian. Countless other adepts over thousands of years have expressed these same great truths of the unconscious/spirit realm, and critics should study these first before casting their stones at Jung (or at me, come to that).

As I was just finishing typing the above, a scene flashed into my mind of one-time actor Henry Fonda running across the plains in the old movie, *Drums Along the Mohawk*. In the scene, three Huron Indians chasing Fonda are after his scalp, and I could actually see this in my mind's eye. So the unconscious was sending up the symbol of 3 + 1, here one positive figure and three negative, in contradistinction to the more usual three positive and one negative or recalcitran, fourth, to complement my conscious thoughts as I was writing. I have actually been chased by three Huron Indians in dreams several times, though this was some years ago as part of my individuation process. This must have been the chthonic trinity in negative aspect and the unconscious was reminding me of it here; or indeed, it was becoming activated again with what I was writing.

Immediately after the above experience, Snow White and the Seven Dwarfs came into my mind, again not just as a thought, but as an image sent and received, as it were. I then realized that it referred to the 1 + 7 archetype, the first or eighth sometimes being female—the Great Mother in Egypt with her seven crocodile sons, for example, or Aditi in India, the Boundless Whole, also with seven sons. This formation of eight, or 1 + 7, was known as the Eight Gods, the *Paut Neteru,* in Egypt, and later in Gnosticism as the Ogdoad. The fairy tale itself, *Snow White and the Seven Dwarfs,* who are miners, displays the same archetypal pattern springing up spontaneously from the unconscious. We must think also of the seven Ali pygmy miners of Ptah in Egypt here, and the seven dwarf sons of the Polynesian god Pinga. As well as dwarfs, the seven are sometimes giants, as with the biblical Rephaim and Zamzumim, the Sumerian Igigi (miners) or the Hohgates of California (who go under the Earth). Also the Chinese Eight Immortals, the eighth one of which is a girl, and even Mary Magdalene with the seven devils that Christ casts out of her reflects the same archetype in negative aspect.

Another dream that I had exemplifies the quaternity structure of the Self perfectly.

> *I am in a hall, rather like a large classroom without the desks. Suddenly, I see four figures some yards above me seated on thrones. These are three male gods and a goddess, the latter sitting to the right of the others as I look (so actually to their left). I say something like, "I believe in wisdom, truth, love, and dignity," although the last one could be "integrity."*

The four figures express a "quaternity," obviously on the positive side, though apparently of the lower spirit. This would not be, therefore, the masculine heavenly Trinity unified with the feminine World Soul, but a quaternity of the Earth Spirit/World Soul (though I could be wrong and it may be the Trinity with the feminine fourth). The four qualities I mention are ones I sometimes think of as quaternary, and so the dream is using this to express the situation.

Since writing the above, I have had a further dream of the four figures, seeing them in the town just a couple of miles south of where I live; therefore in the soul or Earth Spirit aspect. Again, I knew these were gods, though the three males soon disappeared. This left the "Woman," and with her she had her young son.

I asked the "Woman," "Is Christianity the way forward?" to which she replied "Yes. Christianity is the way forward." Now, this is of tremendous importance. It is not the male Trinity pronouncing on this, as we might perhaps expect, but the feminine World Soul. This means that Christ and his mystery have been accepted by the spirit of the Earth, and further spiritual development is to be along those lines—the royal line running from the beginnings of Egypt. So the chance is here for respiritualization if mankind today can take it, and this will be in tune with the eternal powers. We have been falling into chaos for decades, but anyone now who continues on that decline will be running contrary not only to the higher spirit, but to the soul force of nature herself.

There now is a postscript to this: Something seemingly extraordinary has happened, extraordinary, that is, if you do not happen to know the workings of the spirit through the unconscious. I ran into my sister-in-law yesterday, whom I had not seen for a couple of months or so. She told me that her mother, who is almost ninety, is fading a little mentally and is experiencing hallucinations. She says she is being visited regularly by three spirit monks, though the last couple of times a woman has accompanied them with her young son. These figures, the old lady insists, are spirits. This sort of experience also happens with active imagination; the conscious mind lowers partly, allowing unconscious/spirit contents to come through, sometimes even seen as outer visions. My sister-in-law's mother is seeing the very same quaternity that I am experiencing through dreams, three males and a female, the fourth apparently the World Soul with her son. This proves yet again that the unconscious/spirit is another reality we all share collectively and which we may experience in dreams, through active imagination, or as outer visions.

Chapter 7

Squaring the Circle

We regularly find the four in connection with the wheel or circle in mythology and religious texts. The circle containing four parts in some way—meaning the squaring of the circle and the unification of the opposites—is a very ancient symbol, and was not only known to the Gnostics and alchemists, but was the very basis of their tenets; this was certainly the case with the ancient Egyptians. Jung calls it perhaps the main symbol of the unconscious, and of the Higher Self. In India, the cosmic force called Fohat marks the circle vertically and horizontally by moving over it, creating the cross within the circle that quarters it. The wheel in medieval alchemy was called the *circulatio,* partly because the inner processes function in a circular movement. But it was also a symbol of wholeness, and was sometimes divided into four, or eight. There were thus "four bailiffs" associated with the wheel, or the four elements. All of this can be seen in mandala symbolism, of course, where the circle contains four, eight, and so on, with the same meaning. Jacob Boehme, the mystic who lived in the sixteenth and seventeenth centuries, equated the turning wheel symbolically with the "golden child," the infant Higher Self. The alchemical text, *Rosarium Philosophorum* (1550) states, "Our stone is from the four elements," intimating the same archetype.

The four gold keys on the gold key ring that I received from Jung in my dream, and that he received from Philemon in his, form a fourfold mandala, the "circle of four," with the specifically added meaning of the keys as entrance to the mysteries of the Underworld, the unconscious. As we saw, the Egyptian god Shu, "the breath of Ra," provided the keys for the initiate in one version of the mythos, and Shu often holds the ankh cross, the circle and the cross combined. The Four in One, variously emanating from a center, or from a circle, is the foundation of visions and religious symbolism the world over, and Jung tells us that many of his patients produced mandalas with a fourfold structure, expressing the same basic archetype as Ezekiel's wheel, the visions of Daniel, Isaiah, Enoch, and so forth.

In her visions of Christ, St. Teresa of Avila received a gold necklace from which hung a jeweled cross; thus again the fourfold circle, symbol of the god, of the Higher Self. Jung says God manifested in his creation is directly represented by the quaternity, though we can add that God as a circle is Trinitarian, at least from one aspect. When manifested as the Higher Self, God, becomes fourfold, because the "fourth," the Earth or matter/soul, is added. This caused the Gnostics to proclaim, "God is Four." Also worthy of mention is the Gnostic symbol of Jerusalem as the central city having four gates.

While wholeness and completeness can be expressed as a circle, its natural division is a quaternity. We can thus see this archetype in action when the Victorian mythologist Gerald Massey tells us that in Egypt the Great Mother in her Starry Shape, in her four-foldness, was the Beast of the Great Bear Circle, the "Circle of Heaven on the Four Quarters of the Horizon," thus again forming the symbol of the squaring of the circle. (She was also Mother of the Seven Stars in the same constellation.)

I recently saw an account of alien abduction, involving a circle, that expresses the meaning of the 3 + 1 quaternity structure perfectly. I was running through a videotape, silently on slow-forward, of a few items I had recorded some time before, the contents of which I had almost forgotten. Part way through I lost concentration for a few moments, looking away without realizing. But then, "waking up," I turned my eyes back to the screen. What I saw startled me—the tape was still running silently—because there on the screen, if only briefly, was the totality symbol of the Higher Self, the "circle of the four quarters," and indeed, of the 3 + 1 quaternity, though in modern UFO form. What I saw was a colored sketch of a flying saucer from just beneath, which therefore gave a circular shape, and four figures floating up to it, three aliens and a human being, a woman.

When I ran the tape back to the start of the item, it turned out to be one concerning American writer Budd Hopkins, who has investigated hundreds of cases of humans supposedly abducted by aliens. He was now speaking of a case, the most important account he has ever come across, he said, that occurred in New York on November 30, 1989, involving a woman named Linda Cortile. Linda had awakened from her sleep one night in the bedroom of her twelfth-storey apartment to find a small, grey-skinned alien moving up on her. She threw a pillow at it, but then felt herself becoming paralyzed for a time. Two days later she underwent hypnosis in which she regressed to experience what were now three aliens floating with her through the bedroom window and up to the flying saucer that was hovering overhead. This is what the illustration I saw on the TV screen was depicting, making a circle with four figures of a 3 + 1 structure, three aliens and a human female. Inside the saucer, Linda was lain on a bed and her nose examined, and then, after a few surprising pleasantries exchanged with the aliens, she suddenly found herself back in her own bed again.

Strangely, she had seen a doctor some time before this concerning an unexplained bump on her nose, and after examining it, the doctor had informed her of a scar inside her nose. She had also experienced a paralysis creeping up her legs several times, and had written to Budd Hopkins about this, but after the latest abduction, she instead telephoned him to tell the tale.

The above incidents with the aliens could be interpreted as merely dreams, and perhaps—where Linda threw the pillow at the alien—as a confused half-awake reaction. This sort of thing sometimes occurs. But what happens later becomes too involved and complicated for that to be the case here. Fourteen months after the incident, two special police officers sent Hopkins a report stating that on a certain date in 1989, they had seen three "ugly" aliens accompanied by a woman in a nightgown float up to a UFO, a flying saucer. They had seen the UFO then plunge into the river by Brooklyn Bridge. The date they saw all this happen was November 30, fitting in with Linda's experience precisely.

The two officers, called Richard and Dan, had been bodyguards of a former secretary of the United Nations, Perez de Cuellar, and all three were in a car that had stalled under Brooklyn Bridge at the time of the UFO/Linda incident. So Cuellar had also witnessed the alien abduction. Likewise, other cars stalled on the bridge, and even the bridge's lights went out.

As it turned out, about twenty other people had either witnessed the abduction, or had undergone strange experiences themselves connected with the incident. The story becomes so involved, complicated, bizarre, ludicrous, and even hilarious—yet deadly serious—that I cannot go into all of it here. Anyone wishing to know more could read Hopkins' book, *Witnessed* (1996) or Colin Wilson's account in *Alien Dawn* (1998). But an important item is that the two officers later found themselves by the seashore, where they saw Linda digging in the sands with the aliens. Showing the officers a dead fish, she remarked, "Look what you've done."

The illustration on the screen of Linda floating up to the flying saucer with three aliens, forms the quaternity of wholeness, the squared circle of 3 +1, the classic symbol of the Higher Self, of the unification of spirit with matter. It fits in perfectly with all the examples I have given above, the "circle of the four quarters," etc. If anyone asked me to draw the simplest symbol of the Higher Self, I would do a cross within a circle, the Gnostic symbol that squares the circle. If I were then asked to amplify the symbol with a further drawing, I would do a circle with the four figures of a 3 + 1 nature, most probably three males and a female. In other words, the Linda Cortile incident is the same phenomenon as, say, the four sons of Horus on a lotus, the fourth one of which was originally female, though all of the examples I gave earlier, the visions of Enoch, Daniel, Christ and the rest, with the 3 + 1 structure, have the same basic meaning.

It is not the case, as certain investigators would have it, that the historical examples are really UFO experiences that were interpreted as religious ones by the ancients, but rather that they are all actually experiences of spirit that have been interpreted today as UFO experiences, understandably so in the extremely scientific/technological culture that the West has become. The same disturbed and almost mesmerized state of the onlooker is there with both types, the ancient religious and the modern UFO, but the feeling of holiness is lost with the UFO interpretation because it is a lessening of the meaning, and is therefore a misinterpretation. The myths of the Dogon people of Mali contain much similar symbolism, but for them the whole phenomenon is a matter of great sacredness. They do not, as yet, suffer from the atheistic dissociation malady of modern Man (see *An Order Outside Time* for an explanation of the Dogon myths).

The Linda Cortile experience involves the collective unconscious to high degree, and the return to the river of the UFO, while being untenable as a fact of physical reality, fits perfectly with known archetypal events of the unconscious. The main symbol of the collective unconscious is water; the sea, a river, a lake and so on, and the submerging of the UFO into the river returns the archetype to its source. Furthermore, the world of the conscious is symbolized by dry land, and so the seashore is the meeting place between the two different realities of the conscious and unconscious, which is where the two officers find Linda with the aliens.

The dead fish she shows to the officers is also highly symbolic, for as we saw above, a fish is one of the main symbols of the Higher Self—Christ is the Ichthys, the Fish. The flying saucer could mean the symbol of the higher spirit aspect and the fish the lower spirit aspect. Certain actions of the officers—earlier they had picked Linda up off the street for questioning, for instance—had apparently disturbed the processes so much that the fish, as part of the present processes, was killed off. The Higher Self, being immortal, could never be killed off. Linda herself is the mortal aspect or part of it, representing matter/soul, that joins the three of spirit in the flying saucer, in the Higher Self totality, completing the quaternity of the circle, and repeating the age old symbol, the "circle of the four quarters."

I must make clear again that the Higher Self, though usually becoming reduced and personified to us in "human" form, is nevertheless gigantic and contains a large part of otherworldly reality within its nature. As the Logos, it is part of the infinity of God and, though actually both eternal spirit and soul, can be symbolized by UFOs, fish, stars, and a few hundred other things. We are all parts of its wholeness, and while possible actions in physical reality are necessarily limited, literally anything can happen in the collective unconscious. It is another reality existing behind, or surrounding, the physical universe, and we are connected directly to it, so we should not be too surprised if the two realities merge at times and very strange things occur. But though they may seem weird and crazy to us, they are ultimately very meaningful, more so than invasions by aliens from other planets would be. However, we should not become complacent and believe that everything will automatically turn out well because we are experiencing spirit rather than aliens. Certain obligations are required of us as caretakers of the planet, and we are not fulfilling that responsibility. In any case, this aspect of the spirit is not experienced as numinous and holy; it just functions as real aliens would apparently do.

We can experience the Self through processes of the unconscious, and we can study and assess the processes on a scientific basis, but ultimately it is a highly numinous and religious experience that should cause us to drop to our knees in awe and wonderment. Beside such an experience, "scientific evidence" shrinks to almost nothingness, even though we have to study the experience "scientifically." It is very difficult to impart the numinous experience to others, to the world, so it is necessary to try and prove such claims by whatever evidence we can assemble. Jung realized this quite early, but knew the difficulty in adequately conveying what has been experienced. You can read all about being in a car accident, but the real thing is quite something else again. Yet at least the car involved would be known to be real. How many believe in the forces of the spirit?

When the experience occurs unconsciously and is projected outwards into the world, or is otherwise seen as an outer event breaking through the veil, the numinosity may be somewhat lost because of the interpretation, or rather misinterpretation; as flying saucers, for example. Because the experience of the Self "transcends consciousness," and is ultimately collective, it is possible for large groups of people to participate in it, as in the Linda Cortile experience. But even when no outer phenomena are involved, it is still possible for a certain *participation mystique* to occur, as in the Mass, as the Mass is in essence a summation and symbolization of processes involving the Higher Self—"the rite of the individuation process," as Jung expressed it.

When channeled in a religious way the meaning is much nearer to the true nature of the actual phenomena than mere rationalistic scientific interpretation could possibly be. (UFO/alien interpretations are rationalistic ones basically, in that they reduce archetypal/spiritual occurrences to physical ones, albeit extra-terrestrial.) As with the Mass, in ancient Egypt "Osirification," the divine process of resurrection, was gradually allowed to all of the people after originally belonging to Pharaoh alone. Indeed, most of the rituals and symbolizations in the religions of the world have their origins as mystical experiences of the unconscious, and the same is true of myths, legends, and fairy tales, though the source may not be known to consciousness.

Jung says dogma lasts for many hundreds, or even thousands, of years, whereas one scientific theory quickly supersedes another. He says that while scientific theory expresses only conscious ideas and opinions, dogma expresses the truths of the inner Great Man. The dogmatic formula of the Higher Self in the West is not quite complete, as the evil principle is missing from the Trinity, and so exists separately. But as we have seen, the fourth is not only the evil principle, it is also the Earth, soul/matter, as opposed to the purely spiritual Trinity, and is usually feminine. In 1950 the Catholic Church proclaimed the Assumption of the Virgin, which takes matter very much closer to spirit. In fact, Linda Cortile joining the three aliens, the threefold spirit, in the flying saucer, is symbolism similar in a way to the Assumption of the Virgin, who joins the Holy Trinity in the Blessed Bridal Chamber. There are medieval depictions of Mary sitting at a round table with the three figures of the Trinity, and this is precisely what the Linda Cortile experience involves. Nor is this unique: In the thirteenth and fourteenth centuries certain women mystics found themselves unifying with the Trinity during inner spiritualizing processes, forming the Holy Quaternity of 3 + 1. We could say the Linda Cortile experience is the same as that of the women mystics, but seen in modern UFO/alien terms.

The Church thinks in a Trinitarian way, while the unconscious processes insist upon a quaternity ultimately, and so they seem irreconcilable. Yet if the Church would accept the discoveries of depth psychology concerning the fourth that completes the three, the Trinity and the quaternity are unified. Nothing has been lost; the Trinity is still the Trinity and Christ is still Son of God; but much has been gained. The conscious human being, let us say Jesus the man, (or Linda Cortile) is joined to the Higher Self, as is also is the largely feminine realm of matter, to which Man belongs, and so the Trinity becomes a quaternity also. It further allows Christ to be both spirit and flesh without any contradiction; indeed, renders perfectly acceptable all of the impossibilities that have driven the masses away from the Church. This is the further development of Christianity, or a substantial part of it, that Jung saw as the central part of his work, and to which I too have devoted my energies for some years. Nevertheless, from another angle Christ represents only the light side of the Self, not the dark, which is represented by Antichrist, or Satan.

Further Mystery Quaternities

I was watching a documentary about King Arthur recently, which contained a shot of a stained glass window in an old church in England. On the window, the four Evangelists, Matthew, Mark, Luke, and John are depicted, but the thing is, John appears at first to be female, a young woman, the four apparently expressing, therefore, the 3 + 1 quaternity. As has been said, certain Holy Ghost movements sprang up all over Europe in the Middle Ages that were largely based on the quaternity with the feminine as fourth, seeming to be in conflict with, but actually completing, the Trinitarian thinking of the Church. This is part of the mystery of *The Da Vinci Code,* where John is claimed to be Mary Magdalene in Leonardo's painting of *The Last Supper.*

On seeing the documentary about the stained glass window again and considering further information, it has become clear that the fourth figure is not female, but rather a gentle-looking youth. John's symbol of the eagle is depicted above him, which states clearly that it is meant to be John. There have been many depictions of John through the centuries, but while he sometimes has long hair and may look female, at other times he has short hair and is more clearly male. Furthermore, as is pointed out in *The Serpent Grail* (2005), John often carries a chalice. This has been interpreted as Mary Magdalene with the Grail (sometimes she carries an alabaster jar of ointment), but considering what I have just said, it is obviously John that is meant. Yet the 3 + 1 archetype could still have been at work unconsciously, and it may partly be the reason why John was sometimes depicted as feminine looking, perhaps to fulfill the archetype of three males and a female. Having said that, it is believed by many that John the apostle was the John, called "the Divine," who wrote the Book of Revelation, and as this was written many decades after the Crucifixion, John must have been very young when he was with Jesus.

Of the four Gospels, the Synoptics—Matthew, Mark, and Luke—largely agree, while John is somewhat different, being Gnostic in character. Some Gnostics valued the feminine spirit, Sophia or Mary, as co-equal with Christ, and the feminine element in the Middle Ages was likewise included in the quaternity structures of the Holy Ghost movements, so there would have perhaps have been the unconscious urge to make the Gospels fit the three males with a female archetype. Yet this notwithstanding, perhaps the most important of all is the fact that for many centuries, especially at the time of the Renaissance, young men *did* have long hair, *were* clean shaven, and *did* look somewhat feminine. It is also a fact that the 3 + 1 nature of the four Gospels does fit the structure of the quaternity archetype very well.

This and the Linda Cortile experience with the three aliens, fitting the same pattern, reminds me of the painting by Nicholas Poussin, *Les Bergeres l'Arcadie (The Shepherds of Arcadia)*, that is part of the mystery of Rennes-le-Chateau. This was brought to light by Baigent, Leigh, and Lincoln in *Holy Blood, Holy Grail* (1984). In 1895, a priest in a village of Languedoc in the South of France, discovered a parchment in one of the pillars of his church, supposedly leading to a treasure that had belonged to King Dagobert II. There is no proof of this treasure at all, but the priest, Beranger Sauniere, seems to have suddenly become well off, paying for certain construction and renovation work done at the village. This included a new public road, a water tower, and a new villa for himself that included a tower to house his library.

Some of the story has now been discredited and it is said Sauniere gained his sudden cache by selling artifacts, Masses, and so forth, to tourists. This seems an inadequate solution to the full puzzle of what was happening there, and other mysteries still remain apart from the sudden acquired wealth, one involving a tomb (now demolished) and the painting by Poussin. These depict three shepherds and a shepherdess peering at the tomb of a distinguished lady named Marie de Blanchefort. Study of the painting is said to reveal certain clues, pentangles (or pentagrams) and other geometrical designs, which, however, have actually led nowhere. But the thing that strikes me about the painting is that it contains the 3 + 1 structure of the three shepherds and the shepherdess, the classic archetype of the "quaternity of the Self," of the union of higher masculine spirit with feminine soul. So apart from anything else, a mystery does exist here (though apparently no one has noticed it), which is, why is the classic "quaternity of the Self" portrayed in the painting?

It is a fact that the high civilization of Europe was founded and maintained upon a religious system that is exclusively Trinitarian. The quaternity and anything associated with it, alchemy, Hermeticism, etc., was always therefore heretical and of the occult. (The Philosopher's Stone of the alchemists, for example, is fourfold, not threefold.) So the 3 + 1 formulation of the figures in the painting and depicted on the tomb, are based upon an archetype that is basically heretical to the orthodox Christian Trinitarian position. This may be connected with the quaternity of the Holy Ghost movements of the Middle Ages, which would have been continued esoterically, and always aimed at in processes through the unconscious.

The Arcadia of the painting is a semi-mythological rural region, where innocent contentment and peace supposedly reign, although the place-name itself did actually exist, in Greece. Nevertheless, in medieval times Arcadia symbolized a sort of Paradise of Peace, and a fountain and an underground stream were connected with this. The mythical stream probably derives from the river Alpheus found in the real Arcadia, and which runs underground until it arises again at the Fountain of Arethusa in Sicily. The river Alpheus has always been considered sacred, and water being the main symbol of the unconscious has meant rivers, wells, and lakes being sacred all over the world since earliest times. Alpheus even means "source," and running underground, therefore alluding to the Underworld, so to speak, obviously symbolizes the realm of the unconscious. We can see why it would be considered sacred above all other rivers. A fountain is similarly that "spring of pure water" that was the elixir of life to the alchemists, these being the waters of the collective unconscious, the *aqua permanens.*

Underground, the Underworld, has always been associated with the esoteric Mysteries, and Poussin was apparently well acquainted with them himself. All in all, the symbolism of Arcadia, the Paradise of Peace, with the sacred underground river Altheus, and the magical fountain would seem to allude to the unconscious and the "kingdom" of the Higher Self. In such circumstances we can expect to also find the motif of the 3 + 1 structure, of three males and a female, and there it is in the painting with the three shepherds and the shepherdess, *The Shepherds of Arcadia.* There are other details to the mystery, of course, but the above is its essence. The unconscious, the other reality of eternal spirit and soul, has always constituted the greatest mystery of all for mankind. There is no need to search for hidden pentangles and such.

Another part of the mystery is the supposed secret hereditary bloodline descending from Jesus the man and Mary Magdalene. This is the *San Greal,* or *sangreal*—Holy Grail—interpreted, or misinterpreted, as *Sang Real,* literally Blood Royal, then claimed to be the physical, biological bloodline of Jesus and the Magdalene. A secret society, called the Prieure de Sion (Priory of Sion) has supposedly been dedicated for centuries to the preservation of this line, and indeed, to the restoration of the descendants of Jesus and the Magdalene to the thrones of Europe. However, it seems that the Prieure de Sion is a modern twentieth-century invention. Sauniere's small village church was dedicated to the Magdalene in 1069, and Sauniere centuries later dedicated his tower to her, calling it the Tour Magdala. Bestselling books from *Holy Blood, Holy Grail* to *The Da Vinci Code* have been based upon these mysteries, though they are largely full of fallacies.

It seems to me that the quaternity with the feminine spirit, or soul as the fourth completing the Trinity, is again the basis of these mysteries. Jung discovered that the forces of the collective unconscious function in both Trinitarian and quaternary ways; the fourth completes the three. Therefore the feminine spirit completes the exclusively male Holy Trinity. As we have seen, this has been known from most ancient times and all the major male figures of the Bible unify with feminine spirit; first comes the syzygy at human level, and then ultimately the divine forces themselves in the *Hieros Gamos* at collective level.

This has also been known through later centuries, and indeed, I have lived through the phenomenon and experienced it all myself. This was always the great Mystery of religion, the *Mysterium Magnum*, and it was particularly prominent in the twelfth to fourteenth centuries, when the Holy Grail and other spiritual movements blossomed forth. The nineteenth century would have known of it to a degree, and this was almost certainly the mystery in which Sauniere became involved in some way.

We have, in fact, seen the same quaternity at work in the modern world with the Linda Cortile experience, and indeed, centuries earlier with the Holy Ghost movements, based upon the quaternity structure of 3 + 1. The three gods and a goddess I saw on thrones in a dream given earlier represent the same structure, of course.

Mary Magdalene herself has become the Holy Grail to some modern writers, the carrier of Christ's blood, therefore of the child of Jesus. Others are busy digging up the ground at Rennes le Chateau, convinced that the Holy Grail as a physical object is buried there. But the real meaning of the Holy Grail, and indeed, of all these Mysteries, lies with processes of spirit/soul reality, which, of course, involves the feminine as much as the masculine.

Returning to what I was saying above about *The Shepherds of Arcadia,* it is quite interesting that a copy of this motif appears on a monument at Shugborough Hall in Staffordshire, in the middle of England. The image, however, is in reverse, though not, of course, the inscription that appears upon it, ET IN ARCADIA EGO. In *The Tomb of God* (1996), which is about this whole subject, the authors, Richard Andrews and Paul Schellenberger point out that ARCA, part of "ARCADIA," is the Latin for "tomb." However, the name of the realm, Arcadia, seems to come from something other than this, and indeed, *Holy Blood, Holy Grail* informs us that Arca was the name of the god of Arcadia, and this means "bear." Arcadia itself means "People of the bear" or "Worshippers of the bear." The god Arca was the son of a form of Artemis, who was chiefly symbolized by the bear. She was goddess of the Great Bear constellation, and the Welsh form of her was the goddess Arth—the Welsh word for "bear" is *arth*.

The women followers of Artemis were said to be fiercely independent and as children were usually tomboys. They were often bisexual, or fully lesbian, but if they did take male lovers they would discard them after a time—they would never marry them. They were also later the maiden aunt of the family, but certainly not the shy, retiring type, rather the opposite, fierce and aggressively independent. I mention all this because when I visited the monument at Shugborough Hall it was with a woman who has a personality fitting the Artemis type closely. We knew nothing of the bear association with ARCADIA on the monument until we researched it later. But the thing is, my companion had been experiencing the presence of a bear for at least a year previously. One morning she awoke to find a huge bear in bed with her, and it was very friendly. As Jung tells us, the bear is one of the main symbols of the feminine side of the collective unconscious, and certainly of Artemis (and of her son). I have experienced it several times over the years in my own processes, and it can be dangerous. It was repressed quite early by higher religion, particularly Christianity, and as a force of the unconscious would very much like to resurge. Indeed, with the great weakening of Christianity in the modern world it is doing so, as are other feminine archetypes.

Later my friend experienced a lion close to her when waking, one of the main symbols of the alchemists for Mercurius, the spirit of the Earth/unconscious, and again of Artemis—the lion and bear were her main symbols. King David in the Bible kills a lion and bear to save a lamb. The lamb is the divine child, the infant Higher Self as Savior, and the lion and bear are the powers of the unconscious that try and kill it off. The lion and bear as powers, though seemingly slain can never be permanently so, only rendered harmless, or sometimes even amicable, but the bear is a danger to Christianity. As we saw, Daniel in his vision sees a lion, bear, leopard, and a beast "dreadful and terrible" rise up out of the sea as the quaternity expressing the lower Son of Man (the creatures therefore having been rendered amicable and friendly), and Jeremiah also experiences the lion and the bear. Thousands of years later these archetypal forms are still very much alive in unconscious/spirit reality.

Chapter 8

Visions, Dreams, and the Afterlife

Death into Life

In 1944 Jung broke his foot, suffered a heart attack, and almost died. Perhaps significantly, his nurse stated that a bright glow emanated around him at this time. Jung later said he seemed to hover about a thousand miles above a gloriously blue Earth, where he viewed certain countries of the East. When he turned around so that his back was to the Indian Ocean, he saw a giant black stone in front of him, as large as his house at Bollingen, which also seemed to be a sort of temple. Inside sat a black Hindu in the lotus posture, wearing a white robe. As Jung approached the steps, all of his worldly desires and hopes fell away from him, an experience he felt as quite painful.

Yet not everything had gone because conversely and in a strange way he now consisted of—became—all the things he had ever done and had ever happened to him on Earth. He became, he said, his own history, and this was therefore what he had forged himself into in life. Yet many questions still needed to be answered. Why had certain things happened, and others not? Why had his life taken this particular course, or that particular course, and so on? But he did realize he would now know the answers to all of these questions when he entered the rock temple.

Just then, he saw a shape floating up from the European continent, which turned out to be his own doctor in primal form, as a Basileus (a King) of Kos, Kos being the site of the temple of Asklepios, and the birthplace of Hippocrates. The doctor had a message for Jung, which was that he must now return to the world. This actually disappointed Jung as he realized he was required to enter the "box system" once more. It seemed to him as though every person on Earth is contained in a little box, suspended on a piece of string in a world that has been artificially constructed, which is like a prison for each person. This is a view I have held since I made my own journeys through the collective unconscious. It is then our worldly lives that seem so limited and contained, though it is absolutely essential that we live out our lives to gain the fullest knowledge, experience, and wisdom possible while we are here. This is added to the Higher Self when we finally pass over, as Jung realized.

When Jung returned to his body, he knew the doctor was going to die because he had seen him in primal form, which meant that he now already belonged to the "Other World," and must soon return hence. Jung tried to warn the doctor of his impending fate, but to no avail—what could be done in any case?—and soon the doctor fell ill and took to his bed, to die of septicemia.

Jung then had a number of visions as he lay ill, of Sacred Marriages—the *Hieros Gamos*—that were all very beautiful. These concerned Tifereth and Malkhuth in the Kabbalistic marriage, the Marriage of the Lamb in Jerusalem, and Zeus and Hera in a Greek amphitheatre. He describes these visions as truly glorious ones in which he floated in the purest bliss. These were not dreams as such, but rather waking or half-awake visions that took place between bouts of sleep as he lay ill. He even felt the visions were somehow himself in a strange, inexplicable way. Gradually, they faded away as he returned to life and health, but he says they were the most beautiful experiences he ever had in his life, and that he never saw the world, or full reality, in the same way again. He never again lost the feeling that the three-dimensional world that we know has been set up for us to live the small box existence within, and that we are required to live through our time on Earth for some ultimate purpose.

I had a dream—a number of dreams—that expressed the same thing. In one, I was informed, "Reality is not what human beings think it is. Life is a con trick." By this I gathered that it has all been set up to delude us, but for the best purpose. Since that time, I have viewed the world and life from the viewpoint of that other reality as something staged, to be acted out. The world, therefore, and the universe as we know it, is not full reality, but is rather a mere part, a fragment, of something much greater that is overflowing with deeper meaning, ultimately involving the Self and God, that can only be understood, if at all, in religious/spiritual terms. This means that the whole of reality is one vast religious complex, and the more we become lost in the material world, the more we lose the meaning and true nature of full reality.

As to visions, whether seen outside or experienced within—sometimes projected—they are fairly normal to human nature in that people have experienced them at all times and everywhere. In *Psychology and Religion,* Jung says, "God is a primordial experience of man, and from the remotest times humanity has taken inconceivable pains either to portray this baffling experience, to assimilate it by means of interpretation, speculation, and dogma, or else to deny it."

The wisdom of the East tells us that the world of matter is illusion, and we can well understand what that means. One day all life as we know it will be no more, and even the physical universe will cease to exist as it now is; everything that exists is in a constant state of change. But the unconscious states that otherworldly reality is timeless and unchanging permanence. In the meantime, we must live out our earthly lives and develop our souls as best we may, becoming mixed up with the world and its processes. It is our task, laid upon us by the fact that we are agents of spirit forces beyond physical/conscious reality.

In America in the early 1950s, Orfeo Angelucci had a series of visions in which aliens—actually spirits—appeared from a sphere, informing him that we humans are sent here by "the gods," the immortal powers, to experience physical reality on their behalf. The symbolic contents of Angelucci's visions followed processes of the unconscious so closely that Jung had no doubts about their validity. Angelucci, Jung stated, had been touched by God. He even bore the stigmata of a point within a circle on his chest, a potent symbol in the esoteric Mysteries since earliest times. This is a symbol of the Higher Self, of the Gnostic Christ, of the Buddha, and one of the main symbols of Pythagoras. All of the contents on the surrounding circumference are attached to the center, the point that is the One. While the surrounding parts may be in opposition to one another, in conflict, each nevertheless relates to the center, and in this way total harmony is achieved.

Jung's opinions on life after death and reincarnation were very positive, due to his own dreams and visions, his vast experience of the unconscious, and his recognition of the validity of the experiences of many other people. It was not certain knowledge in the sense that knowledge of matter is (though it becomes ever more certain with gained experience), but he could see how reincarnation would be necessary to fulfil our Karma over many lives. One of his male patients had a series of dreams that seemed to confirm this, but Jung would give no details of the dreams. Regression hypnosis, in which people are taken back to previous lives, has become well-known since Jung's day, and there are many genuine cases with evidence that is irrefutable. The system that is life may as well function that way as any other, and we can see how it may work better that way, though the full picture remains mostly unknown to us. What is really beyond belief is life here on Earth itself, but since it is nevertheless concrete fact, then extensions into other dimensions and forms of reality should not surprise us too much.

The Gnostics, the "heretical" religious sects at the time of Christ and afterwards, generally believed in reincarnation. They believed the goddess Sophia (Wisdom), or the Goddess of Justice, led the soul of the deceased to further incarnations, while Christ led to liberation from this. We each wear a body like a suit of clothes, and when this wears out it must be replaced. This is reincarnation at soul level, with Sophia. But, certain sects taught, if we win freedom from the chain of rebirths by overcoming worldly desires in this life, we survive to higher spirit reality with Christ. We are then no longer required to return to another life on Earth.

I have experienced a number of dreams in which reincarnation was given to be fact. I have been taken up to the higher place to which we return after each earthly life, to a sort of cosmic wheel containing many lives. There I was informed of certain previous lives I have lived on Earth—and the unconscious does not lie. It may be brutally frank at times, and may even destroy the conscious personality in extreme cases, although it has no basic wish to do so; but it does not lie. Many years of experience through the unconscious have taught me to think, "It is just so." I have seen the spirits of people who have recently died in dreams, before they passed over, and I see no reason at all, even from a rationalistic standpoint, why this should not be so. I have also seen the spirits of those who have returned again for some reason. My best friend of fifty years returned in a dream a short while after he died, and he kept changing shape to demonstrate to me that he now had no earthly form and could assume any shape he wished. The same happened with my father. The real wonder is life itself; prelife, present life, and afterlife, all parts of a continuing line, and it all makes so much more sense that way.

In one interesting dream I was with a man who had suffered all his life so far and would continue to do so for the rest of it. A dog was standing a few feet away, sideways to us, and I said to the man, "Do you see the dog over there? The empty space behind it represents its previous life, the dog there now represents its present life, and the empty space in front of it represents its next life. We must learn to see our existence over many lives, and then we come to realize that everything evens out, the bad with the good. You have suffered much in this life, but in the next you could be very happy, though our eternal life is not here on Earth." It was not so much myself saying this, but the unconscious putting the words into my mouth. The unconscious *knows* these things to be so, and as I said, has no reason to lie.

A man I knew should have come to visit me one afternoon but failed to turn up. Later that day I learned he had suffered a stroke and was very ill. That night I dreamt his spirit was trying to enter and take over my body, so that I had to fight him off fiercely. He said he had no body of his own now, so he wanted mine. It was a hard fight but I finally managed to drive him away. The next day I learned that he had died the night before.

Another man I knew died in particularly tragic circumstances. His wife had left him to live with another man some time before and he had suffered greatly emotionally before suffering greatly physically. He was not a close friend or relative and so I more or less forgot about the tragedy. Some months later I dreamt that his spirit was still on Earth and that he refused to "go over." He wanted revenge on his wife and the man she had left him for. It took some persuasion to convince the man that for his own future development he must go over, and that the life he had just left was over forever. The tragedy he had suffered was not too important in his eternal existence. Again, it was not really myself saying this but the forces of the unconscious, which were using me to get him to move on, which he finally did. This is how the forces of unconscious/spirit work.

My mother almost died from a heart attack, and she experienced a great eagle that flew down to fetch her over. The eagle had the most beautifully colored plumage imaginable, she said afterwards, like no earthly eagle could possibly have, and it had come to take her to the afterlife. But she was not ready to go yet, and so the great, beautiful bird flew up and away again, while my mother regained consciousness.

A few years later she had a second heart attack and this time my father, who had died since my mother suffered the first attack, came to fetch her over. My father took her up to a sort of great hall, like in a cathedral, filled with the most beautiful religious paintings. But again, she was not ready to leave Earthly life yet. My father tried to persuade her to go over, but still she refused, and she left the hall and came down to Earth again, and slowly regained consciousness.

NDEs (Near Death Experiences) are so common they fill bestselling books (some should perhaps be called DEs, Death Experiences, as in certain cases the person seems to actually die briefly). One interesting account that occurred in the ancient world is told by Plato in his *Republic*. This involves Er, a soldier supposedly killed in battle. Er is put on his funeral pyre twelve days later, though his body is not decomposed Suddenly, he revives to tell a strange tale.

Er had found himself in a land strange and wonderful, where two judges sat between two chasms in the sky that were countermatched by two chasms below in the Earth. Other souls were present, making similar journeys to Er's. The judges told Er he must take note of everything very carefully, and he then witnessed certain events. Souls that had made earlier journeys came down from the sky, while others came up from the Earth, the former describing the lovely paradise they had reached, the latter mournfully telling of a place not so lovely. Those from Earth were destined for reincarnation, while those from Heaven would return there.

The Three Fates told those to be reborn that no Guardian Angel would be allotted to them. They would choose their own, those who had now progressed choosing the good, while the sinners would choose otherwise. Their fate, whichever it was, would not therefore be the fault of God, but due to their own choosing, which would actually be due to the lives they had lived They were then required to drink at the River of Forgetfulness, so that they would remember nothing when reborn. But Er, who was to be reborn himself, did not drink, for he was being allowed remembrance so that he could inform people on Earth of the afterlife situation. He then found himself awake on his pyre.

Very many people have had experiences of the afterlife in some way, but rationalists will always cook up all kinds of arguments against them, as though they have a religious mission to disprove the possibility of anything except purely physical existence. I always imagine these rationalists, when they themselves pass over, arguing just as vehemently against there being Earthly reality as they formerly did against there being spirit reality. Jung spoke of the "urban neurosis of atheism," adding that atheists are habitual groaners who suffer from chronic bouts of indigestion.

Jung had a dream in which he saw a marvelous arrangement of flowers on an altar, and in front sat a yogi in meditation. The yogi seemed to have Jung's face, at which point Jung awoke with the thought that he himself was the yogi's dream. When the yogi awoke, Jung would cease to be, just as the yogi would when Jung awoke. I ascended a pyramid of steps in a dream, and at the top on a throne sat a god-king who looked a little like myself. This was the Higher Self, or at least a representation of the phenomenon, just as Jung's yogi was, and the resemblances experienced by Jung and myself expressed the fact that ultimately we are one with the Self.

The night Jung's mother died, but before he knew of her death, he had one of the most frightening dreams he ever experienced. He was in a dense, almost primeval jungle when suddenly the whole universe seemed to be filled with a piercing whistle. This shook him profoundly, but more was to come as from the underbrush emanated sounds of crashing. Almost immediately, a huge wolfhound came thundering out, its great jaws agape to grasp a victim. Jung, his blood turning to ice, knew this was the hound of the Wild Huntsman, ordered to snatch away the soul of a deceased human individual. He awoke petrified, and that very morning news of his mother's death arrived.

Jung says that from the negative view, this could be seen as a soul being taken by the Devil, or more specifically by Wotan's "wild horde," Wotan being mythologically the Wild Huntsman. (Nietzsche also had a prophetic a dream of the Wild Huntsman and a piercing whistle. See part 2.) But Wotan has his positive side as well as negative, and Jung saw it rather as his mother being returned to "the blessed folk," which represents the lighter, more positive side of the Wotan mythos. This, Jung continued to say, lies beneath the realm of Christian morality and represents the return to the spirit of nature; Pagan certainly, but in a positive sense.

I cannot help contrasting this with my own mother's near-death experiences, which seems to have been Christian in nature. Though my mother never considered herself a full Christian believer, she was certainly one by good thoughts and deeds. However, the spirit of Wotan was resurging powerfully in Germany at the period of Jung's mother's death, presaged by Nietzsche's experiences, as Jung himself declares, stating that Wotan lay beneath the thinnest veneer of Christianity. The whole of Germany, and perhaps surrounding area, was to become deluged by the spirit of Wotan in negative form at that time, though as Jung says, it seemed to be the positive side with his mother.

This is reinforced by the fact that, though Jung had suffered two great shocks, one, his mother's death, almost shattering him with grief, and the other the wolfhound of Wotan coming for her soul in the dream, he was not entirely unhappy. As he returned home on the train journey, he seemed to hear the laughter and music as at a marriage, so that part of him found it impossible to be depressed. He explains this as due to the fact that, though from the view of consciousness and the world, death is a terrible blow, from the view of spirit reality it is something joyful, the return of the soul to its source and true home. It is therefore the return to true wholeness. This place we call the world, of worldly life, is not our true home; that lies in the afterlife. If we are required to continually return to worldly lives, it is in the interest of our eternal life with the Self, where we and the Self are One.

Jung's mother was "uncanny" and "psychic" by nature, very deep and dark, while his father, the pastor, Paul, was a brilliant scholar, particularly gifted in languages. Their son Carl inherited both traits, and in just the right amounts to enable him to experience the phenomena of the unconscious personally, at first hand, while at the same time possessing the high intelligence to study the material empirically and objectively. Too much of one or the other and we would not have had Jung and his works as they stand today.

Affirmation from the Unconscious/Spirit

Jung had another experience that further confirmed his belief in spirit reality and the afterlife. Shortly after his wife died, he had a vision of her in a dream, although he knew that it was not really his wife as she had been. She was young again, aged about thirty, but it was more a representation of herself that she was setting up for him, the vision somehow seeming to contain their whole married life together. Jung commented later that we become speechless before such visions of wholeness, and that the "spirits" have to present themselves to us in three-dimensional forms as in physical reality, in time, but that they are now actually formless and out of time; therefore timeless.

Such meaningful dreams and visions can be assigned to wish fulfillments, chaotic fantasies, psychic meanderings, dream compensations, delusional neuroses, and sundry other causes, but is there any solid reason why their contents should not be real as the necessary counterpart of fuller reality? After all and as said, the appearance of a perfectly functioning universe out of nowhere and from nothing (except chaotic prima materia, which itself has to be explained), complete with living, thinking creatures on its planets, is an extremely unscientific proposition in itself, even or *especially* from the rationalist standpoint. There *has* to be more to it, for something, whatever it may be or become, cannot come from nothing, from out of nowhere and nothingness. And indeed, there are good solid reasons for believing in survival after death, and for Man's visionary and paranormal experiences to be perfectly valid, that have frequently happened to Man throughout history. To repeat: there are ultimately no sound reasons why matter can be real while spirit cannot. Jung's dreams and visions display an extension of normal reality that fits his Earthly life like a glove, filling it out and extending it as the necessary counterpart existing in the eternal scheme of things. Some of my own experiences are similar, and so too are those of so many other people.

Since writing the above, my mother has died, and certain things occurred near the end that are worthy of note because they support much of what I say throughout this work, and indeed, what Jung has said. In her last few days, my mother's conscious mind started to fade a little, allowing the unconscious to rise up at times and merge with consciousness to a degree; not the personal unconscious so much, but the collective. My mother then started to see another reality, or rather contents from it, the eternal realm that exists behind the whole of material reality.

Among the visionary items she saw were three dogs, four cats, and two yellow canaries, sitting at various places in the ward she was in. This was quite pleasing to her and she said "I like it here." She had suffered in her illness and had definitely not liked it in the ward before the visions. To me it meant that her worldly life was coming to its close and that she would soon be returning to the haven of peace and wholeness in the Higher Self, to which we all return at our worldly end, though it must be a higher association with the Self for some, and a lower one for others, the majority.

As to the symbolic creatures my mother saw; dogs refer to masculine spirit—dog-spirit, etc.—as does the number three; the Trinity, and so forth. I have had many dreams where this has been so. By contrast, cats and the number four represent feminine soul—the four directions, the four hollow places of the World Soul (of the prophet Enoch's visions), and so forth. In Egypt, Anubis, the dog-god, was spirit guide through the Underworld, the unconscious, (as well as being a form of the divine Son, Horus), while the cat goddess, Bast, symbolized soul and life.

The two yellow canaries refer to higher spirit—yellow is the color of higher spirit in the processes, and birds are not tied to the Earth and can descend from the skies, therefore symbolising spirit. The birds here possibly represent the twins of the Self in higher spirit aspect; in fact, it was two feathered beings that took Enoch up to higher spirit reality in his visionary experiences. So the three dogs and four cats represent masculine spirit and feminine soul in the 3 + 4 = 7 archetype. (Nu and Noah having three males and four females with them in their respective boats means basically the same.) All of the symbolic contents in my mother's visions represent a state of unification and wholeness in the Higher Self, to which, as I say, she would soon be returning.

Jung believed—and over half a century of investigations into the realm of the unconscious seemed to prove—that we are required to continue with our inner development after death. All of his lifelong experience pointed strongly that way. He had another dream, in which he found himself in the South of France with his wife, who was now continuing her studies into the Holy Grail legends there, having died before completing them. As they were part of her spiritual development in life, she now had to continue with them, as they were still relevant to her in a spiritual sense. Long experience had taught Jung that we are more in tune with our true selves, and with the true nature of full reality itself, when we accept such things as part of that fuller reality. The unconscious itself insists upon such things as *facts*, and when we refuse to accept them as valid truths, we become dissociated not only from the unconscious, but from otherworldly reality and its meaning; ultimately from God. All of this does not conflict with reincarnation, which may happen more quickly with some. We just do not know how the full system works.

I am reminded of a dream in which I was above in the afterlife, at a meeting of famous figures of the nineteenth and early twentieth centuries. I started to make a speech about the real meaning of religion, but while one or two of those present more or less accepted what I was saying (as much as they understood) most did not.

> *I go to a hall where there is a debate taking place. This is about 1890 or so and all the great minds of the time are present, including Thomas Huxley and H. G. Wells. The debate is about God, evolution, religion, etc., and there is something ghostly about it all, as if it is a supernatural happening. In fact, it is taking place in another reality just above the Earthly one, the afterlife, though with a nineteenth-century setting. Wells has just spoken but I say in reply to his remarks, "You are wrong, God really does exist. Spirit is real. I know because I have experienced them. I can prove it; at least, as near as anyone will ever be able to." Now, Wells and the others are all great men, while I am just a small unknown voice, yet Wells, who has been sitting high up at the back, comes down to the front to look closely at me and to hear me better. He wants to hear more of what I have to say.*

It is difficult to know what to make of this dream. If it were only an argument between religious experience and materialistic prejudice it would be easier to understand; but the debate is a supernatural occurrence, as though I had stepped through the veil of time into the past, though also into another, higher spirit reality in the present. On the other hand, if it were happening now, in a higher spirit reality, the distinguished company should know much more about spiritual matters than I do. But I know that the words I speak are true. God and spirit can actually be experienced, while in the dream the spirit figures themselves (Wells, etc.) have no knowledge of this.

The dream illustrates that the immediate afterlife is no more spiritually aware than we are on Earth, even less so here in the dream, and it would therefore seem that the teachings of the East that only the saints win through to Heaven are correct. The rest go to a lower or parallel-to-the-world realm, probably to be reincarnated. This is what the spirit of my father told me in a dream before he was to be buried the next morning, only the saints go to Heaven; everyone else goes to a sort of "pool," he said. This must be a lower aspect of the collective Self, shared by all. Yet if that is the case, why have not Wells and the others been reincarnated? Why are they still up in the afterlife? However, we should not limit the possibilities of spirit reality by our conceptions of what is possible from this our Earthly base. The truth of such things will not be as we imagine, and will probably not follow rules as we understand them.

In another dream, I was again in the afterlife, and it was the same sort of thing, not holy like Heaven is supposed to be. I thought, this is no more religious than earthly life is, just a continuance of it. I somehow knew in the dream that higher spirit reality was still above somewhere, and that only the saints, of all types and creeds, manage to reach there. So most of us go on to the lower type of existence, not much above the worldly, presumably to continue with further incarnations, while those who have progressed sufficiently spiritually would be freed from them, which is what Eastern philosophy has taught for thousands of years. (I had another dream where the Self was a huge wheel, like at a fairground, which we all go to when we pass over—all, that is, except those who win through to the higher Heaven reality.) The Gnostics said a few go above to join Christ, while the rest go below with a goddess to be reborn.

Accusations Against Jung

I think it important to mention here the accusations hurled at Jung by certain writers concerning his supposed "anti's" and hatreds, that is, anti-Christianity, anti-God, anti-Semitism, "hatred of Freud," etc. Here is the situation as I understand it.

After the Second World War, Jung was accused of having been a Nazi sympathizer and of a certain amount of collaboration with the Nazi authorities in the early 1930s. Jung was also accused of being anti-Semitic because of things he had written about the Jewish mind and character being, in certain ways, different to the Germans. As to the first charge, it is true that Jung edited a psychology magazine early under the Nazis, but this was because he cared very deeply about keeping his psychology school alive in Germany, where it could be of some use in understanding the collective psychic forces that were now breaking loose.

In any case, the idea that such a natural humanitarian as Jung could be a Nazi sympathizer runs completely counter to his works. Freud once asked Jung how could he keep from being disgusted by some of his more extremely insane patients, to which Jung answered astonished that it had never occurred to him to view them in that way. Each was a unique human being with a tragic story that could perhaps reveal the secret cause of their insanity. These unfortunates carried the greatest burden of human existence, and Jung stated more than once that if he were going to be disgusted by anyone, it would more likely be by certain of the superficial rich and famous. True, Jung was violently anticommunist, but it is a mistake to believe that he was therefore automatically a supporter of the extreme right. In fact, he frequently warned of the crass materialism of the West, political materialism as well as soulless big business.

It is not generally understood that during the individuation process a transcendental religious position is reached that renders obsolete the extreme political ones. In such a situation the initiate no longer thinks politically, or in any other materialistic terms. He now thinks from the transcendental religious position that is above, and this was the case with Jung. This is the higher position of the One, the Self, in which all opposites find harmony. The initiate becomes extremely influenced by this and then automatically thinks in a religious/spiritual way, rather than one materialistic side or the other.

There is also Jung's early dream where, with the dark-skinned primitive, he shot down the Germanic hero, Siegfried, meaning the killing off of the "heroic will to power" of the "blond beast," and the "Germanic urge to dominate." (Naturally, this slaying of Siegfried has been seen as the slaying of Freud!) Jung came to realize there are far higher things, and that the true nature of full reality is a great complex that unites all opposites within its full nature. By the 1930s and Nazi rule in Germany, Jung was well on the way along the spiritualizing path to individuation, the dream of Siegfried many years past. It would have been impossible for him to have supported the Nazis in such circumstances. Jung was a very intelligent and gifted man, definitely a genius, and in an even deeper way than many geniuses are. His books are extremely profound, and I personally know how much this is so because I have travelled the unconscious trail of individuation myself. They are very wise in a way that is totally at odds with Nazi mentality and philosophy.

Jung wrote in the early 1930s that Germany was a new nation with culture forms yet to be developed, and Nazism, an unknown factor at that time, may have been a positive part of this. He had, furthermore, experienced the archetypal forces of the collective unconscious, which had greatly enriched his life and personality. He therefore had early hopes that the forces of the unconscious now erupting in Germany could be contained and utilized in something more positive, as, for example, the Roman Empire had eventually become redeemed through unconscious forces in the form of Christianity. But he soon realized there was no chance of this kind of positive redemption in Germany, and he was then warning of the great danger of resurged Wotanism, so that his books were eventually banned. Indeed his life would have been forfeited had he fallen into the hands of the Nazis. Certain other well-known figures had positive hopes for fascism in the early days, some to become opponents later, yet none of these have been branded fascist sympathizers. Winston Churchill himself is on record in the late 1920s full of praise for Mussolini and fascism.

Fears concerning the negative side of the collective archetypal forces were proving only too real for Jung, in the same way that a scientist finds his fears about a threatening epidemic proving correct. In fact, Jung soon came to realize that Nazi Germany was living proof of just how the collective archetypal forces can scoop up a culture and carry it blindly along to catastrophe—or to high culture, if those forces are the positive ones of light and love, again as with Christianity. Jung had come to see how Goethe and Nietzsche had produced Mephistopheles and Zarathustra—real products of unconscious processes—because of personal inflation and lack of compassion. Having genuine fear that the same could happen to himself, Jung had determined to strive for all of the higher religious values they had neglected.

Jung also saw the danger of Nazism in certain unconscious contents of his patients, even in some who were anti-Nazi in consciousness. I mentioned earlier the pupil who while in active imagination and passing through several rooms saw an idiot child smearing itself with excrement, intimating a latent psychosis that had to be covered up at all costs. As said, he was the only pupil of Jung's who ever became a Nazi. However, Jung's own inner experiences included religious visions; a gold/green Christ at the foot of the bed, for example, and no person with such potential for inner spiritual riches could ever be a Nazi; it is a psychological impossibility.

This passing through rooms to an innermost one, where a psychic/spiritual content is found, reminds us of St. Teresa of Avila, who went through seven chambers in a vision and in the innermost found "The King of Glory" (Christ) seated on a throne and bathed in the most radiant light. (This actually repeats an ancient Egyptian text that tells of an initiate passing through seven chambers of the Underworld to find the god Osiris seated upon his throne. There are often seven stages in some way to the Higher Self.) The child smearing itself in the dream of Jung's pupil was apparently the divine child in negative aspect, whereas the King of Glory, Osiris, etc., are positive forms of the Self.

The accusation of Jung being anti-Jewish again shows total lack of understanding on the part of his accusers. Besides pointing out the differences between the Jews and the Germans, Jung mentions the similarities, in the sense that both were split in their own way psychically and culturally. The Germans had been Christianized only a few hundred years, and that by persuasion by the sword. Consequently the old Pagan forces, Wotanism in particular, were still very much alive in the German collective unconscious. This caused a split in the collective German soul between a superficial Christianity on top, and Wotanism just beneath. As history was to show, it did not take much for the Christian veneer to crack and the Pagan forces to burst through. (Jung does say elsewhere that Germany had become a gifted culture in many respects before the Nazis, and we must bring to mind the many visionary mystics of the land in medieval times.)

Jung states that the same was true of the Jews, in the sense that they were of a foreign religion and culture deep in the unconscious, but had adopted, and had been forced to adapt to, foreign cultures on the surface in their conscious lives. The total psyche of a Jew will therefore be somewhat different from that of a European, because Yawehism is still dominant in the Jewish collective unconscious (a positive fact rather than a negative one). So although both German and Jew were sharing the same culture consciously, in the unconscious Wotan now reigned in the one, and Yahweh in the other. So this was not criticism of the Jews in any way on Jung's part—how could it be? —but a mere statement of the facts. It was, however, criticism of the Germans, at least, to some degree.

Jung has been further accused of reducing the persecution of the Jews in Germany to "merely" the conflict between the "master race" (Wotan in the collective German psyche)and the "chosen people" (Yahweh in the Jewish psyche). However, while Yahweh was still alive in Jewish consciousness and had never been repressed, Wotan had historically been suppressed and then repressed by the Germans, but was now flooding consciousness again with some force. (Suppression is conscious and voluntary; repression is unconscious and may be involuntary.) Wotan was certainly at odds with Yahweh, who had, of course, become the God of Christianity, so although the "chosen people" were in conflict with the "master race," so too was the Christianity of the West. It was not conflict between Christianity and Judaism that caused the persecution and mass murder of the Jews in the 1930s and 40s—not this time—but the *loss* of Christianity to Wotanism, resulting in a highly dangerous inflation in the German psyche for which the Jews, and the rest of Europe, had to pay the price. In fact, Jung had earlier predicted that Germanic Wotanism would overwhelm Germanic Christianity, which, of course, it did. (Nietzsche had an early dream in which this happened to him personally.)

When Jung was attacked over his "anti-Jewishness," he defended himself by saying that had he compared the French and English cultural differences nothing would have been said. He added that he had actually said something similar about Western and Chinese psychologies, but had not been accused of being anti-Chinese. At this, certain Jews became outraged and accused Jung of comparing them to the "yellow peril" that some had predicted would overrun Western civilization. This, said his critics, encouraged the Nazi theories that the Jews were a great danger to Western culture. Jung protested again about the stupidity and narrow-mindedness of his accusers, but to no avail, and even today the same unintelligent attacks continue to be made, totally devoid of any real understanding. (When we think about it, the Jews themselves could be accused of racism here, against the Chinese, outraged at being compared to them.) In fact, the actual situation was that Jung had spent some time studying Chinese Taoism, alchemy, and the I-Ching, and was consequently greatly impressed by Chinese wisdom. He also knew the great value of Jewish wisdom, and therefore comparisons between the Jews and the Chinese would be complimentary. Understandably, Jung was greatly puzzled and shocked by the reaction. It is all too ridiculous for words.

One modern biographer of Jung states that hatred of Freud (again!) was the real motivating force behind Jung's "anti-Semitism," and that Jung really meant *"that Jew,"* singular (Freud), rather than "*the* Jews," plural, but again, this is nonsense. By the time the Nazis came to power in Germany in the early 1930s it had been twenty years since Jung and Freud parted company. Jung had since, and long since, confronted the collective unconscious and almost drowned in its overwhelming archetypal depths. But he had survived, and had consequently been able to develop in the individuation process, which enlarges and transforms the original lesser personality. Jung had traveled a long way beyond Freud, who would by now have meant comparatively little to him emotionally, and certainly not negatively. We can tell by Jung's writings that this is so.

If we look at Jung's *Sigmund Freud in his Historical Setting,* for example, published in 1932, we see no trace whatsoever of any animosity towards Freud, let alone "hatred." Of course, Jung disagrees with Freud in the work because he has travelled far beyond him, investigating the collective unconscious, the existence of which Freud always denied. But Jung also expresses the value of Freud as far as the latter goes, and indeed, mentions that although Freud had not penetrated into the deeper, collective levels of the unconscious, "He could not have done so without being untrue to his historical task. And this task he has fulfilled—a task enough for a whole life's work, and fully deserving the fame it has won." (*The Spirit in Man, Art, and Literature,* p. 40.) Where is the hatred of "*that* Jew" here? It does not exist, and in fact, had Jung positively *loved* Freud he could not have written a more praising piece, honestly disagreeing with Freud on grounds of knowledge of the psyche and the unconscious, but nevertheless placing high value on Freud and his life's work. And this was written in 1932, just as the Nazis were coming to power.

As a matter of fact, Laurens van der Post says Jung *had* loved Freud during their association. (*Jung and the Story of Our Time.* 1976) We can see why this would have been so, because Freud had been the guru, the "wise old man" figure, and Jung the disciple. In these circumstances the pupil does love his master due largely to transference (projection). I know this from the love I had for Jung as my own guru, though I never met him. A Hindu master told Jung that it is quite possible for a pupil to have a guru as teacher who is no longer alive, who may even have been dead for centuries. Jung had been dead for about a dozen years when I first encountered him and he began to appear in my dreams. Certain information, which I mentioned earlier, seems to show that it was actually the Holy Spirit taking Jung's form in my dreams, and yet at other times I believe it must have been Jung himself.

As for Jung's theories on Jewish psychology in general, and indeed, that of other races, I would have to fundamentally agree, as would anyone else with an ounce of sense. The collective English character *is* different from the French, and those from the German, but that of the Japanese will be more different still, due not least to layers that descend through the unconscious. (In many ways the British are closer to the Americans than to other Europeans, although America itself consists of many peoples.) The total collective psyche of the Asian immigrants into

Britain will be largely different from the indigenous British, and only if we were all people of mere shallow consciousness could it not be so.

All this is true despite the fact that human beings are nevertheless fundamentally the same, developing from nature and the unconscious. Indeed, are all children of God and Mother Earth. But our cultural differences give us all, of all races and cultures, a psychological and historical depth that mere conscious sameness would lack. Just as the individual's life experiences help to form a certain character—though the basic one is inborn—so a blend of cultural experiences, molded with inborn traits, form the character of the race or culture. Furthermore, the experience of the religious archetypes through the unconscious, though basically similar, will have been expressed in different shapes and forms with each culture.

It is because Jewish religion, developed into Christianity, was so much superior to European Paganism that when the former replaced the latter, European high culture was forged. It was therefore not the Jews who were the great danger to European culture, but the Nazis who were sinking into a Paganism of a most negative and brutal kind. The Nazis were definitely lacking as human personalities, grossly inferior, but they projected that inferiority onto others, primarily the Jews, who were not only racially different but spiritually superior. As for Jung, he had many Jewish friends, followers, and fellow workers who all attested to the fact that the charge of anti-Semitism was complete nonsense. Indeed, Laurens van der Post tells us that Aniela Jaffe, a Jewish colleague of Jung, defended him passionately, saying that he did everything he could to help Jewish friends and colleagues under the Nazis.

But apart from all this, Jung knew that the old Jewish prophets had been true investigators of the unconscious, and through their religious experiences had gone to the very heights of the inner processes, experiencing the Son of Man/Son of God figure, along with God Himself. Consequently, Jung was full of praise and admiration for the Jews. Besides, the man Jesus, whom Jung called a truly unique human being, who brought about a higher development of consciousness for mankind and a higher relationship with God, the highest the world has seen, was a Jew; so how on earth could Jung be anti-Jewish? As to racial differences, he was well aware that to love one another in our differences is infinitely superior to accepting one another only when we are all exactly alike. It is, in fact, a type of racism to accept others only when we consider them no different from ourselves; but then, we are all of us products of the eternal forces of body, soul, and spirit in any case.

Jung said racists are tortured inwardly and this is correct. The inner division causes pain and upset, whereas empathy makes us feel unified and more whole inside. The person who can relate to not only other human beings but to all life exists in a state of wholeness that is usually felt as holiness. St. Francis of Assisi is a prime example of this.

Just as Jung has been accused of being a Nazi sympathizer, anti-Jewish, and a hater of Freud, he has likewise been called anti-Christian. He supposedly had anger towards God, treating Satan as a split-off complex of Christ, though on a cosmic scale. Frank McGlynn, in his extremely detailed book, *Carl Gustav Jung* (1996), gives two critical quotes that serve to demonstrate the sort of thing I mean. These concern Jung's book *Answer to Job*. The first comment, by Walter Kaufman, claims that certain of Jung's statements in the book are due to an Oedipus complex and unresolved adolescent resistances to his biblical-oriented upbringing, and to God especially. In fact, the writer says that a more obvious example of an unresolved Oedipus complex could not be found. The second comment, by Marilyn Nagy, says that no unbeliever could be as angry with God as Jung is in *Answer to Job*.

These comments typify some of the nonsense written about Jung and his discoveries. I personally have journeyed for long years through the collective unconscious and readily proclaim Jung's statements to be completely in harmony with the facts of the unconscious/spirit as I have experienced them. What the critics lack, of course, is direct experience of the archetypal processes themselves, which means they are unqualified to comment on Jung and depth psychology in the first place.

The truth is, Jung loved God deeply, for he had discovered Him as the greatest light of unconscious/spirit, *as a reality*. This is why Jung wrote to a young clergyman that all of his thoughts were circling around God with irresistible attraction, like the planets around the Sun. Yet this must of necessity involve the experience of God's full nature, which happens to be a *complexio oppositorum*, a complexity of opposites, in its totality, therefore dark as well as light. We experience God's opposites as seemingly complete in themselves and unconnected, but it was always taught in the Mysteries that we love God in His light while nonetheless fearing His darkness. The total God is light and dark, and indeed, male and female, though the God we know is totally the male side.

The theory of Jung's supposed unresolved Oedipus complex is amateurish, to say the least. This apparently posits Jung with hatred of his personal father, this being then projected onto God. (Otherwise how could the Oedipus complex equal hatred of God?) The trouble here is,

Jung loved his father, and indeed, loved God; and even *had* he hated his father, that does not mean he would therefore have hated God. You could even make a case for his loving God as substitute for the personal father he hated, except that he loved his father, and the accusation is that he hated God.

No better is Satan as a split-off complex of Christ. Like God, and indeed, like Man, the Higher Self has his light and dark sides, which is why we find light/dark twin-gods throughout mythology, Horus and Set, Krishna and Balarama, Cain and Abel, etc. The dark twin is just as real and valid as the light twin, and is certainly no split-off "complex," though he always acts contrary-wise, and is in that sense split off. Which side is brought forth in the processes depends entirely upon consciousness, but whichever, it is not only the real answer to the mystery of Christ and all other god-men, i.e., the dual-natured Self, but to all of these critics with their nonsensical theories.

Yet another criticism is that Jung viewed Christianity as a simple-minded projection of more complex and complete inner truths, these being the ones experienced by the alchemists—alchemy, therefore, being truer and superior to Christianity. Again, it is this criticism that is simpleminded, and a shallow oversimplification of the true facts. Jung well knew the inadequacy and the dangers of becoming caught in the lower spirit that alchemy investigated and warned against it frequently, stressing that Christ is the perfect symbol of the Higher Self, and that the scriptures themselves have been largely misunderstood. The Gospels are, in fact, versions of the individuation process of the man Jesus. Jung insisted that the higher spirit of God must rule, but he also knew that that the lower soul depths that alchemy investigated are nevertheless real and should be included in the full picture for wholeness. This is the fourth that must be added to the three, the Osirian Underworld that must be added to the higher Trinitarian realm of Ra.

In such works as *A Psychological Approach to the Trinity* and *Transformation Symbolism in the Mass,* (included in *Psychology and Religion: West and East,* and in so many other works, Jung leaves no doubt as to the inestimable value of both Christianity and the Church; it is just that they are in need of further development, while retaining the central mystery. Jung even states that the only real defense the modern West has against the overwhelming forces of chaos from the unconscious is Christianity. I cannot for the life of me understand how certain people can read all of these works of Jung and fail to see a man who is fighting for the *survival of* and *further development of* Christianity. He warns over and over what catastrophe awaits if we now abandon the religious treasure that Christianity has stored up for us. Although I am a member of no Church myself, I must say that all of my experiences of the unconscious depths bind me ever closer to the Christian mystery. You cannot have numinous visions of Christ, as I have done and as Jung did, without being so affected.

Chapter 9

God Becomes Man, Man Becomes God

Jung saw that the spiritual crisis of modern man has been building up since the first millennium, causing the unrest to set in what has now become hubris—"giantism," as he puts it—which believes that nothing is greater than Man himself. Jung says that when the Christian myth was lost, so too was the belief that wholeness could be attained in transcendent, otherworldly reality. When the myth is lost, the dark forces break loose to fill the gap, and chaos comes to reign. A mythos—that is to say, a religion—is meant to evolve and develop, affecting both Man and God. But this did not happen to a large degree with the Christian myth, so consequently it could not withstand the onslaught of science, with its rationalism, when it came. Indeed, the sluice gates were then opened for chaos in many forms to come pouring through. Western civilization further developed in certain ways, of course, but not with understanding of its own spiritual foundations, which in consequence eventually resulted in the discarded Christ, or as good as.

Jung says self-knowledge is of prime importance for human beings today, because it reveals the great dangers that are looming up from the unconscious depths, caused by the faulty, lop-sided thinking of modern consciousness. Realization that the soul must be given religious meaning, and that Christianity is an inner psychological defense against the dark powers of the unconscious depths, is a theme that runs all through Jung's works. As he says, it is not the scriptures that are to blame for this great modern problem. The fault lies with ourselves, for we have not further developed them, requiring deeper understanding of them, and have, in fact, opposed their development.

We must understand that God in his fullest sense is not only light, but also dark. He is a *complexio oppositorum,* a complexity of all opposites, and Man must realize this to give God his due, to fill out the situation. Man must also aim for the good, while realizing that he himself is capable of much evil. He may then bring forth the light and good side of God. Only when Man is the "good son" does he bring forth God as the "Good Father." However, Jung saw the great danger that modern Man has fallen into. Atheism, materialism, and the hubris to which mankind is prone, plus his frightening technological capabilities and his extreme intellectualism, which so often gives the impression of good-natured intelligence, makes it all the more dangerous. We can well understand why Jung felt so doubtful about the survival of Western civilization.

It is not just a question of mere religious *belief,* which is something of consciousness concerning an outer God above, but of *psychic structures within,* that connect us literally to eternal spirit and soul. It is highly dangerous to break away and deny the existence of these structures. Outer religion works if the symbolism is sincerely believed and accepted, for the symbolism is the product of unconscious/spirit in the first place. But for a thorough respiritualization, the unconscious itself must become activated and send through its symbolic contents. As it stands, we have lost the central myth that holds a culture together and literally supports it. Can we imagine any great civilization of the past without its mythos, its religion? What would be left of ancient Egypt without its spiritual life? Yet that is how we ourselves function today in our desouled world. We are as dead as Egypt would have been without its great religion, its high spirituality.

So ultimately, what defense have we, what answer, to this greatest of all problems, of mythless Man, lost and disoriented, but with the awesome powers of the gods in his hands? Beyond the old gods, in fact, for while they could send floods and destroy a city or two, it was never conceived that they could bring the whole world to extinction in a few short minutes; or slowly poison it to death. Jung sees the only answer lying in the further development of the myth; that is, as a process that involves the strenuous efforts of both the conscious and unconscious realms, so that the two realities come together like two halves of a coin. These opposites, which are in conflict until unified, are first of all personal and may be felt to be so by the individual. But as each atom is part of the whole, so too is the individual. And so the real problem is one affecting the whole of collective society. Only through the symbolism of religion, through spirituality, can the different realities of consciousness/matter and unconscious/spirit—Man and God—come together in harmony.

As God to be whole must be a complexity of opposites, so too must the Higher Self, the divine Son, who is an emanation of God. The mandala symbolizes this wholeness, which is why we find mandalas as religious expressions the world over. Jung says God can only incarnate in, and associate with, man in the form of man when man has become whole. Man achieves wholeness only when he enters into the inner conflict totally, to be then replaced within by God, who becomes man without. This is the meaning of Christ's words, "Who sees me sees the Father."

By accomplishing this, Jung further states, Man brings to God his wholeness, his completeness, as a fact of both conscious and unconscious realities. If God could accomplish this Himself, He would not need Man to do it for Him. Or to put it another way, God uses man to achieve His own wholeness, which appears to be the reason Man was developed specially out of the rest of nature. To do this, to bring God His wholeness, Man has to make the two sides of the collective unconscious conscious, although it not just a case of spirit and soul (matter) but also of good and evil, and masculine and feminine, and so on, all of the opposites. This is for the initiates into the inner processes to accomplish. For the masses in general, they should surround the religious symbol of the god, whether a Higher Self figure or God himself, like the many spokes around the hub of a wheel.

The Christmas story with the divine child, the Wise Men, the Star of Bethlehem, etc., symbolizes the incarnation wonderfully, but what it lacks—what Christ lacks—is the dark twin, the Set to Horus. It is true that Antichrist appeared almost immediately after Christ's advent to fill out the archetype, but it was not generally realized by orthodox Christianity that this represents the dark side of the Higher Self, and that Christ symbolizes the light side. This is not to say that the figures should be together, light and dark, only that it should be recognized that the dark side exists and always lies in wait to take over when the light fails. The largely feminine depths—and heights—of the unconscious that Gnosticism and alchemy investigated should also be part of the totality, although Mary Magdalene the redeemed and the Virgin Mary do actually symbolize those depths, the latter in her role of *Theotokos* (God bearer), giving birth to the divine Son. Thus the base and instinctual World Soul is redeemed to her highest spiritual aspect. (As many myths express, the feminine spirit is also celestial.)

The loss of the central myth that had enabled Western civilization to develop and flourish was Jung's main concern, and though he had doubts, he still hoped it would be rescued. He comments that myth will never be replaced by science, nor can any science ever become myth. Furthermore, myth is the Word of God spoken unto Man, rather than being the creation of Man. This is true of myth the world over, but it is also true that the myth must evolve, and it can only evolve on a line of descent. Buddhism grew out of Hinduism on the ancient line, and Christianity has roots that reach back through Jewish traditions to the source in early Egypt. These are royal lines that evolve through the collective unconscious involving both Man and the spirit, and only in this way can God come through to Man directly in an Incarnation.

Obviously, the central myth of a culture must be dominant in order to be the foundation, inspiration, and creative force behind it. Unfortunately, the West has lost belief in itself as a religious entity, seeing itself now as a great business and technological complex, a devastating condemnation of Western civilization. This is the Tower of Babel situation all over again, and the rest of the world is in the gravest danger of contamination from the West, as certain of my dreams have warned. The only remedy is to stop the rot at its source. Those cultures of the world, with their own particular religions, may be largely admirable and praiseworthy, yet we in the West are ourselves heirs to a very fine and high form of religion, which, as Jung stresses, represents a highly differentiated level of consciousness. It has roots thousands of years old on a definite spiritual line, but is now in such a dilapidated state that it is in the greatest danger of not only dying itself, but of dragging the rest of the world down with it. I say all of this because I know the collective unconscious and how it works through Man, in both positive and negative ways. As Jung said, we must live within the myth; we must have God in some way, or we eventually get the Devil.

It is often argued that if we all discard our religions and traditions, or at least minimize them, we can then live together as rational, enlightened, modern human beings in a modern world. But the fact is, we are not the shallow creatures of consciousness that this would require, rather the opposite. Below the small, conscious part of the psyche lies the vast unconscious that is by its very nature traditional, mythological, religious, and archaic—and yet is ever developing, and which stretches out to the higher spirit and lower soul depths, and which includes, it must be said, the realm of the dragon. As part of the Self, the psyche of Man is connected to these realms. When Man tries to live without these foundations, he literally loses the ground from beneath his feet, and the culture eventually collapses into chaos. So it is wrong to require peoples to reject religious traditions to all become shallow intellectualized fragments in order to "fit in." Religion should always be the solid foundation of culture. If that means separate cultures so that each can find full spiritual expression and development, it is all to the good.

The only way forward, as Jung sees it (and as I see it), is further development of the traditional myth by means of depth psychology. Certain people, perhaps the majority, are not suited to undergo the inner processes themselves and so would be the outer followers, as, for example, are the majority of Buddhists. Experience of the archetypal processes of the inner depths has always been the province of initiates into the Mysteries, and this would still be so today with depth psychology. This notwithstanding, inner knowledge enables us to see other religious systems of the world as valid and tenable because we see the same basic symbolism in them as in our own. The collective soul of Western Man is in a far worse state than he is aware of, and each generation will become worse, if that is possible. It will not be the fault of individuals basically; the fault will lie with the culture into which they are born and raised, and the framework of orientation in which they develop. To bring about the fundamental change necessary to prevent this collapse of civilization into barbarism will require a miracle. Yet miracles do happen sometimes, as I know myself, and if one individual can undergo spiritual transformation, then so too may a whole civilization that consists of individuals. This means, however, that we will have to learn to think in a different way, although it is in essence the age-old way further evolved. It is not just *what* we think that is at fault, it is *how* we think.

We must look at the situation from the view of the collective substratum upon which consciousness rests, as well as from consciousness itself. The collective unconscious is religious by nature and functions in a mythological way. It is apparently timeless, eternal, and infinite, extending far beyond our powers of full understanding. But part of it touches our worldly reality and works through us, using symbols to convey its different reality, its different nature, to us. It is experience of these symbols that causes Man to set up his religions, and then both conscious and unconscious realities can share in the symbols. This, in essence, means the unification of matter and spirit, and from this flows true culture.

Some of the symbols last for thousands of years in a certain form, and, as said, are royal lines direct from spirit reality. But if Man takes them to be literally true, in a physical sense, as he has always done in the West, it was in the cards that one day, with developing scientific and other knowledge, the time would arrive when the religion as it stands would be no longer acceptable to intelligent, thinking minds. Nor perhaps to the masses that follow the spirit of the age. Yet the fact remains that religion is nevertheless true in an *irrational* way, being commensurable with the psychic depths of the inner Man. Some people, the followers, are influenced this way or that, whichever way the wind blows. They will easily be carried along by the tidal wave that can then deluge the culture, believing the chaos to be the very epitome of what is desirable, oblivious to the fact that they are really drowning in the waters of chaos.

By the same token, people may veer to the good, the positive, the spiritual, the latter actually being more natural to Man in that his psyche is then in tune with the total Self. (In fact, to be spiritual is to be in harmony with the true holy nature of full reality.) If people can come to understand to some degree the fact of the inner Self as a "Christ within," this can be the way to Christianity again for Western Man (though Christ is nevertheless also above, as the Church always taught). As Jung says, faith works if people can stretch themselves that far; better still is at least some understanding of the inner mystery. It was Jung's fate to discover, or rediscover, the source of all the forces of chaos, though thankfully it happens to be also the divine source of healing and wholeness, the source of the divine Inner Man. Yet I must say again that the outer cosmic Christ is nevertheless a fact and perfectly valid as the Logos, and indeed, Jung continues to say that Christianity is a powerful defense against the dark forces of chaos that well up from below. We have just not realized it.

Jung comments that though Christian symbolism is our true heritage we have wasted it, the house our fathers built thus falling into decay. With this dissipation of our natural heritage the spirit of fire from above has become heavy water, and with "Luciferian presumption" the spirit enthroned has been usurped by man's intellect. We can therefore say that, whereas Christ changed the water into wine (i.e., spiritualized matter), we in the modern world are changing the wine back into water again.

As to the full Self as spirit, the lower aspect seems to cover the whole of nature from the very lowest level up through the higher animal to the human level. This represents the Earth Spirit or World Soul, or part of it. But it also reaches up to the spirit above, which is largely unknown to us, though certain of its contents come down to our experience. Consequently, the contents of the Self may appear to us in any shape or form, and from any level. Sometimes it is a mixture of several of them, forming what appear to be bizarre conglomerations, seen as "composite animal figures" in ancient Egyptian depictions. Ultimately, the two aspects, above and below, are, as Jung puts it, like two princes with two separate realms. I call these Higher Self and Lower Self.

The appearance of the Self as Son of Man figure, or as Son of God, is a *representation*, as not only does the figure have no actual physical form, but would be so vast and immense if it did, that we could not possibly take it all into our conscious minds. So it must reduce to human form for us to be able to experience and assimilate it. As said, this is not merely a figure but a realm, even two, above and below. Only religion or mythology can express this great phenomenon at highest and fullest meaning, and so it may be comprehended why the loss of religion is so harmful to the individual and so devastating to culture: It means dissociation from an immensely higher and wider reality, from God himself, and being reduced to little more than an isolated fragment, or as an animal of lower intelligence that has no need of deeper meaning. There is nothing wrong with animals at lower level—a lot that is right with them in fact—but Man has been raised to a higher consciousness, and so must now live a higher way in that he has association with the spirit. This is why he was developed out of the rest of nature. Man now unites the reality of matter with that of the spirit; as a truth believed for some people perhaps, but as actual fact for the successful initiate at the highest level of the spiritual quest. If Man rejects all of this then he seriously malfunctions.

The Symbolic Relevance of the Mass and the Cross

In "Transformation Symbolism in the Mass," Jung tried to demonstrate that the Church Mass is based upon inner psychic processes that connect us literally to the spirit. The Mass is the summation of the life and death of Christ, which is actually the inner spiritual transformation processes of the man Jesus, rather than his outer biography, and so the Mass is really "the rite of the individuation process."

Jung quotes 1 Corinthians 11:23ff on the Last Supper where Christ offers bread and wine to the disciples, which, he says, are his body and his blood. He breaks the bread and says. "*Take, eat, this is my body which is broken for you: this do in remembrance of me.*" He then takes the cup, sups, and then says, "*This cup is the new testament in my blood: this do ye, as oft as ye drink it, in remembrance of me. For as often as ye eat this bread, and drink this cup, ye do shew the Lord's death till he come.*"

But it is perhaps expressed even better in John 6:53–6. "*Then Jesus said unto them, Verily, verily, I say unto you, Except ye eat the flesh of the Son of man, and drink his blood, ye have no life in you. Whoso eateth my flesh, and drinketh my blood, hath eternal life; and I will raise him up at the last day. For my flesh is meat indeed, and my blood is drink indeed. He that eateth my flesh, and drinketh my blood, dwelleth in me, and I in him."*

In fact, earlier at John 6:56 Christ has said: "*He that eateth my flesh and drinketh my blood, dwelleth in me, and I in him.*" Jung also quotes John 6:5: "*I am the vine, ye are the branches.*" He then says that the Mass involves essentially *thysia* and *deipnon,* which intimate "sacrifice" and "meal." The Old Testament, at Prov. 9:5, says: "*Come, eat of my bread, and drink of the wine which I have mingled.*" The King of Righteousness, Melchizedek, who has been called "the first Messiah of Israel," offers bread and wine to Abraham, and the spiritual transformation processes of King Saul involves three loaves of bread and a bottle of wine, forming, of course, a type of 3 + 1 quaternity.

The bread and wine (flesh and blood) obviously represent very much more than merely themselves, including—as solid and liquid—matter and spirit. Also, the bread is white and the wine red, and from time immemorial these colors have symbolized the opposites. As Jung comments, the white bread is female (soul), at least at times, and the red wine male (spirit). But the event in which these are unified in celebration is not just an historical event of the past, it happens again in the Mass, and indeed, at all times. The Upper and Lower Kingdoms of Ancient Egypt had crowns that were white and red respectively. When the kingdoms were unified so were the crowns into one of white and red. But the two kingdoms also represented soul and spirit realities, and so these too were symbolically unified with the white and red crown. Actually, the bread and wine we see in the Mass were usually white bread and red ale in Egypt, but it was the white/red colors and solid/liquid natures of the substances that mattered. A ritual in the Book of the Dead says, "Give me bread and red ale. Let me be made pure by the sacrificial joint, together with white bread." The followers of the god Mithras drank a mixture of bread and wine, while Dionysus was associated with wine and the vine—he was "drunk" by his followers. The goddess Ceres was the grain that was fertilized by Dionysus the wine.

As said, there are two aspects of the Mass, divine and human, and the whole drama of the Christ processes are commemorated by it, involving Incarnation, Passion, Death, and Resurrection. During the Mass, the eternal life of Christ unfolds into human existence for a brief moment in time. All of those who take part come together in "mystical unity," and the One who offers Himself in sacrifice is God, while at the same time the Son offers himself in atonement to the Father. God and Son are One in eternity, but separate in the Incarnation when the Son becomes mixed or merged with his human aspect. But all are included in the divine drama, God, Son, and Man. Christ tells the people in the Gospel of John, *"You in me, and I in God."*

There is no exclusive human purpose to the Mass, as it does not serve primarily Man; it is an end unto itself with spiritual purpose. But it seizes Man and involves him and is a miracle because during it God actually does come forth. This may seem unbelievable to some, or to most, but Jung points out that it is the most improbable claims of all, the religious ones, that last for many thousands of years—or for eternity we might add. This is because they express eternal truths beyond Man, yet include him in a sense, elevating him out of a reality that seemed limited to mere matter. The wholeness of a human individual is not confined to just the conscious mind but extends to the personal unconscious, and then to the collective unconscious, the latter having no known limits. The unconscious/spirit may possess the limited ego-consciousness of the individual and utilize it for its own purposes. In positive form this may amount to a religious mission for the human individual, but in negative form something more sinister and in the end disastrous.

Moved and mover are ego and Self, called in the Greek Mysteries "eidolon" and "Daemon." The ego sacrifices its will to the Self, and so the ego is the sacrificed and the sacrificer the Self. However, as the ego is part of the Self, the Self must feel the sacrifice as being partly of itself. If my hand is injured, not only is it injured itself, I as the totality of which it is part am also injured. So in the same way what happens to the human aspect happens also to the Self. What the unconscious/spirit is in itself is not known, but in coming through to our experience, to consciousness, as the Self it becomes Man. As the ultimate Self is part of God manifested, or *is* God manifested, this means God's incarnation. It happens in unconscious/spirit reality, but nevertheless happens.

The parts of the Self are scattered in the unconscious/spirit realm, but in the individuation process are made conscious, and at the same time assembled, to the center that is the Self. Thus in the Egyptian Book of the Dead the soul of the deceased in the Underworld, which is really ego-consciousness in the unconscious, assembles the seven Akhu spirits to the ultimate Ka, which is Horus the divine Son. Likewise, in the Bible, Joshua conquers seven kingdoms to attain the Promised Land. The human individual is born out of the unconscious and so is the child of the latter. But in the individuation process the Self is born to consciousness as the divine child. Thus ego and Self are, at one and the same time, both parent and child.

Jung says the Mass, though concerning mainly eternal reality, is deeply rooted in the human soul, and that it is the most important mystery of the Catholic Church. That is to say, the Mass symbolizes processes that are of unconscious/spirit reality, the gateway to which is, and which involves, the personal unconscious. The human soul is transformed symbolically by the Eucharist feast (part of the Mass) into the totality of which it is part, of which Christ is the symbol, or is unified with the totality, thus the mortal being with the Self. God and Man both undergo transformation in the processes symbolized by the Mass, which is why Jung calls the Mass "the rite of the individuation process."

Mythologist Gerald Massey, whose works, scorned by twentieth-century conformist scholars, are becoming ever more popular, tells us that the Mass, and in particular the Eucharist feast, is basically the same as the ritual of Osiris in ancient Egypt. Osiris as bread and wine, or bread and red beer, was "the food which never perishes" and this was transubstantiated by the descent of Ra as Holy Spirit. The bread in the Mass, Massey points out, is broken and not cut, just as the bread was broken in Egypt and not cut, to symbolize the tearing apart of Osiris' body by the evil Set. All of this is again symbolism of processes concerning the Higher Self, though Massey adds that in very early times, the sacrificed was a woman, and the bread torn actually the flesh of her body. Massey says, in *Ancient Egypt* (1907):

> The dogma of the incarnation was an Egyptian mystery. Baptism, regeneration, transfiguration, transubstantiation, the resurrection and ascension, were all Egyptian mysteries. The mystery of an ever-virgin mother; the mystery of a boy at twelve years of age transforming suddenly into an adult of thirty years, and then becoming one with the father, as it had been earlier in the mysteries of totemism; the mystery in which the dead body of Osiris is transubstantiated into the living Horus by the descent of the bird-headed Holy Spirit; the mystery of a divine being in three persons, one of which takes flesh on earth as the human Horus, to become a mummy as Osiris in Amenta [the Underworld], and to rise up from the dead in spirit as Ra in heaven. These and other miracles of the Christian faith were already extant among the mysteries of Amenta.

Although some of the symbolism regarding Christ would have been taken from the Egyptian mysteries and the Old Testament, it must be remembered that the phenomenon of the incarnation of the Logos as Son of God was occurring anew within the man Jesus. A lot of the symbolism would thereby have occurred in the inner processes of Jesus directly. Massey tells us that the Son of God is the "ever-coming son," but what he could not have known is that this is literally so as a fact through the unconscious, i.e., as the Self or Logos.

In the same work, "Transformation Symbolism in the Mass," Jung quotes the "round dance" from the *Acts of John,* in which the disciples hold hands to form a circle moving around Christ at the center. This expresses the totality contained in the One that is the Self, sometimes the Ogdoad, or eight as 1 + 7, or sometimes 1 + 12, as in the "round dance." The opposites contained in the totality are opposed and in conflict and therefore find no unification with each other—like a clock face where twelve is opposite to six, nine is opposite to three, and so on. But each finds its connection to the center, like spokes of a wheel to the hub, and so all come into harmony with the center that is the Self or Christ. This is the essence of Buddhism, and of many religious systems worldwide. Moses erects a circle of twelve stones (himself at the center of the twelve-fold circle), and one of the main symbols of Pythagoras was a circle with a centerpoint. (There is no doubt that Pythagoras would have been a Gnostic Christian had he lived five hundred years later, as indeed, would Plato.) Jung comments that the circle with a centerpoint has been a symbol of deity since ancient times. This is one of the chief meanings of the mandala, perhaps the main abstract symbol of the Self. The Self, though the point at the center, contains within itself all of the opposites that are on the circumference. Jung says the "round dance" is a "psychic phenomenon" and a paraphrase of the Eucharist.

At its ultimate meaning, the cosmic Logos contains all souls of Creation, so that all share the One. However, although we may experience certain contents of the Self in a personal way, in its fullness it remains mostly unknown to us. The light that is the Self may as well not exist for those who neither see it nor believe in it, but whosoever knocks on the Self—Christ—will find the door opened. When the contents then begin to come through to experience, they are "phenomena of assimilation." This is what Jung says and he is right.

He adds that when we concentrate on the traditional form of Christianity, particularly on Christ's crucifixion and resurrection, it activates corresponding contents through the unconscious, giving rise to much relevant symbolism. This is why the cross, for example, used to inflict the most horrendous torture, becomes a wondrous symbol of holiness, becoming of far greater importance than the actual cross that was used with Christ. The cross has many associated meanings, a main one being as a fourfold mandala, forming the "quaternity of the Self." The cross divides into opposites, hence torture for the Self, but it also synthesizes the opposites into harmony, for the four directions—and therefore total reality—are unified in Christ at the center. The mandalas produced by the unconscious are matched by the crucifixion of Christ on the cross—the Gnostics in particular grasped this. I personally have seen crucified figures in dreams resembling Christ, though beardless to distinguish them from the original Christ who is bearded in our conceptions of him. These were appearances of the Self in that specific situation, of course, the "Christ within." This is perhaps as Son of Man more so than as Son of God, therefore Lower Self rather than Higher Self.

The suffering of Christ on the cross is caused by God's becoming Man (this refers to the suffering Self rather than the actual crucifixion of Jesus the man). So the archetypal Christ is crucified at his "coming" rather than at his "going." That is to say, as the Self comes through to the world—still in the unconscious—in the individuation process, becoming consciously aware crucifies him between his opposites. He becomes pulled in all directions, a veritable state of crucifixion. (This is one meaning of the crucifixion; there are several. Jung comments that the conscious and the unconscious are rejoined when the cross is concentrated upon.)

Jung quotes the valedictory words of St. Peter as he was supposedly crucified upside down. I included some of this in *The Four Gold Keys*, but it is very relevant here, as it reveals certain deeper meaning to the cross.

> O name of the cross, hidden mystery! O grace ineffable that is pronounced in the name of the cross. O nature of man that cannot be separated from God! O love unspeakable and indivisible, that cannot be shown forth by unclean lips! I grasp thee now, I that am at the end of my earthly course. I will declare thee as thou art, I will not keep silent the mystery of the cross, which was once shut and hidden from my soul. You that hope in Christ, let not the cross be for you that which it appears; for it is another thing, and different from that which appears, this suffering which is in accordance with Christ's. . . . Wherefore the Lord says in a mystery: "Except ye make the things of the right as those of the left, and those of the left as those of the right, and those that are above as those below, and those that are behind as those that are before, ye shall not have knowledge of the kingdom." (M. R. James. 1924.)

There is a hidden secret to the cross here for Peter, involving the wholeness of the god that is the Self, the Christ Logos.

One Gnostic view, given for example in *The Travels of Peter,* was that the vertical bar of the cross represents the spiritual Christ as Logos and the horizontal bar the human Jesus. This fits partly with a dream I had in which three strange figures (i.e., Trinitarian) became the vertical bar, saying that perhaps the most difficult part of the processes is the horizontal bar, representing the flat plain of the Earth.

In the *Acts of John,* as the crucifixion of Jesus is taking place, the apostle John sees a vision of Christ in a cave. Christ tells John that as spirit he is not being crucified as the body of Jesus is. Christ speaks of the Cross of Light, which is ". . . the boundary of all things, and the harmony of things unstable, and the harmony of wisdom, and the wisdom that is harmony" The Cross of Light is the "Redeemer and Emancipator" of the soul depths, and lies in between the Pleroma and Kenoma (spirit reality and worldly reality, though the latter as more than just mere matter). In this way Christ from the Pleroma rescues Mary Magdalene from the Kenoma. It was even said that Christ was crucified on one side of the cross and Jesus, the man, on the other.

The Gnostic cross was usually a cross within a circle, similar to the Celtic cross, which almost certainly derived from the Gnostic. But the circle divided into four, or squared, is actually one of the oldest symbols of mankind. Jung says that it is the main symbol of the Self through the unconscious. In dreams over the years I have experienced both types of the cross, orthodox and Gnostic, though it was quite a while before I realized that these two systems were coming through to me. I eventually came to understand that as these two streams were divided two thousand years ago, it is now time to unify them again, as my inner processes actually do.

Getting back to the Mass, in *Psychology and Alchemy* ("The Lapis-Christ Parallel"), Jung explains how both the Philosopher's Stone of alchemy and Christ are, in the final analysis, symbols of the Self, or of aspects of the Self, hence the "lapis-Christ parallel." As alchemy was based upon similar processes of the unconscious as the Mass to a degree, alchemy and the Mass express the greatest truth of Man, though at different levels—higher spirit and lower spirit. In yet another work, "Transformation Symbolism in the Mass," (contained in *Psychology and Religion: West and East),* Jung demonstrates the similarities between the dream visions of Zosimos of Panapolis, a third century A.D. nonChristian Gnostic-alchemist, and the symbolism of the Mass. Jung lists eleven similarities between them, which are based on the unconscious archetypes of sacrifice and transformation, and then gives eight differences.

There is no need to list the similarities and differences here, but I must say that even among the differences there are certain similarities. For instance, Jung mentions a bloody and gruesome human sacrifice occurring in one of Zosimos's visions, but states there is nothing comparable to it in the Mass; there is only the bloodless sacrifice of the bread and the wine. Yet the bread and wine sacrifice is associated with a deeper, bloody sacrifice, that of Christ himself, which is also the symbolic sacrifice of the Lamb. Jung further says that the meaning of the sacrifice in the visions of Zosimos is the production of the divine water, connected with the birth of the Higher Self, but that the meaning of the Mass is Communion of Christ with the flock. This is partly so, but elsewhere Jung clearly states that the meaning of the Mass expresses the symbolic birth, life, crucifixion, and resurrection of Christ. So both the birth of Christ, the Higher Self, who has his human aspect, and his bloody sacrifice, are parts of the Mass. Thus the gruesome human sacrifice with Zosimos and Christ are comparable, for both forms symbolize certain processes of the unconscious regarding the Higher Self.

Jung's says there are both human and divine aspects to the ritual of the Mass, literally involving man and God. The Last Supper and whole Incarnation, Passion, Death, and Resurrection are commemorated by it. So according to Jung's own words, the visions of Zosimos and the Mass both symbolize a similar phenomenon. It is really a divine event, and the humanization of it only a symbolization. Jung knew that the divine event is repeated with the rite of the Mass, and although it happens above, in the divine realm, Man is nevertheless included in it, through the unconscious.

As the Mass repeats the symbolism of the Last Supper, this unifies the opposites in ourselves and in reality as a whole. Thus the division—and even soul sickness—within us is healed. So religion (here, Christianity) is not just a matter of faith and belief, it is a healing system. I had a dream that actually said this.

I had another dream which said that the sickness of the Roman Empire caused Christianity to appear as the cure. Rome with its "love of power" was transformed into Christendom by the "power of love." Jung says the same, although he adds that Christianity was forced to defend itself against certain of its adherents, including the Gnostics, as well as against obvious enemies. In the case of the Gnostics, this meant against extreme irrationality, forcing the Church to develop rationalism as protection. When later added to by scientific rationalism in general, this caused the chronic state of psychic dissociation that overwhelmed the West in the twentieth century, meaning loss of soul that now threatens the world with chaos.

Yet the Church never succumbed entirely to the rational, for Christ as divine Son of God remained its main teaching. Jung says we must be extremely grateful to the Church for preserving the phenomenon of the God-man for so many centuries and warns of the catastrophe that will befall if we should lose Christ entirely. Christ is the great bringer of order, and indeed, the Higher Self is the epitome of order. So Christ remains the panacea for Western culture today as he was for the Roman Empire all those centuries ago. Nevertheless, Jung sees the revival of Gnosticism as now very necessary, to help those who can no longer accept the literal, orthodox teaching to understand the *Mysterium Magnum*. Yet Jung insists that focusing attention upon the cross is valid for all, as it helps gain oneness with the center, the "Christ within."

Jung knew the true nature of Christ but fully realized that other people did not. He knew he could see through the "dividing walls" to what was happening behind conscious reality, whereas to others the walls were opaque, which meant they could not see what was happening. This "x-ray vision," the ability to see behind surface reality, gave him inner certainty, though it also meant loneliness because to possess such powers separates us from others. Even today, or especially today, Western Man has little inkling of the true nature of Christ, and of his deep meaning and importance for Western civilization. This was Jung's main task, to try to make others see as he saw, and to grasp the urgency of "the evolution of the religious spirit."

Religious/spiritual truths, far from being outmoded and defunct, are actually the most alive and vibrant truths of all, being symbolic eternal truths of unconscious/spirit reality to which the human psyche is literally attached. The point is, all of the symbolism we find in myths and religions represent psychic/spiritual processes taking place within individuals, yet involving another reality in which the God-man, the Higher Self, comes to be born.

At the same time we should be aware that the individuation process can be dangerous, at least for many people, as they seem unable to experience these greatest of truths directly without identifying with it, which means inflation. So Jung believed that the Church displays much wisdom in not making too much of the "Christ within."

The further development of the Western myth of Christ, the Higher Self or Logos, was the central goal of Jung's life and work. He said that his earlier goals had been scientific ones, but that he then discovered a "stream of lava," whose fires completely altered his orientation to reality itself, placing upon him a great task that would last a lifetime. He was a true trailblazer and pioneer, and his discoveries the most important for any age, and certainly the most urgent for our own. Jung completely alters reality itself for us again, restoring to us our own souls; restoring to us the Son of God, the Higher Self; restoring to us God Himself; and indeed, to the feminine spirit. Surely no one could argue that this is not the true gold. Jung died in 1961. I sometimes see lists of the twentieth-century's greatest figures with his name missing. Freud is always there, of course. Yet Jung was the greatest light of his and many another age, and I know it because I know that the things he discovered are *facts*.

Note

I have recently acquired a large book on philosophers, mostly modern, and it illustrates yet again, and quite blatantly, just how dissociated our thinking has become today. These philosophers are regarded as the greatest intellects of their age, some being professors at great universities of learning, but it nevertheless highlights the enormous task facing those of us who know that our way of thinking must be radically changed. Jung is not mentioned at all in the book, though as we would expect, Freud and his theories occupy one of the sections. Yet unless philosophers—scholars in all fields—come to understand that all ideas and postulations must take into account the discoveries of depth psychology, then the conclusions of those scholars remain no more than the limited, over-intellectualized exercises of fragmented and cramped consciousness.

Jung's discoveries, and if I may say, my own experiences, reveal that reality in its fullness is religious/mythological by nature, although it is so easy to split away from the whole to exist in a lesser form of reality, in materialistic fragmentation. But an iota of real experience may totally override the faulty opinions of dissociated consciousness completely. That experience is worth a wagonload of intellectual conjecture, no matter how brilliantly reasoned out.

Part Two

Blavatsky, Nietzsche, Marian Vision, UFOS, and Aliens

Chapter 10

Madame Blavatsky, Prelude to Jung

> He who dwells in all beings yet is apart from all beings, whom no beings know, whose body is all being, who controls all beings from within. . . . There is no other seer but he, no other knower but he. He is your Self, the inner controller, the immortal. All else is sorrow.
>
> —The Upanishads

The Basic Blavatsky

In part 1 we saw that Carl Jung through depth psychology discovered a whole realm of spirit and soul lying beyond the personal unconscious, which must in fact lie behind the whole physical universe, and indeed, extend out into infinity and eternity. Part of this other realm touches the personal unconscious so that the personal unconscious must be a minute part of that other realm, the first layers of which Jung called the "collective unconscious," though he freely admitted that the term is somewhat inadequate.

Human beings have dreams that apparently take place in the personal unconscious, usually to do with the personal life of the dreamer in everyday settings. But sometimes strange, or awesome, or terrifying—or sometimes religious or spiritual—material is experienced that may leave the dreamer stunned, shocked, or conversely, elated. This is when what are known as archetypal contents breaks through from the other spirit/soul reality, the nature of which runs the whole gamut of possibilities. These contents form symbols that are used to convey to the dreamer whatever meaning and message is intended, which range from the animal to the abstract, from demon to angel, and include male and female, and good and evil. Further, because, being spirit/soul, the archetypes have no actual physical forms, ones are chosen by the unconscious/spirit from the outer world that seem appropriate to convey the meaning and message.

As we saw in part 1, myths and religions all over the world since time immemorial have been founded on direct experience of archetypal symbolism from the collective unconscious, which actually form inner processes of development. Initiates into the psychic/spiritual depths have always followed these processes, discovering that they build up to what the East calls the Higher Self. (There are many names for the phenomenon according to the culture: Logos in the Greek Mysteries, Anthropos to the Gnostics, etc.) This is really the basis of the gods, goddesses, demons, monsters, and magical animals and happenings that form the structures of myths and religions worldwide. This is why upon comparison of their symbolism, they are all found to be basically the same, varying in degree of development according to the level of the culture. For example, the fish and the star have been symbols of the coming of a Savior, representing respectively lower soul and higher cosmic aspects of the Self, since the very first culture we know of, Sumeria. This is why the first symbol of Christ, even before the cross, was the fish, and why he has his Star of Bethlehem, the Star in the East. This is why certain unorthodox sects of the early centuries A.D., called Gnostics (literally "knowers") referred to Christ as the "Christ within," because he was a version—probably the most highly developed ever—of the Higher Self, ultimately and literally Son of the spirit totality we call God.

We must now continue that investigation with a couple of other personalities. This will necessitate a return to the time just before Jung. In the nineteenth century, two figures appeared who exemplified the deeply problematic situation of modern man, caught between the discoveries of science and its material and the largely atheistic stance on the one hand, and the deeply spiritual and meaningful hopes and aspirations of the human soul on the other. Chronologically Jung comes just after the two figures we must now explore, but it was necessary to investigate Jung and his discoveries in the part 1 in order to gain some understanding of what follows in the second. Part 2 concludes with certain material concerning visions of the Virgin Mary, known as Marian visions, and UFO sightings and aliens encounters, which form parts of the developing picture of man's spiritual/supernatural experience in modern times.

From the time of the Renaissance, Western Man's worldview became increasingly limited to the investigation of matter. In the nineteenth century, particularly with the discoveries of Darwin, there arose a seeming conflict between the evolution and Creation theories, between science and religion, that has not been resolved even today. (That is, in the general view. In actuality there never was any real conflict.) Yet it was not so much that the Church was in conflict with evolution, for many clergymen accepted evolution as God's *method* of Creation. Ultimately, it was not the Church that rejected science, but science that rejected the Church and its religion, society *en masse* eventually following suit.

Philosophical alchemy, which sought the spirit hidden within matter, and the Holy Grail quests, though genuine routes to the spiritual treasures, had not helped Western Man generally to understand the great mystery of the "Christ within," simply because alchemy and the Holy Grail themselves had not been understood. Despite the many spirit experiences of the mystics, which were taken ever less seriously as the centuries passed, Christianity could only grow weaker, having no real answer but faith to the great challenges posed by the discoveries of science and its general atheism. This is not to say Christianity was therefore proved false or its teachings untrue, only that the Church failed to understand and further develop its great mystery, meaning that it could not stand up to science and its definite material truths as they unfolded. Nevertheless, as Jung says, we must be very grateful to the Church for preserving the *Mysterium Magnum* over the centuries, fighting as it has for the sacredness of spirit reality, and for its importance to the human soul.

The scientific rationalism that developed in the nineteenth century was a force that little could oppose, and it is a fact that many were not troubled by the loss of soul that followed in the twentieth century. Some even thrive under such conditions. But the nineteenth century abounds with personalities that could not rest contented in so negative a situation. One such figure was Friedrich Nietzsche, for whom the "death of God" was a life-shattering blow. When the immense significance of Darwin's discoveries sank into his mind, and indeed into his soul, his personality was basically too deep simply to continue as if nothing of great importance had occurred. Nietzsche, suffering years of inner torment, had to find an answer to the death of God. His great tragedy was that he eventually did find an answer; totally the wrong answer, more dangerous than atheism itself, and it destroyed him.

The other figure who quite literally searched the world for an answer that neither the Church nor science could supply was Madame H. P. Blavatsky. She too finally found her solution, this by becoming, partly, a Buddhist. But she was to say that while Buddhism and certain other esoteric teachings satisfied her religious thirst intellectually, deep in her heart she always felt an inexplicable love for the Russian Orthodox Church.

Buddhism, great and valid religion that it is, is not a satisfactory spiritual answer for Western Man, for it does not speak to the Western collective unconscious, as demonstrated by the fact that Blavatsky herself felt such deep love for the Russian Church within her soul, which she never fully understood.

Both Blavatsky and Nietzsche devoted their lives to this greatest of problems—loss of God, loss of spirit, loss of soul—that afflicts mankind even more today. They sought their solutions in completely opposite directions. Madame Blavatsky finally discovered the spiritual extension of mankind in the Higher Self, finding that morality and compassion are imperative to this immortal entity in positive form, and indeed, to mankind itself. Nietzsche on the other hand abandoned these most important of values in his inflation of the conscious mortal man into a Superman.

It may be asked, with justification, why my investigations of the royal line of the Western spiritual Mystery, which for the past two thousand years has been specifically Christian, include a woman who largely rejected her Western religious heritage to adopt that of the Far East. The answer is that coming to understand the esoteric foundations of the Eastern forms of religion—and those of the rest of the world to some degree—eventually gave Blavatsky the key to the real meaning of the Western forms, causing her to declare that, as the Higher Self and a form of the cosmic Logos, Christ truly is a divine being. This belief—knowledge, I should say—was not based upon mere superficial appreciation of Eastern doctrines. Blavatsky's works reveal that she possessed deep understanding of the archetypal processes of spirit/soul reality involved in the phenomenon of the Self, indeed, at times displaying extra-special insight.

Her perception, about a hundred and forty years ago, that Christ was a form of the cosmic Self that descended into the human initiate Jesus (the highest form ever of the phenomenon) deserves much respect from us. The Theosophical Society she cofounded constituted in certain ways perhaps the most important religious group since the Middle Ages, forming the link to Jung, though his discoveries were to be mightier than any that had gone before. Through depth psychology Jung came to *prove* the religious truths that Man had always believed to be real and incontestable. (The initiates and mystics who experienced them directly had always known, of course.) Yet Blavatsky herself made a magnificent attempt to bring some of the world's sacred esoteric experiences together in a secret wisdom philosophy, while the rest of Western philosophy tumbled into a rationalistic atheism that was basically pessimistic and negative.

H. P. Blavatsky—HPB as she was generally referred to—has become a figure of ridicule for some today, for her critics look only at certain aspects of her works, her views on the "seven root races," evolution, Atlantis, and so on, though even with these there is some need to defend her. She was writing only a few years after Darwin made his discoveries, at a time when literally anything was still possible, when science had not yet drawn the outline, let alone filled in the details, so that some of her ideas concerning these things consequently seem somewhat naïve and unintelligent to us now. By comparison, HPB's most important work, concerning deeper understanding of religious forms and symbolism generally—particularly of the Higher Self—has been largely neglected, presumably because her detractors are bereft of understanding of the phenomenon themselves. Even so, her theories of seven root races are not just her own thought-up ideas, but are taken from the esoteric teachings of the Hindus, though no one sees fit to heavily criticize those. But we must ask, who else of her day was saying that Christ as the immortal Self looked down upon and instructed Jesus, his mortal aspect below? For that matter, how many are saying it today?

She frequently stressed that the Theosophical Society she cofounded, though often expressed in Buddhist and Hindu terms, covers in fact all religions and inner quests for wisdom and truth. She writes that the aim of Theosophy is ". . . namely to reconcile all religions, sects, and nations under a common system of ethics, based on eternal verities." Nevertheless, it is still true that the majority of her concepts and teachings are Buddhist and Hindu, though she does explain that she calls herself a Bodhist, a lover of wisdom, rather than a Buddhist, *Bodhi* meaning "wisdom."

My first encounter with H. P. Blavatsky was quite by chance. I knew of her reputation as a medium—some say cheat and charlatan—but had not read any of her works until, browsing one day in a second-hand shop, I spotted a six-volume set of *The Secret Doctrine* (1888), her most important work. Opening one of the books, the first words I saw were, "Thus every mortal has his immortal counterpart, or rather his Archetype, in Heaven. This means that the *former* is indissolubly united to the latter in each incarnation, and for the duration of the cycles of births."

Now the first sentence is decidedly Jungian, especially the mention of "archetype," and the rest concerning reincarnation is something that Jung had come to believe to be very probable. Furthermore, it expresses perfectly my own experiences involving the Higher Self after years of undergoing the individuation process personally, so naturally my interest was much aroused. Thumbing through the rest of the volumes I came across similar sentences, all of which seemed to reveal that HPB possessed a large amount of knowledge concerning the inner mysteries of the soul. I too had been searching for the same great answer, and as fate should decree. seem to have been led to it, though for me it turned out to lie in the Western religious forms, rather than in those of the Far East.

I bought the books quite cheaply and as I read them it became obvious HPB was no mere medium, either gifted or charlatan. On the contrary, I found her highly intelligent, a true philosopher in the original meaning of the word—a "lover of wisdom," as she herself declared—possessing insight and wide breadth of vision, so that even when mistaken in her conclusions it is due more to the lack of scientific knowledge in the age in which she lived, rather than to her own basic wrong way of thinking.

(I later told writer Colin Wilson of my discovery of HPB, and soon afterwards was greatly surprised when a large heavy package arrived containing some of her works. Colin had long been an admirer of HPB's talents, though I hadn't known it, and thought he would help me along with my studies.)

The Secret Doctrine covers a vast range of subjects and sub-topics, from evolution and solar theory, to the deepest concepts of Hinduism and Buddhism; from gravity and the Life Force, to "Psychic Journeys to Other Planets." (This referred not to any journeys of her own; but to the possibility of them generally). Her mind was able to encompass them all, and she explains them in a well-reasoned and intelligent manner, though her style of writing is often difficult for the modern reader to follow, as indeed it must have been for her contemporaries. The work was written in the 1880s and a vast amount of scientific knowledge has come to light since then, yet she stands out as one of the most positive thinkers of an age that intellectually had already begun the dark descent into regarding spiritual matters not only with negative scepticism but stark denial.

The discoveries of Darwin and certain other scientists were actually welcomed by HPB, and she was well able to embrace both extremes of thinking, the religious and the scientific, within her wide breadth of vision, as though they belong naturally together (which, in fact, they do). She takes the view that, of course physical evolution is true, how else could it be done? But she also stresses the necessary spiritual counter-position for completeness. How many people of her day, or even of today, could accept such extremes quite so readily, and as the necessary counterbalanced halves of a religious philosophy? She was really a very religious person, the foundations of her beliefs being profound esoteric knowledge known to the East for thousands of years. This she called her "Wisdom Religion"—Bhodism we could say—and we now know by way of the discoveries of depth psychology that these teachings are totally valid as archetypal truths of and through the unconscious.

Brief Biography

She was born Helena Petrovna Hahn in 1831 in the Ukraine, the daughter of a colonel descended from the German nobility but now settled in Russia, and a mother whose forebears reached back to Rurik, first ruler of Russia. As a child, HPB is said to have been very deep of soul, and possessing an extremely vivid imagination would visit an old peasant living in the forest who filled her eager mind with weird and wondrous tales of the supernatural. She would then tell these, and especially stories of reincarnation, to other children, continually holding them spellbound. At the age of seventeen, being self-willed and very obstinate, she married a much older man, because, it is said, a governess taunted her that, with her temper, no man would ever have her, not even an old one. However, this seems improbable to me as it is difficult to see HPB ever doing anything she really had no wish to do in the first place.

"Old" General Nicephore Blavatsky, well over three times her age (HPB later claimed), had always found the girl delightful, so to spite the governess, HPB charmed the general into proposing to her. (Some say the general was only forty at the time. This does not tally with HPB marrying an old man to spite the governess, and even if the man were forty, which seems doubtful, that would have been somewhat old to a girl of seventeen.) The attraction to the General may have involved the projection of the "wise old man" archetype, and was perhaps other than physical, the marriage possibly not being consummated. But whatever the situation, HPB left her husband after a very short time. The probable truth is that ultimately no human individual could give her what she most craved, though she would not know what this was herself for some time. What her soul really needed was the magic and numinosity of the spirit, of the inner Self and the spiritual wisdom it brings, and she would have been unconsciously driven towards attainment of that goal, to fulfilment in the Self, as lovers of wisdom invariably are.

HPB began to travel the world, visiting various countries including England, Mexico, Canada, Egypt, and Tibet, finally becoming a medium when she returned to Russia. In 1873 she left for America, and an incident occurred as she was about to make the journey that displays the basic kindness that those who knew her well proclaimed was a main feature of her personality. A peasant woman with her children had somehow been swindled out of the passage money, and so HPB gave the woman her own first class accommodation, though she herself was then forced to travel steerage, being short of further funds. It was frequently said of HPB that she would always try and help the poor and needy.

In America, HPB met a lawyer, Colonel Henry Steel Olcott, who became her life-long friend and supporter. The friendship may or may not have been platonic, but a little later when she married again briefly, a younger man, Olcott criticized her for the deed. Some think this marriage too may have been platonic, and indeed, the relationships she had with several men may have been of the same nature, but then perhaps not. She had a young boy with her for some time for whom she obviously felt much love, and some claim it was her own son, but she herself insisted she had adopted the boy. Certainly, when he died, still a young boy, it affected her extremely deeply.

It is true that sexual abstention increases spiritual powers, as the libido, and indeed, the whole focus of existence, is switched from the physically sexual to the spiritual, the latter then becoming more developed and intensified. This may nevertheless lead to a union of the sexes, but of a higher kind, of a spiritual nature So we can at least say that HPB's mediumistic powers, and later her adeptship on the path of spiritual Enlightenment, would have been much enhanced by sexual abstinence. She always gave this advice to those who wished to follow the extremely difficult path to spiritual Enlightenment themselves.

Eventually, with Olcott, William P. Judge, and Charles Sotheran, HPB formed the Theosophical Society. She wrote her first two-volume work, *Isis Unveiled,* in which she covers more or less the same ground as in her larger later work, *The Secret Doctrine.* The earlier work is understandably less developed in certain ways, though it is nevertheless quite an achievement as a panoramic exposition of the secret wisdom of the ancients, and of the two works it is the easier to read. *Isis Unveiled* was a great success, but then the Theosophical Society decided to amalgamate with another movement in India, called the "Arya Samaj," and so HPB and her companions sailed for Bombay to join the other group.

Theosophy comes from *Theos,* meaning "god," and *Sophia,* meaning "wisdom," hence "Divine Wisdom," therefore her "Wisdom Religion," or Bodhism, as I mentioned above. As well as explaining that the aim of the Theosophical Society is to reconcile all religions, she adds that, "The key that opens one, opens them all, or it is the wrong key." She points out that certain of the figures of the Eclectic School in ancient Alexandria had also tried to bring the many wisdom systems under one canopy, including the great Valentinus, Clement, Origen, Basilides, Bardasanes, Plotinus, Porphyry, Athenagoras, and Ammonius Saccas, the latter being given the title *Theodidoktos,* "God taught." The Bible was certainly full of the hidden wisdom, HPB declared, and Jesus himself certainly wished to restore the old wisdom doctrines in a new light, so as to provide a new development of them in a new age. But all of the above-mentioned figures claimed that divine wisdom was to be gained through dreams and visions, a fact that Jung was to prove and that I came to acknowledge.

Theosophy was not a new religion, but the age-old system of wisdom teachings gained through experience. All religions and none were welcomed into Theosophy, providing they followed the basic principles of wisdom, truth, and love. The aim of Theosophy, as well as adding to knowledge, was to relieve human suffering, physical if possible, but even more importantly, moral and mental.

Things went well for a while, and Colonel Olcott visited Ceylon, where he wrote a book called *A Buddhist Catechism.* This became a roaring success, giving Olcott a high standing in his own right. There were now two authors in the group who had gained wide recognition for their Western interpretations of the Eastern Mysteries, and largely due to this, HPB found herself leader of one of the top religious groups in India. Then, after a sojourn of five years there, she decided to return to Europe for a visit. While in London she agreed to have her spiritual claims investigated by the Society for Psychical Research, which was actually to be the cause of her downfall, although the downfall seems to have been only partial.

Besides her fame as a writer on the occult, HPB was reputedly a very gifted medium. But a former housekeeper, a certain Madame Coulomb, a friend who had obviously become an enemy, claimed that many of the effects brought about in the seances were frauds. HPB was thereby discredited, though there is some possibility that Madame Coulomb, who seems to have been of dubious character herself, concocted the evidence with her husband. Inflamed, HPB denied fraud and intended to sue, but her lawyers advised against it. Most people are suspicious of mediums to begin with, without there being evidence and witnesses to fraud, which supposedly there was with HPB.

As fate decreed, HPB had not too long to live anyway, and she spent her final few years writing *The Secret Doctrine,* which reputedly gushed out of her to become a mountain of jumbled papers. After her death, her friends arranged, typed, and prepared the papers for publication, and Annie Besant, who was to become the leader of the Theosophical Society, wrote in the preface to volume 5 of the second edition:

> The papers given to me by HPB were quite unarranged, and had no obvious order. I have therefore taken each paper as a separate Section, and have arranged them as sequentially as possible. With the exception of the correction of grammatical errors and the elimination of obviously un-English idioms, the papers are as HPB left them, save as otherwise marked. (1897).

And of her effect on posterity Besant commented:

> Her pupils are well aware that few will be found in the present generation to do justice to the occult knowledge of HPB and her magnificent sweep of thought, but as she can wait to future generations for the justification of her greatness as a teacher, so can her pupils afford to wait for the justification of their trust.

Madame Blavatsky died in 1891, at the age of sixty, and it was the consensus of opinion, even including some of her enemies, that she had been a truly remarkable woman.

The Spectrum of Evolution from Matter to Spirit

We can with much justification place the works of H. P. Blavatsky above those of most philosophers of the nineteenth and twentieth centuries, for the simple reason that she discovered the deeper meaning and route to religious truth, to direct experience of the spirit, albeit mostly in Eastern forms. This utmost necessity for Western Man—to find valid meaning to religion, crippled as he was becoming under the yoke of scientific rationalism and materialism—has become even more urgent in our modern day, but HPB was one of the first to seek that deeper spiritual meaning. As said, though remaining a Buddhist—most of her terminology is Hindu/Buddhist—she had come to understand the true nature of Christ as the two combined natures of Jesus the man and the cosmic Self (the Logos), and through understanding of the deeper natures of Hinduism and Buddhism, had also realized that the same psychic/spiritual structures are the basis of all genuine religious systems of the world.

Gradually she compiled her wide studies and experiences to form her Wisdom Religion, finding she could easily accommodate both evolutionary theory and the profoundest religious doctrines within her broad view, because she could see reality from both extremes. Her contemporary, Gerald Massey, said much the same, that evolution in matter is one end of the spectrum and the workings of the spirit the other. Long before I read any of these works, I wrote that experiences of the collective unconscious had demonstrated to me that in complementation to the ascent of matter through physical evolution there has occurred the descent of spirit into matter. The higher matter evolves, the more soul and spirit can further flow into it. That is, matter reaches *up* to experience spirit/soul, which appears to be the basic plan of what we call life. In this way, God and evolution are not in conflict, and both HPB and Massey realized it fully, though, following the Eastern teachings, HPB replaced God with the very remote Parabrahman, while Massey became a Spiritualist.

HPB comments,

> . . . man was not "created" the complete being he is now, however imperfect he still remains. There was a spiritual, a psychic, an intellectual, and an animal evolution, from the highest to the lowest, as well as a physical development—from the simple homogeneous, up to the more complex and heterogeneous; though not quite on the same lines traced out for us by the modern evolutionists. This double evolution, in two contrary directions, required various ages of diverse natures and degrees of spirituality and intellectuality, to fabricate the being now known as man.
>
> —*The SecretDoctrine*

Speaking of the specialization of evolution, and in particular, of Man, she says:

> This is perfectly scientific, and we have nothing against that; for it all relates to the shell of man—his body, which, in its growth, is subject, of course, like every other once so called morphological unit, to such metamorphosis . . . The types of life are innumerable, and the progress of evolution, moreover, does not go at the same rate in every species. (ibid.)

For someone of the latter half of the nineteenth century this is a very enlightened view, but for one who for years had been enmeshed in the occult teachings and deepest processes of Hinduism and Buddhism, it is highly remarkable. But then HPB was not one-sided, in the way that materialists—even great scholars, or perhaps especially them—are.

She did not see natural selection as a "Great Power" behind nature, as many evolutionists did (and do), but only as natural occurrences that could not happen any other way because of the given circumstances. If the food source were up in the trees, for instance, those creatures that could obtain it in some way would survive, whereas those who could not would starve. Obviously a healthy person would have a far better chance of surviving in severe conditions that an ill or crippled one. So Natural selection, which quickly became corrupted to "survival of the fittest," was merely the natural outcome of certain chance situations, and was not a creative force, or "power," in itself. Natural selection is not a laid-down law, therefore, but merely the obvious outcome of the chance circumstances involved. (As a matter of fact, this is how I assessed the situation myself long before I read HPB.)

However, although all physical life may evolve upwards at varying rates, HPB considered the ape to be a special case of the degeneration of Man—not later Man, but an offshoot and degeneration of an earlier stage of Man's development. In other words, the ape was produced from a descent of an earlier type of Man. Consequently, there were no apes before first Man. (If this seems an unreasonable proposition to us now, it must be remembered that the theory of evolution was quite new in HPB's day and that anything was still possible. Up to that time, most people believed in a sudden Creation, and that the world had come into being in 4004 B.C., though we can be sure HPB had never believed this herself.) Elsewhere, she says that apes will evolve into humans again eventually, though "This will take place, of course, million of years hence. This picture of cyclic precession of all that lives and breathes now on Earth, of each species in its turn, is a true one, and needs no 'special Creation', or miraculous formation of man, beast, or plant, *ex nihilo.*" (ibid)

Another point she makes, though she is shifting her position a little, is that as Man has passed through all lower stages of evolutionary forms, " . . . there is nothing very degrading in the idea of having an Orang Outang as an ancestor of our physical form. Quite the reverse; as it would most irresistibly forward the Occult Doctrine with regard to the final evolution of everything in terrestrial nature into man." (ibid.) She seems to have come around to the usual ideas of evolution here.

Actually, the last quotation above fits in with Jung's statements that all the lower evolutionary stages are still contained within the collective levels of the human unconscious, which is, of course, human only at the highest level. Jung's individuation process begins at the psychic level of the ape, when an ape of some description may begin to appear in dreams. But as the process proceeds, symbolic animal forms down to the insect level will also be experienced, as well as forms from the higher spiritual level; again, in keeping with HPB's teachings. None of this is worthy of ridicule, and is actually quite logical and reasonable, given the time that she lived and wrote.

Of evolving life-forms, she comments:

> The Occult Doctrine . . . teaches a cyclic, never-varying Law in Nature, the latter having no personal 'special design' but acting on a uniform plan that prevails through the whole Manvantaric period and deals with the landworm as it deals with man. Neither the one nor the other has sought to come into being, hence both are under the same Evolutionary Law, and both have to progress accordingly to Karmic Law. Both have started from the same Neutral Center of Life, and both have to re-merge into it at the consummation of the Cycle. (ibid.)

She concludes: "[The Occultist] maintains that Spirit and Matter are two *facets* of the unknowable *unity,* their apparently contrasted aspects depending a) on the varying degrees of differentiation of Matter, and b) on the grades of consciousness attained by man himself." (ibid.)

She thinks of Man as a spiritual entity who comes to inhabit a shell or mold, so that there are two distinct parts of him that come from completely different directions and realities, the spiritual and the earthly. Not only does this view make more sense than any other, it is basically the view of Man historically the world over. It is also in keeping with experiences of the collective unconscious, where the initiate goes down to the depths of soul/matter, but also up to the higher spirit realm. These eternal opposites meet in Man, and in very exceptional circumstances may unify in the Sacred Marriage, the *Hieros Gamos.*

Chapter 11

Blavatsky, Jung, and the Higher Self

Madame Blavatsky becomes most interesting when she goes into the mysteries of myth and religion. Even when wrong about certain details, it is because, as said, she lacks the knowledge that was to come with discoveries made in depth psychology. Had she lived some years later, there is no doubt she would have taken hold of Jung's findings solidly, for they are precisely what she needed to adjust and complete her own ideas. She knew of the psychology theories of Eduard von Hartmann (1842–1906) and others of her day, but these were very limited conceptions of the unconscious, and it would be some years before Jung came up with the collective unconscious and its vast implications.

As it is, there are certain differences between HPB and Jung, although most of them would not have been unbridgeable. In her works, HPB covers Gnosticism, original Christianity, the Greek Mysteries, alchemy, the Kabbalah, Masonry, Sufism, Hinduism, Buddhism, the mythologies of Egypt, Babylon, Greece, Persia, Scandinavia, and many other areas, stating that it all derives from the same source and expresses the same basic truths (though as said, her terminology for the ascending spiritual structures are Hindu/Buddhist). But whereas Jung knows that the real source of all is the collective unconscious, HPB, while knowing that certain religious phenomena are experienced within the individual, involving deeper and higher planes of reality, nevertheless ascribes myths (or did when writing parts of her works) to the records of historical events in the far distant past; therefore to racial memory, etc. Even today, many people would agree with her.

She asks: "But what is myth . . . to begin with? Are we not told distinctly by ancient writers that the word means tradition? Was not the Latin term *fabula,* a fable, synonymous with something told, as having happened in prehistoric times, and not necessarily an invention?" And:

> Creuzer, the greatest of all the modern symbologists, the most learned among the masses of erudite German mythologists, must have envied the placid self-confidence of certain sceptics, when he found himself forced in a moment of desperate perplexity to admit that: "We are compelled to the theories of trolls and genii, as they were understood by the ancients; [it is a doctrine] without which it becomes absolutely impossible to explain to oneself anything with regard to the Mysteries of the Ancients, which Mysteries are undeniable." (ibid.)

In other words, we must see myths as the ancients saw them, and evaluate them accordingly. However, the ancients and subsequent cultures saw their myths as mostly spiritual happenings, if partly involving worldly events. To the ancients, myths expressed the same type of truth as Christianity does to devout Christians.

It was precisely the same symbologist, Friedrich Creuzer, whom Jung was studying when he had the first inklings that myths originate as processes of the collective unconscious. Jung states that rather than *inventing* myths, the primitive mentality *experiences* them. Neither is myth fiction, but rather consists of facts observable over and over and repeated continually.

Neither Jung nor HPB accept that myths are inventions, the difference being that, whereas Jung declares them due to processes of the unconscious/spirit, HPB assigns them to events in the far-distant past. Yet HPB almost had the answer herself, nearly coming to Jung's conclusion several times. For instance, she says that when the hero fights the dragon (one of the main mythic themes), it means he must defeat his own sensual passions, for in defeating his own instinctual appetites, the hero also overcomes the onslaught of temptations from the instinctual depths of the unconscious, symbolically the dragon. Furthermore, she knew that the phenomenon of the Higher Self occurs *within* the human individual, the Self descending from the spirit dimension to the soul of the adept, while the soul of the adept goes to meet the Self. So she understood that certain mythological material occurs *within* the human being (though not limited to the collective unconscious, rather extending beyond), but just fails to grasp that it is the key to all of it.

It will be interesting, and it may be important, to compare a few of

HPB's statements with Jung's regarding the Higher Self , as they are in the same vein here. I shall come to these in a moment, but as said earlier, the fact of the Higher Self is of uppermost importance for mankind as a whole and for every individual personally. Nothing else matters so much, for the Self completely alters the very nature of reality for us. It means nothing less than that Man is attached psychically and spiritually to an immortal being existing in higher and deeper planes of reality. So while the reductionists and materialists of the nineteenth and twentieth centuries were busy encaging man in the straightjacket of limited matter, HPB, and later Jung, each in their own way, explored the phenomenon of the Higher Self that the East had taught for thousands of years, but which the West only knew in a projected, unaware, way. (It must be said that while Jung went directly to the psychic/spiritual depths, HPB did not—not knowingly, at any rate.)

We must ask, did HPB experience the Higher Self personally? Well, she spoke of the higher Masters who were guiding her, and one in particular, whom she called Koot Hoomi, was supposedly a manifestation and humanization of one. No one seems to have seen Koot Hoomi other than HPB herself, but he wrote letters to various people, and many swore they were not in HPB's own handwriting. I personally believe that she was the kind of personality who would help the truth along a bit to make it seem more authentic and acceptable, so long as she knew it was definite truth in the first place. This should not cause us to disbelieve her claims regarding the Higher Self in any way, for this in itself is irrefutable, which means that the foundations of her Theosophy and Wisdom Religion are in themselves unshakeable.

The individuation process that produces the Higher Self was without doubt at work within her depths, and it would have been activated in her more so than in most other people. Koot Hoomi may well have been a representation of the Self, and it is quite possible for this to be projected outside. She was certainly on the religious quest that leads to the Higher Self, on the path of spiritual development and enlightenment, and many have spoken of her self-sacrifice to this end, though as far as I can tell she was consciously or fully aware of undergoing the individuation process.

She says, "To live as a conscious Entity in Eternity, the passions and senses of man must die before his body." We must overcome the world of the senses if we wish to triumph over death (when we die). "But if Apophis (the Serpent Power) conquers the Soul then it cannot escape a second death." *Isis Unveiled* (1877) Yet of the select few who have seen the "divine instructor," she says, " . . . each Adept felt the great 'Self' within himself. The Atman, the Self, the mighty Lord and Protector . . ." (ibid.)

She asks, "But who is Padmapani?" and then answers, "Each of us must recognize him for himself, when he is ready. Each of us has within himself the 'Jewel in the Lotus', call it Padmapani, Buddha, or Christ, or whatever name we give to our Divine Self." *The Secret Doctrine*.

Thus the Higher Self is a universal experience of mankind. Jung says that to the Far East it may be the Atman, Buddha, or Tao, to the Americas Mondamin or Quetzalcoatl, to the Near East Khidr, and to Kabbalism Tifereth.

HPB, speaking of the Greek term *Theophania* remarks that it " . . . does not simply mean a manifestation of God to man by actual appearance—an absurdity by the way—but the actual presence of God in man, a *divine* incarnation . . . that power that causes the Divine Self to enshrine itself in its lower self—man." A very important sentence. She further explains: "For it is not only the presence of a God, but an actual—howbeit temporary—incarnation, the blending, so to say, of the personal Deity, the Higher Self, with man—its representative or agent on Earth." (ibid.)

Long before I read these words, or any others written by HPB, I wrote an almost identical sentence, stating that the human individual is the agent of the Higher Self on Earth. It is what experience of the processes of the collective unconscious teaches us. HPB continues: "Throughout the whole mystic literature of the ancient world we detect the same idea of spiritual Esoterism, that the personal God exists within, nowhere outside, the worshipper. That personal Deity is no vain breath, or fiction, but an immortal Entity, the Initiator of the Initiates . . ." (ibid.) (We could, however, say that it exists outside, if we take it to mean behind all physical reality.)

These are not just fine words, but represent the indelible truth itself, for having been through the individuation process that produces the Higher Self myself, I can swear to their complete validity. It is, therefore, as Christ spoke, *"for behold, the kingdom of God is within you"* (Luke 17:21), though, as just said above, it is also outside in the sense that it lies behind all outer material reality.

Earlier, I quoted HPB's words, "Thus every mortal has his immortal counterpart, or rather his Archetype, in Heaven." and we can compare this with Jung's comments that the hidden immortal within the mortal man is perfectly symbolized by Christ, that Christ is at one and the same time ego and Self, part and whole, in that he is what we term a god-man, and that put in religious terms, God's incarnation is due to Self realization.

As we can see, HPB and Jung are saying exactly the same thing (and I could go on and on with similar quotes from each of them), but then, they both speak of the same phenomenon of the Higher Self. Each human being has his or her immortal counterpart in higher, wider reality, and not only can this entity be experienced through inner processes, but can actually come forth to, and incarnate in, the soul of a human being. The world's myths and religions give ample evidence of this phenomenon, and as well as the many positive examples, there are also the negative ones of Set, Satanael, Ahriman, Cain, and in more recent times, Goethe's Mephistopheles. All of these must have been experienced by initiates originally.

On the light side, the inner processes of St. Teresa of Avila, to take an example, concerned the same phenomenon, though these were highly Christian in nature, of course. (Actually, thirteenth- and fourteenth-century Europe exploded into direct experience of not only Christ but of the whole Holy Trinity, a large portion of the mystics involved being women.) The Higher Self attaches to the *values* of the initiate, and to the *traditions* of the relevant culture. Teresa was completely oriented to Christianity, and the collective unconscious of Western man has up to two thousand years of the same conditioning. It would have been useless for Teresa's visions to contain symbolism of the old gods of China, for instance, or symbols from anywhere else. (Can we imagine an Eastern sage in his spiritualizing processes having material come through from Western traditions?) The Higher Self as an independent phenomenon was unknown to Teresa, and so she simply saw Christ (as I have myself several times), but the whole set of her visions is an individuation process *par excellence*, which when put together, reads like a Gnostic myth. (It is also perfectly possible that Christ himself visited her.)

It is essential that due recognition be given to the Higher Self in some way, even if only unknowingly. Otherwise it leads to psychic dissociation, and possibly to inflation—of the ego of the individual primarily, but of society as a whole at the collective level. Inflation may be either positive or negative. Positive inflation in this sense is the belief that Man is everything; that he is the "Lord of the Universe," and that nothing is greater than Man. With negative inflation—deflation—Man is still everything, still the highest power known, but adds up to very little, or nothing at all, so that consequently the whole of Creation is worthless, including Man. Both concepts replace God and the Higher Self with Man, one seeing Man as almost a god over everything, the other seeing him as a worthless worm on a dung-heap, because nothing is worth anything.

The *fact* of the Higher Self, and of God, alters both positions to their proper status. It deflates the one in that it is recognised there *are* infinitely greater powers than Man, which Man must kneel before and even worship, and it raises the other to the realisation that Man *is* connected to and must work along with these divine powers. Man has a very important role to play in an extremely meaningful full reality, but modern Man lost belief in this, resulting in loss of soul.

Recognition is usually given to the Higher Self by means of projection on to such figures as Christ, Horus, the Buddha, Krishna, and so forth. Sometimes the Self figure is missing as such, as with Judaism and Islam, where all the worship goes to God. But even so, the myths of these religions are full of evidence of experiences of the Higher Self; they have just not been recognised as such, and in consequence have been misinterpreted and misunderstood. The Muslim Khidr, for instance, the Verdant One, is a Higher-Self figure (really the lower spirit, or Lower Self), while the Old Testament teems with obvious experiences of the Higher and Lower Self—Abraham/Melchizedek, Moses/Joshua, David/Solomon, the Son of God/Son of Man figures of Ezekiel and Daniel, and so on.

In the Far East, by contrast, nearly all recognition goes to the Buddha, the Higher Self, the Atman, Purusha, etc., and the Father figure is remote, appearing (or perhaps *not* appearing) as Brahman, the Supreme Spirit, or the even more remote Parabrahman, the Absolute. This is certainly not the same concept of God we find in other religions. But as I say, if the higher powers are not recognised in some way, then the ego takes the place of the Self, and mankind takes the place of God. We see evidence of this to a frightening degree in the modern West, where Man believes he can thrive quite well enough by all the forms of materialism. Here is one of my dreams where the unconscious expresses this

> *I see some tall skyscraper buildings that have an extremely frightening effect, making me feel ill. They remind me of Babylonian ziggurats, and there is a bad, negative religious atmosphere about them. Modern man has gone badly wrong and is heading for destruction, it all seems to say.*

What is implied by the skyscrapers and their resemblance to ziggurats is, of course, the Tower of Babel, which symbolizes Man's inflated arrogance, corruption, and matter-worship. Modern man has gone the same way as the ancients in the biblical account, which caused God to bring about their destruction. The Flood did not mean a real, physical event, but a deluge from the dark negative side of the unconscious that flooded and overwhelmed the conscious culture, causing its collapse. When Man turns from religion, which forms the link with God and the realm of spirit, he soon falls into chaos.

For centuries the tallest buildings in Christendom were the cathedrals and churches in every city, town, and village. What dominate now are the tall office blocks, cathedrals of business, erected for purely materialistic purposes, monuments to Man's greed and arrogance. All of this makes me feel ill in the dream, and understandably so, because I know what the terrible implications are.

The unconscious gives warnings of dire consequences, but also offers help. Only a few nights ago I dreamt of the Christian cross, which was gold, but instead of the crucified Christ upon it, there was a lovely boy—the divine child, though not crucified. This child, the infant Higher Self, is in ultimate aspect the Son of God, so we must surely ask, what are tower office blocks, i.e. the world of big business, compared to such holiness and meaning?

We must not worship the wealth and power of the world. Our highest values must be the spiritual and holy, for the Self is the very center of our total being, both personal and collective. All souls are contained within the cosmic Self as the Logos, and we unconsciously project our own "Christ within" upon such a divine figure, (though the Christ with the Logos actually is Son of God). With the modern world's rejection of this, we return to the same matter-worship symbolized by the biblical Tower of Babel, which came before and actually caused the Flood, the "dragon of chaos" that deluges a corrupting and degenerating culture.

Blavatsky herself recognized astutely the immense value and necessity of religion, knowing its absolute validity. Although she went mainly to the Eastern traditions, she defends all genuine religions, recognizing they are founded on similar archetypal experiences. Jung discovered that those experiences are rooted in timeless unconscious/spirit reality, but whereas HPB journeyed to the Far East for spiritual meaning, Jung remained committed to the Western forms, stating the immense importance of the further development of the traditional royal line through the Western unconscious.

Jung thus says they uproot themselves who believe they can simply go over to Eastern forms of religion, which are not rooted in our Western past, striking no chords within our innermost being. The Western spirit developed on an entirely different line to the Eastern, and so we are inextricably rooted in Christian soil.

When I first began to experience the archetypal processes myself,

Christianity had died for me and I was searching into the Eastern religions and other sources for possible spiritual answers. Yet when archetypal material started to flow through from the collective unconscious in dreams, I was greatly surprised that some of it was in Christian forms—some biblical, but some Gnostic, alchemical, Holy Grail and ancient Egyptian, yet all on the same royal line. Western religious traditions are a perfectly tenable, and indeed, necessary way to eternal truth. HPB found her own answer in the East, and had primarily been captivated by the ancient Egyptian mysteries, but then found that the Far Eastern were still living ones, which obviously suited her better. Yet, this notwithstanding, we must not forget her statement that, deep in her heart, she loved the Russian Church, even more so than Buddhism in a way. So it seems to have been the case of her head—that is, her intellect—going one way and her soul going the other, following the collective Christian forms in the unconscious, for which she had great feeling.

Jung himself valued the Eastern forms highly, but while visiting India and becoming fascinated by Hinduism and Buddhism, he had a dream about the Grail Castle and medieval Christian Europe, and took this as a sign that he must get back to the European traditions. Like Blavatsky, his conscious mind was on one track, Hinduism/Buddhism, but the unconscious was functioning on the traditional Western forms, specifically concerning medieval Christian symbolism. As Jung says, we are rooted in Christian soil.

Madame Blavatsky gives her position on Christ the Western Higher-Self figure as follows. After comparing Krishna and Apollo with Christ as the "Good Shepherd," she asks:

> Does all of this take away from the dignity of Christ as an ideal, or of Jesus as a divine man? Not at all. On the contrary, made to stand alone, glorified beyond all other "'sons of God," he can only foment evil feelings in all those many millioned nations who do not believe in the Christian system, provoking their hatred and leading to iniquitous wars and strifes. If, on the other hand, we place Him among a long series of other "sons of God" and Sons of divine Light, every man may be left to choose for himself among those many ideas, which he will choose as a God to call to his help, and worship on Earth as in Heaven. *The Secret Doctrine*

This is highly enlightened, and we can only admire her for her view, with which Jung would have concurred—though perhaps with certain reservations. For instance, it is also true that those "many-millioned nations" were just as prejudiced and often more fanatical than the Christians of her day. Furthermore, we are all connected to our traditional collective forms, far more than we realize, so that we are not always so open to choice. Nevertheless, she rightly separates Christ and Jesus the man, putting the phenomenon among a long series of other "sons of God." (Jesus is a "divine man" because Christ, the Higher Self, is within him, and he is within Christ.) Nevertheless, we must remember HPB's own statement that while the Buddha attained the sixth stage of the inner processes, Christ attained the ultimate seventh. In any case, Christ as the Logos would equal the Atman, while the Buddhi, so HPB tells us further, is rather the vehicle of the Atman that is within reach of humanity.

The Soul, Death, and the Second Death

All through her works HPB comes across as an intelligent, enlightened person, possessing a great deal of insight, although you can well imagine her as a somewhat explosive and larger than life personality. But her responsible attitude concerning the esoteric powers was displayed when the Kabbalist, Eliphas Levi, stated that the true Magus punishes those who do him evil by casting a spell over them. She commented, "This is incorrectly expressed. The true Adept of the 'Right Hand' never punishes anyone, not even his bitterest and most dangerous enemy; he simply leaves the latter to his Karma, and Karma never fails to do so, sooner or later." (1888).

Whether it is possible to punish another person with esoteric powers is not the issue here. It is rather HPB's response, which shows she was not involved with any kind of magic but with the serious religious quest of the true initiate. What she says of Karma is similar to Jung's teachings that whatever we do outside, in the world, we do also to our souls within. Thus the cheat cheats himself, the thief steals from himself, and the murderer murders his own soul.

Jung tells of a certain patient of his, a woman doctor, who so desired the husband of her best friend that she slowly poisoned the friend to death. She then married the husband, but he too died after a couple of years or so, of natural causes, apparently. The woman doctor eventually sought Jung's help, the burden of guilt weighing very heavily upon her—even animals refused to remain in her presence. She only visited Jung once, to tell the tale, to try and ease the torment in her soul a little, and he never knew what became of her after that. She may well have committed suicide, or perhaps slowly ebbed away in her darkness and misery. She had crossed the Rubicon, from whence there is no return, committing the ultimate of crimes and of sins, from which a normal person can have little or no respite. This would not trouble certain dark personalities, of course, but the woman doctor was probably a decent person basically, and such a person may escape the law, but not conscience and the effects upon the soul.

This has always intrigued and shocked me, this murder of one's own soul, because it is so devastating and does not depend upon Man's justice at all. The brutal killer, though he may walk in the midst of living people, is nevertheless one of the living dead, because his soul, or spirit, the real life, is dead. With Man and the worldly powers that govern us, justice is a hit and miss affair. So often those who should be paying for their crimes against humanity, against life itself, ride the crest of the wave, while those who deserve better suffer the injustices of existence. But that is by no means the whole picture, for we all have to leave this worldly life eventually, and what we have written upon our souls will be read out in the Great Hall of Truth and Justice in Amenta, as the ancient Egyptians expressed it, where we become whatsoever in life we forged ourselves into. We could say we begin life with a book of empty pages, and all of our future deeds, and even thoughts, fill this in. The Egyptians said that when we die, we take the book with us to the Hall of Justice in the afterlife, to be judged as to whether we deserve to continue to survive or not. Those who did not were destroyed in various ways, evil souls being gobbled up by crocodiles.

HPB, following the East, believed that the evil person may lose their soul literally during life. She calls this the "second death" and remarks, "Thus the chief and most important secret with regard to that 'second death,' in the Esoteric teaching, was and is to this day the terrible possibility of the death of the Soul, that is, its severance from the ego on Earth during a person's lifetime. This is a real death (though with a chance of resurrection) which shows no trace in a person and yet leaves him morally a living corpse." (ibid.)

In other words, it seems that through evil the severance of the soul occurs during life, and with the death of the body, is lost, it being therefore a second death. Even if the soul dies first and the body second, it is that of the soul that is accounted the second death.

"Real life," HPB says, "is in the spiritual consciousness of that life, in a conscious existence in Spirit, not Matter; and real death is the limited perception of life, the impossibility of sensing conscious or even individual existence outside of form, or at least, of some form of Matter." (ibid.)

But there are actually two kinds of loss of soul. She explains: "Thus we find two kinds of soulless beings on Earth: those who have lost their Higher Ego in the present incarnation, and those who are born soulless, having severed from their Spiritual Soul in the preceding birth." (ibid.) These people have cunning developed to an enormous degree, she adds, and we would never suspect them of being soulless. Jung may have agreed with at least part of this, as he states a number of times in his works that Man has always been threatened with loss of soul from the very earliest times, and consequently was always very afraid of it. He also says there are old souls and new souls, and that the latter are light and frivolous and therefore drawn to the superficial things of life.

Chapter 12

The Dragon-Fight an Inner Process

The main symbol of the collective unconscious is probably the sea, "the Waters." Spirit is symbolized as coming from the skies and space, with dry land, which is in between the sea and the skies, representing the world of consciousness, which in a sense is in between the realms of spirit and soul. As Jung says, because unplumbed depths lie hidden beneath its reflecting surface, the sea is the perfect symbol of the collective unconscious. And Blavatsky speaks of, "The shoreless ocean of universal truth, love, and wisdom, reflecting its radiance on Earth." (*Key to Theosophy,* 1889.)

HPB says the ancients knew the sea as the "Abyss of Learning" and the "Sea of Knowledge," for as we now know, the unconscious was where true knowledge and wisdom, the Gnosis of the ancients, are to be found. But because it is also the realm of the feminine depths, in both light *and* dark aspects, it is designated "Great Mother Chaos." She also states, "Water is, in another sense, the feminine principle, Venus Aphrodite in the personified Sea, and the Mother of the God of Love, the Generatrix of all the Gods, as much as the Christian Virgin Mary is Mare the Sea, the Mother of the Western God of Love, Mercy and Charity . the Celestial Virgin of the Alchemists, and even the 'Waters of Grace' of the Modern Baptists." And, " . . . the 'Waters' is another name for the 'Great Deep,' the Primordial Waters of Space, or Chaos, and also . . . Akasha, the Celestial Virgin-Mother of the visible Universe. Furthermore, the 'Waters of the Flood' are also called the *'Great Dragon'*, or Ophis Ophiomorphis." (1888).

However, HPB is somewhat mistaken when she says that the dragon was never evil to the ancients; though it depends, perhaps, on what we would term "evil." The crocodile—the dragon to the Egyptians—is highly dangerous and would devour us if given the opportunity, but we would not call it evil. On the other hand, the dragon may be greedy for blood and death and so may be deemed evil in this respect. Like everything else in the unconscious, it has dual aspects.

Of the quest for the Self and the necessary fight with the dragon, HPB says that the latter was sometimes called the "Dragon of Wisdom," and the hero dragon-slayers were known as "sons of the Dragon" because they would gain the dragon's wisdom after the slaying. But while this is true in a sense, I have to say that it is mainly because the hero is able to defeat the dragon that he is wise. He is able to choose higher spirituality rather than falling to the baser instincts, which the dragon represents. In other words, it is not the dragon that is really wise, that possesses wisdom, but the heroic choice of the hero; the defeat of Satan, *"that old serpent,"* by Jesus in his temptation, for instance. The serpent, close kin to the dragon, is wise, of course, *"Be ye therefore wise as serpents"* (Matt. 10:16), but this is because it, and the dragon, guard the great treasure, which involves higher wisdom. Only by slaying the serpent-dragon can the treasure be won, and as the eternal unconscious functions on the system of compensation and complementation, it is the descent into the dragon depths that invokes the appearance of higher spirit.

Blavatsky realizes the real meaning of the myth of the dragon-fight when she says:

> Furthermore, the "War in Heaven" is shown, in one of its significations, to have referred to those terrible struggles in store for the Candidate for Adeptship—struggles between himself and his . . . personified human passions, when the enlightened *Inner Man* had to either slay them or fail. In the former case he became the Dragon-Slayer, as having happily overcome all the temptations, and a "son of the Serpent" and Serpent himself, having cast off his old skin and being born in a *new* body, becoming the Son of Wisdom and Immortality in Eternity. (ibid.)

Here she has it. The dragon-fight is not a fantasy; neither does it symbolize happenings in outer reality, or refer to an historical event. It is an inner struggle within the human individual against the instinctual passions. Although these are personalized and affect us personally, they are nevertheless part of the collective soul, which the dragon symbolizes. The rain falls on everyone and is collective, but if a man puts up an umbrella, he has defeated the rain as it affects him personally. The defeat of the dragon is the same sort of thing, the personal defeat of a collective phenomenon. All over the world in myths, heroes slay dragons—Marduk, Horus, Bel, Quetzalcoatl, Vishnu, Sigurd, Thor; the list is long, and these are only the "winners." How many "losers" have there been? Some of those quoted are gods, of course, but the original dragon-fight always involved ego-consciousness as hero.

In actual fact, even the "winners" seem to lose in the end, as Moses fails to enter the Promised Land (though he is part one of a two-part process and would have to fade at the end of part 1 for Joshua to continue part 2). Yet the hero, despite the apparent defeat, may nevertheless install a period of high culture that may last hundreds or even thousands of years. Sometimes the hero is defeated by wild boars or pigs, these being the creatures of the Mother-dragon symbolically, or of the evil Self. The pig was associated with Set in Egypt, and sometimes with Dionysus in Greece and Crete, representing greed for the flesh that destroys spirituality. I always believed that at least Jesus and the Buddha held out, although Jesus was crucified before the rot had time to set in (which is not to say it *would* have done so, of course). The pig and boar represent great danger for the hero. HPB supplies a piece of information that reveals that even the Buddha was to fall to the instinctual forces of the dragon, though she apparently fails to realize the full significance of her words.

She states:

> In the profane history of Gautama Buddha he dies at the good old age of eighty, and passes off from life to death peacefully with all the serenity of a great saint, . . . Not so in the Esoteric and true interpretation which reveals the real sense of the profane and allegorical statement that makes Gautama, the Buddha, die very unpoetically from the effects of too much pork, prepared for him by Tsonda. How one who preached that the killing of animals was the greatest sin, and who was a perfect vegetarian, could die from eating pork, is a question that is never asked by our Orientalists. (ibid.)

So it seems the Buddha too went the way of all flesh, in *this* life, and it fits in too perfectly with the symbolism of other mythic defeats for it to be untrue. When the processes of the unconscious on the path to enlightenment are fresh, the battle, though the hardest of all, may be won by the initiate. But as the years roll by and even the greatest of spiritual truths become everyday ones to the conquering hero, what then? He may be celibate for years on his quest, but perhaps then a distant memory of sex may rekindle sleeping desires (or perhaps they are still wide awake) and the dragon, never totally slain, may find renewed powers of temptation. Then opportunities may inundate from all directions to the once-hero and be laid at his feet. Can a saint be a saint forever? Some saints may have had low sex drives, but then there is no real battle with the instinctual powers. Yet again, the drives may be ones of power rather than of sex, as in the case of Jesus the man. There the Devil to be defeated was the "Will to Power," the "power devil" that was afflicting the whole Roman Empire. As for sexuality, a figure from above in a dream informed me that to defeat it entirely is such an achievement that the person who does so becomes godlike.

As we have seen, with alchemy the dragon represents the *prima materia* and must be slain—or the dragon creates itself and destroys itself. Jung comments that this idea is fundamental to alchemy, seen anciently when the matriarchal world of Tiamat with her dragon attributes is replaced by the patriarchal world of the Father, when Tiamat is slain by Marduk.

This is what I meant when I said that although the dragon-fight is a personal one for the hero, it may have immense consequences for collective Man. Marduk changes a matriarchal society to a patriarchal, and Christ ultimately Christianizes the whole Roman Empire, for the Savior-hero brings and institutes higher culture. Across the world we find myths where a Savior figure causes a blossoming of higher culture.

But then the dragon is not the only content to come from the sea. (The dragon, by the way, also resides in caves and forests and all dark places that represent the unconscious.) The magical fish, the Ichthys, is also "drawn from the deep" and while the Ichthys symbolized Christ, the symbol was actually thousands of years old by then. HPB comments:

> And it is the Jews—whose forefathers made the word *Dag* signify both "Fish" and "Messiah" during the forced development of their rabbinical language—who are the first to deny this Christian claim. And what of the further facts that Brahmans connect their 'Messiah', the eternal Avatara Vishnu, with a Fish and the Deluge, and that the Babylonians also make a Fish and a Messiah of their Dag-On, the Man-Fish and Prophet. (1888).

In what better way could the Higher Self as Savior coming through the collective unconscious be symbolized than as a magical fish rising up from the depths of the sea? I have experienced the fish myself in dream visions several times, and it alters our whole conception of reality. This and other visions bring about inner transformation, and all of the old myths and religions become alive and true as eternal facts of the unconscious, which involve Man. The fish was well-known in alchemy, and one of the main aims of alchemy was the defeat of the dragon.

HPB says that the alchemists had undergone similar processes as those experienced by the ancient initiates into the Mysteries. This knowledge has been lost by science today, she says, and by the modern world in general. Thus she warns: "Science will be as far (in the future) from the solution of its difficulties as it is now, unless it comes to some compromise with Occultism, and even with alchemy—a supposition that will be regarded as an impertinence, but remains, nevertheless, a fact." (ibid.) By Occultism HPB always means the widest possible interpretations of the word, and Jung certainly agreed that a science that denies the symbolic truths of myths, religions, and the Mysteries is dangerously one-sided. Jung, of course, was to show the world the symbolic relevance of alchemy, as Blavatsky had forecast.

HPB comments that with the alchemists, as with initiates into the religious Mysteries, there was the need for sexual abstinence. She says that in the production of

> the Elixir of Life and the Philosophers' Stone . . . the spiritual help of the woman was needed by the male alchemist. But woe to the alchemist who should take this in the dead-letter sense of physical union. Such sacrilege would become Black Magic and be followed by certain failure. The true alchemist of old took aged women to help him, carefully avoiding young ones; and if any of them happened to be married they treated their wives for months before and during their operations as sisters. (ibid.)

Jung comments that gold was the *material* goal of alchemy, which they saw as the elixir of life, but that the higher goal was *spiritual* rebirth out of the darkness of matter, the pneumatic out of the flesh's corruption.

Jung contrasts alchemy with the celibacy of the priesthood, and says that both projected union of the sexes into another medium; the one into matter, the other into spirit, outside rather than within. However, there were alchemists who knew that inner union was taking place, just as there have been priests who experienced inner mystical union. Neither would have gone very far to begin with had they enjoyed a vigorous sex life. HPB insists several times that initiates must become celibate to have any chance of success at the higher levels of the spiritualizing processes, and this is in keeping with the teachings of the profounder religious systems the world over. This is why the many modern books that claim a physical relationship between Jesus and Mary Magdalene are greatly in error. Mary represents the anima in the unconscious, personal and collective, and so the union with Jesus was an inner one, leading to the *Hieros Gamos*. For certain Gnostics and medieval mystics, and so too for the Templar leaders, Mary Magdalene represented Sophia, Wisdom—or she was the first stage of the feminine element while the Virgin Mary was the second.

This reduction of spirituality to physical sexuality is actually very Freudian, but then the modern world has been brainwashed to an amazing degree by materialistic interpretation, and it is now usual practice to reduce genuine spiritual phenomena to mundane, physical occurrences. Our way of looking at reality has been warped, and this has meant the reduction of life to the level of gross matter, which symbolically is the realm of the dragon. Consequently, man is ruled by the darkness, not by the true light, which would raise him. We see this fall from the spirit exemplified in the degenerate pop and celebrity culture of today. Even the festivals at Glastonbury express the Earth spirit, even the dragon depths, rather than the holiness of higher spirituality. Its connections with the Holy Grail merits Glastonbury a holier appreciation than it receives at the moment. Jung said that modern life lies on top of layers and layers of trash, and he said this decades ago. I recently browsed through a Sunday newspaper and became deeply depressed to yet again have it brought home what trash, often dark and negative, we are now sinking in. Captured in the embrace of the dark side of Mercurius, as Jung put it, or Wotan let loose, as his wife Emma expressed it.

Of scientists and their materialism HPB says: "For all their wonderful discoveries will go for nothing and remain forever headless bodies, unless they lift the veil of Matter and strain their eyes to see beyond. Now that they have studied Nature in the length, breadth, and thickness of her physical frame, it is time to remove the skeleton to the second plane, and search within the unknown depths for the living and real entity, for its SUB-stance—the noumenon of evanescent Matter." (1888).

This is wholly Jung, particularly the last sentence, which could have been written by him. HPB almost puts SUB-conscious, instead of "SUB-stance," the subconscious being the limiting Freudian term for the Jungian unconscious. Even so, she speaks of the "search within the unknown depths" for the noumenon of Matter, and where else could that be sought but in and through the unconscious? Just a little more information or realisation would have told HPB that the unconscious/spirit is the true source of all of the myths and religious Mysteries, rather than records of the past. She already knew that the alchemists underwent similar inner processes in their opus as initiates of the religions, and *their* experiences could not be consigned solely to the distant past.

Root Races, Trinitarian Thinking, and the Spiritual Path

I recently watched a television series about the Third Reich and the occult, which stated that the early founders of Nazism based much of its philosophy and doctrines on the teachings of HPB. It was an excellent series, very informative, except for the impression it gave that HPB was an early Nazi, or racist, which is quite wrong. Indeed, nothing could be further from the truth, if her profuse writings are correctly understood.

She believed, basing her theories on certain ancient Hindu and Buddhist texts, that there are seven "Root Races" of mankind, and each of these has sub-races, with various offshoots. Lemuria, or Mu, was the third Root Race, Atlantis was the fourth, and we today are the fifth. The sixth race, which follows ours, will be a mixture of the white, black, and yellow races. This, she says, has already begun to happen in America (this was in the 1880s), and the crossing of races always has occurred and always will occur. This is so counter to Nazi racial doctrines that it is amazing they did not condemn her as a dangerous degenerate. But the Nazis did exactly the same with Jung, claiming that his discoveries supported their doctrines, at least, at first. Both HPB and Jung taught precisely the opposite, the dignity and meaning of the human soul and its relationship to the higher, spiritual Self.

In fact, considering that all nineteenth-century Westerners felt superior to other races of mankind, even those who had benign feelings towards other races, HPB stands out as one who sees mankind as a whole, from beginning to end, all forms originally coming from the same root and eventually merging into the same species. As she says, "the root of mankind is *one*." She saves her criticisms and condemnations for scientists and materialists (for denying spirit reality and religious truth) on the one hand, and for certain of the clergy on the other, (for bigotry and narrow-mindedness, and for failing to realize that the basis of all religions is the same hidden wisdom, her "Wisdom Religion"). As for her belief in Atlantis, this was a very plausible possibility in her day, and still is to many people today, a number of bestselling books having been based on Plato's ancient tale.

This is not the place to go into this controversial subject, so suffice it to say that there may have been an ancient civilization that fits in with Atlantis, or a number of them worldwide, but the myth of a corrupt society that loses contact with the higher gods and consequently sinks beneath the waters of chaos is archetypal, and alludes to the sinking of the culture under the deluge of negative forces from the unconscious. The sea flooding the land quite simply means the lower negative depths of the collective unconscious—the dragon of chaos—deluging collective consciousness, and the civilization, which arose in the first place because of the light of higher consciousness, now succumbing to the dark, negative forces. HPB's ideas concerning Atlantis and Root Races are based mostly on a mixture of Western and esoteric Hindu and Buddhist texts, the latter alluding largely to symbolical contents of the inner realm, rather than to any definite events of the outer world. There are flood myths from all over the world, all with the same basic motifs: loss of the higher spirit, sinking back into the hylic depths, and the upsurging of the formerly suppressed depths of chaos.

(The Atlantis myth, which Plato says the Egyptian priests of Sais related to Solon, probably concerns, at least in part, the last of the Egyptian seven great Cycles of Time involving the heavens, its demise brought about by a deluge. This was said to have occurred in 9600 B.C., precisely the date of the supposed sinking of Atlantis. See *An Order Outside Time* for an exploration of the subject.)

As said above, HPB, following the Eastern path, did not believe in God the Father in the traditional view of the West, though she went along with the Hindu doctrine of a very remote, eternal Supreme Spirit, the Absolute, or Parabrahman, the Causeless Cause. The Atman or Higher Self is part of the Absolute, but only the Self is experienced as Being or Entity, because it, or he, manifests through the unconscious. When Moses experienced God and the burning bush on Mount Horeb, therefore, HPB believed it was not actually God who spoke, but rather the Higher Self. However, an angel is present in the burning bush and this can only be the Higher Self, though God speaks. *"And the angel of the Lord appeared to him in a flame of fire out of the midst of a bush . . . God called unto him out of the midst of the bush, and said, Moses, Moses. And he said, Here am I."* (Exodus 3:2–4.) A human individual is part of the Self, and the Self is part of God; thus the Self functions as mediator from Man to God. There is no other reason for the angel to be there in the burning bush except as mediator, the Self, between Moses and God.

This is one of the reasons why Jung believed that we must keep to our Western traditions. The experience of the Western line is of Father and Son, and the Son is the angel with Moses; Christ and the Son of Man with Jesus; the Son of Man with Daniel, Ezekiel, and Enoch; and so on. Earlier in Egypt, Ra manifested as Horus, Ptah as Iu-em-hetep, Atum as Tum, and Amun as Khonsu. All are examples of the Son or Self at ultimate level come forth and manifested out of God.

For myself, I can only say that through processes of the unconscious I personally came to experience the Higher Self, and then through this figure, God. I experienced them separately and also together, with the Self at the right hand of God—all in dreams, of course. So I obviously followed the Egyptian-Judaic-Christian traditions, and it is a mystery why the Indian experience is of the Higher Self alone, and not together with God. However, this may be answered in the following way.

The connecting power between God and the Son is the Holy Spirit, and Jung says that in alchemy the Holy Spirit sometimes appears as "ligament of body and soul," similar to its role of "spiration," the binding Father and Son in religion.

The binding power of the Holy Spirit, together with God and Son, forms the Holy Trinity, which again is experienced through the collective unconscious, and which may also, in a sense, be experienced as an outer reality. But where is the comparable Indian experience of the Trinity? HPB answers by saying that there are certain manifestations of it, commenting, "The notion of a triple hypostasis in One Unknown Divine Essence is as old as speech and thought. Hiranyagarbha, Hari and Shankara—the Creator, the Preserver, and the Destroyer—are the three manifested attributes of it, appearing and disappearing with Kosmos; the visible Triangle, so to speak, on its plane of ever-invisible Circle. This is the primeval root-thought of thinking Humanity; the Pythagorean Triangle emanating from the ever-concealed Monad, or the Central Point." (1888).

Another version is the Trimurti, comprising Brahma the Creator, Vishnu the Preserver, and Shiva the Destroyer and Regenerator. So the "triple hypostasis in One Unknown" equals the Three-in-One Deity that is God to the West.

Jung says that the Holy Spirit is the motivating force behind Trinitarian thinking (sometimes called "thinking in the magic circle of the Trinity") and that this allows expression of complicated happenings through the psyche. But this is not limited to the personal psyche, for as Jung explains, these happenings actually involve needs way beyond mere personal ones.

In other words, Trinitarian thinking is unconsciously motivated to give expression to something far greater than mere consciousness, something that is "divine and holy," as Jung himself says. Jung then goes on with an inspired paragraph the gist of which is that man must integrate these holy contents that come through the unconscious or he becomes mere ego, a split-off fragment, and then the "divine contents" appear in their dangerous and negative forms. He finishes by saying that, not receiving any reply to the problem he set mankind, the Holy Spirit was thereby compelled to fade.

HPB and Jung both point out that the Jewish concept of spirit is feminine *(Ruach-El)*, and that it was also the case with certain early Christians and Gnostics, thus giving a Trinity of Father, Mother, and Son. In the Chaldean Kabbalah, according to HPB, spirit was sexless, as is the case with the Indian Narayana, the Mover on the Waters. (Kneph, a form of the Holy Spirit in Egypt, moved over the waters.) If the sacred doctrines of the Egyptians, the Gnostics, the Kabbalists, the alchemists, and so on, are difficult for us to grasp (easier when we have the key, the symbolism of the unconscious processes) the Indian are even more so. Nevertheless, HPB seems to have possessed an excellent understanding of them. That her initiation into the religious Mysteries was totally sincere, and that she knew she was on a genuine spiritual path, is shown not only by the great learning and knowledge HPB acquired, but also by the serious warnings she gives to other initiates of the responsibilities and dangers of the great task. Some people are unaware of the moral implications of their deeds, she says:

> But the case of each who is pledged to the Higher Self is quite another matter. You cannot invoke this Divine Witness with impunity, and once you have put yourselves under its tutelage, you have asked the Radiant Light to shine and search all the dark corners of your being; consciously you have invoked the Divine Justice of Karma to take note of your motive, to scrutinise your actions, and to enter up all in your account. The Nip is irrevocable as that of the infant taking birth. Never again can you force yourselves back into the matrix of Avidya [without knowledge] and irresponsibility. Though you flee to the utmost parts of the Earth, and hide yourselves from the sight of men, or seek oblivion in the tumult of the social whirl, that Light will always find you out and lighten your every thought, word and deed. (1888).

There she has it again. Once you have awakened and activated the slumbering depths of the unconscious, you are into the most serious business possible. All of your actions, and indeed, your every thought, are weighed and balanced and have effect. Woe betide any who have dark motives in the processes, for one day they may well meet their own Mephistopheles as the dark counterpart in the unconscious; in other words, as their Higher Self. Once on that spiritual path herself, HPB obviously knew that it takes all of the virtues to ensure positive results, but even then it is a very risky affair.

Although HPB was clearly influenced by the unconscious to some large degree, it appears to have been mostly unconsciously so, and she was therefore only partially aware of what was happening. I can see no indication that she literally went down to the psychic depths herself on her quest, *consciously.* Nevertheless, I could be mistaken here, and if Koot Hoomi is a manifestation of the Higher Self, HPB may have projected the inner manifestations of the figure outwardly. This is quite possible and it occurs with certain people more often than is realized. However, as she paid no attention to dreams and rejected the theories of von Hartmann on the unconscious, she probably had no conscious knowledge of the phenomenon taking place within her psychic depths, which would have been an extremely powerful individuation process. So although the unconscious obviously affected her a great deal, she was apparently only aware of the surface effects.

Wisdom Religion, a Way to the Self

Ancient wisdom was a reality because it was based upon processes involving the unconscious/spirit, which unite Man with the eternal powers. Modern Man has largely lost that link, even in the projected form of the Church and its dogma. But such souls as Jung and Madame Blavatsky are too rich and deep to accept a reduced, materialistic view of reality, and so each sought the true meaning that lies behind the façade of matter, of conscious life.

It is only with the discoveries of Jung that we now realize the ancient wisdom was factual, being based, as said, upon archetypal processes of the collective unconscious. But HPB had studied Hinduism/Buddhism and the wisdom of the ancients, and was able to declare herself:

"The whole of the ancient and mystical literature is symbolical. The *Books of Hermes,* the *Zohar,* the *Ya-Yakav,* the Egyptian Book of the Dead, the Vedas, and the Upanishads, and the Bible, are as full of symbolism as are the Nabathean revelations of the Chaldaic Qu-tamy." (1888).

It is imperative that modern Man fully appreciate the way of thinking that produced these philosophies, doctrines, mythologies, and religions, because it is precisely what he needs to restore real meaning and psychic balance to his existence. The truths of spirit, soul, and Self are *real* truths that lie behind physical reality, and these must come through and be accepted by Man. A man is not a god, but he should be aware he is *connected to* one. HPB gathered these truths together to form her Wisdom Religion, a magnificent attempt to assemble Man's esoteric experience of the divine Self as expressed in much of the world's mythology, while also encompassing ideas on the then-new theories of evolution and natural selection.

Can there be anything more important? Man, the human individual, is connected to—is the agent of—an immortal being of higher reality that is, in turn, part of God. This phenomenon can literally be experienced in life, and that he exemplifies wisdom, truth, nobleness, and love (and also, it must be said, the opposites to these in his totality). What, then, is the worth of wealth, power, and worldly success, compared to the truths of the spirit? What are they worth when we know we return to the immortal Self at death, taking with us to the Self the sum total of our worldly life to add light or darkness, as the case may be? Of what real worth are the "ten thousand things" the Hindu mystics warn us enchain us to the heaviness of matter? If we can take wisdom, truth, and love to the Higher Self, and decency and warmth of heart, then with this growth of our souls, the Higher Self is added to and greatly enriched.

Surprisingly, along with others in her day HPB could not believe that myths contain any sort of divine revelation. (At least, she did not at the time she wrote this in *The Secret Doctrine*.) In fact, it would have been considered absurd in the nineteenth century to ascribe revelatory meaning to myths in any way, as it would generally today. Yet ultimately, that is precisely what myths are, symbolic revelations of the unconscious, including especially, revelations of the divine. To HPB and others of her day, they expressed meaningful behavior patterns of the past, which were not divine revelations in themselves. But it must be realized that conscious life is the child, while the great unconscious/spirit is the parent. Conscious life is limited and temporary, while the unconscious widens out to infinity and eternity.

When archetypal contents, sometimes of a divine nature, filter through and are experienced by consciousness, usually in dreams, and these are then taken to form myths, how else could it be designated but as divine revelation? (The phenomena can certainly appear as types of outer visions.) HPB was adamant that the Higher Self is an inner experience of the initiate, and she points out that this, in one form or another, is expressed in myths and religions all over the world—as I quoted above, she says all the sacred texts are full of symbolism. Therefore, she should have understood that myths and religions actually do express divine revelation. She as good as says it, but just fails to grasp it. But then, Jung's discovery of spirit reality through the unconscious was still some years hence.

HPB was accused by certain figures, who again completely failed to understand her, of dabbling in magic. This is absurd; her purpose was much higher. Colin Wilson writes that when he was a young man, he considered magic "no more than a crude attempt at science," though he has long since altered that opinion. Jung similarly stated that magic is a crude attempt at religion, a lower form, and usually an aberration of it. Those who seek and receive "magical" powers do so from the lower soul or Earth Spirit side of the collective unconscious, rather than from the higher spirit side. But as the wish to possess such magical powers derives from selfish, negative motives, the results themselves can only be seen by the normal person to be negative—and certainly dangerous. The wise investigator of the unconscious realm says, "I refuse such powers. I seek only wisdom, truth, and meaning," and then he or she may continue further with relative safety.

At some point HPB took the higher path to spiritual Enlightenment, along which the initiate must fight to overcome all selfish motives and impulses of the senses—to become filled with the love of wisdom and truth, etc.—if the highest levels of the processes are to be attained. Indeed, the appearance of a magician in the processes, unless he comes as a bitter enemy, is a dangerous if not catastrophic sign. The appearance of a friendly magician signifies compatibility, hence being motivated by the same negative impulses as the magician. It would necessitate radically altering the conscious position immediately, or seriously risk becoming possessed by, and the tool of, the lower forces. Aleister Crowley, the early twentieth century Satanist, for example, did not so much possess magical powers, *they* possessed *him*, he becoming their "thing."

It may be as true that the unconscious forces likewise possess the initiate on the Right Hand Path, but these are the higher ones of light, wisdom, and love. Such a person may then be possessed by divine spirit, being filled with it, but it is a positive state or condition. (Pharaoh Akhenaten is a good example.) Because the initiate has unselfish motives and wishes only to serve God and humanity, he is then able to take the spirit, the Light, to his fellow human beings. The magician, by contrast, desiring to serve only himself—and indeed, to have others serve him—brings only darkness to the world. HPB realized this, as her writings testify, and she frequently warns that once the higher path is taken, every thought is known, weighed, and registered by the higher power within. This is the real business, and if the Royal Road is followed to its ultimate destination, then the day of reckoning will have arrived. The Higher Self will appear in the unconscious as either a Savior or a Set – that is, in positive or negative form. It depends which side the initiate develops on the quest.

HPB travelled to the East, to Egypt, India, and Tibet, to try to discover the true source of the secret wisdom. Perhaps it was necessary at that time to literally search the East, as little was known in the West of the inner mysteries and their true source. But these outer journeys are no longer necessary (and never really were), for we now know that the true source of all esoteric wisdom—and magic powers, if you like—is the unconscious, or the other reality of spirit and soul through the unconscious. It is therefore possible to travel to the secret place of hidden wisdom while sitting in an armchair by the fire at home, or asleep in one's bed. Furthermore, if the processes go far enough, symbolic material will be experienced similar to those upon which the (once) religion of the initiate's culture is based. (However, this will be found to have both light and dark aspects, and much other countermatching material will be experienced.)

It is extremely difficult to get people in the West to understand that Christianity itself, like all genuine religions, is based upon the most "magical" esoteric mysteries possible. Religions evolve, however, as everything else, like a skyscraper constructed from one storey to the next, and Christianity is one of the highest evolved. HPB knew this, and it is perhaps significant that she does not mention the Holy Grail, and the quest for it, in the whole of her vast work, *The Secret Doctrine*. The hero's search for the Grail involves some of the best examples of the initiate's quest for the Higher Self on the path to Spiritual Enlightenment that have been seen since Christ and the Gnostics. But HPB chose the Eastern forms, which themselves are extremely highly developed, and though she knew the validity of the Western forms, they could not have been alive for her, at least consciously. HPB mentions dreams only briefly, so apparently the unconscious processes were occurring within her and motivating her unknowingly, though she almost came to realize it at times herself. The individuation process would certainly have been at work in her, which explains her "inexplicable" love for the Russian Church. Its rich symbolism would have spoken to her through the unconscious.

She could have done invaluable work on behalf of Western religion directly had she returned to it, bringing her gained knowledge to the further understanding of Christianity. As it was, the West was not going to fall over itself *en masse* to follow the Eastern doctrines; it is Christianity itself that was and is in urgent need of further development.

The collective unconscious speaks its own language, which is almost always according to the traditions of the culture of the initiate, though this covers a wider area than is generally realized. Ultimately, God desires to come through to the world of matter, and does so by way of an incarnation. This occurs in the soul of a human individual through the unconscious, and can only be achieved by an initiate undergoing processes successfully. This is the development and ultimately the incarnation of the Higher Self that both HPB and Jung insist upon, and which I know myself to be *fact*. This is the possibility mankind has evolved into. As matter/soul ascends through evolution, spirit is able to descend, thus making possible the Incarnation and Sacred Marriage.

The hidden wisdom at work behind religion has been little understood in the West, but by going to the East and gaining its wisdom, HPB was able to comprehend its validity. Those who followed her applied the gained wisdom to Christianity. Annie Besant, who became leader of the Theosophical movement herself after HPB's death, wrote a number of works, such as *Esoteric Christianity; or the Lesser Mysteries*, (1918), in which she demonstrated the true meaning of Christ as the Higher Self, and how this is the inner truth of us all. When Besant speaks of the Trinity needing to be united with the "feminine fourth" to form the quaternity, this is pure Jung. HPB's biographer, William Kingsland, wrote *The Esoteric Basis of Christianity* as early as 1895, and this too endeavours to show, as the title suggests, the inner fact of Christ as the Higher Self.

Besant had been married to a clergyman but finally could no longer suffer literal Christianity—nor her husband either, apparently. Divorcing him, she became an atheist and socialist, helping the poor and campaigning for rights for the lower working class. But she eventually met Blavatsky, being so impressed by Wisdom Religion that she became a Theosophist and a follower of Blavatsky. This led her to Buddhism, but though becoming and remaining a Buddhist all her life, she nevertheless wrote her works on the truth and relevance of the symbolic figure of Christ.

The Theosophists, through esoteric Wisdom Religion, possessed at least part of the answer to the imperative spiritual development of the West at the very time when Freud and many other materialists were destroying its religious heritage. HPB and her followers were pioneers of a new and deeper understanding of the mysteries worldwide, which though necessitating understanding of the profound Eastern forms, has its real source in the unconscious itself, where Jung made his major discoveries.

Jung's discoveries in the unconscious went further, but the Theosophists did important pioneer work towards it, making them perhaps the most important religious group of the last few centuries. What let the Theosophists down, however, was literal interpretations of such legends as Atlantis and Lemuria (the continent with a high civilization that supposedly sank before Atlantis), which there is no doubt are purely mythical, although true in a symbolical way. Orthodox Christians were criticised for taking the Bible stories literally, yet HPB and the Theosophists did the same with the Atlantis and other myths.

However, when HPB spoke against the Church, it was against the arrogance, hypocrisy, and narrowness of the Church in her day, which said that Christianity alone could be right; all other religions were heathenish at best, and some even devilish. HPB knew, however, that the Christ had descended into the man Jesus and that his immediate followers were worthy of praise—she particularly admired St. Paul, the great adept and visionary of the mysteries of Christ and the spirit.

It is now well over a hundred years since the death of Madame Blavatsky and it is time she came into her own, to be recognized as an important figure who should have, but did not, but who yet may still, help us forward to further and deeper understanding. As said previously, we cannot now accept some of her ideas because of our modern knowledge of the physical universe, but others contain real and genuine wisdom, for which she obviously had great love. HPB and Nietzsche possessed diametrically opposed philosophies and values, inhabiting completely different realities, the one extending out to the eternity of spirit, the other extremely limited to a matter-only universe. She was right and he was wrong.

Chapter 13

Friedrich Nietzsche, Herald of the Antichrist

> God is dead. God remains dead. And we have killed him.
>
> —Friedrich Nietzsche

Journey to Nihilism

Friedrich Nietzsche's life and philosophy are the counter-position, as it were, to everything I say in my books concerning the royal line of the spirit that has run from the beginnings of ancient Egypt. He denied the otherworldly reality of spirit/soul, denied God, denied the possibility of Christ and therefore of the Higher Self, all of which means he ultimately denied any deeper meaning to human existence. Yet he was truly prophetic in saying that the future man would be an Antichrist, for that is the way things are working out in the modern world (though there has now arisen a countermovement instigated and motivated by the spirit through the unconscious).

The "main experience" of Nietzsche's life is in some ways similar to my own, both of us becoming isolated from the world to some degree, destined to pursue similar goals, driven by the need to find an answer to the nihilistic view of reality, to the great existential problem of Man lost and alone in the middle of meaningless eternity. Nietzsche eventually came up with a message for mankind, but while Nietzsche's may seem positive in its vitalism and joy of the Earth, it is nevertheless negative from the view of overall truth, which must include the spirit to attain completeness. But there are no "roots in eternity" for mankind with Nietzsche, which ultimately destroys hope and meaning. Furthermore, while Nietzsche's philosophy was formed on lines of outer conjecture (though tremendous forces were unknowingly at work within his depths through the unconscious), my own message springs from full conscious awareness of *direct experience* of the archetypal processes of unconscious/spirit reality.

Nietzsche was largely overlooked in his lifetime but was to gain ever-increasing popularity in the twentieth century, with factions ranging from the Nazis to Women's Lib movements, and including certain types of dissociated intellectuals, all to a degree seeing in Nietzsche just what they wanted to see. Many say he really meant this, or really meant that, but in the final analysis we must take him at his own word, or we fail to do him justice (though that may not necessarily favor him), and we are left with our own ideas, rather than his. Yet I too can only say that as far as I can determine, this is what Nietzsche is about, this is what he means. Elements in Nietzsche are widely contradictory, but while truth itself may sometimes seem to be so, contradictory aspects find a kind of harmony in the totality of fuller truth. This involves unification of body, soul, and spirit, Nietzsche completely denying the existence of the latter two.

Certain scholars consider Nietzsche a genius, even some that for the most part disagree with his philosophy. But a genius has to be ultimately right in what he says or accomplishes, whereas Nietzsche was ultimately wrong; and not only was he wrong, he was *very* wrong.

Born at Rocken, Prussian Saxony in 1844, the son of a Lutheran minister who came from generations of Lutherans, Nietzsche as a boy and youth was intensely religious, being called "the little pastor" at school. He intended to devote his life to God and Christianity, but then in his late teens it all fell to pieces when it suddenly struck him like a dark and profound revelation that the cherished faith of his forefathers was all folly and naive illusion, a load of nonsense. This realization brought him no measure of satisfaction, but to the contrary caused him to fall into a deep, nihilistic depression that was to last for some years. Nietzsche probably possessed a religious soul (of sorts), and Jung comments that he was extremely over-sensitive and full of emotion, so we can see why, when the axe fell and all of his cherished beliefs and ideals crumbled to dust, it was such a devastating blow. The upshot was that he abandoned his religious studies. Turning to philosophy and philology, he became a brilliant young scholar and then professor of philology at Basle University. This was not to last, however, for Nietzsche was forced to retire when still relatively young due to poor health, having to live for the rest of his life on the small pension he received.

At the age of thirty-two, Nietzsche began to produce books that are among the most skeptical ever written, in which he demolishes all of the moral and religious ideals of mankind, declaring them to be merely functional, provisional, and expedient, thereby reducing everything to physical causes. He wrote at this time that so-called living creatures are only a form of the dead, which in religious terms the "soulless" are, and that the truths of life are actually "irrefutable errors." Then, in perhaps his most well-known statement of all, he finally declared, "Is there any up or down left? Are we not straying as if through an infinite nothing? Do we not feel the breath of empty space? Has it not become colder? Is more and more night not coming on all of the time? Must not lanterns be lit in the morning? Do we not hear anything yet of the noise of the gravediggers who are burying God? Do we not smell anything yet of God's decomposition?—Gods too decompose. God is dead. God remains dead. And we have killed him." (*The Gay Science,* 1882).

For Nietzsche, God was dead and would never again be reborn, not as an eternal, moral God of spirit, and this to the highly sensitive young philosopher was a soul-shattering event, which indeed, it should be and is for the whole of mankind. To a finely tuned philosopher, poet, artist, or indeed, any person possessing a religious soul, reality in this way may become a terrible black abyss from which there seems no escape, only death. I know this only too well from my own lost and painful years. I too felt that God and all of the higher truths, the spiritual values, were slipping away, so that I was left with nothing of worth or quality. Reality itself was nothing, only stark meaningless matter. I can confirm that it causes a terrible inner—and outer—darkness, and in my own case, too, it lasted for years.

Yet against all this, I never quite felt that God was dead, not quite—reason and instinct telling me at times that my negative view, though seemingly valid enough, must be wrong. At the same time, something from within, mightier though very vague, something separate from my conscious reasoning, opposed the negative assessment. But it was a very uncertain state in which I was wavering between nonbelief and a very shaky hope. Nevertheless, for some time the universe remained cold and threateningly silent, and Christianity itself, Western man's path to God for up to two thousand years, had died for me, as it had for Nietzsche.

After some years undergoing my inner dream processes, when I had developed the Higher Self to some extent, I had a dream one night (one of many thousands over the years). Here is the dream.

> *God is in the clouds above me and is very angry with mankind, particularly with Western civilization. I am very much afraid of God's wrath, but then I see a rainbow, which gives me some hope. God actually speaks*

> *of his anger, but I was so amazed by it all that when I awoke, I completely forgot what God's words were. (In the years that followed, God was to appear very occasionally in my dreams, sometimes with the Son at his right-hand side.)*

This demonstrates that Nietzsche, and indeed, the general scientific-rationalism that possessed Western man in modern times, were and are wrong in their denial of the existence of God, and further, that those are wrong who admit to only some kind of vague, abstract idea of God that cannot be seen in religious terms. As said, it was only one of thousands of dreams I was to have containing archetypal/religious material which demonstrated that the religious/spiritual view of reality is the only true and valid one ultimately.

I have no doubts whatsoever that it was actually God himself speaking to me from the clouds, and that is how it has been symbolized from the earliest times. God took "human" shape in the dream, but not very clearly or specifically so, and it seemed to be just the top half of God, coming through from spirit reality. Clouds and their movement are signs of God's movement, His approach to mankind, though God in my vision is angry because we have rejected Him, worshipping all the forms of matter, from science and technology to big business and sex satiation.

The human species was developed especially out of the rest of nature to be nearer the spirit so that God can communicate with the material side of reality. As Jung pointed out, it is God's desire to incarnate into the world. Orfeo Angelucci in his visionary experiences in America in the early 1950s was informed that man was developed on earth to live human life on behalf of God (or the gods), but if man then denies the existence of God and spirit reality, man has malfunctioned and is not fulfilling the purpose for which he was created. We must understand that we are always watched by the "Watchers" and by God, as the ancients well knew. ("The Watchers" was one of the terms in the ancient world for powers, often sevenfold, that seem to watch mankind from above. Cultures all over the world have tales of these.)

However, in the dream I see a rainbow, the meaning of which I was unaware of at the time. I later discovered that God tells Noah that if ever the covenant with Him is broken, He will use the sign of the rainbow to remind Himself and mankind of the covenant. I also came across Jung's words in which he more or less says the same, that God instituted the rainbow as a sign of the covenant between Him and mankind to keep it fresh in the memory. The rainbow would then appear in the future to remind Him and mankind of the contract in the event that God was provoked to send thunder clouds, floods, and lightning. Such a terrible deluge would not be a physical one that takes place as an outer, meteorological event, but one from the collective unconscious that causes civilizations to collapse.

If I speak of this vision of God in something of a matter-of-fact way here, it is because I am so used to it now, after all these years undergoing the inner processes. God is as real and natural to me now as anything in the material world (eternally permanent, of course). Christ said, *"No man cometh unto the Father but by me,"* and he is speaking as the Higher Self, or Logos. I personally have now developed the Self to the degree that he is the intermediary (or mediator) to God, as he always was historically.

Thus the dream; but it can never be anywhere near adequately expressed what the "death of God" means for both the individual and society collectively. For the individual it means psychic and spiritual dissociation from the whole, the effects of which, though not always felt fully in consciousness, nevertheless causes conflict in the unconscious, in the total psyche. As Jung stresses, atheism causes a profound disturbance in the Higher Self. This is the age-old loss of soul, and when enough individuals feel the same way, the whole culture is thereby affected. If the condition persists and dominates for too long, it may even lead to the death of the culture.

A child separated from its parents, feeling completely lost and alone, obviously needs to be integrated into a warm and secure home again with its parents, where there is love and some degree of contentment. This is what the adult needs with God and the spirit. It is the deeper meaning and inner harmony that acceptance of God provides, one second of time in tune with the whole of eternity. This is why Jung says the authority of the parents over the child should be replaced by the authority of God over the adult. The parable of the Prodigal Son told by Jesus exemplifies the psychic separation from God the Father and then the return to Him, when all becomes well again. This is not going back to a childish attitude or position, but forward to a truly adult one. We need to shrink our ego from the arrogant to the humble, realizing we are but a second of the eternity of time that is God. It was Nietzsche's tragedy that he suffered the loss of God but did not, and could not, return to Him. Nietzsche had a religious soul (otherwise the "Death of God" would not have affected him so tremendously) and so had to come up with an answer, a substitute for the loss of God. Eventually, of course, he did indeed come up with an answer, but being the wrong answer, it was to destroy him.

For some years Nietzsche carried on in his negative state, producing depressingly nihilistic works, and although we can see his bludgeoning down of traditional religious values and moral truths, his smashing of the old tablets, as being partly a reaction against the narrowness of his Lutheran upbringing, there were yet certain other strong influences that worked on him to form his so negative worldview. Nineteenth-century materialism was a very powerful force that was eventually to change Man's whole way of thinking in the twentieth century, and scientists, philosophers, and other scholars in Nietzsche's day were becoming largely atheistic and materialistic in outlook. Decades earlier, Shelley had declared "the necessity of atheism." Freud was a product of the same negative materialism, and indeed, any serious scholar, thinker, artist, etc., who took the religious view of reality in the twentieth century stands out as a sore thumb, as an oddity almost. But it would be a mistake to think of Nietzsche as an ordinary materialist, for there were other forces at work in him, very deep ones, which we will come to in a moment.

Will to Power the Solution to Nihilism

Nietzsche was much too sensitive a personality to suffer so nihilistic a state indefinitely. An answer had to be found that would soothe the pain-filled vacuum in which he found himself, in order to change his gloom-filled worldview into a more positive one. He was asking soul-searching questions, such as how can we bear to suffer existence once we realize what life really is, and so forth. Possessing a basically religious soul, which his negative dissociated consciousness could neither enrich nor satisfy—as Jung was to say, Nietzsche was no atheist, but his God was dead—he could not continue to exist in such a state indefinitely. Only if we understand this can we understand fully what happened to Nietzsche. What does a basically religious man do when he finds himself in a meaningless, Godless reality that he finds painfully intolerable, where there is only Man and the Earth? Well, one solution is to make a god of Man and worship the Earth, which is precisely what Nietzsche was to do. However, that is still only part of the story. As said above, deeper forces were at work in him that were not of conscious reality, which he did not so much *know* as *feel*.

He had come to feel a strong, irritated reaction to Western philosophers, whom, he felt, retreated into their intellects to bandy about their purely intellectual ideas, and his rejection extended even to Schopenhauer, an atheistic, pessimistic Romantic who based everything on "the will," and whose teachings had earlier impressed Nietzsche. Being full of emotion himself Nietzsche despised piled-up intellectual knowledge, the German variety in particular. So-called great scholars were walking encyclopedias full of cold facts with no real life in them. My own reaction to Western philosophy was similar to this when I was searching for my answer, my way out of the abyss. I wanted wisdom that was concerned with feeling, experience, and *being*, not just over-intellectualized mental exercises and intricate arguments (no matter how brilliantly structured) that could seemingly be made to prove anything and everything. Nietzsche said that he had no understanding of purely intellectual problems and that he put his whole heart and soul into everything that he wrote, which is why his writings are brimming full with passionate expression. But the answer that was to develop within his inner being led him to go whole hog, preaching surrender to the world of feeling to an extreme, almost uncontrollable degree, in contradiction to the fact that the answer he found, ultimately the "Ubermensch," or Superman, was supposed to be the higher and fuller evolved state of Man.

Nietzsche's answer, while promulgating Life, energy, vitality, and the Will to Power, at the same time scathingly denounced Christianity and its morality as sickly and weak, fit only for slaves and the herd, and perhaps not even for them. Initially, he postulated that common humanity exists to serve the uncommon man of genius, the true leader, but later he developed the idea of the latter, the special man, into the Superman, the be-all and end-all of Life, of existence. So the ideal society would consist of those who labor and those who lead, the latter including those free to live their lives in the pursuit of philosophy and art. It would be wrong to implant the ideals of the high culture, the elite, into the low culture, as it would create too much dissatisfaction and unrest; the ignorant masses are better staying ignorant. Nietzsche praised the pre-democratic age of Greece, the age of tyrants, and hated in particular the "false" democratic ideals and spiritual values of Socrates and Plato that came afterwards. Virtue, justice, and morality were degenerate, Nietzsche now believed, but the unspiritual Superman would cure all of this.

Nietzsche never explains exactly what he means by the Superman, but it is obvious when we consider the facts. Having, as he says, "murdered God," and asking if the deed is not too great for ordinary men, he asks, "Must not we ourselves become gods simply to seem worthy of it?" (*The Gay Science* 1882). This one sentence sums up Nietzsche's whole philosophy of the Superman, and his own eventual collapse into insanity. Man, or the individual conscious man of genius, must become a god.

As there is no High God or spirit, Man will take the place of God as ruler of the universe. This is hubris on a grand scale and dangerous enough, but Nietzsche was to unconsciously undergo the hero's individuation process in which the Higher Self may come forth. Possessing the nature of a god, if unrecognized as such and instead identified with the human personality, it may shatter mere mortal consciousness. This is what happened with Nietzsche. He had no higher framework of the spirit in which to place the Self as a separate divine entity, as something greater and independent, and he consequently identified it with what human consciousness may become. Furthermore, as he taught the rejection of morality and compassion in order to serve the Will to Power, he could then only develop and bring forth to his own unconscious the dark, heavy side of the Self, so that the catastrophe was doubly inevitable.

But let us not go too far too quickly. Let us try and sort out Nietzsche gradually to build up the case. Certain incidents in Nietzsche's young life reveal clues that show how he was eventually to reach his answer. I can do no better than to quote Colin Wilson's *The Outsider* (1956) on a couple of them, the writer realizing that far more was taking place in Nietzsche than mere intellectual philosophizing. Nietzsche was an "outsider" personality, and while certain people may come to *understand* the great spiritual problem of an age (though the majority usually remain oblivious to it), the outsider figure may be forced to *live the problem out.* It may shatter him because the problem is collective, involving forces beyond the personal level, or it may make of him a great personality, and the two conditions are at one and the same time very far apart and very close together.

The great religious/cultural problem (it has also been called the existential problem) pulls the outsider to pieces because he feels it so intensely personally, so that it becomes imperative that he find a new way to put everything together again in a position that is whole and unassailable. Only then can he rest content to any measure. Because it is also a collective problem, if he should find that new way and accomplish his task, it becomes the answer not only for himself but for the whole culture. Such a figure then becomes the culture hero, a Moses, Christ, Buddha, etc., actually because he has brought forth and developed the Self, the epitome of the unification of opposites into wholeness. But if the outsider fails to find the right answer he either remains shattered, or comes up with an inferior substitute answer that may seem appropriate for a time, but which in the end fails to work and may even be highly destructive. Adolf Hitler fits into the latter category to a degree, as does Nietzsche. But I must add that the answer discovered—experienced—by the outsider must in the end be a truly religious one. Further, it may seem a new way, but it is really the age-old one merely wearing a new coat; Horus, Moses, David, Daniel, Christ, are really repetitions of the same phenomenon on the same royal line.

But to quote from *The Outsider* on Nietzsche's early experiences.

> The first is related in a letter of 1865 to his friend Von Gersdorrf:
>
> "Yesterday an oppressive storm hung over the sky, and I hurried to a neighbouring hill called Leutch . . . At the top I found a hut, where a man was killing two kids while his son watched him. The storm broke with a tremendous crash, discharging thunder and hail, and I had an indescribable sense of well being and zest . . . *Lightning and tempest are different worlds, free powers, without morality.* Pure Will, without the confusion of intellect—how happy, how free."

Wilson then comments:

> The experience seems simple enough, and yet its effect on his way of thinking was far reaching. Normally the sight of blood would seem unpleasant to him; now the exhilaration of the storm combined somehow with the smell of blood, the flash of the knife, the fascinated child looking on; and the result was the sudden intuition of pure will, free from troubles and perplexities of intellect: an intuition which was release from the thought riddled nature which had so far been his chief trouble.

The author then tells of another incident that Nietzsche related to his sister Elizabeth when she asked about the origin of his Will to Power philosophy. This came to him, he said, when he was tending the sick as an orderly during the Franco-Prussian War. He had been up to his eyes in blood and gangrened limbs but was now walking alone just outside Strasbourg, totally worn out. Troops then approached, which turned out to be his old regiment, and as they passed by he was filled with the conviction that "the strongest and highest will to life does not lie in the puny struggle to exist, but in the Will to War, the Will to Power." Wilson remarks: "In a sense they were 'mystical experiences'. Normally Nietzsche was imprisoned in the 'thought-riddled nature'. These experiences point to an exaltation of Life." (We could, of course, call war the exaltation of killing and death, particular as Nietzsche views the situation.)

Wilson also quotes from Nietzsche's first book, *The Birth of Tragedy,* in which the philosopher says that "blissful emotion" and Dionysian feeling have analogy with drunkenness. Nietzsche mentions the great joy of nature when Spring arrives, awakening the Dionysian feeling that may lead to complete and joyful forgetfulness. Primitive Man often experiences this great force that springs from the depths of nature, and indeed, lives it, as does all nature. Wilson again: "Nietzsche *knew* this emotion; it became the acid test by which he judged everything."

We can see in all of this the joy of life, the joy of Spring, the joy of nature, and so forth, plus the overcoming of a negative mental state changed to a—seemingly—positive one. But right away we also detect dangers, ones that we see in Nietzsche throughout his works, sometimes blatantly expressed. In the first quotation above, where the kids are killed, Nietzsche says significantly ". . . . *free powers, without morality.* Pure Will . . . " and over and again he would pose the same question; "Why does the way to happiness have to be morality?"His answer clearly is that it does not. He even became interested in criminals because their lack of any moral considerations gives them a certain energy and power.

Other people have more of a built-in regulator, emphasized by social orientation, which creates a conflict between consciousness and the unconscious shadow that is in us all, which naturally curtails the energy available to consciousness somewhat. Consciousness wishes to go one way while the shadow wishes to go its own selfish way, which in turn consciousness opposes with its moral values. (This is not to say that morality springs from consciousness alone, for the unconscious is also highly moral itself in part.) It is the inner upsurge of power when morality is dispensed with that so interested Nietzsche, and we can well see his point.

Just for a moment, imagine doing something dark and forbidden without any moral or guilt considerations and you will feel a sudden upsurge of energy. This is due to the effects of the shadow let loose that we normally keep in check. However, the normal person soon begins to feel guilt if such an impulse is given way to, and will wish to set things right, whereas the natural criminal continues to follow the shadow impulse unperturbed by conscience.

The idea of dispensing with morality to increase the desired inner power is one of the basic tenets of Nietzsche's philosophy. Morality and virtue are weakening, according to him, and not only did he reject Christianity for this and for its spirituality, but Plato and Socrates for their teachings of morality and of the immortal soul of Man. The idealistic young man who had wanted to be a pastor now rejected all teachings of morality and Man's immortal soul as weaknesses, and had stepped over to the counter-position, even proclaiming himself to be an antichrist.

Yet having said that, as far as we can tell Nietzsche never actually abandoned himself to his own philosophy of rejecting the moral. Although he wrote a work called *Beyond Good and Evil,* he apparently never arrived at that place himself. It would be impossible in any case, for such a position does not exist; we can only fail to arrive at the *distinction between* good and evil, never go beyond it. Only a person with an undeveloped brain, or one drugged to the state of oblivion, or morally insane, could be unaware of the eternal opposites of right and wrong, morality and immorality, good and evil. This would not be going beyond them, but, as I say, failing to arrive at the distinction. The truth is although Nietzsche was an "outsider" who took the hero's path to the point of self-sacrifice, his philosophy is not only selfish but unintelligent. We could even say that his was self-sacrifice to selfishness. We can reject moral considerations and act selfishly, but it is not going beyond to a position where moral considerations do not apply.

Nietzsche's reaction to the "blood sacrifice" of the kids on the mountain with the accompanying lightning is also a little disturbing, because blood and death are bound up with Will and elation, with the lightning surely intimating the power of the gods. We are reminded of Abraham on the mountain about to sacrifice his son Isaac, when a lamb is substituted at the last moment. Isaac too would have looked on and witnessed the animal sacrifice, as did the boy with Nietzsche. (Actually, the Isaac sacrifice story is symbolical, the "sacrifice of the Lamb," as the great-minded early Christian Origen pointed out, but it fits the situation with Nietzsche in the same way.) The sacrifice is tantamount to an archaic Pagan version for Nietzsche, a sacrifice to raw power and ecstasy, and he *feels* it, is elated by it. Is it only coincidence that not long afterwards the youth of Germany would make animal sacrifice to the old Pagan gods with the same emotional fervor that had elated Nietzsche, and which was, in fact, to overwhelm the whole German nation? And what can we make of "the Will to war, the Will to power" that elated Nietzsche in the Franco-Prussian War other than that this was soon to be played out on the largest scale imaginable in two World Wars. (There is also the point that since ancient Egypt, the lamb/sheep has been the symbol of a Savior, with the kid/goat representing the opposite power. In Egypt, those who followed the divine Son Horus were the sheep, while those who followed his evil twin Set were the goats. This happens again with Christ in the Book of Revelation.)

The elation of the Will to Power and craving for joy for Nietzsche blots out any consideration that war is horrendous, and certainly not elevating. In fact, just a short while before his experience of elation at the passing troops, Nietzsche had been steeped in the bloody gore and unendurable suffering caused by war. Why was he not sick to his soul at the pure horror of it all, instead of feeling the elated "Will to War, the Will to Power"? He later stated that war is a remedy for a nation that is weak with doleful peace, and that Europe had become so enfeebled by peace that it needed not merely wars, but the most horrendous wars. It was soon to get them, of course. We must seriously ask, was there something wrong with Nietzsche mentally? Where is the extreme sensitivity and basically religious soul that Jung speaks of, or had Nietzsche completely stifled that part of his nature? Was he now entirely dissociated from it? Elsewhere, Jung calls Nietzsche a psychopath.

Dionysus the Dismembered God

Part of Nietzsche's philosophy is the surrender to almost unconscious emotion, untroubled by any considerations of morality and pity. Running through his works are references to Dionysus, the old Greek/Thracian god of frenzy and ecstasy. Dionysus represented for Nietzsche much that he himself was promulgating, and he wrote *Dionysus Against Christ,* so who is this god who, at least for Nietzsche, must be in contradistinction to Christianity and its values?

Though in some versions of his mythos he is a Savior born of a virgin, whose advent occurred on December 25th, Dionysus was associated more with nature and the Earth than with the higher spirit. He was perhaps a Phrygian god originally, being son of the Earth goddess, Zemelo, which makes of him a type of Osiris and Mercurius, the latter "the age-old son of the Mother." Zemelo, however, became the mortal virgin Semele with the Greeks (the Old Mother of mythology as World Soul is also the young virgin, and everything else in between, including the terrible dragon). Dionysus was the Ram and Lamb in some places, though more often the Bull. In rites for Dionysus, a bull would be killed and distributed to the worshippers to be eaten, while its blood was drunk.

As a god of fertility and nature, Dionysus was elsewhere associated with the goat, giving him devilish connotations for the early Christians (again bringing in the association of the kid with Nietzsche). This tells us that he had opposing aspects, seen with twins Osiris and Set, light and dark sides of the Earth Spirit in Egypt. Furthermore, Dionysus was said to have been nurtured on sow's milk, linking him directly with the sinister side of the gods. Pigs in mythology, like the goat, are always connected with the dark powers, highly dangerous to the god of light; the evil Set, for example, who murders Osiris, sometimes takes the form of a pig, and as such blinds Horus in one eye. Dionysus is therefore the Earth Spirit who contains the positive and negative aspects of Osiris and Set within his nature.

Dionysus became mad for a time—he also made certain mortals insane—but was helped and guided by Cybele, goddess of the land, whose cult was associated with frenzy and violence. This suggests Dionysus' unification with the World Soul in negative aspect. The companions of Dionysus were the satyrs, called "demons of the countryside," depicted as part human with horns at the head, and goat-like below, like little devils. They were associated with unbridled and even uncontrollable sexuality. The cult of Dionysus in this form was widespread in Crete, and was associated with Zeus there, who was far more like Dionysus than the Greek Zeus. So it was Dionysus as god of unconstrained ecstasy and earthiness that Nietzsche had become deeply interested in, which is not surprising considering his denial of the higher God of spirit.

Seen from the view of depth psychology, Dionysus is a type of the Earth Spirit of the lower unconscious, or the Lower Self, which, as we have seen, is dual natured. Dionysus is contrasted above by the aesthetic god Apollo, and we may say that while Apollo roughly speaking equals Horus and Christ as divine Sons above, Dionysus corresponds to the lower twin gods Osiris/Set in the Egyptian mythos, and Mercurius in Roman mythology and alchemy. In other words, the Earth Spirit in Egypt is differentiated into two gods, Osiris and Set, light and dark, while Dionysus and Mercurius are not so divided into two beings, though they are dual natured, light and dark. As Osiris is dismembered and resurrected, so too Dionysus in the form of Zagreus is torn to pieces and devoured by the Titans and then reconstituted, though Dionysus never seems as good as Osiris or as bad as Set. Nevertheless, Nietzsche would unknowingly become possessed through the unconscious by this lower Earth Spirit, though to confuse the issue more, really in the Germanic form of Wotan.

A version of Dionysus corresponds to Christ in certain ways. The great Greek mystic Pythagoras (fifth century B.C.) studied the resurrection mysteries in Egypt for over twenty-two years, also visiting India and other lands. Taking Osiris as his model, he made Dionysus into a version of him, hence the Osiris/Dionysus spoken of by certain scholars today. In this aspect, Dionysus was a type of Christ, though in lower aspect—Christ actually has higher spirit and lower spirit aspects. (Even the Catholic Church takes Osiris to be a prefiguration of Christ.) Obviously, Nietzsche was not interested in this version of Dionysus, and it is doubtful he even knew of it. The followers of Pythagoras were peaceful and nonviolent, teaching the immortal soul of Man, sharing everything in communal equality, like certain original Christian sects. Decidedly not what Nietzsche had in mind; the idea of the equality of people was abhorrent to him. The Will to Power could not be further removed from the teachings of Pythagoras and his form of Dionysus, or of course, from Christ and the original Christians.

Nietzsche would come to preach his own "Gospel of the Earth," one of self-overcoming, yea-saying, and life affirmation, but with consciousness inflated to the state of the Superman, yet involving near-unconscious Dionysian ecstasy. The Superman is actually a projection of the Self from the unconscious, but blindly seen as further evolved mortal man, a tremendous limitation of the Self, making him a sort of super but soulless human entity, motivated by the Will to Power. This is an enormous inflation of consciousness and devaluation of the Self.

This was to be Nietzsche's answer to the tortuous, unbearable state of nihilism. In a sense, Nietzsche was to achieve his goal, the aggrandizement of consciousness, but actually in a Dionysian state of unconscious possession, which meant that he was to lose not only full conscious awareness, but eventually his sanity. Often in a state of megalomaniacal grandeur he would sign his name Dionysus, or Zagreus (or the "king of Naples," etc.) and would refer to himself as "the Crucified." The Titans tore Dionysus, as Zagreus, into fragments, and this has the same basic symbolic meaning as crucifixion. Considering that he was to violently oppose everything Christian and aesthetic, and to glorify the Earth and the uncompassionate Will to Power, we can well understand Nietzsche becoming a follower of the earthy Dionysus, though as Jung says, it was really as Wotan that the lower spirit got into him. Jung further points out that Nietzsche's denying Christ while yet experiencing the phenomenon inwardly and unconsciously meant that he himself was fated to become "the Crucified."

As I relate more fully later, Dionysus had certain women followers who would work into a state of frenzy and tear to pieces animals—and, some say, any unfortunate men—that happened to cross their path. While Wotan had the effect of "insane fury" on certain followers, Dionysus had the same on these women, which Jung significantly calls "female storm troopers."

Anyone who goes down to the collective unconscious to experience its depths will discover that it divides into two opposing realms, which apparently extend to infinity and eternity. One is of the higher spirit, and the other of the lower spirit that animates matter, all over the universe presumably. The feminine side of the lower spirit is the *anima mundi,* or feminineWorld Soul, with the masculine side the spirit Mercurius; sometimes Mercurius is the "age-old son" of the mother. The alchemists termed the spirit of the unconscious Mercurius, after the Roman god, and because he was dual natured, symbolizing the opposites, he was said to be "good with the good, and evil with the evil," which gives us the twins Osiris/Set, and the dual-natured Dionysus. We develop and bring forth out of the unconscious whatever our conscious values and motives are. Consequently, the alchemists stated that all of the Christian virtues must be adhered to in the work to ensure that the good light side prevailed. One of Nietzsche's major errors, therefore, is that he rejected those Christian virtues, so that the good god of light could not develop within his depths.

Wotan the Wild Huntsman

The early Christians equated Mercurius (the Roman god) with the Devil, as they did Dionysus, and indeed, some of the symbols of Mercurius, the raven, the toad, etc., are also symbols of the Devil. But the Germanic peoples would sometimes identify Wotan, their god of wind, storms, war, and magic, with Mercurius. As the god of frenzy who "inspired" the berserkers, Wotan is very similar to Dionysus. Both are really the spirit of the lower unconscious, or of the Earth, as is Mercurius. However, while Dionysus and Mercurius in highest aspect parallel Christ to a degree, Wotan never does. It was this that led Jung to insist that if we read the works of Nietzsche with even a little comprehension, we are left in no doubt that though Nietzsche writes of Dionysus, it was actually the spirit of Wotan that so deeply affected him, and, eventually, the whole German people.

At the age of fifteen, Nietzsche had a nightmare that would prove amazingly prophetic, and this explains his whole enigma. He was wandering about in a wood in the dream, when suddenly he heard a "bloodcurdling shriek" from an asylum nearby. He then came face to face with a huntsman, whose countenance was "wild and uncanny," and Nietzsche discussed with him whether he should go to the town of Eisleben, the "town of Luther," or to Teutschenthal, the "Valley of the Germans." The huntsman then blew a tremendously shrill blast on his whistle causing Nietzsche to faint, to then immediately wake up in his bed. The rest of Nietzsche's life was to show he had not chosen the "town of Luther," (the Christian path), but rather the opposite, Pagan path, the "Valley of the Germans" associated with pre-Christian forces. Many years after the dream, Nietzsche was to make his Zarathustra/Superman a sort of hunter storm-god: "And like a wind I shall come to blow among them," and, "smitten by thee, cruel huntsman, Thou unknown—God!" (*Thus Spoke Zarathustra* see *Symbols of Transformation,* p. 290.) In a poem, "Mistral Song," Nietzsche would write "Raging storm-wind, how I love thee," the storm-god being Wotan (see Jung's essay *Wotan*).

Wotan, storm-wind and god of war, (similar in some respects to the Scandinavian god Odin, though there are also wide differences), was the Wild Huntsman in German mythology, and it is obviously his representation that Nietzsche saw as the "wild and uncanny" huntsman in his dream. Wotan would ride across the night sky like a hurricane, leading the Wild Hunt composed of dead warriors, leaving a trail of fire in their wake. But Wotan was not only the god of war, he was also the god of inspiration, magic, and cruel sacrifice, and on the same night that the unstoppable Wild Hunt thundered across the night sky, witches would ride out to employ their evil magic. In the old book, *The Norsemen,* (c. 1900) H. A. Guerber expresses it excellently:

> [Wotan] was most generally known as The Wild Huntsman, and when people heard the rush and roar of the wind they cried aloud in superstitious fear, fancying they heard and saw him ride past with his train, all mounted on snorting steeds, and accompanied by baying hounds. And the passing of the Wild Hunt, known as Woden's Hunt, the Raging Host, Gabriel's Hounds, or Asgardreia, was also considered a presage of such misfortune as pestilence or war . . . Even after the introduction of Christianity the Northern folk still dreaded the on-coming storm, declaring that it was the Wild Hunt sweeping across the sky.

Wotan was a god of the Underworld (the lower unconscious), and he was said to have received his powers of dark wisdom and magic from Erda (or Jord), goddess of the primitive Earth and daughter of Night, though at the price of blindness in one eye (just as Dionysus received his powers from Cybele, goddess of the Earth). Later as Odin, he received the wisdom at the Well of Mimir, or Fountain of Wisdom, which, referring to a well, fountain, pool, lake, etc., means again the soul depths of the collective unconscious. Mimir, whose name is said to mean "he who thinks" (though I would say that it is connected with water, "Mir," "Mer," etc., i.e., the unconscious), was the keeper of wisdom, and is to some degree a Jethro figure, the "wise old man" archetype who teaches Moses the secret wisdom of the unconscious at the well of Midian. Mimir has seven sons as Jethro has seven daughters.

The losing of one eye means that though visionary gifts may be gained, part of the personality is nevertheless taken by the unconscious. Samson, by being totally blinded, loses all his powers to the dark forces. There is the type of priest-magician who loses consciousness in his visions and who therefore is taken over completely by the unconscious during them The other type of "mouthpiece" of the unconscious, who has visions due to his higher and wider state of consciousness, not only sees clearly with both eyes, but further and more clearly than other people. He sees things others do not. He is a true "seer" and is sometimes said to have "snake's eyes," for the snake represents true wisdom. This figure loses nothing to the unconscious, but gains much.

A shaman who loses consciousness belongs to the first type, while Moses, Jesus, etc., who attain higher and wider consciousness, belong to the second. Both types have visions, but the difference is obvious, and the type of unconscious state of ecstasy that interests Nietzsche is clearly the lower, unconscious kind. This is understandable, as he has rejected the higher spirit reality that Moses, Christ, and other clear-sighted "seers" experience. Nietzsche was fated to lose his sanity, the clear sight of consciousness, to the overwhelming forces of the unconscious. The initiate may lose one eye temporarily, but then may resume the fight to ultimately win. Horus is blinded in one eye by Set, but nevertheless survives to eventually slay his evil adversary.

The name Wotan probably comes from the old German *wut,* which means "extreme excitement," "fury" and "frenzy." Odin means "furious rage," and the modern German word, *wuten,* means "furious battle." In contrast to Wotan, Tiwaz was the higher Germanic god of the sky, though still a god of war. (All the Germanic/Scandinavian gods were warlike, much more so than the Greek or Egyptian gods.) The Anglo-Saxons derived Tuesday from their form of Tiwaz, *Tiw,* and Wednesday similarly from Woden, a variation of Wotan. We could say that Tiwaz represents the sky and the higher spirit, like the Sun-gods Apollo and Horus, while Wotan belongs to the Earth and the Underworld. Odin as the father-god is more like Zeus or Ra in this aspect than Wotan. Zeus resided on Mount Olympus with the other Olympian gods, while Dionysus belonged to the spirit of the Earth and the Underworld, like Wotan. Dionysus, though occasionally included among the Olympians, never really belonged on Olympus with them. Dionysus and Wotan both receive their powers from a goddess of the Earth, while Odin receives his from the "wise old man," Mimir, the Jethro type. This is perhaps significant, for as I say, Wotan and Odin are different and even opposing forces in certain ways.

The higher counterpart to Dionysus in the Greek mythos is the sky-god Apollo, just as the counterpart to Wotan is the sky-god Tiwaz. So we can clearly see close similarity between Wotan and Dionysus as lower Earth gods. It seems pretty certain that Tiwaz and Wotan represent the higher and lower aspects of the Self, though perhaps in inferior form than, say, Horus and Osiris, and perhaps even Apollo and Dionysus. It is also interesting to note that the ancient Hittites had a god of light called Tiwat, they and some of the original Germanic tribes certainly sharing a common origin. Indeed, the Hittites were the Hatti, or Khatti, and one group of the Germanic tribes were the Chatti, or Khatti. So Tiwaz is apparently of the same origin as Tiwat.

All of the above indicates quite strongly that while Nietzsche continually speaks of Dionysus, it is the Germanic counterpart of Dionysus, Wotan, the Wild Huntsman, that is really taking possession of his soul—"smitten by thee, cruel huntsman," as Nietzsche himself writes. And we must remember that Nietzsche's dream at the age of fifteen concerned the Wild Huntsman, therefore Wotan.

Incidentally, when the bravest Germanic warriors died in battle—the ideal death for them—they would ascend up to the massive golden hall of Valhalla, where they would train for battle, or enjoy frequent battle itself, to then spend their nights in drunken orgies. These seem to be the pursuits that Nietzsche greatly praises; the glory of battle and wild states of intoxication.

But returning to *The Norsemen* and the Wild Hunt of Wotan that left a trail of fire across the sky. A paragraph appears in the book that is extremely significant, though I need only quote part of the first sentence: " . . . sometimes it left behind a small black dog, which, cowering and whining upon a neighboring hearth, had to be kept for a whole year and carefully attended, unless it could be exorcised or frightened away."

A dog is one of the first forms the Self takes in the inner processes, and a black dog symbolizes its dark side. This is why in the German tales an attempt had to be made to exorcise it, when left behind by the Wild Hunt. A black dog has appeared frequently in my own dreams, countermatching a white poodle. In Goethe's *Faust,* the dark Mephistopheles first appears as a black poodle, which was originally a hunting dog, fitting in with the black dog of Wotan, the Wild Huntsman.

In *The Four Gold Keys,* I mention an account given by Colin Wilson in *Alien Dawn,* which tells of paranormal activity, including a black dog, at a farm in Quebec at the turn of the twentieth century. This can only mean experience of the Higher Self and the accompanying phenomena, and indeed, an angel-type figure also appears, in a starry white robe, with rays emanating from his head. This reminds us of a certain medieval Anthropos account, where an angel wears a white robe and a crown of stars (in *Aurora Occulta,* 1659, see Jung's *Alchemical Studies,* 1968). In countermatch to this figure, a spirit announcing it was the Devil appeared in various forms at the farm, including that of a black dog. The paranormal activity at the farm is certainly material symbolic of the individuation process, which is always both positive and negative in nature. So this is the significance of the black dog with Wotan; it is a symbolic representation of him as the Self.

Experiences of the Self may be from the lower Earth Spirit and at the other extreme ultimately from God, but Wotan with the black dog represents the lower Earth spirit in negative form. The appearance of the black dog in unconscious processes usually forebodes much danger, although it is better if it comes as an enemy, which means that consciousness is taking the opposite positive position to it. In the Irish myth of Finn McCool, to give just one example, Finn's companion is a white dog called Bran, and Bran leads the hounds of the hunt. But Bran fights and kills a black dog, which means that the light side of the Higher Self prevails over the dark side in the processes.

Chapter 14

Nietzsche's Zarathustra, Prophet of Immorality

As Jung rightly says, all of these Pagan forces were still very much alive in the German collective unconscious in Nietzsche's day, just below the Christian veneer, simmering under the surface and ready to boil over. These were to have a profound effect upon Nietzsche. In what is reckoned his greatest work, *Thus Spoke Zarathustra,* (1883), the "hero" Zarathustra is not actually the Superman, as is often believed, but the prophet-magician who proclaims the coming of the Superman. Yet prophet and Superman are connected, like two aspects of the same being, one the smaller, the other the greater; almost one the mortal, the other the immortal, (though, not quite, because Nietzsche does not recognize any immortal power).

But it is obvious to anyone who has knowledge of the unconscious processes, that Zarathustra the prophet and the Superman he proclaims are really Nietzsche and the Higher Self, though that is not to say Nietzsche himself was aware of the fact, rather the reverse. Nietzsche would have hotly denied that a god of spirit (which is what the Self ultimately is), or spirit itself, could actually exist. However, we can see in the prophet Zarathustra a mixture of both the initiate and the archetype of the "wise old man," a sort of Mimir, which Nietzsche had obviously activated in his search for an answer to his painful nihilistic state. (With myself, the "wise old man" took the form of Jung.) On the light side the archetype may be expressed as priest or prophet; on the negative side it appears as the magician or evil sorcerer.

Nietzsche's Zarathustra is not a true prophet, for a true prophet is the "mouthpiece" of the gods, of otherworldly reality, of which Nietzsche denied the existence. Zarathustra does not speak on behalf of spirit reality, for the Superman he heralds and proclaims is only a mortal, no matter how further developed or evolved—"super"—he is supposed to be. Furthermore, in his so-called "superiority," the Superman lacks morality and compassion, so that it can only be an inferior type of "superiority" that Nietzsche champions. But we must look at another aspect here, at something that played a fundamental role in the formation of Nietzsche's philosophy.

Nietzsche was very much influenced by the theory of evolution, which was relatively new in his day, and he clearly accepts it as fact, as the foundation of Man, and indeed, of all life. In his *Zarathustra,* we can see this even at the beginning, in the prologue. We do not fully appreciate today the great impact Darwin's discoveries made on many thinking people in the middle of the nineteenth century, even on certain of the clergy of the Protestant Church. Madame Blavatsky accepted evolution enthusiastically as part of her wider Wisdom Religion simply because her breadth of vision could encompass the fuller truth of ascending matter and descending spirit as countermatching aspects of one total system. Likewise, the pronouncements of Zarathustra reveal the powerful influence the evolution theory was having on Nietzsche. (At one point he says he is anti-Darwin because the struggle is for Power, rather than the struggle for existence, as it is with Darwin, but Nietzsche clearly propounds evolution as the life system.) Nietzsche states:

"You have made your way from worm to man, and much in you is still worm. Once you were apes, and even now man is more of an ape than any ape." So although Nietzsche accepts the process of evolution, he is unhappy with the results so far. Nevertheless, he has his solution.

> Behold, I teach you the Superman.The Superman is the meaning of the Earth. Let your will say: the Superman shall be the meaning of the Earth!
>
> I beseech you my brothers, *remain faithful to the Earth,* do not believe those who speak to you of otherworldly hopes!
>
> Once sin against God was the greatest sin, but God died, and thereupon these sinners died too. To blaspheme the Earth is now the most dreadful offence, and to esteem the entrails of the Inscrutable higher than the meaning of the Earth.

The prophet Zarathustra, who, of course, is really Nietzsche, then suggests that men should ask, "What good is my happiness?" "What good is my reason?" "What good is my virtue?" "What good is my justice?" "What good is my pity?" and he tells them, "It is not your sin, but your moderation that cries to Heaven, your very meanness in your sin cries to Heaven!"

He then goes on to speak of the tightrope walker:

> Man is a rope, tied between beast and Superman—a rope over an abyss.
>
> A dangerous going-across, a dangerous wayfaring, a dangerous looking back, a dangerous shuddering and stopping still.
>
> What is great in man is that he is a bridge and not an end; what can be loved in man is that he is a *going-across* and a *going-down.*

Then Nietzsche speaks for a page or so about how he loves "him who does not want too many virtues," "whose soul is lavish," and perhaps most significantly:

"I love those who do not seek beyond the stars for reasons to go down and be sacrifices: but who sacrifice themselves to the Earth, that the Earth may one day belong to the Superman."

Then a little later: "I love him whose soul is deep even in its ability to be wounded, and whom even a little thing can destroy; thus he gladly goes over the bridge."

". . . but his heart drives him to his downfall . . . they prophesy the coming of the lightning and as prophets they perish."

And then finally in this part:

"Behold, I am a prophet of the lightning and a heavy drop from the cloud: but this lightning is called *Superman.*"

I could go on and on throughout the whole work, but there is no need. What is stated here says clearly enough what Nietzsche's whole position is, and it all ties up with what I have said on earlier pages, and what Nietzsche has said himself. Recognizing what was to him the sickliness and weakness of Christianity (Lutheranism especially), and seeing clearly the truth and relevance of the evolutionary process, he sees Man as a bridge, as part of that process, entirely physical and of the Earth. Consequently, he has come to reject the whole of the spiritual or metaphysical position, the effect of which had been to cast him into gloom and nihilism until he finally found an answer, a cure for the pain. This was the Superman, the being that the person of genius can and will become, through evolution and Will to Power. (As Colin Wilson says, "The idea of Zarathustra began as a reaction against Nietzsche's own soul sickness;

it was the attempt to give body to the idea of great health.") By sheer Will to Power, according to Nietzsche, Man can approach this state, though perhaps not actually achieve it fully, now. Nevertheless, we can help the process on its way. Again, only the few elite men of genius will attain to this, the rest of mankind being the common herd that will serve.

Man, rising from the ape, is at this moment a low, somewhat worthless creature, but is nevertheless a bridge to the Superman that he can become, though this entails going beyond good and evil and compassion. Yet whereas we would have thought Nietzsche to have considered the path to the Superman a "going up" the evolutionary scale, it is a sort of going down for him, because the Earth is down.

We must surrender with joy to the Earth and not oppose its forces and processes—helping them, in fact, to be fulfilled. We must not concern ourselves with morality, we should rather be "beyond good and evil," for "What good is my virtue?" Neither should we make compassion our priority, for we may be required to "rise above" that in our Will to Power, so "What good is my pity?" We must certainly be prepared to sacrifice ourselves on behalf of the Will to Power and the Superman and be happy to go over the bridge. The prophet of the lightning will perish, so Nietzsche, the prophet who goes over the bridge, will himself perish. Whether Nietzsche realizes this is what he is saying, that he himself is the doomed, self-sacrificing prophet, is unclear, but that is what it amounts to.

At the same time, though Nietzsche is robustly glorifying the Earth and the Will to Power, there is also a feeling that he is strenuously forcing it all, forcing his conscious mind and his will with great effort, while the real position is that underneath he is weak and vulnerable. In other words, his solution, his philosophy, is partly based on personal compensation, or perhaps more truly, over-compensation. That does not necessarily invalidate his solution, and the solution for one man may turn out to be the solution for all mankind. Do not all those who push themselves to extremes to find truth and meaning compensate, at least to a degree, for the emptiness, weakness, and fear within themselves, that only something truly great can assuage, fill, and strengthen? Furthermore, the initial lost, disoriented state and sense of great impending danger of the mythical hero—actually the religious hero—reflects at bottom the true condition of his whole culture, so that the cure for the individual is the cure for the collective. However, Nietzsche's standpoint and goal is the development and aggrandizement of the few, the genius and ultimately the Superman, even at the cost of the rest of mankind and without compassion for them. There can be no such weaknesses as morality and compassion in the Will to Power. This is what Nietzsche himself not only defends but *proclaims*.

Because Zarathustra comes down the mountain to make his speech it has been called "the sermon *off* the mount," but what an eternity of difference to Christ's Sermon *on* the Mount.

> Blessed are the poor in spirit: for theirs is the kingdom of heaven.
>
> Blessed are they that mourn: for they shall be comforted.
>
> Blessed are the meek: for they shall inherit the earth.
>
> Blessed are they which do hunger and thirst after righteousness: for they shall be filled.
>
> Blessed are the merciful: for they shall obtain mercy.
>
> Blessed are the pure in heart: for they shall see God.
>
> Blessed are the peacemakers: for they shall be called the children of God.
>
> Blessed are they which are persecuted for righteousness' sake: for theirs is the kingdom of heaven.
>
> Blessed are ye, when men shall revile you, and persecute you, and shall say all manner of things against you falsely, for my sake. (Matt. 5:3–11.)

We must ask, which is worthy of evolved Man in a higher state of consciousness? Ultimately, which is reasonable and which is totally unreasonable, Christ's "Sermon *on* the Mount" or Nietzsche's "sermon *off* the mount?" Jesus with the Christ and Nietzsche with the Superman are extreme opposites here, diametrically opposed. This is why Nietzsche says the future man will be an Antichrist, because the Superman is a type of Antichrist. Nietzsche calls ordinary humanity the "Ugliest Man," wishing to be high above this, in close identity with the gods though not believing in gods as such. (Yet he has asked "Must not we ourselves become as gods?") By contrast, Jesus the man unified with the cosmic Higher Self, a god, humbles himself to identify with lowly, frail, and faulty humanity, with the poor and the sick, not with the princes of this world, the Caesars and the Herods. The greatest must humble itself to the level of the lowest, or it would not truly be the greatest. Nietzsche could never comprehend this, and his whole way of thinking, his whole philosophy, goes the opposite way.

Nietzsche believed that high intelligence and a warm kindly heart could not exist together in the same human being. The warm kindly person has low intelligence, and a highly intelligent person is above a warm kindly heart. By this thinking, the man Jesus, of the warmest kindliest heart has low intelligence. But Nietzsche gets out of this by saying that Jesus would have altered his thinking had he lived, had he not been crucified. His beliefs and teachings were all due to the folly of youth! This is tantamount to saying that Jesus, and through him Christ, would have become an Antichrist had he lived.

According to Nietzsche, the Christian God is hostile to life and is certainly a sign of decay, a "miserable God." But then, Nietzsche denies God in any case, promulgating the Will to Power and the necessary dispensing with of morality and pity. He says in *The Antichrist* (1888) that when a man feels pity he loses power, and therefore becomes inferior. Christianity has waged war on the higher man (who feels no pity), calling him a villain, but only such a man can conquer, with the Will to Power. In this way, despite what supporters of Nietzsche claim or deny, Nazi Germany—at least in its "ideals"—was the implementation of his teachings and partly the fulfillment of them. In other words, follow the path that Nietzsche lays down and despite his claims of "beauty" and "truth," Nazi Germany or something similar is what you arrive at.

This is not to say Nietzsche would have liked or approved of the Nazis, but he apparently failed to realize the ultimate outcome of what he was preaching. Nevertheless, it has been said more than once that a Hitler is the consequence of Nietzchean doctrine. Nietzsche says there are a "master morality" and a "slave morality," and while slave morality may think it needs compassion and the other Christian virtues, the strong master morality knows differently.

It is often forgotten that the Nazis were idealists—of a negative type, yet trying to produce the ideal man, the Superman, in the ideal state. As with Nietzsche, the human virtues could not be part of it. In fact, it was imperative they be rejected, for what was noble and ideal was what was hard and the pitiless. The law of natural selection is thwarted by pity, preserving that which is ready for death. The weak must not be saved; only the strong are worthy of survival. Horrible and sick as all of this sounds, it is what Nietzsche actually says, and is it anything other than Nazi philosophy?

Yet, unlike the Nazis, Nietzsche was not anti-Semitic, and he would steer clear of anti-Semites generally. He was close friends with composer Richard Wagner for a time but never liked Wagner's racist ideas on the Jews. Indeed, another close friend of Nietzsche's for some years was Paul Ree, who was Jewish. Nietzsche admired the strength and determination of the Jews, saying they were the healthiest people in Europe, though he detested their religion for teaching of God and otherworldly reality, and for being the parent of Christianity. He had no wish to banish from Germany the Jews who were already there, but believed that enough were enough. However, he did believe that "brawling" anti-Semitic Germans *should* be banished from Germany, and this seems to show that Nietzsche was no racist. His personality was apparently not that of a true Nazi; when people met him he seemed different from his harsh writings. Yet the fact remains that he condemned morality and compassion, proclaiming rather the hard and the pitiless, totally despising "soft" humanity and in particular "Christian weakness."

By a God Possessed

But there is actually much more to Nietzsche than merely his conscious thinking and proclamations. While he is telling us something from a limited conscious standpoint, with limited understanding and conclusions, in reality tremendous, unseen forces from the unconscious depths are scooping him up and carrying him along like a whirlwind, *the conscious standpoint being much too limited for those tremendous forces.* This returns us to Wotan, the spirit of the Self that has now entered Nietzsche, literally "in-spiriting" him, and this is why he says he is a "prophet of the lightning," that is the Superman. Put simply, Nietzsche may postulate the Superman in consciousness, but it is the Wotan archetype possessing him in the unconscious, as the dream of the Wild Huntsman foretold. This is why in *Thus Spoke Zarathustra* he says he feels smitten by a cruel god.

> Thou huntsman behind the clouds.
> Struck to the ground by thee,
> Thou mocking eye that gazeth at me from the dark:
> Thus do I lie,
> Twisting, writhing, tortured
> With eternal tortures,
> Smitten
> By thee, cruel huntsman,
> Thou unknown—God
> (trans. Common 1904)

> And again in *Ecco Homo:*
> And now
> Self-hunted
> Thine own quarry,
> Thyself pierced through . . .
> —(trans. Lodovici 1911)

Nietzsche is wounded "with arrows" just as we find with certain mystics who were undergoing the inner spiritualizing processes. This is the fate of the religious hero, for it is the Self that pierces. The problem is, Nietzsche has rejected religion and the spirit and identifies everything with consciousness and matter. An individuation process is occurring within his depths of which he is largely unaware and is completely misinterpreting. It would of necessity be of a negative kind in any case because of his selfish conscious values. An Osiris cannot develop within him, but a dark Set might, and what is Goethe's Mephistopheles but a type of Set? Yet even an Osiris would be very dangerous if identified with the conscious man, for the mortal man is not a god, nor should he wish to be. Consciousness must always separate and humble itself before the spiritual phenomenon of the Self. Nevertheless, even with a positive individuation process there is much suffering and danger, and feeling pierced and injured is felt all the way through.

Jung compares this with Christ the Crucified pierced by the lance (Nietzsche was to refer to himself later as "the Crucified"). It expresses a mortal, deep in the processes of the unconscious, smitten by a god, the Higher Self. As Jung comments, the affliction does not come from without, rather from within, a man tortured at one level by his own opposites, but much more so tortured because he is attached—nailed, crucified—to the god, causing a horrendous conflict. As Jung again says, the Self does violence to Man, though it must be added that in turn Man does violence to the Self.

This is where the Devil, or in this case, Wotan, spies his chance, for Nietzsche in his denial of God and Christ and all of the virtues, now becomes suitable prey for the opposing negative forces. Wotan as a god had his positive side, but Nietzsche's negative conscious values would not bring forth this side. In the same way, Dionysus in higher and positive aspect had certain attributes in common with Christ, but these would have been totally rejected by Nietzsche. (He could not have known of the higher "Christian" side of Dionysus.) The Pagan force of Wotan as bringer of war and conquest lay just below the Christian veneer in Germany at that time and was ready to soon burst forth; Nietzsche was one of the first to be overwhelmed by its enormous power.

Jung comments that Wotan sprang awake at that time like a volcano that had been thought extinct. (Mythologically, Wotan lies in wait in the mountains for the time when he will be called forth.) German youth became restless wanderers, infected by Wotan, the restless, roving god. By 1933, however, they ceased their wandering, for now the Nazis marched, filled with this power. They stirred up the whole German nation like a whirlwind, possessed by the god who is not far from the Devil in some aspects. Jung wrote in 1936 that while it was believed to be fair weather, a hurricane, a "mighty rushing wind god" was on the loose in Germany. He also said that all that is not rooted deeply is in great danger when the great gale force through the unconscious blows. It is also important to remember that while Dionysus, a force similar to Wotan, is at times still under the authority of Zeus, Wotan is never accountable to anything similar. As well as being a very primitive force of battles, storms, and frenzy, Wotan is a magician of occult nature, and it is a fact the magician and Savior are diametrically opposed in processes of the unconscious. Jung insists that only Christianity could have saved the Germans from the Nazi onslaught at that time, but Wotan proved the stronger.

Here is a dream of my own suffering in the inner processes. Help came from a quite unexpected source, so opposite to Nietzsche's answer.

> *I am due to start work on a new job but feel so ill with my nerves that it is impossible to do so. The inner processes are weighing me down heavily. As I walk down a street, I realize that I have forgotten my tinted glasses, which would help to protect my eyes from the world. I cannot face the world at the moment. A teenage girl comes along and I explain to her just why I cannot start the job, apologizing for it, and this causes her to weep on my behalf. My suffering and despair weigh so heavily on me that, falling to my knees, I too begin to sob. With head bent I say that my heart is broken and I cannot go on any further.*
>
> *At that moment, Christ walks into the dream, wearing long white robes, his arms and hands bleeding, and walking up to me, he lays his hands on my head as I kneel. But not only am I on my knees in the dream, I am also watching all of this from a few yards away, just inside the line that divides the sleeping state from consciousness, so to speak. So I then watch as Christ leaves the "me" who is on my knees, and walking right past me as I stand there, he walks out of the dream again. Though I see him very clearly from the front, I do not actually register his face.*

For some time after this dream I kept asking myself what (besides the appearance of Christ) was different about it, different from normal dreams, but could not put my finger on it. Then it suddenly came to me one day when I was out in the fields with my dog. Christ had walked in and out of the dream as a real figure, and was not just an image of the dream as such. I had watched the dream as though from conscious reality, and Christ had come from behind me, from higher consciousness, higher reality, not just from the world. An earlier dream had featured the magical green fish, the Ichthys, the symbol of Christ as Savior, and now he had appeared in person.

As with appearances of Christ in other dreams, I have long wondered if this was the Higher Self as a Christ equivalent, or the original Christ himself, or the Holy Spirit taking the form of Christ. I am still unsure. All I can say that he must have the same basic meaning as the original Christ or he would not appear in that form.

The "Christ within," or Anthropos, of the Gnostics; the Son of Man of the prophets Ezekiel, Daniel, and Enoch; Melchizedek with Abraham; Horus, Iu-em-hetep, and Khonsu in Egypt; the examples of Atman, Purusha and Vishnu in India; Quetzalcoatl in Central America; Ahura Mazda in Persia; Vatea in Polynesia; and Kwan Shai Yin in China are expressions of the Higher Self found around the world. Of Kwan Shai Yin, Madame Blavatsky says, "He is the Self Manifested: in short, the 'Son of the Father'. Crowned with seven dragons, above his statue there appears the inscription. 'Pu-tsi-K'ien-ling, the universal Savior of all living beings'." (1888). The Dalai Lama is said to be one of his incarnations, and the name Kwan Shai Yin means "The Lord that is seen," in one sense "Divine Self seen by Self." All of this applies equally to Christ, to the Anthropos, to the Son of Man, and to all of the other God-man, Higher-Self, figures. Just as Kwan Shai Yin is crowned with seven dragons, Christ has seven stars or seven candlesticks, Horus has Seven Lights, Vishnu has seven Rishis, and so on.

In the dream above, I am unable to go on, and break down sobbing, which reflects my mental state at that particular time In my suffering, the suffering Christ hears me and comes and performs the "laying on of the hands." As well as indicating healing, this could also perhaps mean to confer blessings and grace. Christ himself is bleeding in the dream, which reminds us of how Christ sweats blood in Luke's Gospel 22:44, *"And his sweat was as it were great drops of blood falling to the ground."* This repeats Osiris Tesh Tesh in Egypt, the god who suffers in agony and bloody sweat. Because blood is red, it is said that the Red Sun suffered his agony in the Underworld. The High God, Atum, as the Sun, symbolically set in a red pool, intimating blood, and even the red, scarlet, or purple robe of Christ is connected with the blood caused by suffering.

Just as Christ is said to redeem the world by his "bloody-sweat," so the alchemists believed that the blood sweated from their Stone would produce a Redeemer. Not Christ himself, but his parallel, hence the "lapis-Christ parallel."

Jung comments (1963b) that in the individuation process at ultimate level, the adept experiences a transformation that may be compared to the Passion of Christ. This is because the Higher Self attaches himself to the Christ image, so that it may even involve a correspondence to Christ, rather than an "imitation." Always the original experience in the depths is repeated anew, though this must involve self-sacrifice.

Hippolytus, one of the Church Fathers who wrote on the Gnostic sects, writes: "The Naassenes speak of a nature of man at once hidden and manifesting itself, which they say is within man, and is the kingdom of heaven that is sought after." (*Against Heresies* vol. 7.) Furthermore, the Naassenes understood that the other young dying gods of the Pagan myths expressed the same truth as Christ, though as Jung tells us, Christ is the highest development of all.

I have not developed the higher Self as a Christ figure yet—that occurs with the processes later—so who is the figure in my dream? The original Christ? the Holy Spirit? Who? (I now know this was the Christ from the higher spirit, the Logos, ultimately from God, not the Christ copy produced by the Earth Spirit/World Soul to countermatch Christ.)

The Original Zarathustra, Prophet of Morality

We must now look at Nietzsche's choice of name, and indeed, model, for his prophet-magician, Zarathustra. The philosopher himself actually explains it to us in his autobiography, *Ecce Homo* (1888). Speaking of the ancient prophet of the Persians, he writes:

"Zarathustra was the first to see in the struggle between good and evil the actual wheel in the working of things: the translation of morality into the realm of metaphysics, as force, cause, end in itself, is *his work*. But this question is at bottom its own answer. Zarathustra *created* this most fateful of errors, morality: Consequently he must be the first to recognize it." Nietzsche then goes on to say that Zarathustra is more truthful than any other thinker, but that, "The self over-coming of morality through truthfulness, the self over-coming of the moralist into his opposite—*into me*—that is what the name Zarathustra means in my mouth."

In other words, the original Zarathustra was responsible for the error of the elevation of morality, of good and evil, into a major metaphysical problem, but he, Nietzsche, as a sort of returned Zarathustra, will now correct the error. Nietzsche is therefore the counter-position, in a sense, like the Antichrist to Christ, and not only the elevation of morality, but the very concepts of the moral and the metaphysical themselves, are in error.

The original Zarathustra probably lived in the seventh century B.C., although some authorities have put the date very much earlier. He is credited with writing the *Zend Avesta,* the Holy Book of the old Persian religion of the Parsees. The Persian Zarathustra was obviously an initiate into the unconscious processes who experienced the Higher Self, in this instance Ahura Mazda, leader of the seven Amesha Spentas—Ahura Mazda, or Ohrmazd, is actually the creator of the other six, or sometimes seven. This corresponds to all of the other Higher Self examples with the Seven Powers; Oannes with the seven Annedoti, Vishnu with the seven Rishis, Horus with the seven Akhu, Christ with the seven candlesticks or seven fishermen disciples, etc. Zarathustra becomes partly godlike, and his birth, like that of Jesus and certain other hero/Self figures, is said to be miraculous.

When Zarathustra is conceived, his mother—indeed, the whole house—becomes bathed in a great light, and for three days before his birth the whole village shines with so bright a luminosity that the villagers think it is on fire and abandon it. After the birth they return to find the baby Zarathustra radiating the great light—and he is laughing! (Nietzsche would have liked that, though he would have denied the possibility of a divine birth.) A star of great radiance watches over the birth, following the archetypal pattern, for we find a star connected with Higher Self figures right across the world, from the Wichita Indian Savior, the Flint-man, to Kwan Shai Yin of the Far East. Christ has his Star of Bethlehem, of course.

Dark forces try to prevent Zarathustra's birth happening, and endeavor to destroy the child after it has been born, again following the archetypal pattern (King Herod with Christ, King Kansa with Krishna, Pharaoh with Moses, etc., all of whom have all the baby boys killed). But Zarathustra survives to grow up to serve his God, Ahura Mazda, of whom he has visions in trance-like states, or in dreams. The opposing god of evil, incidentally, is called Ahriman, or Angra Mainyu, the "Demon of Lies." The divine birth in this and certain other myths, Jesus, Moses, the Buddha, is taken to be the physical one of the human hero, when it is really the birth of the Higher Self in the unconscious, the immortal whom the mortal prophet brings forth and experiences. (While Jesus as the Christ is thought of as a god, the others are not and remain human.) Ahura Mazda, as well as being a Higher Self figure, is like the High God in some ways, and his sacredness, goodness, and morality are greatly emphasized in extreme contradistinction to the evil Ahriman. (In the Zoroastrian creed, Ahriman, the evil principle, comes into being when a doubting thought enters Ahura Mazda's mind.)

In his visions, Zarathustra is told by Ahura Mazda to begin a new religion, in which the followers must likewise be emphatically good and moral. Ahura Mazda has fathered twins who are spirits, one of which is the Beneficent Spirit, and the other the Destroying Spirit, following the archetypal pattern of the twins of the Self (Horus and Set, Cain and Abel, etc.). The accompanying Amesha Spentas, the Holy and Bountiful Immortals, are spirit representations of moral powers, being Righteousness, Good Thought, Sovereignty, Piety, Weal (well being, prosperity), and Immortality. Ahura Mazda, God of Truth and Light, is the One who contains the other six within himself, making seven. However, as the Beneficent/Destroying Spirit is dual as two aspects of one, Ahura Mazda is then 1 + 7, which fits the archetypal situation fully—the first gods of Egypt were the Company of Eight Gods, which were Nu with seven companions. By bringing all of this to the knowledge of mankind, Zarathustra highlights the eternal *moral* problem of good and evil—in metaphysical as well as in earthly terms. Other versions give the six as pillars of the Throne of Ahura Mazda, three male and three female. The male are Good Will, Supreme Truth, and Benevolent Power, while the female are Holy Piety, Sacredness, and Immortality.

Zarathustra instructs all Mazdeans of the distinct choice between good and evil, and that they must choose the good. Evil will not be tolerated, and, in fact, the moral difference between good and evil then becomes so accentuated that it is said to have led to Dualism, the eternal opposing principles of good and evil that can never be unified. (However, in my own humble opinion, the situation is little different than with certain other religions, particularly Christianity.) Ahura Mazda, the "good and holy," is seen as a divine flame that can spiritualize the whole world, like the Holy Spirit, although every human being possesses the flame, or solar light, to a degree. (Thus the Logos disperses himself into all mankind, and perhaps even all of nature.)

Schure's Version of Zarathustra's Quest

In his book *From Sphinx to Christ* (1928), Edouard Schure relates a version of the central myth of the adult Zarathustra that demonstrates a Higher Self experience—indeed, the whole individuation process—of a human individual clearly and excellently. The author may take poetic license, but the original Zarathustra must have experienced his individuation process in more or less this way, and so I will give part of Schure's version here.

Zarathustra, called Arjasp at first, is on a journey one day when he comes upon a lovely pool of pure spring water, "blue as the sky above," and by the pool kneels a beautiful woman. She is dressed in white linen, with her hair tied up in a circlet of gold, and she is drawing water from the pool. Arjasp asks her to whom the place belongs, and she replies: "Here reigns the patriarch Vahumano, Guardian of the Fire and servant of the Highest."

Arjasp then asks the woman her name, and again she replies: "I have been given the name of this spring, which is called Ardouizur, meaning 'source of light.' But be careful, stranger! The Master has said, 'Whosoever shall drink of this water shall burn with an unassuageable thirst, and only a god can quench it.'"

Blue lightning and golden arrows dart from the beautiful maiden's eyes, but she then disappears, leaving Arjasp kneeling himself to drink from the palm of his hand of the clear blue water.

Some years pass before Arjasp sees Ardouizur again, when she is captive of the worshippers of Ahriman, Demon of Lies (or Lord of the Demons), and undergoing much suffering. Her arms are tied behind her and she is covered with blood, certainly with no lightning and magic in her eyes now, only the look of death. Arjasp is told that she is to be food for the two evil serpents of Ahriman, but that he, Arjasp, can have her for himself if he will bow down and worship Ahriman. Arjasp, despite his longing for Ardouizur, refuses to do this, and so she is led away, leaving Arjasp burning with the desire for vengeance. However, he remembers what Ardouizur had told him of the wise old patriarch, Vahumano, and so he quickly gallops off to the mountains to seek the old man's help.

After some time, Arjasp comes upon a sword lying on a stone altar, flowers forming a cross beside it telling him that he is nearing his destination. Soon he finds Vahumano in a village, sitting in a tent dispensing justice to his people. "His eyes were like the Sun that rises above the snow peaks; his greenish-white beard was like the lichens that cover the ancient cedars of the Alborji Mountains."

The two then discuss the plight of Ardouizur, and Arjasp is asked by Vahumano, "Have you the patience that outlasts the years? Are you ready to give up everything for your task? For you are only at the beginning of the test, and the suffering will endure throughout your life."

Arjasp answers that he is indeed ready for all things, and Vahumano continues by saying, "Then I can help you. Come and live here for a time. Disappear from among your own people; when they see you again you will be another. From this day forward you will be called Zarathustra, which means 'Star of Gold' [or 'Splendor of the Sun'], and you shall become the prophet of Ahura Mazda, who is the aureole of the Omniscience, the Living Spirit of the Universe."

"You will be another" reminds us of that other "wise old man," Samuel, telling Saul that after his visionary experiences he will become another man. Zarathustra thus becomes follower of the "wise old man," Vahumano, the chela to the guru.

The myth as told so far overflows with symbolism of the unconscious processes. The pool of spring water represents the depths of the collective unconscious, largely feminine, while the woman Ardouizur clearly means the feminine anima/soul, connected with the World Soul, the gold circlet in her hair being the symbol of this. In one of my dreams the collective anima appeared to me as the old Nordic goddess, Freyja, who herself wore a gold ring, necklace or circlet. She presented me with a gold ring that had eight squared insets—the "Ring of Freyja," as it was referred to in the dream. Christ was in one of the insets, and so the ring was a mandala that contained both the feminine and the masculine spirits, representing the Higher Self in its totality. There are many stories of heroes and prophets meeting a special woman by a pool, spring, or well; Isaac and Rebekah, Jacob and Rachel, Moses and Zipporah, Jesus and the woman of Samaria, and so on. Celtic mythology is also rich in this symbolism, including the Lady of the Fountain, etc., and in the Arthurian/Grail tales we find the Lady of the Lake and the Star Woman rising from a pool.

As we saw, the anima tends to become lost in the lower instinctual unconscious during the inner processes—captured—so to speak, which is why she has to be rescued by the hero on his spiritual quest, just as Jesus is said traditionally to redeem Mary Magdalene from her lost state. However, just as Mary Magdalene and Rahab, the prostitute/dragon with Joshua in the conquest of the Promised Land, and Sophia in her lower aspect represent also the whole feminine depths that must be won over to higher, purer aspect; so too must Ardouizur. So sometimes the instinctual depths capture the anima/soul, while at other times she is in the depths to begin with, but the meaning is the same. Anima/soul must be rescued or redeemed.

The sword Arjasp is associated with a stone—Ardouizur is like a Lady of the Lake. (King Arthur, and Sir Galahad in his Grail quest, pull swords out of a stone.) The flowers forming the cross with the stone reminds us of the Gnostic symbol of the union of opposites. In another of my dreams I am at an ancient religious center, like Stonehenge, and a voice says,

"The stone and the cross." The special stone is known throughout religions, myths, and legends, including the White Stone of Egypt and in the Book of Revelation, the black stone of Mecca, the Bethel stone of Jacob, St. Peter the rock or stone, and the Philosopher's Stone. There is also the Toad Stone, of which Shakespeare writes:

> Which like the toad, ugly and venomous,
> Wears yet a precious jewel in its head

This refers to the reptile guarding the treasure of the Higher Self, found in myths worldwide.

As for the sword, I too was given a special sword—with a stone in the pommel—in my own processes, with which to cut my way through the unconscious depths. Schure may be using poetic license here with Zarathustra to amplify his tale, but he seems to know the individuation process excellently, which the original Zarathustra most definitely underwent.

The patriarch Vahumano, to whom Zarathustra turns for help, represents the archetype of the "wise old man," which Jung calls "the personification of spirit." As I say above, he is most clearly seen in the figure of Jethro, father of Zipporah, from whom Moses learns the secret wisdom. Mimir, as guardian of the Fountain of Wisdom, from which Odin drinks, represents the same figure, though a somewhat lower version, being also a magician and sorcerer. Merlin fills a similar role, of course. In my own processes, Jung was the wise old man who taught me the secret wisdom of the unconscious, and I know the truth of the statement that once you have tasted of the waters on the quest, you will not rest until you have encountered your god, your Higher Self, and even God Himself.

But to continue with the account. Some time later, Arjasp, now called Zarathustra, has acquired a certain knowledge and wisdom, and he takes his leave of the old patriarch to go and live in solitude in the mountains. Resting in a cave, he is tormented by dark visions sent by the evil Ahriman, as well as being tortured by thoughts of the sufferings of Ardouizur. Phantom demons assail him from all sides, and then he sees the vague and sinister shape of a woman hovering over him, all black at first, though over subsequent visitations gradually growing lighter until she becomes pure white, at which time she chases away the demons. She points towards the rising Sun, which symbolizes Ahura Mazda, and then miraculously seems to be absorbed by the rays. Zarathustra is convinced this was Ardouizur, or her soul, and that he will now never see her again, which throws him into even deeper despair than before, if indeed this is possible. Losing all hope, he climbs to the very top of the mountain in which the cave is set, where, completely exhausted, he becomes aware only of death; not just his own, but of the whole of Creation.

This terrible melancholy lasts for three days and nights, but then it happens! Schure describes so well the appearance of the god, the Higher Self, that I will let him tell it:

> But the third night, lying in this condition, he heard a great voice like the rolling of thunder, which died away in melodious murmurings. Then a hurricane of light seemed to hurl itself upon him with such violence that he thought his soul must be driven from his body. He felt that the unnamable Cosmic Power that had haunted him since childhood, that had plucked him from his valley and led him to the mountain top, was going to be made manifest to him by means of the language in which the gods speak to men. And the Lord of the Spirits, the King of Kings, Ormazd, the Solar Word, then appeared to him in human form. Clothed in beauty, strength, and light, He shone upon His fiery throne, which was supported on either side by a winged bull and lion, while the wings of an enormous eagle were spread beneath it. Around Him in three semi-circles stood seven Cherubim with golden wings, seven Elohim with azure wings, and seven Archangels with violet wings. [In the *Zend Avesta,* Ormuzd is Ahura Mazda; the Cherubim are the Amesha Spentas; the Elohim are the Yzeds, and the Archangels the Feroher.] From moment to moment a blaze of light issued from Ormazd, penetrating all three spheres, and the Cherubim, Elohim and Archangels shone like the God Himself with the dazzling whiteness of snow, and thus reassumed their former colors. Bathed thus in the glory of Ormazd, they manifested his unity; glowing in gold, azure and violet, they became His prism. And Zoroaster heard a melodious voice, vast as the universe, which said: "I am Ahura Mazda, who created thee; I have chosen thee. Hear now my voice, O Zarathustra, best of men. I will speak with thee by day and by night, and reveal to thee the living word."
>
> Then there was a blinding flash in which Ormuzd and the attendant Archangels, Elohim and Cherubim, seemed to grow colossal, till they filled the whole valley and hid from sight the jagged peaks of Alborji. The light spread itself over the whole firmament and for some seconds the constellations glittered through the wings of the Cherubim. But then the vision faded into space, though the echo of the voice of Ahura Mazda rang through the

mountains like distant thunder, and died away in palpating vibrations. (pp 134–5.)

That describes a classic vision of the Higher Self, reminding us of very similar ones in the Old Testament and elsewhere, of Isaiah, Daniel, Ezekiel, and Enoch. Whether Zarathustra was awake, or asleep dreaming the vision "in the night visions," it amounts to the same thing; the coming through—manifestation—of God to man in a specific form. Furthermore, it matters not how much of the retelling is due to Schure's poetic imagination; it describes the phenomenon excellently, and the event is Earth-shattering in its beauty and meaning; God, or the Son, or both, incarnating to Man, and it is an age-old archetypal experience.

From then on Ahura Mazda instructs Zarathustra in what is required of mankind; to recognize good and evil and to choose good, to love peace and not war, and so forth. In fact, the whole *Zend Avesta* is really a continuous dialogue between Zarathustra and his God, although perhaps only the Gathas contain the original teachings. One thing I particularly like for its natural "common sense" wisdom, is the following. "What is the thing that gives most pleasure on Earth?" "When a pure man walks upon her." "What is the next most pleasurable thing?" "When a pure man builds his house where there is a fire, where there are cattle, and fine flocks, where there is a woman with children. For in such a house is abundance of righteousness." Simple, homely truths; an honest family living a decent life in harmony with their God and nature; and yet whole civilizations depend upon such simple truths. It is such simple truths that will save mankind, if anything does, not the mind-boggling possibilities of science, or the cleverness of dissociated over-intellectualized ideas. Yet at the same time, the truths that spring from the divine source are very complex, involving spirit reality through the unconscious, and ultimately God. Nevertheless, Man must have a simple, honest heart before God.

At the end of his life, according to this account, Zarathustra, though serving his god faithfully since the first encounter, still feels a yearning for Ardouizur, the woman of the pool of pure spring water. But then, when the time comes that he finally dies, he finds her waiting for him, even more beautiful than she had ever been in her earthly appearances. She tells him she was his soul in life, and that he has forged her into what she now is, what she has now become, by all of his good deeds and teachings during his lifetime. They then merge into one being, becoming partly one another, Zarathustra and his beautiful soul Ardouizur finally unified as One.

This reminds us of when Jung almost died and found himself up in higher reality, where he literally became all that he had ever done in life. He says he became his own history, all of which he would now have to take to the Higher Self (though as we know, he was suddenly required to return to Earth again, to life).

The above account concerning Zarathustra tells of inner processes, of the "symbolic life," involving the spirit and the soul, not the outer life. As with all other mythological heroes, Moses, Christ, the Buddha, etc., only the symbolic life matters. The human life is of no consequence except in relation to the spirit. Zarathustra is said to have married three times in real life and to have had children, but how much of this is actual real life and how much is part of the inner processes we cannot know. (The real life of the man Jesus has little importance for it would not have swayed the world; only the symbolic life can achieve that—or at least, a blend of the two. Jung says very little can be left of the man Jesus in the Gospels.)

The first thing that strikes us about the teachings of Nietzsche's Zarathustra is that they are in direct contradistinction to those of the original Zarathustra, like a dark parody of them, in fact; but this is what Nietzsche himself has told us. His aim, his very vocation, is to show all the error of the earlier prophet, and to now take himself the counterposition. The good and the moral as opposed to the evil and immoral are not for Nietzsche and his Zarathustra eternal and metaphysical problems, nor are they everyday ones. (They are, of course, both eternal and metaphysical with the original Zarathustra.) Nor need they concern us, according to Nietzsche, for we can step beyond them, "beyond good and evil." The metaphysical and the holy are false teachings in any case, for only the Earth exists. And even if those higher things did exist, they would not be the choice; the Earth must be the choice. As Nietzsche says: "But we certainly do not want to enter into the kingdom of Heaven: we have become men, so we want the kingdom of Earth."

The difference between the positions of Nietzsche's Zarathustra and the original Zarathustra is as enormous as it is possible to be (as also with Christ), and so we can understand the completely different outcomes. Nietzsche himself became insane, while the German people were to become embroiled in and largely responsible for two horrendous world wars in their dreams of conquest, their Will to Power. The original Zarathustra, on the other hand, attained a state of holiness and wholeness, the precise opposite of insanity, united with his god, the Higher Self, and with his own beautified soul, teaching peace to his people, and bringing a higher state of culture and civilization.

Zarathustra was of the aristocracy of a people who had conquered a weaker and culturally inferior one, but he instructed the conquering nobles to help the conquered people and to teach them the higher way, rather than enslaving them. Jung says somewhere that God has not been served best if he has not been served in beauty, and the original Zarathustra can only be said to have served his god in beauty. Nietzsche did not serve his god, the Superman, (really the Higher Self unconsciously), in beauty, for how can "free powers, without morality" and "the Will to War, the Will to Power" ever be beautiful? Paradoxically, Nietzsche often writes about beauty, is a champion of it—but not moral or spiritual beauty. In truth, we develop the Higher Self and bring forth whatever *our own* values are, for the Higher Self, consisting of all opposites, is all possibilities.

Chapter 15

The Irreconcilable Themes in Nietzsche's Philosophy

Thus sayeth the Lord God; . . . thou hast said, I am a God, I sit in the seat of God, in the midst of the seas; yet thou art a man, and not God, though thou set thine heart as the heart of God.

—Ezek. 28:2

The Deep Dichotomy

There is actually a deep dichotomy in Nietzsche's thinking, a large contradiction, because although on the one hand he preaches return to the Earth and a near unconscious state of ecstasy, his Superman is nevertheless a supposedly rising-above, a development to, a super-developed consciousness, not in the spiritual sense, but in the physical/evolutionary sense; what conscious Man may become. These extremes with Nietzsche are not only irreconcilable, but full of dangers. The fall into the Dionysian, as Nietzsche means it, is the return to animal feeling and the near unconscious state of pure emotion, with little conscious awareness. It is also the unconscious visionary state of the shaman-magician who serves the Earth. In ancient Greece, in the Dionysian orgies, women followers, called *Bacchae, Maenads,* or *Thyiades,* would tear living animals to pieces in frenzy, and even any unfortunate man they happened to come upon, according to some authorities. This was apparently done to imitate the tearing to pieces of Dionysus by the Titans, and it is interesting to note that the frenzied women would blow shrill blasts on flutes, similar to Wotan with his whistle.

The frenzy is also similar to the berserker state mentioned earlier, in which the old Germanic and Nordic warriors would become entranced in an elated frenzy of blood and violence. Yet Nietzsche's Superman is supposedly the other extreme, consciousness developed above and beyond normal Man even as he is now, the latter being designated the "Ugliest Man" by Nietzsche. This reminds us of the Superman ideal of the Nazis, supposedly superior, yet a cruel, unprincipled opportunist without morality and compassion, dedicated to conquest and the Will to Power, and all too ready in its own inferiority and gutter logic to annihilate what it deigned inferior. Nor is it possible to be any fairer to Nietzsche here, for he posited Cesare Borgia as a superior type of man. (Borgia was engaged in the same type of Will to Power and murder of opponents as the Nazis.)

Nietzsche says that as a rabble can become a nation by great discipline, so the individual can will himself to joy. But as he personally tried to implement his ideas within his own personality rather than achieving self discipline, he lost more and more self-control as an enhanced emotional state took over, so that at times he would not go out because his eyes were red with unrestrained joyful weeping. On other occasions when out in the streets, he would have uncontrollable fits of grinning that would last half an hour or so, these certainly being signs of emotional unbalance, or morbid euphoria. We can all weep for joy at certain times, but with Nietzsche it became so uncontrollable that he lost all control, and therefore lost that Will that he proclaimed would control all.

With the Berserker or Dionysian state of ecstasy there is very little conscious will, if any. In fact, besides meaning "fury," an associated meaning of *wut* (from whence Wotan) is "insane," a state where all control has been lost. A recent writer on Nietzsche mentions Dionysus and morbid euphoria together in the same paragraph, but then assigns Nietzsche's morbid euphoria to the effects of syphilis. This without reflecting at all that morbid euphoria and Dionysian possession are both states of uncontrolled emotion, and that Nietzsche in that sense, was achieving part of his goal, the "going down" into uncontrolled joy. The "going up" in evolution to the Superman would have been impossible to achieve, not least because it is in direct contradistinction to the "going down," which Nietzsche says is the requirement. How is it possible to have super consciousness and near-loss of consciousness at one and the same time? As to syphilis, there is absolutely no evidence of this with Nietzsche. It was Jung's opinion that Nietzsche's mind burst with the onslaught of the super-personal forces through the unconscious that he experienced but denied.

As a matter of fact, Nietzsche did make an inadequate attempt to unite in art the higher Apollonian and lower Dionysian sides of reality. Loosely interpreted, the Apollonian means the world of the higher intellect and aesthetic serenity, respect for law and order and divine harmony, while the Dionysian refers to the realm of the Earth, the animal, and the emotional. (These have also been termed the "Apolline and Dionysiac.") Nietzsche sees the extreme opposition between these two positions as giving birth to a third way that contains both. But this idea was nothing new to either art or philosophy, and we see it in ultimate and truly evolved form in myths and religions as the unification of spirit with soul. Nietzsche's version was anything but this, being an inferior misconception of the idea. Although there is a connection of sorts with the Dionysian, it would be a serious mistake to connect Nietzsche's Superman with the higher Apollonian in any way, or to think that Nietzsche did, so that the unification of Apollo with Dionysus would be a sort of unification within the Superman. Such was not the case. Nietzsche's Superman is a material aberration, in no way comparable with the refined grace of the spiritual Apollo, the god.

Apollo the Sun-god is of the higher spirit, a divine Son equal to Christ in certain ways, who does everything on behalf of Zeus his father, instilling order and divine harmony. Dionysus, on the other hand, is something of a free agent, connected with the lower realm of the Earth; on the positive side the god of rich vegetation and abundant health, on the negative side, a disruptive god of wild orgies and uncontrollable frenzy, though in the end even he is accountable to Zeus. Nietzsche did not recognize the spirit, so the true Apollonian could not be incorporated within the Superman any more than Christ could. But we can see why Nietzsche was searching for a way to unite his so-called higher evolved Superman and the Will to Power with the lower, near unconscious state of ecstasy, because otherwise his whole philosophy falls literally in two. As the two extremes are irreconcilable, that is what happens; the two halves of Nietzsche's philosophy fall apart as irreconcilable opposites, each inferior and undesirable in itself.

It is true that the soul depths or Earth Spirit must not be denied, but integrated to the higher spirit in totality, but this has to be within the boundaries of higher and wider reality, which of necessity must involve higher and lower spirits. Only the transcendental position of genuine religion can fully unite the opposites in the *Hieros Gamos,* the Sacred Marriage, but Nietzsche rejects the spiritual and the opposites cannot unite within his inferior material perception of reality. All opposites become unified in the center that is the Self, symbolized by Christ, the centerpoint that unifies the opposites that surround. This is a sort of all-embracing canopy involving a metaphysical position that Nietzsche completely denies.

The two opposing aspects—gods we could say—had long been after Nietzsche's soul, and we know that this plagued him from the time of his dream at the age of fifteen of the wood and the Wild Huntsman, when he was required to make a choice between Christian and Wotanic paths. We know what choice he made and what god won. So although Nietzsche saw himself as a materialist in that he refused to accept the spirit, vehemently rejecting and opposing Christianity—one work of his was called *The Antichrist*—conflict would have raged in the collective unconscious between the higher spirit of Christ and the opposing lower spirit Wotan. Each of us is connected to these immortal forces of light and darkness through the unconscious, and with our lives we make the choice between them in how we live. But in order to unify higher and lower positions we first have to recognize them, which Nietzsche did not.

Nietzsche writes: "Christianity as a dogma was destroyed by its own morality; in the same way Christianity as a morality must now perish too; we stand on the threshold of this event." (*Gay Science,* 1882). In this he was prophetic, for Western civilization as a whole no longer possesses Christian morality, or much real morality of any sort, and indeed, is no longer a Christian culture. Yet Nietzsche knew that the loss of God and the spirit would mean chaos, unless the West aimed for a new order to replace the old one. But his own solution, rejecting all Christian values, which he saw as weaknesses, means chaos itself in the end, like a return to the Roman Empire at its worst.

Actually, Nietzsche saw the Roman Empire as the greatest achievement of history, ruined by decadent Christianity. Preaching otherworldly reality and morality, Christianity drained the life's blood out of the magnificence and might of Rome. The Will to Power and all it had achieved had been in vain, drained of blood by the "anemic vampires" the Christians. But Nietzsche is mistaken yet again, for the real truth is that the decadent, rotting Roman Empire was rescued and transformed by Christianity, giving it renewed life and a higher way to follow, so that it eventually grew to become Western civilization. True Christianity does not deny life, but adds to it and expands it, for the Higher Self, the Logos, upon which Christ is based, is the greatest and higher truth of us all. I speak objectively when I say that true Christianity is the greatest product ever of evolving mankind; the spirit through the unconscious has declared this to be so in several of my dreams and those of other people.

I need only reflect on my own soul sickness when the material world was weighing down heavily on me, crushing me in my atheistic neurosis. Then, not only *like* a miracle, but literally *as* one, I discovered Jung and the collective unconscious, and the spirit came pouring through to my direct experience like a transfusion. This is the meaning of blood in religious/mythological symbolism. As blood permeates and brings life to the physical body, so the spirit brings true life to material existence. Through the living spirit I personally was filled with new and invigorating life, new inspiration and eternal meaning. Life was no longer a heavy burden to carry. So the actual situation is the precise opposite to Nietzsche's claims of "Christian vampires," it is the lack of higher spirit that means lack of true life, therefore of blood symbolically. This is the meaning of the Waste Land in the Holy Grail stories; only the blood of Christ in the Grail can restore new life and fertility to the land. So while Nietzsche claims that Christianity drains the life's blood, it is actually Christ's blood, his divine essence, that gives true life.

Here is a dream I had that exemplified the deep problem—and answer—for me.

> *I am helping load a lorry with goods, but when I pick up a side of beef, my legs almost buckle under me with the weight, it is so heavy. It is a great strain to carry it, but I finally manage to throw the beef onto the wagon. My sister says to me, "The reason it is so heavy is that it is lifeless. It is white," I then pick up a gallon bottle containing blood and I say, "This is what it needs."*

In the dream my sister represents my anima, my feminine side in the unconscious. Red and white have symbolized spirit/matter contents since early Egypt, seen with the wine and bread of the Mass. The beef is so anemic it is white, and it is this that makes it such a burden to carry. In other words, the flesh needs the blood; the mortal man needs the soul and the spirit to give him true life and meaning. Then the flesh, the world of heavy, meaningless matter, will no longer be such a burden. I was to find soul and spirit and the greatest meaning possible through the unconscious processes, and then the burden that is life was no longer so heavy to carry. But mankind as a whole must realize this. Society itself cannot exist without the living Red and White spirit, for the floods of chaos soon deluge the culture.

In his last "sane" writings, Nietzsche displayed signs that he was beginning to doubt at least some of his more extreme ideas. Though still making virulent attacks upon Christianity, he would say that only he who lived his life as Christ had is a true Christian. "Such a life," Nietzsche comments, "is still possible today, for some people even necessary: genuine, original Christianity will be possible at all times." (*Antichrist,* 1888). So near the end it looks as though Nietzsche was altering his views somewhat, but apparently too late. Actually, he had always admired the man Jesus as a strong personality, but hated Christianity generally. But just to admire Jesus for his strength of character, his willpower, is an aberration of the real meaning of Christ.

What Nietzsche did not realize is that all over the world at all times cultures have flourished after a coming forth of the Higher Self in positive form, which ultimately amounts to God's incarnation, and that Christ is the highest form to date. For this to occur, all of what we call the Christian virtues are necessary within the human initiate, and the reason that such an incarnation seldom happens is that those virtues are so superior and difficult to maintain. It is far more difficult to reach and maintain the unselfish ideals of Christianity than it would be to implement the selfish ones of Nietzsche's Superman, though in the end the former constructs healthy culture while the latter destroys it.

Scholars Freke and Gandy say that Jesus Christ never lived and that the biblical writings are nonsense as the Word of God (1999). Yet the truth is the Bible consists of individuation processes that go to the highest levels, to the spirit and to God, and are prefigurations leading up to Christ as Son of God. The biblical texts are true Gnostic processes, the Gospels involving the inner journey of the man Jesus in his individuation process, ultimately to God. Nietzsche and Freke and Gandy are opposites in that while Nietzsche promulgates the love of power, Freke and Gandy proclaim the power of love, so the latter say. Yet both sides agree in that they deny Christ and the Bible itself as valid truths of the spirit.

As to the Superman, this ideal state of Nietzsche's is not attained by "self-overcoming," as he claims, but rather, according to his philosophy, by surrender to the baser instincts and then selfishly pushing forward with them in the Will to Power. True "self-overcoming" is the overcoming, to begin with, of all the selfish and instinctual drives within ourselves, involving the great struggle to implement in their place the higher qualities of modesty, humility, morality, and pity, the very qualities Nietzsche sees as weaknesses to be cast aside. Nietzsche's Superman, therefore, is actually a weakling compared with the true priest or initiate (or any other person trying to live an unselfish life) who has a harder task on his hands than to even conquer the world; that is, to conquer the *inner desire* to conquer the world (and indeed, other desires). This means in essence to conquer oneself; true "self-overcoming." Near the end of his long quest for the Holy Grail, Perceval realizes, "I have been fighting myself," to which Gawain comments, "Thou hast conquered thyself."

No matter how far Man—or *a* man—may advance with the Will to Power, it can never be in the spiritual or the moral sense with Nietzsche, who makes sure we are under no illusions that the Superman is either spiritual or moral. We must also ask how much of the personal shadow, the dark side in the unconscious, was playing a strong, or even dominant role in Nietzsche's personality, as it was soon to do on a large scale in the whole German nation, for Wotan as the unbridled spirit of conquest personifies the dark collective shadow of the unconscious. Nietzsche had simply realized that the then prevalent form of, and literal interpretation of, Christianity was unacceptable as it stood, and his consequent train of thought is not hard to follow. If the spirit and morality are no longer tenable, then we must turn to the physical Earth and if not stark immorality, certainly amorality. Yet we must ask why other people who came to the same realizations concerning the literal interpretation of Christianity did not themselves see fit to abandon morality and pity? Did Nietzsche have no innate instinct for these things, as many people do? In fact, if there were no God to ensure the eternal validity of morality and compassion, surely that should cause we ourselves to fight to implement those values all the more, rather than abandoning them?

We have evidence in myths from the earliest recorded times of how Man has experienced the spirit and soul processes of the collective unconscious, and they clearly involve the question of morality more than any other single thing. The gods of mythology are diversified to represent different aspects of the eternal forces, but the main division is between good and evil, light and dark, what is right and what is wrong, and Man realizes—is often instructed—that he must live by the one and fully oppose the other. With his higher-developed consciousness, Man was able to discriminate, to make the moral choice, whereas, before, this Man was not able to discriminate, not able to make the moral choice. It is not, therefore, as Nietzsche sees it, that man as he evolved *created* morality for expedient or provisional reasons, it is rather that he was now able to *discern* between the two positions due to his higher conscious awareness. Indeed, *it became his responsibility to do so.* In other words, Man did not *create* morality as he evolved, he *grew into it* and discovered what already existed.

Jung calls Christianity, along with Buddhism, the highest point of evolved human consciousness, actually the highest development of evolution itself. Nietzsche's shirking of the responsibility this brings, his very denial of it, in order to indulge in unreflecting or even unconscious selfish joy, is not therefore a rising above, or going beyond, good and evil to an advanced state, but precisely the opposite. It is the return to an archaic state where the moral problem of good and evil has not yet arisen. A fully conscious being, whether human or superhuman, can never go beyond the fundamental problem of morality, he can only try to deny it and endeavour to become unconscious of it. This would not be, nor could it be, "Beyond Good and Evil," as Nietzsche believed. Yet we can understand why Nietzsche considers abandoning morality, and why he glorifies the Earth; *because it may add power, strength, and exuberance to his own weak, unhealthy, and nihilistic state.*

I tried to tread Nietzsche's path for a while before I discovered Jung and experienced the archetypes in the individuation process, and so I know why Nietzsche went the way he did. But I know what a false way it is. The truths of spirit/soul reality are real and Man must live in close association with them or he eventually goes to pieces.

The Effects of the Unconscious on Nietzsche

When the Higher Self is experienced in the individuation process, it becomes evident as a tremendous fact that, as the complexity of opposites *par excellence,* it has its light good side and its dark evil side. This is power beyond Man stretching out to and in to God (and on the other side, to the Earth Spirit/World Soul). Therefore good and evil form part of the fundamental metaphysical set-up extending into God and into eternity. All of the evidence shows that Nietzsche was undergoing the individuation process himself, though mostly unconsciously, and was open to these extreme metaphysical opposites. I say "mostly unconsciously" because from his dreams he must have realized, or at least suspected, that something far beyond the normal was happening. We do know he paid some attention to his dreams—as did Goethe, whom Nietzsche greatly admired, and who based his *Faust* on dream processes stretching over decades. Jung states that the Nietzsche phenomenon is definitely Faustian.

Jung also tells us that Nietzsche had a recurring dream of a toad, which in itself is highly significant. A toad in the individuation process represents the lower, darker side of the chthonic unconscious, and as we know from myths and folklore, it is a creature associated with the dark side of reality, even the Devil. As my own dreams have demonstrated, the toad forebodes an approaching experience of the dark Self, which has to be endured for completeness; both light *and* dark sides must be experienced. St. Teresa of Avila saw a toad in one of her own visions, for she too was undergoing the individuation process, experiencing the divine source through the collective unconscious. The toad is one piece of evidence that the nonpersonal forces of the unconscious were affecting Nietzsche, inspiring and carrying him along, though in his case in a negative sense.

As a young man, Nietzsche found himself sitting next to a young woman at a function. Telling her of a dream where a toad had sat on his transparent hand, which he had then gulped down, the young woman laughed, and Nietzsche was greatly puzzled, unable to understand why. We know such appearances occur during the individuation process, but Jung comments that Nietzsche had a predilection for loathsome creatures. Jung also states that Nietzsche swallowing the toad meant swallowing his own disease, which was to overwhelm him later. This is so, for the toad, the dark content, though needing to be experienced, must ultimately be rejected rather than "taken in" and accepted. (I must add that in alchemy the toad was deemed necessary to the processes to weigh everything down, so that certain airy contents would not float away on the clouds.)

Nietzsche's early prophetic dream of the wild, uncanny huntsman, and the "blood-curdling cry" from the lunatic asylum is a significant pointer to his ultimate fate. He had a choice—the Lutheran town, Eisleben, or the Valley of the Germans, Teutschenthal—pathways to opposite fates. In my own processes, a church often appears in some form or representation, and it symbolizes not just a creed, but the full religious position as a whole. A church is a symbol of the Higher Self, as a temple was in the ancient world. The unconscious, or the spirit itself, has to use some known form to convey itself to us, and as I believe the Catholic Church (despite its many failings) in many ways expresses archetypal symbolism better than any other Christian creed, that is the form the spirit sometimes takes with me. It represents the religious side of the unconscious, and ultimately the Higher Self. (I do sometimes see Protestant churches.)

So Eisleben in Nietzsche's dream would not have merely represented Lutheranism, but the whole of the higher religious position itself, with Teutschenthal pointing to the dark Paganism that would destroy all Christian values for him, and for Germany itself as it turned out. The wild, uncanny huntsman in the dream obviously represents the lower spirit, Wotan, for is not Wotan the Wild Huntsman of Germanic myth? He, or his representation, had come forth in the dream, and was obviously Nietzsche's choice. As for the terrible cry from the nearby asylum, can this presage anything other than Nietzsche's own insanity years later, because he was to make the wrong choice? It is to be Christ or Wotan, and Nietzsche chooses the latter.

In *Thus Spoke Zarathustra,* the "prophet" Zarathustra says to the buffoon after his fatal fall, "Your soul will be dead even sooner than your body," which again is so prophetic of Nietzsche's own fate. The unconscious knows these things in advance because it sees all sides of all situations, the overall picture of everything, including where present events and decisions will eventually lead. As to Wotan, a quote from Emma Jung and Marie-Louise von Franz is particularly relevant here, that Christian humanity today has been inflicted with a deadly spearthrust by Wotan.

There is yet one other point concerning Nietzsche's early dream that I should mention before we go further, and this is where the Wild Huntsman "blew such a shrill blast" on his whistle that Nietzsche fainted. Now, as "leader of the souls of the dead," in medieval times, Wotan was sometimes identified with the Pied Piper of Hamelin. Of this H. A. Guerber writes: "In this myth Odin [or Wotan] is the piper, the shrill tones of the flute are emblematic of the whistling wind, the rats represent the souls of the dead, which cheerfully follow him, and the hollow mountain into which he leads the children is typical of the grave." In the individuation process we would say the rats represent the disease of evil, while the hollow mountain is the unconscious.

So again, with the shrill blast on the whistle, can we have any doubt what god, or force, Nietzsche was experiencing in his dream, that had come through the Other World of the unconscious? Can we have any doubts that he was experiencing Wotan when he writes of the "wild hunter god" that pierces him? Make no mistake, these eternal forces do exist in that other reality to which our conscious world is attached. They are real, though thankfully there is also the light side, represented by Christ, Ahura Mazda, Vishnu, and so on. Jung says that Nietzsche himself has become the sick prophet crucified due to the denial of Christ, actually expressed in terms of the earlier dismemberment of Dionysus-Zagreus.

However, as Jung says elsewhere, it is in the *Germanic* form of Wotan that Nietzsche experiences the Earth-god, and we could not expect it to be in any other form. A Hindu does not experience the archetypes in the same forms as an Eskimo, any more than a Frenchman experiences them in the Chinese forms.

Perhaps if Nietzsche had lived in another time his tragedy might not have occurred. (His father became insane, due to brain disease apparently, but that in itself does not mean that the son was bound to suffer the same fate, though the proposition is at least as valid as the theory that the insanity was due to syphilis, the presently prevalent though almost certainly erroneous explanation.) To be alive when all the discoveries of science were declaring (at least, to many intellectuals) that the literal interpretation of the faith of Nietzsche's ancestors, of his family, social group, and culture was outworn and defunct, while the powerful Pagan spirit of pre-Christian Germany, never far beneath the Christian surface in any country, was beginning to make its resurgence, was an unfortunate mixture of circumstances for a man of Nietzsche's highly-strung temperament. Had he been able to find a way back to higher religious meaning, then despite the world-shattering age in which he lived—world-shattering because a complete revolution in Man's thinking was occurring, when all the old tablets were being smashed—his energies, and the inner archetypal forces of the unconscious, could have been channeled to run in the opposite direction to which they did with him—a "going up," rather than a "going-down." Not a going up that would deny the Earth, but one that would unify it with the higher spirit in a wider, total reality.

Did Nietzsche know any of the works of his contemporary H. P. Blavatsky? It is difficult to say. But if so, they could have made no impression upon him at all; his own view remained at the other extreme. And yet HPB could have demonstrated to him so many other original Zarathustra figures who experienced the Higher Self and spirit reality directly, who brought great light to the world, and who insisted upon morality and compassion above all else. Nietzsche was a highly educated man, a classical scholar, and so would have known these figures, but he did not possess any kind of key to them or their real meaning, and so would have rejected them and their teachings. He was conversely to become filled with the opposite spirit, the lower side of the gods in negative aspect, of which Mephistopheles was a comparatively recent example.

Nietzsche does seem to have been impressed (though perhaps not in too pleasant a way) by the original Zarathustra's idea of Eternal Recurrence, sometimes called Eternal Return, which Nietzsche misinterpreted to mean that although the particles of the universe are many billions in number, they are nevertheless still limited. As change continuously takes place, the life-patterns in Creation will constantly be repeated no matter how many billions of years it takes. This is similar to the old idea that if you set a chimpanzee plonking away at a typewriter indefinitely, sooner or later it will produce the works of Shakespeare, and if it continues to plonk away for eternity, it will produce those works again and again. This may partly be an attempt by Nietzsche to gain some sort of permanent meaning, permanence for existence, to compensate for his philosophy of impermanence, a sort of reincarnation that does not involve the spirit, though obviously a poor substitute for reincarnation itself. Even if Eternal Recurrence were a fact, what possible meaning could it have for Man? It would not be we ourselves who are repeated, but completely detached similarities. There could be no link between the separate lives, as that would necessitate some kind of spirit as the connecting thread. Nietzsche does not seem to have realized this, otherwise how could it have interested him? It would be no different than two people alive now, alike entirely by chance, yet having no other connection.

In his autobiography *Ecce Homo,* Nietzsche says: "The doctrine of 'eternal recurrence,' that is to say the unconditional and endlessly repeated circular course of all things—this doctrine of Zarathustra *could* possibly have been taught by Heraclitus. At least the Stoa, which inherited almost all its fundamental ideas from Heraclitus, shows traces of it."

However, in the old Persian texts, Zarathustra's doctrine of Eternal Recurrence *does* involve spirit as well as matter. In the teachings Ahura Mazda and the Amesha Spentas, the Holy Immortals, as well as the Demon of Lies, Ahriman, are spirit forces, and the soul of a human being lives on and is eternal, whereas Nietzsche's version involves only physical recurrence, for only the physical exists. Yet again, Nietzsche gets it wrong.

The original Zarathustra asks Ahura Mazda, "When one of the faithful departeth this life, where dwelleth his soul on that night?" Ahura Mazda's answer is a long one, but the gist of it is that a good man lives on in bliss, meeting and merging with his feminine soul in a fourfold Paradise. For though the soul may be lovely, the good man makes her lovelier still with the good deeds of his life. (It is also true for a woman with her masculine soul, of course.) Furthermore, Ahura Mazda states, it is useless to care about worldly things for they all perish, including, especially quickly, the human shell that is eventually left behind. This obviously is entirely different to Nietzsche's interpretations and ideas.

Other Flaws and Dangers in Nietzsche's Ideas

Of all people Jung would have been the one most qualified to make a long and intensive assessment of Nietzsche, but he unfortunately did not do so, though he mentions the philosopher fairly frequently in his works. Jung was at Basle University not too many years after Nietzsche had left there, and a lot of people still remembered the philosopher, who remained, in fact, one of the main topics of conversation. Jung was influenced by Nietzsche in his early years, but realized that the philosopher was in a fever, in the grip of nonpersonal powers that were giving him quite a different psychological outlook to anyone else. Nietzsche was fascinating to those interested in the real and fundamental issues of the time, as Jung was. However, Jung was to realize that the phenomenon of Nietzsche was based on the power drive, just as Freud was based on the sex drive, and we can add that it was the archetype based on power—and lack of morality—that Nietzsche had activated in the collective unconscious. We should understand that it was not so much the erotic freedom in Dionysus that interested Nietzsche, but the increased feeling of power, ecstatic joy, and strength.

Nietzsche dethroned God and denied the religious instinct within himself, but then, replacing the latter with the power instinct, deified the Will to Power. The Will to Power is not the same as ordinary will power, which we all need to accomplish any task, particularly unpleasant ones, or to reach any achievement. The Will to Power is by comparison that totally dominating force that extinguishes all other impulses, including better ones, to reach the goal; i.e., the inner power that could be developed to make a man—a sick man, such as Nietzsche—into a Superman. By total contrast, a person like St. Francis of Assisi, though possessing tremendous will power, was nevertheless devoid of the Will to Power, being filled rather with the power of love. For him, to be simply human was enough because God and Christ were the greatest powers possible. They were also his center in the same way that St. Paul says, *"I live, yet not I, but Christ that liveth in me."* (Gal. 2:20). There is the power of love and the love of power, diametrically opposed opposites, and it is the latter that Nietzsche proclaims.

As for St. Francis, what a marvelous understanding of the true nature of reality he had, where everything that exists was his brother or sister, all things being literally related in holiness and wholeness. This realization that all things are parts of God in One-ness, body, soul, and spirit, and that this is the actual truth of full reality, can cause a person to marry poverty, or even death itself—but also life. St. Francis had great joy of life, which is what Nietzsche sought, but in the opposite way; that is, in anti-Christian form. Yet which of the two lost their reason, St. Francis or Nietzsche?

Jung says that when younger he personally had the fear of Faust within himself, for knowing that the nonpersonal forces were at work in his own unconscious, he felt afraid that he too was in danger of bringing forth a Mephistopheles. I must add that I too suffered the same fear, which caused both Jung and myself to adhere to all the moral qualities that both Goethe with *Faust* and Nietzsche with *Zarathustra* saw fit to neglect, and even deny. When the Nazis took power, Jung wrote that the wind god of old, from the barbaric past, had taken possession of the German people, indeed, as it had Nietzsche. He added that Nazism was most certainly a religion, though opposite to the higher religions. Not only in that it was of a darkness contrasted to light, but that whereas the higher religions teach of the moral responsibility of each individual, Nazism was based on mass unconsciousness, where a whole people would be carried away blindly to catastrophe as if by a terrific storm-wind. This fits in precisely with Nietzsche's storm-wind, and "complete forgetfulness," untroubled by morality, but motivated by the Will to Power. (When Nietzsche speaks of love for the "raging storm-wind" it is an actual force through the unconscious, that force being represented by Wotan, the wind god.) We get the mental pictures of Wotan leading the Wild Hunt across the night sky to war and destruction, of the Pied Piper leading the rats and children across the river to their destruction, and of the Nazis leading the whole German people across Europe to destruction.

If we abandon the higher forms of the spirit, the lower forms sweep in, and sometimes this may happen despite ourselves, and despite our best intentions. Our cleverness not only may be no defense, it may even add to the problem, and in certain cases—as in dissociated intellectualism—may even constitute the basic problem itself. That Nietzsche was a clever man there seems little doubt (or so people say), but though his writings themselves have great style and force, at times the flaws in his basic philosophy are so simple as to render it naïve, even unintelligent nonsense. When I was partly in agreement with Nietzsche in my own lost state of nihilistic dissociation when younger, searching for my own answers, I was then helped enormously by Jung and the forces of the unconscious (many of these appearing in Christian forms). These could have been the making of Nietzsche, too. Instead, maintaining negative values in consciousness that were unsound, he was destroyed by the unconscious. The denial of God and the spirit can be very dangerous for some people.

Chapter 16

The Return of the Pagan Shadow

When Nietzsche was on the hill and became elated at the lightning, and what amounts to the Pagan blood sacrifice of the kids, his reaction was in full concordance with the events. But such blood sacrifices—of cattle, in fact—was one of the things that the original Zarathustra forbade his followers to carry out. Such sacrifices represented the archaic lower Pagan state, which Zarathustra insisted they must overcome in order to serve the new higher God of Light, Ahura Mazda. This would mean a higher state of consciousness and of culture. In the very same way, when Jesus saw Jewish priests making animal sacrifices, he remonstrated with them, stating that God does not wish cruelty from Man, but love. Surely then, Nietzsche's own reaction of ecstatic elation at the events on the mountain can only mean the return to the Pagan and the barbaric, for he is ecstatic at the Pagan state that Zarathustra and Jesus reject. It is as though this incident were heralding the exuberant return to Pagan Wotanism that was soon to possess the whole German nation.

The old Pagan rituals of Wotanism, including animal sacrifice, were revived by the Nazis, and as has now become well known, the Nazi leaders were themselves initiates into the new form of the old Pagan religion. Festivals of great fervor rejecting Christianity and reviving Paganism were held at Nuremberg and elsewhere, and pictures of Christ were taken down from above the altars in the churches, being replaced by ones of Hitler, the new Messiah, or rather anti-Messiah, or Antichrist.

Wotan, using magic, had mythologically rescued the ancient runes, the ancient magical symbolic writings from the depths, and now all SS officers had to study them. Again, can we see all of this as anything else but the wider fulfillment of the Pagan spirit that had ignited Nietzsche on the mountainside, and which actually flowed into him from the realm of the unconscious? Jung wrote that the Superman, the personification of these negative forces, which Nietzsche projected into conscious reality, is the greater personality—here in negative form—that may sometimes burst the shell that is the brain.

Of course, Nietzsche would not have approved the cruelty and mass murder of the Nazis, but we cannot help but believe that in the early days he would have been carried along by the great surge of Paganism and Earth-worship and the attempt to create the Nazi Superman, despite the fact that it is said to be in some ways a lower version of his own ideal. We find the same contradiction of moral regression mixed with so-called progressiveness both in Nietzsche and the Nazis. Nietzsche would have had high hopes for Nazism, though one difference was that ultimately the philosopher was an individualist who proclaimed the development of the individual man, whereas Nazism soon proved to be the loss of the individual into the mass Man. Nevertheless, what else is forgetfulness in ecstasy but the loss of the individuality that comes with consciousness? And we must remember that Nietzsche's freedom was for the elite minority, whom the inferior masses would serve.

Again, there is no doubt that Nietzsche would have been utterly horrified by the Nazis' attempt to exterminate other races. He was neither a racist nor a cruel man, and as said earlier, he disliked anti-Semites in general. He had Jewish friends, and said that if anyone should be driven out of Germany it should be the anti-Semite louts who caused violence on the streets. As said earlier, when people met Nietzsche for the first time after reading his works, they were very surprised that he seemed affable and even likeable. He was not like the ideas in his books, though some report they could detect great loneliness in the man. But we must remember that he said Europe needed a great war, which it was to get, two of them, the horrors of which affected the whole globe. As to Nazism, the world was saved from this great evil not solely by the greater armies of the Allies, but also by the basic decency of Western peoples, nurtured by many centuries of Christian influence (helped by many other decent peoples of the world). This was the true bulwark against the Nazis, the very antithesis of Nietzsche's teachings.

Despite his opposition to religion, Nietzsche did have the insight to see that once religion had vanished from the world, mankind would no longer produce beauty and great works of art. In this there is no denying he was truly prophetic. Where is the beauty in our modern world; where is the great art? We have to go to the past to find it. Nietzsche was under no illusions that mankind would be improved by the loss of God, at least, initially, for he believed that the "false" values of religion would be replaced by no values at all; indeed, that horrible process had happened to him personally. So he preached that Man must create values himself, and must be elevated to create great art, which would, of course, be the task of the special individual, or the Superman, who would be the result of the Will to Power. But we must ask, as the Superman denies the finer qualities that make even mortal men worthwhile, how could he produce great art? How could beyond morality, beyond pity, beyond good and evil, the Will to War, the Will to Power, ever be great or beautiful?

Nietzsche's rejection of God and Christianity and the elevation of the Superman does not give hope to mankind, but rather condemns it to mere physical existence, no matter how evolved and advanced the Superman is supposed to be. And in any case, the majority, the "herd," are not to benefit, only the gifted few. But the whole point of evolution is to reach higher consciousness. To experience and reflect upon higher realities, largely of the spirit, is Mans' main business; no other creature can do it. So would we ever want Nietzsche's "ideal reality," where the greatest meaning possible is, and ends with, the Superman, the creature that lacks morality and pity, and with the herd in servitude? Or do we not cry out from the depths of our souls that reality is so much more than this, and that there are far more things in Heaven and Earth than in Nietzsche's philosophy? The Superman is nowhere near adequate to express the real truth of Man, or of reality itself, for the Higher Self is Man's greatest truth, and beyond that, God, whereas the Superman is a grossly inferior and manifestly dangerous, substitute.

Christianity itself guarantees the value of all people under God, where even the lowliest have souls that are immortal; indeed, the lowliest soul may rank the highest with God. If such a person were to spend a lifetime in kindliness, in helping others, they would rate much higher than any selfish genius or Superman. These are realities of unconscious/spirit, not mere ideas of consciousness. There are stories around the world in which a tyrant ruler dies but in the afterlife finds that he has a lowly position. Seeing his old stable hand in a high position, the former ruler complains. Surely there has been as mistake here; surely the positions should be reversed. But he is told that though he had a high position in life he brought only suffering to his people and the world, whereas his stable hand, though lowly, was a man of great kindness and truth, who always tried to help his fellow human beings. Unlike on Earth, in spirit reality things appear as they truly are and should be.

In any case, how could any superior being lack morality or go beyond it? The very lack means an inferiority, and even God Himself would be inferior to Man if he lacked morality. Given Nietzsche's view—that God did not exist—he should have insisted upon morality in both Man and the Superman all the more, as the prime requisite for both the good of the individual and for a higher state of culture. Christianity, the continuance of the divine Son of Egypt, the cosmic Higher Self, eventually replaced the old Pagan forms of religion in Europe. Nietzsche's experience was, at least in part, the abandonment of the former and the regression to the latter, albeit mixed up with ideas of a super state of mind. There is no doubt that Nietzsche's philosophy, though denying the validity of religion, is nevertheless partly a return to Pagan Earth worship, mixed in with ideas of a super elite. Jung tells us we should have no illusions as to just how primitive and cruel the old Pagan religions could be.

When certain modern intellectuals believe there is a more "subtle" meaning to Nietzsche when he rejects morality and pity, I suggest they talk to the survivors of the Nazi death camps for their opinions on what the lack of morality and pity—subtle or otherwise—can really mean. In the same vein, another modern writer on Nietzsche says in support of his rejection of pity that the only way to treat others as whole and equal is not to feel pity for them. This is over-intellectualized claptrap, though perhaps more dangerous than mere claptrap would be. (A Jungian writer says more or less the same, and it is still claptrap.) Ask a starving Ethiopian if he minds not receiving pity and compassion because it prevents him and his people from being whole and equal. Only when we feel pity are we truly moved to help those who are suffering, who may even die otherwise.

We must understand that Nietzsche really means what he says when he asks why morality and pity should be the way forward, and answers that in his opinion pity is weakness and only hardness can win. Hardness is noble, and that which is ripe for death is preserved by pity when it should die. Further, a man who feels pity loses power. Is Christian love weak and inferior to this?

My dictionary interprets "morality" to mean "principles of conduct based upon distinction between right and wrong," and "pity" to mean "compassion—grief, sorrow, sympathy felt for the sufferings of another; to show mercy to." How can Man ever dispense with these highest of qualities, no matter how we try to see deeper meaning in their abandonment? Man becomes a dangerous beast whenever he does abandon them, as history has shown only too clearly. In fact, we can say that it is the ability to feel and distinguish these qualities of morality and compassion that make Man truly evolved and human. They are proof of it. A person is devoid of these essentially human qualities we classify a psychopath. (As Jung did Nietzsche at one point.) Nietzsche was deeply interested in criminals because they seemed to possess added strength and vitality, due to their lack of morality and consideration for others, and this demonstrates that he actually did mean dispensing with morality and pity. His philosophy, from his point of view, is invalid otherwise.

I would like the reader to understand that I was for a few years lost in a nihilistic state myself, and that I considered Nietzsche's ideas an answer, when my inner suffering was at its most unbearable. I desperately needed the strength and power that criminals seemed to have, and that I seemed to lack in my own weak state. Nietzsche apparently felt the same. He had a love of the Renaissance, which I share, and was fascinated by Cesare Borgia, and this too was the case with myself, though I knew nothing of Nietzsche's feelings at that time. (My fascination for Borgia was due to my shadow wanting recognition. At that time I knew nothing of depth psychology.) But I had no illusions about Borgia as a "superior" type of man as Nietzsche thought, and I certainly never admired Machiavelli as Nietzsche did. More than the beauty associated with the Renaissance, Nietzsche would have enjoyed the power intrigues, being unconcerned with their immorality and even blind to their cruelty.

In fact, Nietzsche loved militarism, and speaks of the *"affirmation of war,"* and even his personal appearance was based on that of the prototype Prussian officer, with the "sweeping-brush" of a moustache he wore. As far as I can detect, his mind seems to have blinded itself to the horrors of war. Even when he personally was up to his eyebrows in blood and death in the Franco-Prussian War, he could only see the glory of war and the Will to Power. It is a fact that that while much of Europe was enamoured with the glamor and romance of militarism at that time, the German obsession went further. The German was a soldier first, devoted to the "Iron Will," and belonged to his own profession or trade second. Nietzsche loved all of this, partly because he saw it as an exhilarating antidote to the abject nihilistic state he had suffered for years.

True nihilism is a state of profound inner torture, and in such circumstances the personal shadow of the unconscious usually plays a large part in finding an answer. Spying its chance, the shadow leaps in, and though it may indeed bring an upsurge of renewed vitality at first, in the long run, if allowed to run unchecked, it leads to catastrophe. A person may come to an understanding with the shadow, to a degree and of a kind, but it must be on *moral* terms laid down by consciousness.

In my own case I was lucky in that I stumbled upon Jung and depth psychology, which then led to my individuation process through the unconscious. During this process I encountered stark evil many times, but always help came flowing through from the light side. (Both sides must be experienced for completeness.) I eventually had the dream given earlier, where I could no longer go on, sinking to my knees sobbing and broken. But suddenly the wounded Christ, his arms and hands bleeding, walked into the dream and laid his hands on my drooping head. Christ, in whom I did not believe at that time, had pity and brought me grace. I came to know by direct experience that God and a true Christianity are the greatest things that Man can know, and that morality and pity are not only noble in themselves, but are also the truest kind of health, to ourselves and to our world. The answer for mankind is therefore to be found in the opposite to Nietzsche's philosophy—in humility, compassion, and morality; ultimately in Christ and God.

The collective unconscious is the foundation of all consciousness, of all being, the Primordial Ocean from whence all life springs, and if you should you ever come to experience it directly, then you will learn to have morality and pity as your values, if they are not so already. Or, as H. P. Blavatsky and Jung warn, not even God will be able to help when the day of reckoning arrives, when the Self appears in the form you have forged. I once had a dream that told me that the only true answer to everything is "Christian love," if we can manage the enormous task of filling ourselves with it.

It always seems to me that Nietzsche lacked simple humanity. I have always been an outsider myself, searching for the same answers he sought, and this has meant isolation from other people to some degree. It is not even a choice, for the great inner thirst has to be quenched above all, and at any cost. But we must never lose track of our simple humanity; indeed, the necessity of humanity is one of the things we come to realize with a successful quest. Strangely, although experience of the Higher Self separates us from our fellow human beings to a degree, it also integrates us with them, so that a Moses or a Zarathustra, while drawing close to their God, nevertheless lead their people and are an integral part of them, caring deeply for their welfare. When it comes to Nietzsche, we are forced to ask not where is his greatness, but where is his smallness, his identity with his fellow humans and his compassion for them? But then, they are the herd, and he calls the ordinary mortal the "Ugliest Man," the inferior who must be rejected on the way to the Superman. But it is from this lowly position that we better appreciate our empathy with others. Christ mingled with the poor, the sick, the lowly; the greatest reducing itself to the smallest.

I recently came across reference to a letter Nietzsche wrote to Lou Salome, the woman he hoped to marry, but who rejected him. He writes that he wants to learn how to be human once more, that he is tired of being lonely. He knew he was losing his humanness, and so wanted another chance at it. As said, it is necessary on the quest to become isolated from our fellow humans for a time, at least mentally, but ultimately we must become unified with all of mankind, and indeed, all of nature, as happened with St. Francis of Assisi.

At one point Nietzsche himself felt there is a One-ness of all creatures in the great Whole, but it is an inferior experience, for it lacks the sunlit holiness of St. Francis's mystical experience, or that of the original Zarathustra. What Nietzsche was missing, what he lacked, was the sunlit holiness of the higher spirit, for what light does the Earth possess without the light of the Sun? What light does Man possess without the light of the higher spirit? In other words, we need to be very humble to look up and appreciate the wonder of God. Because modern Man exists largely without that higher light, he naturally lives in a much-darkened world. This is what Jung feared, a return to barbarism due to the loss of the higher spirit. Nothing in Nietzsche's philosophy helps us to reconnect to the higher spirit, precisely the opposite. This is what Nietzsche lost, and what modern Man has largely lost, and what we so desperately need to regain. Christ the Logos, the greatest light possible, disperses himself into humble humanity; we must not deny that light.

Absence of the Feminine Element

Certain women's lib movements have adopted Nietzsche as a supporter of their cause, and indeed, a number of women are now reading and even partly following the philosopher. This seems puzzling, not least because if ever a writer propounds the masculine principle while neglecting the feminine it is Nietzsche. The Earth is largely feminine, Mother Earth, and so on, yet Nietzsche's Earth worship concerns only masculine forces, Wotan and Dionysus. Jung asks where the feminine element has got to in Nietzsche, and concludes that the feminine soul is very undeveloped in the German mind collectively, and this is plainly seen in Nietzsche. All other peoples have Motherlands, but the Germans have the Fatherland. We cannot imagine Nietzsche seeing as feminine the Earth that he so proclaims, and it is Dionysus and more particularly Wotan that inspire him.

It may be true that Christianity itself as it developed was lacking in the feminine element, although the Catholic Church is feminine as the Bride of Christ. Most of the great cultures of the world had goddesses in complementation to the masculine gods, but Christianity, while having feminine spirit originally, largely lost it later. Nevertheless, the near worship of Mary by the Catholics has always gone some way to compensate this, and rightly so.

Nietzsche clearly likes the feminine woman and hates the feminist. He writes, "The struggle for *equal* rights is even a symptom of sickness. The more a woman is a woman the more she defends herself tooth and nail against rights in general—'Emancipation of woman'—is the instinctive hatred of the woman who *has turned out ill.*" He seems to have liked women generally, though he considered them to be privileged and elevated in many ways, and believed that the wisest of them knew it. He also said, speaking figuratively, that when a man goes among women he should take a whip.

So why do women libbers adopt Nietzsche considering the above views? The answer can only be, as far as I can determine, his Earth worship and philosophy of the Will to Power. Men have always had the power and so now it is the turn of women, the libbers reason. The trouble is, many of these women are inevitably ruled in this by their own masculine animus (the male side of a woman in the unconscious), and the main aim of the animus, so Jung tells us, is *power* (his italics). This means that rather than more femininity being brought to the world—which has always been sorely in need of it—more masculinity is brought, albeit the "feminine" variety. So we must conclude that it is Nietzsche's rejection of Christianity, (i.e., the masculine higher spirit), his near-worship of the Earth, which is largely feminine (though not for Nietzsche), and his proclaiming of Power (the main interest of the animus), that attracts women libbers to Nietzsche.

When we think about it, it is Christ who brings the "power of love" to the world—love being considered more a feminine quality than masculine—whereas Nietzsche opposes this with the "love of power." Love and power are opposing principles in the human psyche, so the furtherance of animus power means the lessening of love. Turn up the heat, the cold depletes, and vice versa. Furthermore, Christ has his own femininity highly developed, seen in the transformation of Mary Magdalene, who as anima/World Soul redeemed, becomes the Virgin Mary, whom Jung rightly says is a form of the goddess Sophia. The Sacred Marriage is achieved in Christ's unification with this feminine side, so that the feminine is raised as co-equal with the masculine. The man Jesus in his inner processes would have raised feminine spirit as co-equal with the masculine in order for the Sacred Marriage to take place. So it is Christ who furthers the feminine cause, not Nietzsche. Yet the libbers reject Christ and adopt Nietzsche with his masculine Will to Power, masculine Earth, and no rights for women.

The whole Roman Empire was decaying with "love of power" sickness, which had infected conquerors and conquered alike. This is why power rather than sexuality tempts Christ; it is not Eros that is the main cause of the sickness but the power devil. So it is the Will to Power that Christ must defeat, the very inner drive that Nietzsche promotes and some women libbers adopt. Nietzsche wrote *The Antichrist* because this was the position he took, his philosophical stance. But as Jung says, where power rules there can be no love, and where love rules there is no need for power; which is why of necessity Nietzsche had to discard compassion and morality in the interests of increased power. This was not new with Nietzsche, of course; it is a large part of the story of mankind.

One woman defends the animus power drive in modern woman on the "principle" that the end justifies the means, always the claim of those who have attained the throne of power by dubious methods. But such a throne of power is built upon rotten supports, which is why the throne of the High God in ancient Egypt had to rest upon Maat, truth and righteousness, actually represented and exemplified by a goddess called Maat. It was realized that for the whole of reality to be justified and sustained it must rest upon those qualities, as must the life of each human individual, and their every action. The end rarely, if ever, justifies the means.

My words are in no way an attack on the feminine itself, indeed are rather a defense of it. I have always been a true admirer of women and even as a child realized there must be a feminine counterpart to God, or a feminine side of Him. Equality between male and female is the way reality is structured and it could not be any other way. The world benefits greatly from feminine love and feeling, but that is the whole point; it is the *feminine* it sorely needs, not feminine masculinity fueled by animus *power.* I have long been supported in what I say by the feminine side of the unconscious, which knows that part of my work is to raise the feminine World Soul to the Sacred Marriage with the higher spirit. This has always been the ultimate aim of the religious and esoteric Mysteries. Nietzsche denied all of this, and so there can only be stagnation and degeneracy with his ideas.

Nietzsche's Fatal Illness

We now come to Nietzsche's fatal illness, which some modern authorities assign to syphilis contracted from a prostitute some years earlier. It is assumed that Nietzsche must have visited brothels at times, but there is no evidence of any of this at all, and even if there were proof of such visits, it would still be no proof of syphilis. The facts of Nietzsche's illness, however, do fit exceedingly well with what we know of the dangers of the collective unconscious as it may affect the human psyche. Not knowing the tremendous forces of the unconscious and how it can shatter consciousness under certain circumstances, scholars are left with only possible physical causes to postulate.

To explore a little further what these dangerous psychic effects may be, we must return to the frenzy state of Dionysus/Wotan. In *A History of Religious Ideas* (1979) Mercea Eliade states:

> At the center of the Dionysiac ritual we find, in one form or another, an ecstatic experience of more or less violent frenzy: *mania*. This "madness" was in a way the proof that the initiate was entheos, "filled with the god." The experience was certainly unforgettable, for there was a sharing in the creative spontaneity and intoxicating freedom, in the superhuman force and invulnerability of Dionysus. Communion with the god shattered the human condition for a time, but it did not succeed in transmuting it. (vol. 1, p. 368.)

With Nietzsche it apparently did.

The myth of Dionysus is partly concerned with spiritual renewal and rebirth, and as said earlier, as Dionysus-Zagreus he is killed and dismembered by the Titans, his parts boiled in a cauldron and then eaten. Zeus, learning of the crime, destroys the Titans, and, with the help of one of the goddesses, Zagreus is then reconstituted. This myth, like that of Osiris and many others, including Christ, is based upon processes involving the Higher Self, although the human initiate is also involved and undergoes transformation. Philosophical alchemy was based upon the very same processes, as was the initiation of shamans. But it is also interesting from the point of view of Nietzsche and his experience that the name Zagreus means "great hunter," of which Mircea Eliade comments "which corresponds with the savage, orgiastic character of Dionysus." This brings us once again to Wotan, of course, the Wild Huntsman, whose followers would sometimes fly into savage frenzy. Obviously, the same primal force of the collective unconscious was behind this aspect of each god, Dionysus and Wotan, and there is even the possibility that they originally were the same god, or partly so, of a people who infiltrated both Greece and Germany. Even the wild and dangerous women followers of Dionysus, the *Maenads,* remind us of the witches who were said to follow the Wild Hunt of Wotan. (As said earlier, Tiwat, the Germanic sky-god that countermatches Wotan, seems to be connected with the Hittite god Tiwaz; and this was in what is now Turkey, next to Greece. Furthermore, some say that Dionysus originated in the same region, Turkey.)

But why then did Nietzsche not speak of Wotan, rather than of Dionysus and Zagreus? The answer most probably lies in the fact that Nietzsche, being a professor of classical philology, had been immersed in Greek philosophy and mythology all of his adult life, and possibly even in childhood, and it was therefore second nature to him; plus the fact that the ancient Classical world was greatly admired in his day as representing the epitome of learning and culture. But all the evidence of Nietzsche's writings show that he was constantly affected by the archetypal force represented by Wotan, the Wild Huntsman.

Yet Dionysus also fits the bill partly, for as Mircia Eliade explains:

> Intoxication, eroticism, universal fertility, but also the unforgettable experiences of the periodic arrival of the dead, or by *mania,* by immersion in animal unconsciousness, or by the ecstasy of *enthousiasmos*—all these terrors and revelations spring from a single source: *the revelation of a god.* . . . This is why Dionysus constitutes a type of divinity radically different from the Olympians.

Precisely. Nietzsche, albeit mostly unconsciously, experienced directly the nonpersonal, god-like force that we would equate with Dionysus-Zagreus or Wotan, was "filled with the god," and in his fatal illness he would sometimes sign his name "Dionysus" or "Zagreus."

Rejecting the higher spirit, and religion in general, Nietzsche projected everything into physical reality, but as usually happens in such cases, the lower spirit was able to resurge, and given Nietzsche's basic nature, it resurged with great force and filled him. Nietzsche underwent the processes involving the Self, but in a lower, negative form, and mostly unconsciously, which he then identified with the possibilities of consciousness in the Superman. He obviously intended to try and reach that state himself, but in so doing was identifying with the Self, a truly catastrophic situation. His ego-consciousness was thus absorbed into the Self, becoming identical with it, which burst the all too frail human consciousness, resulting in a state of inflated insanity. He could even be said to have achieved his goal in the sense that he became, to himself, superhuman and godlike, though as everyone else could plainly see, it is no fitting state for a mere mortal. Nietzsche in his sick state not only believed himself to be godlike, at least, at times, he actually partly *became* so, for Dionysus/Wotan was the archetype Nietzsche was absorbed into. As I pointed out, Nietzsche's early words, "must not we ourselves become gods," is a danger sign and warningly prophetic.

Jung says very clearly in *The Archetypes and the Collective Unconscious* that if we read Nietzsche's *Zarathustra* with attention and psychological understanding, it will become clear that with rare consistency and with the passion of a truly religious person Nietzsche has described the psychology of the "Superman" for whom God is dead, and who, because he tried to imprison the divine paradox within the narrow framework of the mortal man, is himself burst asunder.

We find evidence of the unification of the human initiate with the Higher Self in myths and religions across the globe, but the situation is entirely different than with Nietzsche. The "normal" initiate loves the spirit (God), knowing that morality, compassion, and all the nobler values are essential to his quest and to mankind. He knows that he must shrink "to the size of a pea," as Jung puts it, lest he identify with the Self, the god, in positive inflation (similar to, yet opposite to Nietzsche's negative inflation). The nearer we approach the realm of the gods the smaller we must shrink, or, as with Icarus, our wings, which are not true wings, will melt with catastrophic consequences. The wise initiate is extremely aware that the Higher Self is immortal spirit, and that the initiate is only a tiny mortal in comparison. Nietzsche is a warning to us all of what tragic consequences can follow having a reduced and negative attitude towards the eternal powers of the spirit, of which we can know only the part that touches us.

Contrary to Nietzsche's pronouncements, civilizations flourish when Man adheres to spiritual values and morality, not rejecting the Earth but bringing the highest meaning to it with the unification of both. This is why in Egypt, Ra had his seat in Maat, which meant the rightness and fundamental morality of full reality itself. In other words, the truth of

God rests on moral foundations. When Ra incarnates as his divine Son, Horus, it is with the same wisdom, truth, and righteousness. As to the unification of the opposites, Ra, the High God, and Osiris, Lord of the lower spirit in light aspect, came to be unified in harmony, expressed by the heads of both on one body.

Perhaps Nietzsche was meant to be a Christian, a true one, but he lost his way, and the times were against him in that the death of God was to be the new spirit of the age. He was an accomplished pianist and composed music, which, it was said by those who heard him play, was really "church music." This has been ascribed to the effects of his Lutheran upbringing, but surely we would have expected him to compose music in the opposite vein, to show his vehement rejection of and opposition to the Church and Christianity, as in his writings. The truth may be that at the deepest level of his soul he sorely needed (and may even have loved) Christianity and what it represents, or at least part of him did, for the opposite god was to gain control of his soul. In a way, Madame Blavatsky was similar. She became a Buddhist, but deep in her soul the Russian Church still affected her emotionally.

The final word must be that it is not the heavy Earth that truly inspires us, filling and quickening the soul, but the spirit. The Earth has its own beauty and light, and to walk down a country lane on a lovely summer's day is full of delight; but Man needs more. He needs contact with the holy and the divine and to know that it is ultimately moral and compassionate. He needs to know that the soul is somehow immortal, not because of fear or selfishness, but because then there is deeper magical meaning to the whole life process, which is then added to the Earth. Nietzsche had none of this and even his proclaiming of life and the Earth is dark, negative, and selfish. Yet those of us who have been fortunate enough to experience the higher spirit must feel compassion for Nietzsche, taking him along with us to teach him, as it were, rather than rejecting him outright. He had a bad life in what was for him an ugly reality, and his ultimate fate was extremely sad.

Though Nietzsche castigates pity and compassion, what else can we feel for a man who surrendered to what he believed to be "the answer" to the point of self-sacrifice, although that answer was ultimately false and destructive. In this act of self-sacrifice, if in nothing else, Nietzsche truly followed a similar path to the man Jesus, becoming, as Jung tells us, "the Crucified."

Chapter 17

The Spirit in the Modern World

The Vision at Pontmain: Great Mother and Son

It is a fact mostly unrecognized that Western thinking became warped and falsified in the twentieth century due to the influence, indeed, indoctrination, of scientific-rationalism, affecting not solely *what* Man thought, but even more importantly *how* Man thought. If we limit our thinking to the functional process of an electric light bulb, we may be on the mark as far as that goes. But, if having been conditioned to think that the light bulb process constitutes the basis of the whole of functioning reality, we then try to apply the same yardstick to measuring the worth of the human soul, or to the ultimate meaning of the universe, we will fall very much short of the mark. It may be a poor analogy, but such reductionism condemned modern Man to a straitjacket of negative materialism that he not only seemingly cannot escape, nor seemingly has any desire to escape, but of which he seemingly has no inkling that he *should* escape. Nevertheless, his soul knows differently and rebels.

This is the basic cause of the psychic disturbance in society today. Freud claimed that the basis of the human psyche is a sewer. Jung, studying the unconscious in great depth, came to realize that it rather has foundations in the immortal Self, which is ultimately a *religious* phenomenon. Jung began his working life as a young psychiatrist studying the human mind and the unconscious, but upon discovering the archetypes lying beyond the personal unconscious, soon came to link psychology up with religion, which adepts in the hidden Mysteries had actually been doing for thousands of years. We must remember Jung's words that he had been studying the unconscious all his life, but the Gnostics had already known it.

The importance of Jung and his discoveries cannot be overestimated, for Jung came to substantiate the utter validity of all the old religions, and indeed, the mythology of the world generally, as processes of and through the unconscious, the otherworldly reality countermatching the worldly. Everything has been altered for us again with Jung, away from the dissociated scientific-rationalism that desouled us all in the twentieth century, back to a spiritually alive universe that Man had always hitherto inhabited. Spirit/soul reality itself is continually at work within mankind to influence him on to the religious path, in dreams of individuals through the unconscious, but also sometimes seen as outer manifestations that we call religious visions. Some of the latter have concerned the Virgin Mary.

As modern Man became more and more dominated by scientific-rationalism, and as his wars became increasingly terrible and devastating in consequence, due in part to horrible inventions of mass destruction, there arose a corresponding counteraction from spirit/soul reality to try and restore the balance. UFO and alien sightings certainly form an aspect of this counter movement, but there have also been a number of visions of the Virgin Mary, known as Marian visions, which actually began in the first half of the nineteenth century. It is no coincidence that these started to appear just as Man was becoming psychically and spiritually dissociated, when his science began promulgating atheism and a soulless universe, with his philosophy spouting a pessimistic rationalism connected with anything and everything bar "love of wisdom" (*philos* = "love," *Sophia* = "wisdom"). Indeed, "God is dead" more than anything else became the mood of Western philosophy in the modern age. The upshot has been the gradual unleashing of the dragon of chaos as culture falls ever deeper into degeneracy, for only the light from the spirit above prevents the world tumbling into the abyss of darkness below. The light that A. E. Waite called "the Christ-light" has been switched off. The rule of mythology and religion generally is that the higher spirit must redeem the Earth Spirit and that this must be maintained for a higher level of culture to be sustained.

As for Marian visions, it seems to be fact that contents of otherworldly reality, including the most holy ones, are not solely to be reached and experienced through the unconscious. Spirit/soul apparently has the ability to break through and manifest in outer, physical reality, and such seems to be the case with Marian visions. The latter have been experienced largely, though by no means exclusively, by children, and two accounts in particular so abound with archetypal symbolism that we would expect to find in processes of the unconscious that there can be no doubt as to their source and validity, the archetypal material somehow breaking through the veil. We can look at Marian manifestations briefly here.

The first episode I relate is little known and yet is perhaps the most important from the point of view of the symbolism proving its authenticity. This occurred at Pontmain, France, on the evening of January 17, 1871, when Joseph and Eugene Barbadette, aged ten and twelve, were at home sharing a meal with their parents, Cesar and Victoire. During conversation, the boy Eugene strolled over to the door, which must have been open, and gazing up at the dark evening sky, observed a patch that was virtually clear of stars. Suddenly, he was amazed to find that a "Holy Lady" of "lovely countenance" was smiling down at him from within the clear patch. He could discern a gold crown over a black veil resting upon her head, while below she wore a blue gown covered with golden stars. Calling to the others in the room, they joined Eugene at the door, though while young Joseph could also see the vision, the parents could not.

Several neighbors then assembled, including the local schoolmistress, Sister Vitaline, and Joseph commented that he could see three bright stars, forming a triangle, enclosing the head of the Holy Lady. While the newly arrived adults could see the stars, they could not see the head, so Sister Vitaline sent for three other children, all girls, in order to observe their reactions. On arrival, two older girls described exactly the same configuration as the Barbadette boys, though the youngest girl saw nothing. The three stars the others saw were to disappear later when the Holy Lady herself finally vanished. Meanwhile, as the vision continued, the children also saw four unlit candles on a blue rectangular frame encompassing the Holy Lady's body, two candles at her shoulders and two at her knees, these being, of course, below the triangle of stars that encompassed the head. There was thus a triangle over a square, the symbol of unified opposites in the esoteric Mysteries, the Trinity with the quaternity, 3 + 4. Then, as she grew in size, a red cross formed over the Holy Lady's heart, and many other stars attached themselves to her gown, covering it all over even more so than it had been before.

Words then appeared on a streamer at the Holy Lady's feet, which said, "But pray my children," although these soon changed to ones that read, "God will soon answer you." Then, as the Holy Lady's face became very sad, a third message could be seen, "My Son allows Himself to be moved," at which point a large red cross appeared with Christ crucified upon it in a still darker red. Had there been any doubts that the Holy Lady was the Virgin Mary these would now have been dispelled by the appearance of Christ the Son on the cross. However, it may be of some importance that Christ here seems to be Son of the Great Mother, as well as Son of the Father.

The four candles were then lighted in turn by one of the stars, though the crucified figure on the cross vanished. This was followed by the gradual fading of Mary from the feet upwards as a white veil spread over her. The whole vision had lasted a few hours, and it affected the two Barbadette brothers to such an extent that later both became priests, while one of the girls became a nun.

The first thing to comment on is that while Mary traditionally had been depicted wearing a blue mantle over her head and shoulders with a red dress below, reflecting the two aspects of the feminine spirit, celestial and earthly, in the Pontmain vision the gown itself was blue. (The Church had come to declare by that time that Mary should wear a blue mantle over her head and shoulders with a white gown below, the significance of which may mean that Mary has lost her earthiness, becoming rather celestial, at least in Catholic thinking.) This suggests that it was the celestial aspect of the feminine spirit that appeared that night at Pontmain rather than the lower form, considering the blue gown covered in stars. In ancient Egypt, Nut was the goddess of the sky, blue naturally being her color, and the thing is, she is often depicted covered in stars. E. A. Wallis Budge speaks of "a woman, whose body is bespangled with stars; this woman is the goddess Nut." (*Gods of the Egyptians,* 1904).

Nut is sometimes seen covered in stars bending over touching the Earth with her hands, thus forming an arc with her body and representing the sky, corresponding to the arc formed by Mary's mantle. In fact, Nut's arms and legs in this position are said to be the four pillars upon which the Heavens rest. Two of her titles are, "Nut, Lady of Heaven," and "Nut, the Great Lady who gave Birth to the Gods." One of these gods is Osiris. While Budge speaks of her as "the Sky-mother, who has produced her son, the Sun-god," this being Horus, Nut was mother of the Five Gods, Osiris, Set, Isis, Nephthys, and Horus. (There are at least five mothers of Horus I know of in different Egyptian cults, Hathor, Isis, Neith, Sefekh, and Nut.) So while the vision at Pontmain was obviously of Mary, the gown covered with stars connects her to the original Great Mother of All, the same eternal archetypal feminine force well-known to the ancient world. The Sun Woman in Revelation wears a crown of twelve stars, but is not connected directly with the Virgin Mary, or with the Holy Lady in the Pontmain vision, though all are manifestations of the Great Mother.

Nut absorbed several other goddesses of Egypt, most of which were sevenfold, and the Seven Stars, found in the constellation of the Great Bear, was the "Chair of Nut." Originally it had been the thigh or leg of Nut, becoming the chair later. Incidentally, it is usually assumed that the

Seven Stars of the Great Bear used by the ancients were those of the Plough, but while this may be so in certain circumstances, looking at an Egyptian depiction they appear to be seven other stars of the Bear. There are over a dozen stars in the constellation and several formations can be taken from them.

The three stars with four candles below that the children at Pontmain saw have been called "a total of seven lights," and these encompassed Mary in the vision. So Mary here is sevenfold, matching many goddesses and wisdom figures of the ancient world. Several female figures of the Bible represent the feminine spirit and are sevenfold, including Rebekah; Rachel; Bath-sheba; the Queen of Sheba; and Zipporah, wife of Moses, which are later versions of the Egyptian goddess of Wisdom, Sefekh. Mary is often compared with Isis, who has her seven swallows, seven veils, etc. The vision at Pontmain is obviously a version of the sevenfold goddess as Mary, here in Great Mother aspect, again an extremely ancient archetype.

The Seven Powers in one form consist of three of spirit and four of soul unified, and often the goddess in Egypt was sevenfold in her celestial aspect, and fourfold in the Underworld, or the abyss. In one version, Nut is the celestial sevenfold goddess above while Hathor is the fourfold one below in the Underworld, though Hathor had her Seven Hathors in her own celestial aspect, where she was wife of the High God Ra, and mother of Horus. However, Nut herself had two aspects, as Sky-Mother who gave birth to the gods, and as a feminine form of Nun, the Primordial Waters. Later the Greek/Gnostic goddess of Wisdom, Sophia, was sevenfold and had higher and lower aspects. So Mary, the Virgin at Pontmain, is a continuance of the sevenfold ancient Mother Goddesses, and covered in stars equals Nut in particular. These figures continued in the Bible are no longer goddesses, having become humanized by the Jews. But "sheba," or *seba,* means "seven" in Hebrew, and so Bath-sheba with King David and the Queen of Sheba with Solomon refer to the same sevenfold wisdom force, who in one form is Great Mother of All.

Sophia, "Wisdom," obviously derives directly from Sefekh, the Egyptian goddess of Wisdom. Even the name (the k was silent mostly in ancient Egyptian, rendering the name "Sefeh") was the feminine equivalent of Thoth, god of Wisdom and leader of the Seven Sages. Sefekh has a seven-rayed star (or seven-petalled flower) as her symbol, and *sef* was a word for "seven" in ancient Egyptian. Sefekh was mother of "Horus the Golden," so she too fits well as a prefiguration of Mary the Great Mother, with Christ her Son. As we have seen, Christ has dual aspects,

Son of the Father, but also Son of the Mother, as with all Savior figures in their fullness.

As said, the vision at Pontmain containing three stars in a triangle encompassing the head, and four candles below at shoulders and knees, has been called "a total of seven lights." The Seven Powers in the ancient world were sometimes called "the Seven Lights"; the seven Akhu in Egypt were spirit lights. Both the number three and the triangle are symbols of higher spirit, while the number four and the square are symbols of lower spirit/soul. So the vision at Pontmain is possibly a unification of higher and lower feminine aspects in a sevenfold structure. H. P. Blavatsky demonstrates this several times in *The Secret Doctrine* and other works. One example is, "The 3, 4, and 7 are sacred numbers of Light, Life, and Union—three in spirit above, four in life below, and seven in the unification of both." (1888). Certainly, in the Mysteries generally the triangle of higher spirit rests upon the square of the four corners of the Earth.

The children were witnessing symbolic contents coming through from spirit/soul reality, with archetypal details known to the ancient world, of which the children would have had no prior conscious knowledge. In essence, the timeless archetype was breaking through the veil that separates two realities, and the vision could only have been the sevenfold Great Mother that the children saw, here as Mary with her Son on the cross to fit the Western forms. So Christ here is more Son of the Mother.

Now it is something of a mystery why Christ in the Pontmain vision is red skinned, but Gerald Massey (1907) may have the answer. He says that it was common tradition that Christ was red complexioned, and that this was the Virgin's child in mystical character, one symbol of which was the red calf. There was apparently a medieval painting of a red calf that was associated with Christ, mentioned in an old manuscript. It depicts Eleazar sacrificing a red calf, with Christ opposite on the cross with a red skin. This symbolism may have originated in ancient Egypt.

To quote Massey:

> The red Christ, equivalent to the red Horus, is here identified with the red cow and therefore with the red calf of the Ritual, which was a symbol of the little red sufferer, the "afflicted one" in the winter solstice. In some of the mystery-plays the Christ wore a close-fitting, flesh colored garment, through which the nails were driven into the wood of the cross. The resurrection robe was always red. Satan wants to know who this man in the "red coat" may be. And when Horus rises again, in the character of the avenger, it is as the "red god". The manes thus address him, "O

> fearsome one, who is over two Earths; Red God, who orderest the block of execution!" (*Lectures* n.d.) Jesus likewise appears to have been represented as the red god, or the god in red. For 'they stripped him and put on him a scarlet robe."

So it seems that Christ was traditionally the red god, at least in one form, following on from Horus who was the red god and the red calf. Hathor was mother of Horus when the Father was the High God Ra, but Hathor, Nut, Neith, Isis, and so forth, are all interchangeable in certain aspects as the feminine spirit in Egypt, and these with the divine Son Horus are really prefigurations of Mary with Christ. Atum was also the Red God with the red skin, and this is when he is a type of the Son come to Earth, the original Adam. But the line is obviously from Horus to Christ. (Osiris is usually depicted green-skinned, almost certainly to express him as "The Lord of Green Vegetation," i.e., the lower Earth Spirit.)

The red cross over Mary's heart is a symbol of unification, among other things, perhaps of the blue and red partly. This brings us to a figure called the Star Woman who appears in the Holy Grail legends. During his quest Perceval sees a pool, and suddenly a woman rises up out of it. She is called the Star Woman and wears a red gown covered with stars, and as such is the red "Lady of the Abyss," the lower counterpart or aspect of Mary/Nut, the blue "Lady of the Stars" in the children's vision at Pontmain, who wears the blue gown covered with stars. The blue and red Star Women are therefore higher and lower aspects of the feminine spirit, or representations of her. Similarly Mary wears a blue mantel above and red dress below in most medieval depictions to express the celestial and lower soul aspects of her nature.

There is so much older symbolism in the Pontmain vision, of which the simple village children could have had no knowledge, that it has to be genuine. The fact that the symbolism can be found in ancient Egypt in no way lessens its value to us or for the Church, rather the opposite. It demonstrates the validity of the archetype for all times, and Mary is just as valid a form of the Great Mother as Nut and the rest. It is said of Sophia, "Thou Mother of the seven mansions come, who in the eighth hath found thy rest," and she is the "Shining Mother," the "Merciful Mother," and so on. This is why when Jung says Mary is Sophia, we can reverse this and say Sophia is Mary; that is what Mary has become for a large portion of the world's population, a goddess as "Shining Mother." Incidentally, "seven mansions" is connected with the visions of St. Teresa of Avila, specifically with the King of Glory (Christ), although the archetype was originally Egyptian as the "Seven Mansions" of Osiris in the Underworld.

The Visions at Fatima: The Angel and the Goddess

In the Spring of 1916, three Portuguese children, Lucia dos Santos, a girl aged nine, and her cousins, the brother and sister Francisco and Jacinta Marto, aged seven and six, were in the fields near Fatima, a small village about seventy miles north of Lisbon, when an angel suddenly appeared to them. This took the form of a young man bathed in a brilliant light that was like the "Sun piercing a crystal." The angel, which called itself "the Angel of Peace," then said a prayer three times and told the children to pray to Jesus and Mary.

The angel appeared again in July, telling the children to pray to Jesus and Mary and to sacrifice for God. In September, another vision of the Angel of Peace appeared, when it produced a chalice into which dripped blood from the Host (the bread). These remained suspended in the air while the angel said a prayer. It then gave Lucia the Host, and Francisco and Jacinta the chalice, and they were told to partake of the Body and Blood of Christ. They were then instructed to pray fervently and regularly for the sins of Man against God.

The Angel of Peace did not appear to the children again, but on the May 13, 1917, they saw the vision of a white-robed Lady—the "Lady of the Rosary," as she later called herself—who appeared after two flashes of lightning radiated a light brighter than the Sun (as with the angel). She told the children not to be afraid, for they would not be harmed, and when they asked where she came from, she pointed upwards and replied, "I come from Heaven." The children were told to return to the fields every month on the thirteenth day for several months, and then, after instructing the children to say the Rosary every day to bring peace to the world, the Lady in white ascended into the sky, and, moving Eastwards, gradually disappeared.

Of course, word of the miraculous appearances spread, and on the thirteenth of the next month, about fifty people gathered at the same spot with the three children, hoping to see a further vision. But apparently only the children saw the Holy Lady, who again appeared after a flash of lightning. In answer to certain questions, she replied that the brother and sister, Francisco and Jacenta, would shortly "go to Heaven," but that the older girl must do work to promote the "Immaculate Heart" worldwide.

On the next occasion, the thirteenth of the following month, rays of light shot from the hands of the Lady of the Rosary, penetrating the Earth and opening it up to reveal a horrible vision of Hell, full of demons and lost souls. The Lady warned that although the then present war, the Great War, would soon end, if the nations did not turn from their wicked ways, another world war would break out again eventually. If in the future, the night sky were to become illuminated by a bright light from an unknown source, this would mean the terrible war is approaching, and that God is about to punish the world. Russia would then spread its oppression and atheism to other lands, but if Russia were consecrated and converted to the Holy Lady, the war and oppression could be averted, and peace would then reign.

The next month, the white-robed Lady appeared yet again, and then the following month, on October 13, she made her last appearance, this time tens of thousands of people gathering from all over Portugal to watch. The Lady spoke first to the children, saying that a chapel was to be built there in her honor, and it was then that she actually declared herself to be the Lady of the Rosary, adding that the war would soon end. But when the children asked for things for the people, they were told that mankind must mend its ways and that God was already much offended. The Lady then rose into the air and stretched her hands out to the Sun, becoming increasingly brilliant as she ascended. Then she was gone, to be replaced by visions of the Holy Family, though again only the children saw these.

Now, it had been raining heavily, and the clouds covering the sky were black. But these suddenly parted to reveal the Sun, looking like a dull, grey disc, which, therefore, everyone could look at directly. The disc, certain people said, then did a dance, displaying all the colors of the rainbow, before finally plunging to the Earth, causing the congregated crowds to drop to their knees. Then it turned around and shot back up into the skies again, right to its proper place as the Sun. One well attested fact is that the people, whose clothes had been soaking wet from the heavy rain, found to their amazement they were now perfectly dry.

Not too long after this last appearance, in April 1919, the young boy who had first seen the visions with the other children died, with his sister's death following in February 1920, both being victims of complications of influenza. This was as the Holy Lady had spoken, and by then the war had ended as she had also foretold. The surviving child, Lucia dos Santos, later became a religious sister in a convent, and in 1925 had another vision of Mary with the Child Jesus. In 1929 she saw the Holy

Trinity, and then in a further vision Mary spoke to her again. Nearly a decade later, in 1938, Lucia saw the sky light up luminously and unnaturally, presaging the outbreak of the Second World War, as the Lady of the Rosary had yet again foretold. Mankind had not turned to God and away from its wickedness.

Though the brilliant light was claimed by some to be due to the Aurora Borealis, many others, who also witnessed it, said that the light was much too bright and spread over too large an area for it to be that. Furthermore, radio signals were interfered with in a strange way that had not occurred before. In any case, Lucia was certain within herself what it really meant. But even if the luminous light *was* the Aurora Borealis, which it almost certainly was not, it would not necessarily disprove the vision. Visions sometimes manifest themselves in suitable physical phenomena, and such could have been the case here, spreading and intensifying the effect, though there is no evidence that the Aurora Borealis was actually involved at all. Whatever the case, those who have visions always have difficulty persuading others to accept them, for the visions themselves are the only real evidence, which the nonbelievers have not experienced themselves in the first place.

As to the visions at Fatima, the male angel that first appeared offered the children the host, the bread, which was dripping blood, and the chalice. This repeats Christ at the Last Supper offering the bread and wine to the disciples, repeated later in the Eucharist. Blood is more the language of the unconscious/spirit than wine, but both mean the same, the divine essence from above, while bread represents feminine soul. It is possible the angel may be a representation of Christ, and then with the Lady of the Rosary a sacred unification of the opposites could be implied, the blood dripping from the bread into the chalice certainly represents this.

The Lady of the Rosary is, of course, the Virgin Mary, the Catholic representative of the eternal feminine spirit, Sophia to the Gnostics. Mary is *rosa mystica,* the "mystic rose," and medieval mystic poets would compose their hymns to her as such. The Sun becoming a disc is significant because globes and discs represent mandalas, and mandalas are symbols of the unification of the opposites, which is why they are symbols of the Higher Self, the unification of opposites *par excellence.* It may also be why the Sun-disc in the vision plunged to Earth to then shoot to the skies again, as this unites above and below, spirit and matter/soul. However, the Sun is also an age-old symbol of God.

Jung tells of a dream vision of one of his patients that contained a woman, a globe, and the Sun—which is basically, or partly, what the last

Fatima vision contains. Jung explains that the woman in the dream is the anima in collective aspect, representing the World Soul, the *anima mundi,* while the Sun is God. In the dream, the woman, the World Soul, kneels and worships the Sun, the globe being the symbol that unites them; God and World Soul—Mater Dei, as Jung calls her—unified. Only when soul reality is won over to the spirit is unification possible. In the Fatima visions, the Lady of the Rosary, the World Soul in her highest and purest form, needs to be unified with the Sun, the eternal masculine spirit, which is why the disc, the mandala, flies down to the Earth and then up to the Sun again. This does not contradict the union of Christ as the angel with Mary, but rather supports it.

The disc, or Sun, at Fatima contains at one stage all the colors of the rainbow, a totality symbol that reminds us of the "peacock's tail" and "all colors in the white One" of the alchemists (and Joseph's "coat of many colors"). The rainbow has, of course, seven colors within its totality, and so makes an excellent symbol for the Seven Powers forming the totality of the Higher Self, which is also the meaning of the peacock's tail and Joseph's coat.

Man's main task, the reason why he was evolved ultimately, is to unite spirit and matter/soul realities in the *Hieros Gamos,* the Sacred Marriage, which produces the divine child, the full Higher Self. God and the Great Mother cannot accomplish this themselves apparently, which is why a creature had to be evolved for the task. The story of Christ is an example of the phenomenon of the Sacred Marriage bringing forth the divine child, and there are others in the history of the world. However, the visions as a whole concern more than unification, as great a thing as this is.

The events at Fatima included dire warnings of Hell for sinful mankind if it fails to alter its ways, warnings that we find in so many ancient myths. The people of Nineveh listen to Jonah and repent, and all goes well, but obviously not to Noah, or to Manu in the Hindu myth, nor indeed the people in the Atlantis legend, resulting in floods of chaos destroying the cultures. When we look at our modern world, particularly the West, we see we are in a more dangerous condition than ever before, having grown much further dissociated from the spirit in the twentieth century than any culture in the past. Jung said over fifty years ago that modern Man has become captured by the dark side of Mercurius, the spirit of the Earth/unconscious; so goodness knows what he would make of the world today.

Those who see these visions in terms of UFOs or as other purely physical events—or as illusions, mass hypnosis, and so on—are the most deluded people of all, limiting full and meaningful reality to mere materiality. They should ask themselves why so many of the children who see these kinds of visions become priests or nuns later. Obviously it is because of the tremendous effect their experiences have upon them. Orientation to reality changes drastically with the visions, and indeed, as well as with children it usually happens with adults who have visions, a prime example being St. Paul.

There is yet a further episode to add to the foregoing, which may not allow us to be too optimistic concerning the future of our world. Lucia dos Santos, the eldest child at Fatima, had been sworn to secrecy about the predictions of the Holy Virgin, but in 1929 had confided them to the Pope. These became known as the "three predictions." One had been fulfilled not long after the visions occurred, this concerning the ending of the First World War. The second prediction, the coming of the Second World War, was to happen a decade *after* it was told to the Pope. (Actually, another prediction was the death of two of the children, which also came to pass.) But one secret remained concerning the future, and it was not until the year 2000 that it was finally proclaimed to the world by the Vatican. This involves the vision of a descending angel holding a sword in his hand, followed by a white-robed figure leading a procession of priests along a path. Suddenly, hostile figures appear with guns and bows and arrows, and, shooting the white-robed figure and the priests, kill them all. This is the basis of the "third secret."

The Vatican and Pope John Paul II associated the third prediction with the attempted assassination of this Pope that occurred in 1993. But the details of the attempt do not fit with the vision at all well. The white-robed figure in the vision was killed, as were all the accompanying priests, but in the real life event the Pope did not die, and no one else was injured. Furthermore, no arrows were used in the real life event and the types of locations were entirely different.

Nevertheless, the white-robed figure with the priests could refer to a Pope and the Church in a symbolical way, which would mean the death of the Church, and possibly of Christianity itself, intimating an age of dark barbarism that is to overwhelm the world. Let us be clear on this; there is nothing Western Man possesses with which to replace Christianity, except from the opposite, shadow side, and the death of the Church would ultimately mean the collapse of higher culture. It is happening now, in fact, despite optimism to the contrary. Even if the white-robed figure means a spirit entity, rather than referring to a human individual, such as a pope, the meaning would nevertheless be similar, the defeat of the spiritual light by the forces of darkness. The angel at the beginning with the sword reminds us of Christ in Revelation, but there the sword is in his mouth, and the vision at Fatima was of an angel and not specifically of Christ. Furthermore, the forces of light finally prevail in Revelation, but there is no sign of this in the Fatima vision, rather the opposite.

It has been said it could mean that the angel brings and dispenses God's justice, which would not bode well for present mankind. We have not turned from selfish, destructive, materialistic ways, and not only is culture corrupting and degenerating, we are destroying the rest of nature in the process. The last thing we should desire from God is justice, for it would not favor us well.

On the other hand, it has also been pointed out that the visions were experienced in 1917, and that much of Europe came under the control of the dark forces of Pagan Nazism only a couple of decades later. So perhaps this was the death of Christianity in Europe alluded to in the third prediction, though I personally do not feel at all satisfied with this interpretation. In fact, this was the second secret foretold, the Second World War, quite distinct from the third secret. As to any allusion to atheistic communism coming to take over, this danger too has now passed of course. It is possible that the white-robed figure is the Higher Self, of course, and if the accompanying priests numbered seven we would know this for sure. But again, the meaning would be the same, the killing of the Savior by dark Pagan forces; as I say, there is no doubt that the latter are gradually possessing Western civilization. Jung certainly believed this, stating as said above that we have become possessed by the dark side of Mercurius. (I have had dreams that warn of "death of a culture," and this fits with the third secret at Fatima, though conversely, I am sure that the light side of the spirit through the unconscious is trying to bring about fundamental change to respiritualization.)

There is a strong modern tendency to dismiss experiences as those at Pontmain and Fatima either as nonsense, or as mass hallucination, or to interpret them in some materialistic way, even as visits from extraterrestrials. It is then claimed that all religious interpretations of such phenomena are misinterpretations, but it is the materialistic interpretations that are in error. We live with a false picture of reality that puts us at odds with every other age of mankind that ever was, though we believe we are the clever ones. Yet myth and religion are still solid foundations of culture for certain peoples of the world. What great harm we would do (and have done) if we took from them the sacredness of their beliefs, inflicting upon them the same impoverishment of soul that has overwhelmed our Western civilization, substituting lesser meaning for greater, and indeed, meaninglessness for meaning. But it is perhaps the turning of the tide, and even the clash between fundamentalism and New Age spirituality may be a good sign that spiritual truth is being striven for and argued over, albeit at different levels and in different ways.

Experience of the religious archetypes of the unconscious brings certainty. Reality then becomes alive again with definite religious meaning—it is as though a light has been switched on in the whole universe—and matter is reduced to its rightful place, as merely part of a greater whole. The trick is to reach a balance, always remembering that we are here to live a life, though a meaningful one, and on behalf of the Higher Self, as well as for ourselves. The human individual eventually takes the sum total of the lived human life to the Self, of which it is part, which adds to it in either a positive way or a negative way, as the case may be. The Self for the West is Christ, and so in this way we actually exist in Christ.

It seems that such Marian visions occur to remind us in our state of dissociation of our great religious responsibilities, and to reorient us accordingly. It is no coincidence that Marian visions began in the nineteenth century as the West developed scientific-materialism and rationalistic-atheism. This leads ultimately to the final message at Fatima, where the white-robed figure and the priests are all killed. It is not a pleasant vision and should, in fact, cause us some worry, hopefully enough to move us to begin to change our world and the way we run it.

A number of other visions of the Virgin Mary have occurred since those at Pontmain and Fatima, the main ones being at Beauraing and Bannaux, Belgium, in 1932–3; Garaband, Spain in 1961; and Medjugorje, Bosnia, from 1981–91. The most famous of all visions of Mary, predating Pontmain and Fatima, are those of St. Bernadette, which began at Lourdes in 1858. Other experiences were at La Salette, in the French Alps in 1846 and at Knock, Ireland, in 1879. I will not go into the details of these here, but one thing that must strike us is that visions of Mary involve Catholics, and occur in Catholic countries or areas. It can be queried, therefore, that if the Virgin genuinely appears to mankind, then why not to Protestants; or indeed, to Buddhists and Hindus, and so forth? The answer is that it all depends upon the religious forms, values, and preconceptions of the individuals witnessing the visions, and of the specific culture involved. The Protestant Church is all masculine spirit in a somewhat over-intellectualized manner, whereas the Catholic Church, as the Bride of Christ, has feminine soul and feeling highly developed. In other words, the Protestant mentality is not attuned to the Mother Goddess, whereas the Catholic mentality is. I was alone in a Catholic Church when a woman came in, knelt at the statue of Mary, and putting her raised hands together, said prayers to her, rightly making of Mary a sort of goddess.

This was the real motive force behind the Reformation, for the Northern temperament was obviously better suited to the more austere masculine spirit, to the Father and to the intellect, than to Southern emotion and the largely feminine element that constitutes the Catholic Church. And we must remember that Germany, where the Reformation began, is the Fatherland rather than the Motherland, having, as Jung says, the feminine element poorly developed.

It is said that UFO sightings occur more in Northern Protestant countries, and Marian visions in Southern Catholic ones. But then, spirit symbolically has always come from above, and feminine soul from the depths—though also seen above. UFO phenomena without doubt represent the workings of the spirit, which has no actual physical forms and which can therefore assume any it chooses. Spirit itself is a complexity of opposites, which is why it may be beneficent or maleficent; aliens are usually said to be unemotional, disturbingly aloof, and even callous. This is not holy or sacred spirit as we understand it.

Chapter 18

UFOs and Aliens, Activity of the Spirit

UFOs and aliens could be forms of the spirit. I personally am pretty sure they are. (Colin Wilson points out that John Keel, Jacques Vallee, John Mitchell, and Ted Holliday had more or less come to a similar conclusion decades ago.) For one thing, they are often threefold in some way. Various reports made by people of outer experiences contain symbolism known to occur sometimes in dreams. Trinitarian concepts, and indeed experiences, are well-known to religion and it is not just in Christianity, but in those of many cultures reaching back to earliest times. We must ask why Christianity and other cultures saw fit to include such a concept as Trinitarian spirit (or spirit that is somehow threefold) within their religious formulations. It would be an unnecessary inclusion, pointless to any mythos, unless it were a real and living reality that had been, has been, and can be experienced.

The Holy Spirit, though part of the Holy Trinity, is nevertheless said to be a force somewhat independent of God and the Son, according to all teachings a *creative* force, the force that creates in matter. The Holy Trinity is God as the Three-in-One Deity, but the Holy Spirit itself is represented at times as threefold, coming forth, therefore, in a threefold manner. In a similar way, some people report seeing or being abducted by three aliens. (Not always three, it is true.) Reports that abductees have been taken to spaceships and operated on may well be valid, for this would be part of the work of evolution that spirit undertakes in matter. They may well actually have been taken through the collective unconscious to the spirit reality that lies behind the physical universe, and indeed, I am of the opinion that people experience alien abduction as part of their individuation process. I have good reasons for saying this, for I have been abducted by aliens through the unconscious in dreams, though when my individuation process eased off after many years, so too did the threat of alien abduction. I knew after each dream that the aliens abducting me had been spirit, often threefold in some way, and the same seems to be the case with many other people.

Jung was convinced that new understanding of religious traditions of the West through depth psychology could help bring about the necessary leap forward in the evolution of the religious spirit. Yet the spirit itself is always at work, so that as Man becomes dissociated and one-sided, falling into the abyss of matter on the one side, or inflating into the spirit on the other, the spirit itself will attempt to restore the balance. In an age when Man becomes so spiritualized that material life itself is threatened, the spirit eases off to allow the material side to replenish. This is not to say that the designs of the spirit will automatically be accomplished: Sometimes they are not, and the culture collapses. But the spirit is always at work when dangerous dissociation is causing the imbalance that can lead to catastrophe. The workings of the spirit may manifest as outer visions, either in traditional religious forms, or it seems, as UFOs, aliens, abductions, and so on; and certainly to be included in the list are the Marian visions we looked at above.

The whole range of paranormal experience is of the utmost importance for mankind as it is evidence of the higher, wider, other reality to which our world, and we ourselves, are connected, giving us extensions and dimensions that are absolutely vital to us, allowing us to grow more fully, experience more deeply, and evolve still further on the path of true evolution and enlightenment. The alternative, certainly, is that we will stagnate in a reduced, limited, meaningless existence that will stifle us; civilizations soon fall into chaos if they lose their associations with spirit reality.

Some while ago I was talking to Colin Wilson on the telephone and among other things we spoke of the significance of Jung, of the unconscious, and of the possible meaning of UFOs. The upshot of our conversation was that Colin sent me a copy of his book, *Alien Dawn* (1998), which deals specifically with UFO phenomena, including Jung's opinions concerning them.

In this work, Colin comments several times on Jung's *Flying Saucers:A myth of Things Seen in the Skies* (1958).

> Jung appears to be saying that he believes UFOs to be a "projection" of the collective unconscious of mankind—a projection

> being essentially a kind of hallucination, like a drunk's visions of pink elephants. They are a projection of mankind's longing for a Savior—or for what he calls individuation, a state in which all the inner conflicts of the psyche are resolved.

We might also call a projection a sort of mirage in that what we see as happening before our eyes is actually taking place somewhere else, i.e., in the unconscious. But there are two kinds of projection. One is the meaning we ourselves project onto an outer object, which happens at personal level, for instance with love at first sight. This is projection of a usually unconscious image we carry within ourselves onto a figure of the opposite sex who fits the bill. There is also projection from the nonpersonal or collective level, an example of this being the inner Great Man, the "Christ within" or Self, which we project onto such outer figures as Christ, the Buddha, Krishna, and so forth.

Nevertheless, archetypal contents from the collective level, which are separate from and beyond us, may project themselves into outer reality, into the world, so that they appear as outer visions, often as religious ones, or as UFOs, aliens, and so forth. Whether UFOs are able to assume solid physical forms is unclear, but perhaps they do in a way; that is, in the same manner as ghosts, which are there and yet not there, so to speak. (Or indeed, aliens may even have the ability to become solid, having physical effect; indentations have been left in the ground where UFOs have landed.) But it is a fact that appearances of spirit are often triadic or threefold in some way, and I have myself experienced spaceships and aliens in dreams that were often somehow threefold and which I came to realize were visitations of spirit.

The archetypal situation behind physical reality is the real reason why mankind has always tended to arrange his gods in triads, and a triangle itself often symbolizes threefold spirit. Madame Blavatsky says: "This is the primeval root-thought of thinking Humanity; the Pythagorean Triangle emanating from the ever-concealed Monad, or Central Point." (1888). In fact, Pythagoras, Orpheus, and Plato all believed in divine Trinities underlying reality, which they probably derived from the Egyptians originally, though also from their own experiences. I give certain examples of Trinitarian aliens/spirit in a few moments but we must ask, why do experts seem not to see the threefoldness in UFO/alien experiences, which occur in so many instances? They seem oblivious to the fact.

In dreams, outer space and phenomena from it symbolize the realm of the higher spirit, whereas the sea and its depths—or the earth—represent the opposite realm, the World Soul. So spirit is both above and below the physical universe, even surrounding it, and spirit contents may well break through into physical reality and be accessed through the unconscious. Spirit is certainly studying us, and even working on us, which is why people are abducted, though seemingly through to the unconscious/spirit realm. This is perhaps why many abductees are taken from their beds and then say no earthly time has passed when they return, the collective unconscious being a timeless other reality. They were actually taken through to the spirit/soul realm.

The threefoldness of spirit, reflected in the Holy Trinity, the Three-in-One Deity, could usually be seen expressed traditionally in Greek and Latin Christian churches by a triangle in the dome, or above the main altar, containing the Eternal Eye. For the ancient Greeks, the triangle was the "vehicle of the unknown Deity," and the Boetian Zeus was written with the delta, Δeus, as was the Latin *Deus,* as Δeus. Many ancient cultures arranged their gods in triads and trinities, including Egypt, Babylon, and India—the Hindu Trinity is the Trimurti.

Spirit aliens are far more meaningful than aliens from other planets would be, for the latter would still be material beings, as we humans are, albeit from afar. But spirit entirely alters the nature of full reality for us, and our whole way of thinking is changed to how it should be. It appears that we are being watched, not by beings from space, but by spirit reality itself. This is why these spirit powers were sometimes called Watchers in the ancient world.

As I was typing some of the above, I suddenly felt I was on a ship, and was very aware of the great ocean beneath. I felt I was in an audience watching a film on a screen out front, which was about airplanes flying in the skies, but then shown in close-up. It then suddenly came to me that this is the true nature of UFOs. They are projections into the skies from otherworldly reality, just as the airplanes on the screen in front I was watching were projected images from a projector behind. Not projected through human individuals, used as projectors, rather projections from the collective unconscious directly into the outer skies. In other words, UFOs do exist, but are symbolic projections from the unconscious/spirit dimension. So we only think they are in the skies but they are actually projected images from another reality, the two seeming to merge. This is why I feel I am on the sea but watching planes up in the sky, projected up there from below.

In my telephone conversation with Colin Wilson he pointed out that some of the abductees have physical evidence of operations done on their bodies. I suggested these physical effects could be sort of stigmata, physical affects with nonphysical origins. We do not know the ultimate nature of full reality, nor what effects spirit can have upon matter, and vice versa. Who knows what is possible ultimately?

Colin remarked, "There seems to be two aspects of them, physical and nonphysical," to which I replied, "Yes, or they are projections breaking through from another reality, and are not what we usually mean by physical." We agreed that their existence is certain.

As said above, if the UFOs and aliens were visitors from other planets, they would nevertheless be material beings (though, like us, also having their nonphysical aspects). That is why material aliens, though a fascinating prospect, do not throw any light onto greater and more meaningful reality. They would still be mortal beings like ourselves, albeit in different forms. The first questions I would ask physical aliens are: what are your spiritual experiences? Do you have God? Is he a Trinitarian Deity? Do you believe in reincarnation? Do you know of the inner Immortal, the Higher Self, the Christ figure to us, or his equivalent? Such aliens would have the same problems of identity in eternity that we have, and would be in danger of the same possible spiritual disorientation that always threatens mankind.

Dreams and Aliens

Some of my dreams are obviously religious in an orthodox Christian sense, while others seem to use the symbolism of alchemy, the Holy Grail legends and so on. Yet there are also dreams of UFOs and aliens, partly fitting in with Trinitarian symbolism. Here are a few of the relevant dreams and I can see no interpretation other than that they represent spirit as a Trinitarian force coming forth. I give the first dream, of black, three-legged creatures coming up out of the ground, the chthonic trinity, because it was immediately followed by one about three-legged flying saucers, showing how lower and higher contents are connected, and how experience of one invokes the appearance of the other. In other words, they are connected opposite poles of a fuller reality.

> *I lead a party of explorers first to New Guinea and then to Australia, where strange creatures come out of the ground to attack us. They are rather like octopus-spiders, but have only three legs, and are about six-feet high and jet-black in color. They shoot arrow-like spikes at us, and*

one of these sticks in my right hand. I am afraid and tell myself that I must stop invading the land of these creatures. As I think this, the spikes stop.

To go south in dreams is to travel to the instinctual depths, the World Soul or "Realm of the Mothers" as it has been called (it is also partly the masculine Earth/Spirit). You cannot go much farther south from England than Australia, which means, therefore, that I am in the deepest depths of the unconscious. As we also "take in" New Guinea, which has been called the most primitive place on Earth, it is obviously an omen of what we are likely to encounter on our journey. A dark chthonic trinity residing in the depths of matter was revealed by alchemy (similar to the three-headed devil of Dante), the lower counterpart to the higher, divine Trinity. Jung says that though its symbolism shows that the lower triad has definite connections with evil, we must not hastily conclude that it is solely that (1959a).

The black three-legged creatures that come up from out of the Earth can only mean the black, chthonic trinity spoken of by the alchemists and others investigating the depths of the collective unconscious. Here in the dream they do not like this invasion of their domain and they repel us, but my intention to leave this place well alone in future obviously has a placating effect on them. Journeying to these depths means that a response will be invoked from the higher, spirit side of this other reality. That is the law of the unconscious, as the following dream demonstrates:

I am in a space station in Australia and the country—the world—is about to be invaded by alien beings, which arrive in round tripod-like spaceships (having three legs), flying saucers probably. However, we do not actually see them at first, though we are well aware of them, as rays from the saucers are zapping everybody. Then the flying saucers do appear, and though I cannot see the aliens, I somehow know that their essence is Trinitarian or threefold. They continue zapping everybody, either paralyzing or killing them, but when it comes to my turn and I say, "We also have a Holy Trinity, consisting of Father, Son, and Holy Spirit," it causes the invaders to pass me over, though they continue zapping everybody else.

In the last dream I was in Australia where black, three-legged creatures, the chthonic trinity, came up out of the Earth. Now in response, their opposite, the Trinity of spirit arrives *over* Australia. The spirit, though Trinitarian, is not necessarily Christian, and not necessarily good or benign. In fact, as it zaps everybody, the opposite seems to be the case. The fact that when I mention the Christian Trinity I am passed over, however, suggests it is *willing* to be Christian, as the Christian Trinity expresses adequately the light side of its nature.

This may fit with certain modern sightings of UFOs where a light, or disc, joins two others, yet seems partly independent of them, as though the Holy Spirit were an independent entity from Father and Son. It may also fit the saying of Christ that a sin against Father and Son may be forgiven, but not one against the Holy Spirit.

Jung stated that the Christian Trinity is based upon the same model as that of ancient Egypt, and this expresses long and deep experience of their "Other World." As Jung comments, the structure of Father, Son, and Ka-Mutef found in ancient Egyptian mythology was produced by the same archetype through the unconscious that was responsible for the Christian Trinity (1958). I can add that with the monotheistic pharaoh Akhenaten, the sun-disc Aten contained Ra, Horus, and Shu, the latter having a title, "The Breath of Ra." Thus the Aten-disc actually contained Father, Son, and Holy Spirit.

E. A. Wallis Budge was of the opinion that the Egyptians arranged their gods in triads or trinities after the human model of father, mother, and child. In other words, the god triads were projections of the human state. However, with experience of the unconscious processes we know that this is not so. Trinities are the natural order of unconscious/spirit forces, as are quaternities. Those similar to the human model include Atum as Father, Iusaas as Mother, and Tum as Son, the divine trinity at Annu; Amun-Ra/Mut/Khonsu at Thebes; Ptah/Sekhet/Iu-em-hetep at Memphis, Osiris/Isis/Horus, and Set/Nepthys/Anubis. Of the exclusively male trinity type were Ra/Atum/Horus, and Akhenaten's Aten disc containing Ra, Horus, and Shu, which definitely alludes to Father, Son, and Holy Spirit. Massey mentions a variation of the last mentioned, Ra, Set, and Shu.

Here is another of my dreams:

> *I am in the street where I see people dashing about, because they can see a spaceship in the sky, though it is a little hazy among the clouds. It has three fuselages, or bodies, which are interconnected, making it a three-in-one spaceship.*

As we have seen, aliens, spaceships, etc., represent spirit in dreams, and this three-in-one craft can only refer to the Trinity, the Three-in-One Deity. God traditionally appears in the clouds, and this triadic spaceship that appears in the clouds is not just a symbol in a dream. It is God himself coming forth as a Trinitarian symbol, yet nevertheless as *an actual event*. We should all bow down before this, for it really is God. It may be taking place in another reality, accessed through dreams, but it is nevertheless *real*. Just before the dream I had been thinking of the terrible state modern man is in and I asked fervently for God to help us. The dream came in response.

> *I sit in a chair, which then swivels backwards, swinging me up in a huge arc. I lose consciousness and when I awake, I am in a higher reality, lying on a bed like an operating table. I seem to be in a spaceship, which is also higher reality, and a Mongoloid looking young female is at my feet holding a knife. She makes as if to cut off my right foot, but does not, and then I realize that two primitive-looking males are also standing at my side, rather like ancient Egyptians, but with the blood of very archaic primitives in them.*
>
> *However, when they speak, I realize they are actually highly educated superiors, and they are peeved that I took them to be inferior. Then I see that I have a large growth coming out of my chest, perhaps signifying a malignant psychic growth. One of the males puts a bow (a weapon) over my head, as if to show how superior they are, although it may also be a clue to their identity.*

Being taken up into a spaceship to higher reality has happened to me several times in the processes. The dream corresponds to what many other people have experienced in outer reality—alien abduction and so forth. However, dreams involving the collective unconscious are not just fantasies but *events* of another reality, and it is my strong belief that alien abduction, in either inner or outer reality, involves forces of spirit. That is why aliens are seen in so many different shapes and forms; being spirit, they have no actual physical forms, and so can manifest as literally anything. Furthermore, many abductees claim that no earthly time passed during the period of the abduction, but if it was to the collective unconscious, which is a timeless other reality, then no worldly time would have passed. (Some, however, say that time did pass.)

In the above dream, I am taken up to a higher spirit reality through the unconscious, and though this happened several times, I eventually learned how to escape the aliens when they came for me. They were not religious experiences; this kind of spirit is not holy and numinous, just a powerful force. This seems to correspond to the Watchers, Instructors, Builders, Creators, etc. known to the ancient world. These were usually seen above, although the apocryphal Enoch (in the apocryphal Book of Enoch) is literally taken up in his visions to join them, perhaps significantly from his bed.

I cannot explain exactly what the details of the above dream signify, but I would say that as well as being "superior" in some way, the aliens also have their dark, primitive aspect. Everything that exists has its shadow side, even spirit, even God. The aliens probably represent pure spirit, but not the highest form, the Holy Spirit. The bow possibly alludes to Sirius, the Bow Star to certain ancients, but this is far from sure. (There is also the chance it could mean the aliens really are on a more primitive level, suggested by the bow.) In *The Sirius Mystery* (1973) Robert Temple explains the Nommo gods of the Dogon people of West Africa as descending aliens from Sirius, (though this again expresses activity of the spirit, actually as the Higher Self with the Seven Powers).

In *Alien Dawn* Colin Wilson relates a version of the visions of Orfeo Angelucci, which had appeared earlier in Jung's book, *Flying Saucers: A Modern Myth of Things Seen in the Skies,* which Jung had taken to be genuine. These visions are of some importance as they demonstrate perfectly the symbolic processes that are occurring in the collective unconscious, that are coming through to many people in sleeping or waking states; in other words, in dreams or visions.

Some of Angelucci's experiences are similar to my own, the difference being that his apparently occurred in the waking state, while mine did so in dream processes while I was asleep. Angelucci's visions and my dreams, though products essentially of another reality, are nevertheless *real,* for the collective unconscious is timeless, eternal, and unchanging other reality. It can therefore more justifiably be regarded as real than our own material world, which is ephemeral and in a constant state of change.

> *I see an alien from outer space that has a completely nonhuman head. It is rather like an insect's, but has three eyes in a vertical line in the center. The eyes then merge into one and emit a beam.*

The alien represents Trinitarian spirit, and such experiences may account for the sightings of aliens that people believe they have seen in the outer world. These "spirit beings" are apparently able to manifest themselves in the material world, as they also do in unconscious reality. The unconscious is a real "place" and not just one where fantasies happen. It extends to infinity and eternity, and events take place there just as in the outer world and universe. Likewise, the alien I see is *real,* and the threefoldness of its eyes denotes spirit, as we know from examples going back to most ancient times. But the three eyes merge into one, showing that the alien is representative of Trinitarian spirit, that is, from the Three-in-One Deity. The eyes being in a vertical line therefore alludes to from below to above, i.e., to the spiritual, rather than horizontal, i.e., on the flat plain of the Earth.

> *There is utter chaos in a city, with people running about wildly as though there are earthquakes and other catastrophes. I am attacked, accused of being a priest, but I manage to fight off my assailants. Things are so bad, the chaos so great and utter, that I cry out, "Only God can help us now." As I look up at the evening sky, I see three balls of light, two behind a front one. Then the rear two move forward to merge with the front one, the three becoming one, in religious terms the nature of the Holy Trinity, again, the Three in One Deity.*

This may explain some of the sightings people have seen, apparently coming through from higher spirit. An ex-RAF man saw the same formation of three lights in the sky, and though he stated he does not believe in UFOs, that is what he nevertheless assigned the lights to. He was adamant that he knew what he saw. It never occurred to him they could have spiritual meaning, actually concerning Trinitarian spirit. He interpreted the sighting as flying saucers, in keeping with the materialistic bias of our age, although they were lights, or glowing discs, with nothing specifically to do with flying saucers. A relative of mine saw a vision of the same three lights just before she died. (She also saw a "wonderful angel-fish" as she described it, this being the symbol of the Self as Savior.) Two astronauts were recorded in conversation and one suddenly said that two lights were approaching their spacecraft. After a short while they then spoke of a third light coming to join the other two. As I said, this was recorded and I have heard it played myself.

I will give a few other experiences here that were somehow threefold, though there are many more. It is true that some experiences are not threefold, but there may be various explanations for this; perhaps the person involved simply failed to notice it or speak of it. But we can consider this later; here are the threefold instances.

There is film of two discs moving swiftly over a field, which are then joined by a third disc, and they create crop circles as they fly back and forth. Experts say that the film could not have been faked. My godson saw two whirlwinds come to his bedroom window in a dream, which were then joined by a third. They had come to "take a look at him" —the whirlwind was anciently and biblically a sign of God. A whole village in Russia witnessed the landing of a flying saucer, and when a large creature disembarked, one young man drew a sketch of it. It had three eyes. This is similar to the alien that visited me in the dream above, which also had three eyes. There is also the dream of the spaceship with three fuselages, which the dream said had been sent by God.

A sighting at a U.S. Forces base in Britain concerned a strange triangle shape that had apparently landed. This had been filmed and when it was shown, appeared to be the colored outline of a triangle. It eventually took off and became three lights, or a triangular spacecraft. It left three indentations in the ground, made by its legs or feet, so that whatever the "object" had been, it was obviously "tripodic" and solid, at least for a time. (One "expert" claimed the indentations, or holes, had been made by rabbits, but since the holes were equally spaced, forming the corners of an equilateral triangle, this is an example of narrow rationalism in the extreme, or there are some very clever rabbits.)

In part 1 I related the experiences of Linda Cortile, who was abducted by three aliens and taken up to a flying saucer, actually forming the very ancient symbol of a circle with the fourfold structure of 3 + 1. At Socorro, New Mexico, in 1947, a disc-shaped craft crashed to Earth. An army sergeant who investigated reported it contained three dead aliens. When Antonio Boas told of being abducted in 1969 he said he first saw a round object land, three legs emerging from beneath. Three aliens that had three tubes coming out of their helmets then took him up to the craft. There a naked woman, who was somehow very strange, was brought to him and he and she had sexual intercourse. (This sounds like unification with the feminine anima in the collective unconscious.) In 1973 two men on a fishing trip in Mississippi saw three aliens float down to fetch them up to a spacecraft. One of the men lost consciousness when touched by one of the aliens, but the other man recalled being examined by a floating eye. In 1975, one of seven tree-fellers was abducted and in the spacecraft found himself being examined by three aliens that looked like foetuses. A patrolman in Nebraska was shown a film, by aliens, of three alien spacecraft in the sky with the constellation of the Plough in the background. In 1968 a doctor in France saw two disc-shaped UFOs, but twelve days later saw a third that was triangular shaped.

At Bethesda, Wales, Alan Morris was fishing when a ball of light landed. Three aliens emerged that were about seven feet tall, having what looked like antennae on their heads. Morris had his dog with him, which started to run towards the aliens. He called it back but then fainted; when he regained consciousness the aliens and UFO were gone, and so was his dog. In Montana, a youth agreed to undergo tests at a center after seeing an alien outside his home. Under hypnosis he told of being abducted by three aliens to their spacecraft, where he was examined. He was then informed he would remember nothing of the incident afterwards, though he obviously remembered seeing the alien outside his home to begin with.

A woman in Devon, England, was driving home one night when her car suddenly stalled. Getting out to investigate, she was attacked from behind, immediately losing consciousness. On regaining consciousness she was elsewhere and was being examined by three strange beings. Two then left and the third had sex with her, after which she found herself lying by her car again. (This amounts to unification of the feminine element with Trinitarian spirit, the 3 +1 quaternity archetype that was experienced by women mystics in the Middle Ages.) A man called Bob Taylor encountered a landed spacecraft in a forest in Scotland. Two aliens dragged him towards the craft but he lost consciousness; when he came to, the spacecraft was gone. There were only two aliens involved here, at least outside the craft, but when police later investigated the incident they found *triangular* indentations in the ground. In June 1984 a youth in Dale, Indiana, observed a brightly shining object move over his home. The electricity within the house failed. On going out to investigate, he suddenly found he was unable to move. The UFO then disappeared and he was able to move again, but three indentations were left in the ground as if made by three legs.

Colin Wilson mentions (in *Alien Dawn*) the Rev. William Booth Gill who saw a great light in the sky. Three "men" seemed to be doing something "on top," but then it all disappeared. An hour or so later the UFO reappeared, and then a second one, and then a third, so that there were three in all. The next night the three UFOs appeared again, but then no more. Colin also tells of the experience of a Swedish journalist called Jan-Ove Sundberg, who saw a UFO land in the woods behind Loch Ness. Three grey aliens emerged, though they then apparently entered the craft again, which shot off at lightning speed. A couple of pages after the Sunberg incident, Colin tells of the experiences of Pauline Coombes, who in 1977 looked out of the kitchen window of her farm to see a UFO that was about twenty feet across. It stood on three legs and when it took off left a circular burn mark in the ground.

In a number of reported cases the aliens have just three fingers, sometimes webbed, and one report said a round-faced alien had a triangular impression on its forehead. Other sightings have differing numbers of aliens, fingers, etc., but by far the most common number involved is three. As said, a UFO containing three aliens fits Akhenaten's experience of the Aten disc containing Ra, Horus, and Shu—the Holy Trinity—pretty well. (Akhenaten definitely underwent Jung's individuation process, which would have ultimately produced the Aten Trinitarian experience.)

To comment further on the Loch Ness incident here: Lake monsters are known the world over, though nobody has actually captured one or even photographed one satisfactorily or adequately, so that there is no real evidence of a physical creature. But water is the main symbol of the feminine unconscious, and the main symbol of the feminine spirit in instinctual/chthonic aspect is the dragon (occasionally in male aspect, though not too common). A refinement of this is the Lady of the Lake, Lady of the Fountain, etc., and even the Virgin Mary is connected with the sea—she has long been the patron saint of sailors. A form of the goddess Hathor in Egypt was Meri, Goddess of the Waters, and even Neith and Apt in early times were sort of Dragons of the Deep.

Since earliest times, the male Trinity from above has come to Earth to unify with the female Goddess, sometimes through a human woman apparently, giving a 3 + 1 within a circle symbol—the Linda Cortile experience, for example, where she and three aliens ascended to the circular flying saucer. There were also several medieval women mystics who found themselves unifying with the Holy Trinity after undergoing inner spiritualizing processes (Jung's individuation process). But this is what is apparently happening today with UFOs, often containing three male aliens, they seek to unify with the feminine Earth, apparently partly to bring about the further development of mankind as a whole. (A friend of my nephew dreamt of a three-sided, three-colored shape that descended from the sky to plunge into a lake, which symbolizes the same unification.)

These are just a few examples of threefoldness connected with aliens, seen in my dreams and experienced by other people. There is now no doubt in my mind that aliens are connected with spirit, which is often threefold. As my own UFO/alien experiences formed part of my individuation process, I must conclude that other people's similar experiences are part of theirs, at least in some cases.

Jung's "Flying Saucer Vision"

In 1958 Jung had a dream of two gleaming discs that, after hovering over his house, flew down to the adjacent lake. Jung then saw another circular shape coming towards him, and then another appeared that was extended on a tube from a sort of magic lantern. He then realized that while he had always thought of UFOs as being due to our own human projections, this dream was telling him that we are all really projections from the UFOs. This is similar to a dream where Jung thought a yogi was dreaming him, rather than him dreaming the yogi. Eastern philosophy has seen reality in this way for thousands of years, the spirit realm being true reality, and worldly reality actually the illusion. Orfeo Angelucci, whose UFO/religious experiences I mentioned above, was informed by aliens—spirit entities, so they said—that humans are agents in the material world of higher immortals, which amounts pretty much to the same thing as our being projections of the UFOs.

In the same year as the dreams, 1958, Jung published *Flying Saucers: A Modern Myth of Things Seen in the Skies*, in which he explored the phenomenon of UFOs from the point of view of projections from the unconscious; not the personal unconscious, but the collective. Most UFOs are circles and spheres and therefore mandala shaped, and mandalas are symbols of wholeness produced by the unconscious/spirit. Jung believed that the unconscious may be producing the symbolic UFOs in order to bring mankind to reunification with the lost part of reality, the religious/spiritual, and mythological, although we must understand that by the unconscious Jung actually meant spirit reality itself.

But Jung also knew that UFO phenomena are at the same time occurrences in outer reality, happening as outer events of a sort, suggesting they have both spiritual and material aspects, or are rather spirit becoming manifest in matter—still remaining spirit even though they come through to physical reality, like ghosts to a degree (although they do seem to become solidly physical). As he pointed out, UFOs rarely seem to be strictly spaceships, or behave like them, but overall appear compensatory to the dissociated and spiritually disorientated state of modern Man. All of this fits with my experience of being on a ship on the ocean—i.e., the unconscious—suddenly realizing that UFOs are projections from there, like the airplanes I was watching on the movie screen, though again becoming solid apparently.

As well as taking the form of circles or spheres, UFOs may occasionally be cylindrical or cigar-shaped, both types suggesting, therefore, feminine and masculine symbols. (Nevertheless, in ancient Egypt and elsewhere, the circle indicated Heaven and the higher spiritual.) Just as symbols of unification appear from the unconscious urging us to unify matter and spirit, so these shapes in the skies seem to be urging us away from a limited, materialistic view of reality to a balanced one of wholeness involving both material and spiritual sides of one total reality—"*Render unto Caesar the things that are Caesars, render unto God the things that are God's.*"

Commenting on Jung's response to UFO phenomena, Colin Wilson says:

> What Jung has done is to make it absolutely clear why flying saucers have exercised such a powerful influence on the human imagination in the second half of the twentieth century. It is the romantic—and religious—craving for "another reality." . . . Our deepest secret wish is to see the real world transformed . . . it seems that creatures of that "other reality" have decided to pay us a visit. And this is also what Jung meant by "the flying saucer vision" (*Alien Dawn* 1999).

Jung's discoveries, plus my own experiences, show that not only *can* we believe in our dreams, but that we *must* do so. We can know there is another reality existing behind the physical universe, and that our psyches are connected to it through the unconscious. It is religious by nature in the widest sense of the term, and functions in a mythological way; one of the main points about the UFO phenomena is that they are not "scientific" and "technological." They seem to fit better with mythological—albeit space-age—and religious associations than with the boring technology of a launch from the Cape.

Jung speaks of two separate realities that are nevertheless connected, and which sometimes touch, and Colin says Jung knew all of this intuitively. "He knew enough of the world of the paranormal to realize that mankind is being offered a revelation that could amount to a new kind of consciousness." (ibid.)

"Revelation" is the way to describe some of the symbolic contents that come through from the collective unconscious, and which have the greatest meaning and significance for mankind.

As well as *Alien Dawn,* Colin Wilson sent me another book, which he calls "A marvellous book, one of the great books of the 1990s," *The Holographic Universe* (1991) by Michael Talbot. The book demonstrates how certain scientists, though a minority, are taking the view that what we call reality, our universe, time and space, matter, etc., may not after all be as real as we think. It may, according to these scientists, even be a holographic reality; that is, one that is more or less a projection from other reality.

It depends on what precisely the scientists mean, but their conclusions may in some ways fit in with my own experiences, based on information obtained through the collective unconscious itself in dreams. This is to say that what we call our material world has been set up in order for the higher powers—the immortals, ultimately God—to bring about development through human beings, their mortal agents on Earth. This is the opinion of the Eastern religions based upon thousands of years of experience of unconscious/spirit reality.

The support from certain scientists for other realities is welcome, though I must stress that it would be a mistake to regard ultimate reality as "scientific" in nature. The best, and indeed, the only true way of assessing and understanding absolute reality is through religious and mythological symbolism. The ancient Egyptians were not fragmented as we are today, and in their wholeness science and religion came together as parts of the same teachings, although religion dominated by far. They would never have made the mistake—committed the sacrilege—of viewing their gods and full and total reality in a scientific way. For them, as with the teachings of the East generally, and indeed, with the information given to Angelucci, the immortal gods live material lives through their "mortal shadows" on Earth—mankind.

The alchemists began as materialists and little more than chemists, having material goals, but because in their work they touched upon that spirit/soul reality and became involved in its processes, the more intelligent of them underwent inner transformation that spiritualized them. They were forced to parallel their Philosopher's Stone with Christ, because what had happened with the divine Son was occurring in the matter they were investigating, albeit in a lower form (actually the spirit lying within or through matter). Even their terminology became highly mystical and even religious as they aimed for the unification of body, soul, and spirit. As Jung tells us, the spiritual alchemists dropped their work in the laboratory altogether, relying mostly on dreams.

Mankind, though separated from the Higher Self, is nevertheless part of it. And in turn, the Self, though become separated from God, is nevertheless still part of God (and part of the Earth Spirit/World Soul at lower level). Accordingly, Man is directly connected to God through the Higher Self, though at the same time extremely separated. This is why the Logos was the connecting link between Man and God in the ancient world. We humans are all, therefore, extensions of God. The individuation process, which reveals so much darkness and chaos and causes so much suffering, ultimately leads to the greatest order and light possible: the things I speak of are experienced as *facts*.

We must try to view full reality with the eyes of the true philosopher (literally a "lover of wisdom"), the prophet, the poet, the mystic, the seer, the visionary, the saint, and only with the eyes of the scientist for necessary classification. (Though does the mystic need to classify his visions?) And indeed, the Egyptian Pyramid Texts, the Wisdom Texts, the Book of the Dead, the Gnostic codices, the Bible, the Talmud, the Torah, the Kabbalah, the Qur'an, the Vedas, the Upanishads, the alchemical and Hermetic texts, the myths and legends of the world, folklore, fairy tales, and all of the paranormal experiences of mankind, express the nature of the unconscious/spirit, and indeed, full and ultimate reality, far more adequately than science could ever hope to do. As I say elsewhere, science represents the grocery list, not the groceries themselves, and indeed, even the grocery list is somewhat incomplete.

Colin Wilson writes:

> So what we might call the "UFO reality" would seem to be a realm like alchemy and quantum reality, where two apparently incompatible realities come together. In fact, they are far from incompatible; they only appear to be so because we are trapped in our tunnel vision, which assures us that this world is physical and that we are inescapably tied to it. Yet we are always catching glimpses of a larger reality that tells us that this is untrue. (ibid.)

Jung spent the greater part of his life trying to show how this is so from the point of view of depth psychology, from the total psychological experience of mankind. After all, how else would we experience either the material universe or spirit reality but with the human psyche, the depths and heights of which we are only just beginning to plumb and understand.

Chapter 19

Jung and the Apocalypse

UFOs and aliens and Marian visions are by no means the full picture. Jung looks into the Book of Revelation (in *Answer to Job*) to find hints of what could be expected for the future in the visions of its author. Jung was of the opinion that the book was probably written by the John who wrote the Epistles of John. The Epistles are full of love; love of God, love of one's fellow human beings, God is love, and so forth. But in Revelation the shadow surfaces, and this may be partly the shadow of John himself in the unconscious. Nevertheless, Jung suggests it is predominantly the dark side of God that issues forth, and that a seer such as John, who is fated to experience the immensity of God, must be prepared for such invasions. God, therefore, must be feared as well as loved.

The first vision John sees in Revelation is Christ as the Son of Man but apparently in somewhat negative aspect.

"And in the midst of the seven candlesticks one like unto the Son of Man, clothed with a garment down to the foot, and girt about the paps with a golden girdle.

"His head and his hairs were white like wool, as white as snow, and his eyes were as a flame of fire:

"And his feet like unto fine brass, as if they burned in a furnace; and his voice as the sound of many waters.

"And he had in his right hand seven stars: and out of his mouth went a sharp two-edged sword: and his countenance was as the sun in his strength."

The Son of Man in the midst of seven candlesticks is actually the continuance of Horus with the seven Akhu, the seven Shining Lights or Spirits of Egypt, the Shining Ones of Mesopotamia, Moses with the seven candles of the *Menorah,* the seven-branched candelabra, and so forth. The Son of Man speaking of the "mystery of the seven stars" is said to relate to seven churches, of which five are heavily criticized. Again, it is symbolical, the Seven Stars being a symbol of the Seven Powers of the Self or Logos. But further, the numbers seven and five match Joshua's seven kingdoms in his conquest of Canaan, five kings of which he hangs. Seven and five make twelve, of course, and these were always the symbolic numbers of the inner processes, seven and twelve. (A dragon/prostitute occurs in both the Joshua story and Revelation, called Rahab in the former, and the Whore of Babylon, riding the seven-headed dragon in the latter—again meaning that the two accounts in Joshua and Revelation, match in certain ways.)

I personally have seen the Seven Stars fall onto the east coast of America in a dream, and such an event usually presages the birth of a Savior on Earth—in the spirit, not physically. This in the modern world could even point to the Second Coming of Christ, again spiritually, through the unconscious. However, Jung says the divine figure with the sharp two-edged sword in Revelation does not bode well for mankind—such a sword is not for peaceful intent.

Another point Jung makes is that because John's visions were concerned with wholeness, he would have known that after the reign of Christ would come that of Antichrist. Mankind shudders at the prospect of the dark climax to the Christian era that it will have to experience, when the Four Horsemen of the Apocalypse are let loose to ride forth as bringers of doom. Our age seems to be running headlong into this catastrophe, for collectively we have surely rejected Christ and his light, as can be seen in so many ways. John actually sees a Lamb that was almost slain, a lamb with seven horns and seven eyes, open the Seven Seals, which issue forth floods of terror and destruction onto mankind, partly brought by the Four Horsemen.

Jung asks how did John come to terms with the eternal paradox in God's nature, and more to the point, how do we? The answer, Jung suggests, may come by way of dreams, when for example, the motif of the squaring of the circle appears. In part 1 I mentioned that in a dream I received four gold keys on a key ring from Jung, which represents the squaring of the circle, but alluding to the complex processes that were then taking place. Jung also appeared in one of my dreams wearing a tam, a round flat hat, that was turned down on four sides making a square, thus the squaring of the circle. Another answer produced by the unconscious is the divine child, the product of long and complex processes that unify the opposites in unconscious/spirit reality, producing ultimately the Self, the first appearance of which is as the child.

Nevertheless, Jung suggests that as God incarnated his good side with Christ, he may now wish to incarnate his dark side for completeness. I do not necessarily go along with this conclusion. It would certainly bring about the end of Man, to which he is perilously close in any case without God's dark side. The fact is, Man would be much influenced by God's dark side, as he is already by the Dragon of Chaos that is resurfacing from the dragon depths with the loss of Christ. Chaos from the unconscious depths is quite capable of bringing an end to mankind without any assistance from the dark side of God.

Jung, saying there is more dark in ourselves today than in a Christian such as John from two thousand years ago, adds that we are not so able to withstand the evil and so will be deluged by it. What we need, therefore, is more light, more goodness and morality, and also the Goddess of Wisdom. This is the feminine side of the spirit, represented by Mary or Sophia. (According to all this, Revelation is not about John's personal shadow, but rather the shadow side of God, and also the dragon depths.)

Whatever, the dark side of God inundates John, and then the Holy Ghost engenders the divine child in compensation, copying the prototypal Christ. (We must doubt if it really is the dark side of God for then the child would surely be dark and negative, which it is not; the opposite, in fact.) The Sun Woman gives birth to the divine child in Revelation, which Jung identifies with the *filius sapientiae,* the Son of Wisdom, or Sophia. *"And there appeared a great wonder in Heaven, a woman clothed with the Sun, and the Moon under her feet, and upon her head a crown of twelve stars."* (Rev. 12:1.) Jung calls the Sun Woman the feminine Anthropos, stating that she unites the masculine Sun, or spirit, with the feminine Moon, or soul. Of this union is to be born the Son, and indeed, the Sun Woman gives birth. The red dragon, seven-headed and ten-horned, suddenly appears as a great danger to the child, but the archangel Michael with his angels casts out the dragon with its angels *"into the Earth."*

In a later chapter, another woman appears, sitting on the "scarlet colored beast," the seven-headed, ten-horned beast. "And the woman was arrayed in purple and scarlet color, and decked with gold and precious stones and pearls, having a golden cup in her hand full of abominations and filthiness of her fornications." (Rev. 17:3–4.) This is the Great Whore of Babylon, supposedly signifying Rome according to certain interpretation, but she is actually the lower chthonic counterpart to the Sun Woman, and in negative aspect, just as Nut and the other ancient goddesses have both Heaven and Underworld aspects, and light and dark sides. Even Sophia has her dark, negative underside. Apt in Egypt was constellated in the heavens above (in the Great Bear, as a hippopotamus) but was also "The Scarlet Lady of the Ritual," the red hippopotamus below. Sekhet, another Mother Goddess of Egypt, was "The Lady in the Scarlet-colored Garment." Rahab, the dragon/prostitute with Joshua, hangs up a scarlet ribbon as her sign. So the Scarlet Woman as dragon/prostitute in Revelation reaches back to early Egypt.

At any rate, Jung says the Sun Woman is Sophia (a version of her), and that if these biblical events were to occur in a modern individuation process, we would not hesitate to interpret the birth of the child as that of the Higher Self. In fact, the child is not from God but is taken up to God, meaning that it is the lower form of the Self that it is from the Mother, what I term the Lower Self, a lower *parallel* of Christ Son of God from above. Jung states these events are "a slap in the face" to rationalism and the materialistic view, and that we must understand such things psychologically and symbolically. But obviously, we cannot limit such events to personal psychology, because they are of cosmic divine significance in which a human individual has become involved, involving the Earth, the world. Jung says the events indicate the Sacred Marriage in the Pleroma that produces the divine Son, but we must remember that the Earth becomes involved. The Assumption of the Virgin in 1950 was certainly a step towards the Sacred Marriage, and it was reported that the Pope himself experienced visions of the Virgin at that time.

As said, the child is finally caught up to Heaven by God, and Jung says that if the child is Son of both God and the Sun Woman then Christ is repeated—Christ is both Son of God and Son of the Mother. In any case, the child goes up to God while the mother is "nourished by God" in the wilderness and is protected by the Earth. Jung says that the incarnation of the light Son was obviously what mattered in John's time. But the light Son in Revelation is in lower aspect apparently and then taken up above to God; therefore Son of the Mother that becomes Son of the Father. In a certain myth of Egypt, Isis gives birth to the divine Son, Horus, and she asks God, here Atum, if he will take the boy as his own. The child is then taken up to God above, as in Revelation.

With the future Apocalypse foretold in Revelation a fury of destruction is to be expected, with just one hundred and forty four thousand humans surviving on Earth, and these male virgins, *"not defiled with women."* Satan will have been locked up for a thousand years (the length of time is metaphorical) but will then be loosed, although Christ has said that Man will be inspired by the Holy Ghost to do greater works than even He himself. The way to knowledge of God is self-knowledge, Jung asserts, and the beginning of knowledge is fear of God. The God who must be feared is just as real as the loving God, because God is a totality of opposites, as is the Higher Self, and indeed, Man. Can we expect God to be any less than Man? If Man has a shadow extension then God must have this also, otherwise God would be less than Man. But it is our own light side that brings forth the light out of the Self and God.

Jung repeats that the visions of John are part of the heavenly Sacred Marriage, the *Hieros Gamos,* from which is born the divine child. Yet I must explain again here that the child as Son from God Himself seems to come forth whole, and so it is quite possibly the "Christ within," the lower Christ, Son the Mother, that is the divine child in Revelation. I say this because in my own individuation process I saw God as the Sun and part of Him broke away to become the Son—thus the Son directly from God, not involving the Mother. But in another dream a lovely divine child floated in from the sea as Son of the Mother. Jung himself says there are two Sons, one from above and one from below, like princes of two different realms, Son of the Father and Son of the Mother. So the Son from below, from the Mother, is not God's direct Son as such, but is nevertheless accepted by God.

Whatever the case, the divine child in Revelation is threatened by the dragon and this is so in mythology generally. Sometimes the dragon is in human form, like Herod with the baby Jesus, Pharaoh with Moses, and King Kansa with Krishna. Jung says the Sun Woman, the "feminine Anthropos," which is a name of the Higher Self with certain Gnostics, reconciles the opposites, spirit with matter/soul, and light with dark, the union as a complexity of opposites. However, as the Son is associated with the wrathful Lamb with John and will rule the nations with a "rod of iron," Jung sees it as a portent for the future, rather than happening there and then at the time of John.

Another point Jung makes is that the Second Coming of Christ should be on the clouds, but that this does not occur in John's visions; he is rather born from a conjunction of Heaven and Earth from the Sun Woman. Yet the Son of Man with the prophet Daniel comes on the clouds of Heaven, but his association is with the four beasts coming from the sea—the water, and therefore the feminine, the Great Mother. Furthermore, earlier in Daniel, a Son of God has appeared associated with fire, so here again are two Sons, one associated with water, the other with fire, i.e., from the Mother and from the Father. This shows that the Son coming on the clouds can be from the feminine depths. But in any case, Jung's point that the Son does not come on the clouds in Revelation is not altogether valid, for actually he does, earlier, in the first chapter; *"Behold, he cometh with the clouds"* (1:7). However, the divine child is born much later, in chapter 12. But why all the confusion? The answer seems to be that a number of different processes are at work in Revelation, some taken from the Old Testament, from the conquest of Canaan, from certain of Daniel's visions, and so on. This is nothing new, for New Testament material to be taken from the Old Testament; it certainly happens in the accounts of Jesus in the Gospels. However, we will have to explore all of this elsewhere, not here.

Jung comments that though Christ was an actuality in history, he is nevertheless also a symbol, for he expresses the Higher Self, the Christ within us all. Had this not been so, he would not have spread like wildfire through the whole Roman Empire. So again, there are two levels of Christ, one symbolizing our own inner Self, but also, at the cosmic level, the divine Son, the Logos, as manifestation of God. Jung suggests that the Son in John's experiences is the higher version, for John has become mixed up in the divine drama at ultimate level. I personally believe that both higher and lower forms are involved in Revelation, which is usually the case in a full individuation process, but whatever, Jung suggests John's negative feelings have perhaps colored, or discolored, the Lamb so that it comes forth in a wrathful aspect; this is possibly so.

The city of Sophia is the "heavenly Jerusalem" in Revelation, and as Sophia was with God before Creation (in Proverbs), so she will be with Him again in the Sacred Marriage. They were at the beginning One, the universally hermaphroditic archetype of greatest immensity, the ultimate male/female God/Goddess, and they will be together again in the Sacred Marriage that is to occur in the future. Revelation also looks into the future to certain prophesied horrors, which is surely now in view to us in our time. We can terminate ourselves and our planet with the greatest of ease with the hangman's noose we have placed around our collective neck. It depends ultimately on us ourselves, and to help us we are given the necessary information through the unconscious in archetypal symbolism, if we will only strive to understand. If we do not listen and alter ourselves, the processes will continue unconsciously, which will mean the situation becoming even more dangerous. For if the archetypal forces are not accepted in their light, positive aspect, they plough through in their negative destructive aspect.

Yet Jung seems to partly contradict himself with the above. He first says that the dark side of God may be coming forth as the dark Son, and that God may wish this for completeness, to countermatch the light Christ. Furthermore, the dark God could only incarnate in dark and guilty Man. But then Jung later says more light is needed, more goodness and morality to enable us to absorb the dark God. So we need to be dark for God's dark incarnation, but light to absorb it, which seems not to add up. Perhaps I have mistaken Jung here, failed to understand fully. In any case, what comes forth as the result of John's experiences is the light divine child, not the dark, born of the Sun Woman, menaced by the dark dragon, although the wrathful Lamb also plays a role. So although the Lamb was somewhat wrathful at the beginning of Revelation, the divine child born to the Sun Woman later is not.

Jung says Christ's perfection in a sense injures the feminine principle, and so engenders a perfectionist state that has always steered the Church to the masculine side. This leads nowhere, ultimately, and so a balance must be reached by raising the feminine spirit to bring about a state of completeness. Yet the Catholic Church has always made much of Mary historically, and her Assumption goes some way to making of her a goddess, which will fill the need for Sophia and her Wisdom to complete and balance Christ. When God is harsh, Sophia, the highest form of the feminine spirit, is the caring helper of mankind, and Mary is actually Sophia. Jung comments that although the perfectionism in the Jewish Yahweh came to be tempered somewhat by a certain feminine element in Christianity, the patriarchal supremacy nevertheless remained unassailable. So we have not heard the last of the neglected feminine element, for it is sure to surface in the future. We can see how right Jung was here by the way feminism has burst forth on the world like a cannon shot since his day.

The Assumption of Mary (which gives full recognition to Sophia) is John's visions fulfilled in reality, for in the blessed bridal chamber above the Mother is united with the Son, and also with God. It points, furthermore, to the "end of days" and the "marriage of the Lamb." Jung comments that when the people feel a longing for the exaltation of the Great Mother it means ultimately the desire for a Savior. In the hidden recesses of the soul, the Holy Spirit is at work. The Great Mother as Queen of Heaven must join the Holy Trinity to form the ultimate quaternity of wholeness. The Catholic Church may be the Bride of Christ, but it is not good enough. Christ, representing God, needs a personified representation with which to unify.

Christ is God manifested and so is eternal (he is also Son of Mary/Sophia). But it needs to be asked, if God (in total form) is everything already, why does He desire to become Man in an incarnation? We can only conclude that God needs to move, to expand, to function, even to grow, otherwise He would be perfectly still and probably unaware of Himself. In other words, God gains more consciousness through contact with Man. Jung says the incarnation entails a transformation of God that is world-shaking in that God becomes separate from Himself to become the Son, though it is still God. If we take a cup of seawater from the sea, they now become separate from each other, but it is nevertheless still the sea in the cup. One becomes Two, though both are still One. Yet God's incarnation is even more than this because He transforms into Man; in fact, God becomes Man and Man becomes God in the unification. But it is because Man is part of the Self and the Self part of God, that God is able to become Man, and Man God.

Jung says it is now up to Man, for a gigantic task has appeared as if out of nowhere. Suddenly, new understanding of religious processes that take place through the unconscious, beyond anything that could have been suspected, have come to light. The old religious tenets have proved to be true and valid; God is real, Mary (Sophia) is real, the divine Son is real. All of this knowledge coming to light is thanks to Jung. Nevertheless, Jung warns that if Man is to save himself and the world, further "gnosis of the Divine" must be gained. Man must come to understand the metaphysical processes that are taking place through the unconscious, of which we are most definitely a part.

Incidentally, a very important statement made by Jung is that when treating psychoneurosis a doctor is forced, even against his will sometimes, to go into the problem of religion. Often the root of the mental disturbance is a deeper disturbance of the spirit. Man is in between the opposites of matter and spirit, symbolized by the two thieves with Christ at the crucifixion, one of which will go up to higher spirit reality, and the other presumably down to the depths below. People largely live their lives in the modern world without religion, yet this is the deepest aspect of us all, and in the depths of the psyche there is no escaping the conflicts it causes. It is intended for Man to have a relationship with God and the Son, and to deny this is to deny the very reason for our existence. We have malfunctioned and so God may get rid of us and evolve another creature in his work of Creation. God has eternity to make experiments until the right creature is produced.

Conclusion

Jung came to understand the validity of collective dreams and visions as communications from timeless levels of reality. He had learned to assimilate them into his own psychic matrix and life view. He had also come to realize, however, that although the archetypes may last for thousands of years in a certain form, the time eventually arrives when they lose their validity for a culture and so must be further developed, renewed, or replaced. He was certain that the time had now arrived for Western culture to undergo renewal itself or suffer collapse. But he was also aware that the collective unconscious is at the same time very traditional, functioning along a traditional line of development, and would prefer development to follow on along that line. This for the West is the royal line from Egypt to Christ, the "order outside time," as Jung called it. All of this tells us that what is called for is the continuation of Christ, a new and deeper understanding, not his abandonment.

When Jung visited India and had a dream about medieval Europe and the Grail Castle, he took it as a serious message that he must return to his main work at home involving the renewal of the Christian spirit. This could only be accomplished through the unconscious of Western Man, for while Hinduism and Buddhism are part of the wider picture, they are of another line and are not the main and central issue for the West. So while his conscious mind had become deeply involved with the Eastern forms of the processes, and despite the fact he was in India, the collective unconscious was working along its own traditional Western royal line.

Jung was further concerned that the modern world has hurled itself into the future, breaking away dangerously from the past with a speed that is frightening. The penthouse of a skyscraper cannot exist suspended in midair, it needs all of the stories beneath for support. If it were to lose that support, the penthouse would come crashing down into rubble—a definite danger and possible fate for the modern West. Jung writes that we have fallen into a chasm of "progress," which, the more it distances us from our roots, carries us into a future that threatens ever more violence and chaos. Contrary to our conscious way of thinking, we still have much unfinished psychic business not only with the Middle Ages, but with the ancient and primitive worlds.

We have witnessed the further impoverishment of the quality of our world in the years since Jung. We are heavily weighted down with the products of a technology that are as mind-confusing as they are awesome. We rush madly into the future so that the past, to which we are quite literally connected through the unconscious, is left behind, causing a gaping split in our personal natures, in our culture, and in time itself. We are a once-civilization going haywire, having lost our true foundations in mythic/religious reality (therefore, solid foundations in eternity) and Jung knew it to the point of despair.

In our greatly accelerated age we skim over true reality, never really knowing the depths of actual living, of actual being. Jung built a medieval-style house right on the lakeside at Bollingen, to which he would retreat whenever possible. It had no modern facilities—it was lighted by oil lamps, and the water was pumped from a well. Everything was as natural as possible. At least for a while Jung could be at peace—with nature, with time and history, with the unconscious, and with God.

But association with the unconscious/spirit that we knew through Christianity has been broken, and such a split means collapse of a culture into chaos ultimately, unless new association can be reestablished in time. If it happens, it may result in a further and more highly developed form of the old religion. If not, it means culture collapse. We see this situation with Noah, whose society had fallen into degeneracy, sinking beneath the "floods of chaos" (a real, physical flood is not meant). Contact with the higher light had been broken and to lose the light is to be in darkness. However, Noah then establishes a new covenant with God and everything begins to grow and blossom again; the light has been restored. The symbolic flood is an archetypal occurrence that always threatens mankind, and we in the modern world, sinking in chaos ourselves, must reestablish our own covenant with higher spirit. Some years ago I had a dream that said that many people will in the future be affected by the spirit through the unconscious, and this is definitely now happening.

An example of how the thinking of modern man has completely changed, at least for many of us, is well illustrated in a true incident told by Egyptologist John Romer. He relates that he was once in an old medieval town in Italy, and the painting of the Virgin had been stolen from the old church. The news media and art experts had all descended on the place because an important work of art had been stolen. But to the local residents it was not a matter of art. Their holy Virgin, virtually their goddess, had been taken from them, so it was a great *religious* catastrophe. To the modern way of thinking, art—or science, business, or whatever—is the highest value, but the people in the old town had not yet been afflicted with the loss of soul that the modern world now endures, and so the higher spirit still reigned with them. Art to them was nothing compared with the sacred and the religious. As Jung points out, mankind must have its center in God, for those who are grounded in the world have only the pavement beneath their feet.

Yet beyond almost anything we could have expected or hoped for, there are now signs of a definite return to religion, at least in America. Who could have predicted this just a few short years ago? And it is Christianity that people are getting into again, whether traditional orthodox forms or the deeper mystery with its archetypal symbolism, Gnosticism, and so forth. Indeed, many bestselling books concern Christianity in some way—Amazon America has opened a new Christian bookstore because of the demand. Jung's works and those about him or that are connected in some other way are also very good sellers. But then Jung himself was promulgating the Christian mystery—all religions—as the best and truest psychotherapeutic system, essential for the health of both the individual and culture as a whole.

I ask, who could have predicted this, but I must answer my own question, and with a positive answer: the unconscious/spirit did, in my dreams. Although warning of catastrophic consequences if we fail to respiritualize, my dreams years ago forecast that many people would in the future be so affected through the unconscious. A few decades ago it was thought that if intelligent people did get into religion in the future, it would be perhaps Buddhism or some form of the Hindu wisdom that we saw attracting the young in the late 1960s and 70s. But no, it is Christianity that is suddenly seizing people, and this, as I say, is because they are unknowingly being affected through the collective unconscious by the activated archetype. Christ is alive again, is risen in the human soul, and I have experienced this personally in my dreams, though time alone will tell what the ultimate effect on the West will be. Other parts of the world—Africa, for example—are certainly becoming Christianized, each rightly in its own manner, and I was reading that in Communist China it is necessary to book in advance to be able to get into a church for the service because they are packed out. Is the miracle really coming true?

Bibliography

Alford, Alan F. *When the Gods Came Down.* 2000. London: Hodder and Staunton.

Andrews, Richard, and Schellenbergen, Paul. The Tomb of God. 1996. London: Little, Brown, and Company.

Angelucci, Orfeo. *The Secret of the Saucers.* 1955. Amherst, Wisconsin: Amherst Press.

Artis Auriferae. 1593. Basel.

Aurora Occulta Philosophorum. In *Theatrum Chemicum.* 1659. Strasbourg.

Baigent, Michael, Leigh, Richard, and Lincoln, Henry. *Holy Blood, Holy Grail.* 1982. London: Jonathon Cape.

Besant, Annie. *Esoteric Christianity; or the Lesser Mysteries.* 1918. London: Theosophical Publishing House.

Blavatsky, H. P. *Isis Unveiled.* 1877. New York: Theosophical Publishing House.

———. *The Secret Doctrine.* 1888. New York: Theosophical Publishing House.

———. *Key to Theosophy.* 1889. New York: Theosophical Publishing House.

Brown, Dan. *The Da Vinci Code.* 2003. London: Bantam.

Budge, A. E. Wallace. *Gods of the Egyptians.* 2 vols. 1904. London: Methuen.

Charles, R. H. (trans.) *Book of Enoch.* 1924. Oxford: Oxford University Press.

Creuzer, Georg Friedrich. *The Symbolism and Mythology of Ancient Peoples.*

Darwin, Charles. *The Origin of species.* 1855. London: John Murray

Eliade, Mercea. *A History of Religious Ideas.* 1979. London: Collins.

Freke, Timothy, and Gandy, Peter. *The Jesus Mysteries.* 1999. London: Thorsons.

Freud, Sigmund. *The Interpretation of Dreams.* 1899. Leipzig and Vienna: Franz Deuticke

Freud, Sigmund. W. D. Robson Scott (trans.). *The Future of an Illusion.* 1928. New York: H. Liveright.

Gardner, Philip, and Osbourne, Gary. *The Serpent and the Grail.* 2005. London: Watkins Publishing.

Gospel of James. See *The Nag Hammadi Library.* J. M. Robinson, ed. 1990. San Francisco: Harper SanFrancisco.

Guerber, H. A. *Myths of the Norsemen from Eddas and the Sagas.* 1908. London: G. G. Harrap & Company.

Hippolytus, Antipope. *Philosophumenia;* or, *The Refutation of All Heresies.* 1921. London: Society for Promoting Christian Knowledge and New York: The Macmillon Company.

Hopkins, Budd. *Witnessed.* 1996. New York: Pocket Books.

Inman, Thomas. *Ancient Pagan and Modern Christian Symbolism.* 1869. London & Liverpool: printed by the author.

James, Montague Rhodes (trans.). *Acts of John* in *Apocryphal New Testament.* 1924. Oxford: The Clarendon Press.

Jung, C. G. *Psychological Types.* 1921. Princeton: Princeton University Press

———. *The Spirit in Man, Art, and Literature.* 1932. Princeton: Princeton University Press

———. *Psychology and Alchemy.* 1953. London: Routledge and Kegan Paul.

———. *Psychology and Religion: West and East.* 1958. London: Routledge and Kegan Paul.

———. *Aion.* 1959a. London: Routledge and Kegan Paul.

———. *The Archetypes and the Collective Unconscious.* 1959b. London: Routledge and Kegan Paul.

———. *Memories, Dreams,* Reflections. 1963. New York: Pantheon Books.

———. *Mysterium Coniunctionis.* 1963. London: Routledge and Kegan Paul.

———. *Civilization in Transition.* 1964. London: Routledge and Kegan Paul.

———. *Seven Sermons of the Dead.* 1967. London: Vincent Stuart and J. M. Watkins, Ltd.

———. *Alchemical Studies.* 1968. London: Routledge and Kegan Paul.

———. *Symbols of Transformation.* 1990. Princeton, N.J.: Princeton University Press.

Kaufman, Walter. *Discovering the Mind.* 1980. New York: McGraw-Hill.

Kaufman, Walter (trans.). *Thus Spoke Zarathustra.* 1954. Baltimore: Penguin Classics

Khunrath, Heinrich. *Amphitheatrum Sapientiae.* 1609. Hanau.

Kingsland, William. *The Esoteric Basis of Christianity.* 1895. London: Theosophical Publishing Society.

Koepgen, Georg. *Gnosis Des Christentums.* 1939. Salzburg.

Massey, Gerald. *Ancient Egypt, Light of the World.* 1907. London: T. F. Unwin.

McGlynn, Frank. *Carl Gustav Jung.* 1996. London: Bantam Press.

Nagy, Marilyn. *Philosophical Issues in the Psychology of C. G. Jung.* 1991. New York: State University of New York Press.

Neumann, Erich. *The Origins and History of Consciousness.* 1980. Princeton, N. J.: Princeton University Press.

Nietzsche, Friedrich. *The Birth of Tragedy.* 1872

———. *The Gay Science.* 1882.

———. *Thus Spoke Zarathustra.* 1883.

———. *Beyond Good and Evil.* 1886.

———. *Ecce Homo.* 1888a.

———. *The Antichrist.* 1888b. Nordland Verlag.

Phillips, Graham. *The Chalice of Magdalene.* 1996. Rochester, Vermont: Bear and Company.

Reinach, Salomon. *Orpheus, a History of Religions.* 1930. New York: Liveright, Inc.

Rosarium Philosophorum. In *Artis Auriferae.* 1593. Basel.

Schure, Edouard. *From the Sphinx to Christ.* 1928. London: Rider & Company.

St. Teresa of Avila. *Interior Castle (The Mansions).* 1944. London: Sheed and Ward.

Talbot, Michael. *The Holographic Universe.* 1991. New York: Harper/Collins.

Temple, Robert. *The Sirius Mystery.* 1976. New York: St. Martin's Press.

Van der Post, Laurens. *Jung and the Story of Our Time.* 1976. London: Vintage.

Wilhelm, Richard. *The Secret of the Golden Flower.* 1931. London: K. Paul, Trench, Trubner & Co. Ltd.

Wilson, Colin. *The Outsider.* 1956. Boston: Houghton Mifflin.

———. *Alien Dawn.* 1998. New York: Fromm International.

About the Author

Robert B. Clarke was born in Burslem (Stoke-on-Trent), England, in 1942. After a materially- and educationally-poor but spiritually-rich youth in central England, he became severely depressed and disillusioned, having lost the inner certainty of his childhood. Then Clarke stumbled onto the teachings of the great psychologist Carl Jung, and found the path to understanding he had sought. Led through the individuation process by some 30,000 dreams, he went on to become an independent scholar and mystic who delved deeply into the realms of philosophy, religion, and psychology, applying the insight he had acquired to illuminate the meaning beyond day-to-day life.

The record of his many years' journey through the depths of the collective unconscious was published by Hampton Roads Publishing Company as *The Four Gold Keys*, in 2002. In 2005, Hampton Roads published *An Order Outside Time: A Jungian View Of The Higher Self From Egypt To Christ*.

Three additional manuscripts are being published posthumously by Hologram Books:

The Royal Line of Christ the Logos: A Jungian View of the Roots and Meaning of the Orthodox/Gnostic Christian Mystery

The Grail, the Stone, and the Mystics: A Jungian View of the Medieval Spiritual Mysteries

The Sacred Journey: Part One, Jung and His Discoveries; Part Two, Blavatsky, Nietzsche, Marian Vision, UFOs, and Aliens

Robert Clarke died in November, 2009, in Burslem, not far from his birthplace.

About Hologram Books

Hologram Books was founded by Frank DeMarco to publish works of enduring interest regardless of their immediate commercial potential. For a complete list of books published by Hologram Books, go to its website, www.hologrambooks.com.